CITIZEN POLITICS

SIXTH EDITION

Other titles by Russell J. Dalton published by CQ Press:

The Apartisan American: Dealignment and Changing Electoral Politics (2012)

The Good Citizen: How a Younger Generation Is Reshaping American Politics, Revised Edition (2009)

CITIZEN POLITICS

Public Opinion and Political Parties in Advanced Industrial Democracies

SIXTH EDITION

Russell J. Dalton
University of California, Irvine

Los Angeles | London | New Delhi
Singapore | Washington DC

Los Angeles | London | New Delhi
Singapore | Washington DC

FOR INFORMATION:

CQ Press
An Imprint of SAGE Publications, Inc.
2455 Teller Road
Thousand Oaks, California 91320
E-mail: order@sagepub.com

SAGE Publications Ltd.
1 Oliver's Yard
55 City Road
London, EC1Y 1SP
United Kingdom

SAGE Publications India Pvt. Ltd.
B 1/I 1 Mohan Cooperative
Industrial Area
Mathura Road, New Delhi 110 044
India

SAGE Publications Asia-Pacific Pte. Ltd.
3 Church Street
#10–04 Samsung Hub
Singapore 049483

Acquisitions Editor: Elise Frasier
Editorial Assistant: Lauren Johnson
Production Editor: David C. Felts
Copy Editor: Pam Suwinsky
Typesetter: Hurix Systems Pvt. Ltd.
Proofreader: Gretchen Treadwell
Indexer: Author
Cover Designer: Auburn Associates Inc.
Marketing Manager: Jonathan Mason
Permissions Editor: Adele Hutchinson

Printed in the United States of America

Library of Congress Cataloging-in-Publication Data

Dalton, Russell J.

Citizen politics: public opinion and political parties in advanced industrial democracies / Russell J. Dalton, University of California, Irvine.—Sixth edition.

pages cm
Includes bibliographical references and index.

ISBN 978-1-4522-0300-3 (pbk.: alk. paper)—ISBN 978-1-4833-0092-4 (web pdf: alk. paper)

1. Political parties. 2. Political participation. 3. Democracy. 4. Public opinion. 5. Comparative government. I. Title.

JF2011.D34 2013

324.2—dc23   2013001003

This book is printed on acid-free paper.

SFI label applies to text stock

13 14 15 16 17 10 9 8 7 6 5 4 3 2 1

Contents

Part Four: Democracy and the Future

Tables and Figures

Figures

To Penn and Mac

Preface

Experts frequently claim that history follows a circle, and if you wait long enough you will end up where you started. When I began work on the first edition of this book in the 1980s, many political scientists were openly worried about the viability of modern democracy. Claims about an imminent crisis of democracy were commonplace. Against this backdrop, the first edition of *Citizen Politics* (1988) argued that democracy was alive and well in the advanced industrial democracies, whose citizens believed in the democratic creed and wanted their governments to meet these expectations. That book showed that people were becoming more active in the political process, more likely to participate in elite-challenging activities, more likely to vote on issues and other policy criteria, and more demanding of their representatives. If democracy was in crisis, it was one of institutions, not of the democratic spirit among citizens.

Subsequent events seemingly supported this contrarian perspective on democracy. The toppling of the Berlin Wall, the collapse of communism in the Soviet Union and Eastern Europe, and the spread of democracy in the 1990s created a euphoria surrounding the democratic process. Even those who had proclaimed its limits a few years earlier now trumpeted this new wave of democratization. Suddenly it seemed apparent to everyone that democracy represented the start of a new history.

Now we have come full circle. The current conventional wisdom again claims that democracy is at risk—and the citizens are at fault. A host of distinguished scholars cite an apparently unending list of what is wrong with democracy's citizens. Too few of us follow politics, too few are voting, too many of us are cynical about politics, and too often we are intolerant to those who do not share our positions. It's déjà vu all over again, as Yogi Berra used to say.

Watching this ebb and flow of the political debate has deepened my belief that systematic research provides a corrective to the winds of punditry. Things were not so bad during the pessimistic days of the "crisis of democracy" literature, and they were not so good during the euphoria following the Berlin Wall's collapse. We understand the nature of democracy and its citizens not by watching talking heads on television, but by talking to the public and learning how they think about politics and how they act on their beliefs. And while I sometimes subscribe to the line about "lies, damn lies, and statistics," in the long run systematic research can provide a deeper understanding of the true nature of citizen politics.

This book introduces students to what we know about citizens' political behavior, questions about it that remain unanswered, and the implications of findings thus far. The analyses focus on citizen politics in the United States, Great Britain, France, and Germany, with frequent comparisons to other established democracies. This sixth edition engages in the debate on the vitality of contemporary democracy and argues that ongoing processes of social modernization are changing the values and behavior of the public. These changes to the status quo might be a concern to someone who longs for an idyllic past (which never existed), and, indeed, these changes create new challenges and tensions for the democratic process. In the end, however, if democracies successfully respond to these challenges, the democratic process will be stronger.

I hope this book is of value to several audiences. It was written primarily for classroom use in courses on comparative political parties, public opinion, and European politics. The first half (chapters 1–6) introduces the principles of public opinion and the broad contours of citizen action and citizen beliefs. The second half (chapters 7–11) covers party alignments and can be combined with other texts on political parties. The book concludes with a discussion of citizen attitudes toward democratic institutions and the political process and the choices that face the various polities.

At the graduate level, the book is a useful core text for courses on comparative political behavior or Western European politics. It summarizes the existing knowledge in the field and introduces the controversies that at present divide researchers. I hope instructors find that this introductory analysis facilitates discussion of readings from primary research materials. Even senior scholars may find familiar data interpreted in new and thought-provoking ways.

Major Revisions

The basic framework and its findings of this book have remained fairly constant since the first edition. As more evidence has become available, the trends have become clearer and more apparent. This new edition includes several significant changes to improve the presentation.

- Discussion of whether the 2008 Great Recession has reversed the patterns of social modernization and citizen politics—the answer is no.

- Description of new forms of political activity, such as Internet-based activism and new forms of political consumerism.

- More attention to current academic debates over the decline of participation, the erosion of political support, and the implications for democracy. I offer a contrarian view on these points. (Also see Russell Dalton, *The Good Citizen: How a Younger Generation Is Reshaping American Politics*, Congressional Quarterly Press, 2009.)

- Revision of all the chapters to present the latest research and empirical evidence, including new evidence from the Comparative Study of Electoral Systems (CSES) project (module III), and new material from the 2008 U.S. elections, the 2010 British election, the 2009 German election, and the 2007 French election.

- A revised statistical primer (appendix A) to give readers guidance in interpreting tables and figures. In addition, it serves as a reference guide for using correlation statistics to understand the relationship between two traits, such as summarizing educational differences in voting turnout.

- A new data supplement in appendix C based on the 2005–09 World Values Survey. These data are used throughout the book, and a free subset of survey questions is available for class use. The appendix lists the variables, and matching Statistical Package in the Social Sciences (SPSS) files are available from the book website at (www .cqpress.com). Computer-based research projects on public opinion can enrich a course for students and provide a firsthand opportunity to understand the process of public opinion research.

Acknowledgments

For five editions, this research has benefited from the advice and criticism of my colleagues, comments of students who have used this text, and insights I have gained from working with other scholars. Many colleagues offered advice, survey data, or moral support on this new edition: Amy Alexander, Laurie Beaudonnet, Bruno Cautrès, Natalie Cook, John Curtice, David Farrell, Rachel Gibson, Heiko Giebler, Marc Hooghe, John Jackson, Ronald Inglehart, Miki Kittilson, Hans-Dieter Klingemann, Ian McAllister, Robert Rohrschneider, Nicholas Sauger, Roger Scully, Markus Steinbrecher, Francesca Vassallo, Martin Wattenberg, Chris Welzel, Bernhard Weßels, and Paul Whiteley. I also appreciate the advice from the reviewers of this new edition: Terri Givens, Robert Hinckley, Matthew Singer, Boyka Stefanova, and Laron K. Williams. I owe an equal debt to the students in my Citizen Politics course at the University of California, Irvine, who have used this book and shared their mostly positive reactions.

This book would not be possible without the generous sharing of data by the principal investigators of the surveys presented here. The researchers from the national election studies, the World Values Survey, the International Social Survey Program, and other projects invest considerable time and effort to collect data on citizen opinions—and then make these data available to researchers and students. In addition, there is now an international network of social science data archives, such as the Inter-university Consortium for Political and Social Research at the University of Michigan, the Economic and Social Data Service in Britain, and the Center for Socio-Political Data (CDSP) in Paris. The GESIS archive in Germany has been especially helpful; first as the primary archive for many international data-sets (ISSP [International Social Survey Programme], CSES, ESS [European Social Survey]) and for other assistance. My appreciation to these individuals and institutions.

It is a pleasure to work with a great group of professionals at CQ Press. I want to thank the editors who worked on the project: David Felts, Elise Frasier, and Pam Suwinsky. A special thanks to Charisse Kiino who was my original editor at Congressional Quarterly Press and guided the earlier editions to publication.

I also owe a special debt to Ronald Inglehart. Ron was my mentor at the University of Michigan, and his provocative views about citizen politics deeply influenced my own thinking. He developed the World Values Survey into a global resource for social science research; many of the analyses in this book are based upon these data. I have always admired Ron's enthusiasm for social research and his creativity as a scholar. In innumerable ways, I am in his debt.

This book has a bold objective: to provide an overview of the nature of citizen politics in advanced industrial democracies. The task is clearly beyond the means of one individual, but with a little help from these friends, the resulting product begins to outline the political changes and choices that today face the citizenry in these established democracies.

Russell J. Dalton
Irvine, California

1   Introduction

This is a book about you, me, and the people around us—as citizens, voters, protesters, campaign workers, community activists, party members, and political spectators, we are the driving force of the democratic process. The spectacle of an American party convention, the intensity of a French farmers' protest, the community spirit of a New England town meeting, or the dedication of a German environmental group create an impressive image of democracy at work.

Yet, there is now an active debate on the vitality of contemporary democracy. Over the past two decades, we watched in awe as the force of "people power" tore down the Berlin Wall, led to freedom in South Africa, and created a democratization wave on a global scale. At the same time, however, new political challenges emerged in the established democracies. Some of the leading political scientists warn that democracy is at risk (Macedo et al. 2005; Putnam 2000). Various experts claim that social and civic engagement is weakening, intolerance is spreading, and people are becoming skeptical about politicians, parties, and political institutions. They claim that contemporary democracies are facing a malaise of the spirit that arises from their own citizens and that erodes the very foundations of the democratic process. Others criticize the structures and institutions of democracies and their inability to match their democratic ideals (Wolfe 2006; Dahl 2003; Zakaria 2003).

Other researchers are more positive about the present health of Western societies and political systems. Long-term social change has dramatically improved the income and living standards of the average person (Kenny 2011; Easterbrook 2003). Crime rates are down, life expectancy has increased, most people have more leisure time, women and minorities have more rights, and average incomes are higher (even in the midst of the current recession). Social modernization research maintains that the public's skills and values are becoming more supportive of democratic citizenship (Inglehart and Welzel 2005). By some measures, political involvement and political tolerance has increased (Zukin et al. 2006; Dalton 2009a). And various studies come to the conclusion that democracy is working better now than in the past (Soroka and Wlezien 2010; Powell 2011).

Internet Resource

Test your political knowledge and compare to the U.S. public:

http://pewresearch.org/politicalquiz

How can this be the best of times, and the worst of times, at the same time? The previous five editions of this book discussed this ebb and flow in analysts' evaluations of the democratic process and its citizens. Indeed, this is a long-standing debate, because each generation seemingly argues about the vitality of democracy. The two contrasting perspectives are both real. Democracy is a dynamic system, and it changes to succeed and advance. This dynamism causes tensions and strains, but if successful it deepens and enriches the democratic process. The contemporary debate about democracy arises from the tremendous social changes that the established democracies have experienced in the past several decades. The political world is changing, our puzzle is to understand how and why, and the implications of these changes.

This book focuses on the citizen's role within the democratic process, how this role has changed over time, and how these changes are altering the nature of democracy. The analyses are incomplete because we do not study the role of elites, interest groups, and other political actors. We also do not presume that the public is all-knowing or all-powerful. Indeed, there are many examples of the public's ignorance or error on policy issues (as there are examples of elite errors), as well as many instances in which policymakers disregard the public's preferences. The democratic process, like all human activities, is imperfect—but its strength lies in the premise that people are the best judges of their own destiny. The success of democracy is largely measured by the public's participation in the process, the respect for citizen rights, and the responsiveness of the system to popular demands. As Adlai Stevenson once said, in a democracy the people get the kind of government they deserve (for better or worse).

Before proceeding, I must acknowledge the complexity of studying the citizen's role in democracy. It is difficult to make simple generalizations about public opinion because the public isn't homogeneous. There isn't a single public. The public in any nation consists of millions of individuals, each with his or her own view of the world and of the citizen's role in politics. Some people are liberal, some moderate, some conservative; others are socialist, reactionary, communist, or none of the above. Opinions are often divided on contemporary political issues—this is why the issues are controversial and require a political decision. Some people favor strict environmental laws; some see environmental standards as excessive. Some favor international trade; some are skeptical of its claimed benefits. The study of public opinion underscores the diversity of the public.

People also differ in the interests and experiences they bring to politics. A few people are full-time political activists; most have modest political interests and ambitions. On some issues, a broad spectrum of society may be involved; other issues are greeted with apathy. Public opinion generally defines the acceptable bounds of politics, within which political elites resolve the controversies. When elites exceed these bounds, or when the issues immediately affect people's lives, the potential for political action is great. The difficulty is to understand and predict which course of action the public will choose.

In short, as social scientists we deal with the most complex problem in nature: to understand and predict human behavior. Yet this isn't a hopeless task. Scientific public opinion surveys provide valuable tools for researchers. From a sample of a few thousand precisely selected individuals, we can make reliable statements about the distribution of attitudes and opinions (Asher 2007). The survey interview allows the researcher to observe behavior as well as study the motivations and expectations guiding behavior. Furthermore, we can divide a survey into subgroups to examine the diversity in individual opinions.

This book relies heavily on public opinion surveys. I do not claim that all we know about the public is found in the statistics and percentages of public opinion surveys. Some of the most insightful writings about political behavior are qualitative studies of the topic. And yet, even insightful political analysts may make contradictory claims about the public. The value of the empirical method is that it provides a specific standard with which to evaluate contrasting descriptions of public opinion or behavior. Surveys enable people to describe their political views in their own words, and thus survey research is a tremendously valuable research tool for social scientists.

Drawing on an extensive collection of opinion surveys, this book examines public opinion in several advanced industrial democracies.[1] I describe how people view politics, how they participate in the process, what opinions they hold, and how they choose their leaders through competitive elections. These findings should help us to understand the public's role in the political process in contemporary democracies.

Comparing Public Opinion across Nations

If you have ever traveled to a foreign country, you have already learned the first lesson of this book. Human beings have many values and beliefs in common, but there are often differences in our values and behaviors. In simple terms, the British stand in lines; the Germans don't. The Americans love their hamburgers; the French don't. Furthermore, we only realize what is distinctive to a nation by making these comparisons.

There are several advantages to the comparative study of public opinion in Western democracies. Although these nations differ in the specifics of their governments and party systems, they share broad similarities in the functioning of the democratic process and the citizen's role in the process. A comparative approach is a means to study those aspects of political behavior that should be valid across nations. General theories of why people participate in democratic politics should apply to people regardless of their nationality. Theories to explain party preferences should, for example, hold for Americans and Europeans if they represent basic features of human nature.

In most instances, we expect to find similar patterns of behavior in different democracies. If our theories do not work similarly across nations, however, then we have learned something new and important. Science often progresses by finding exceptions to general theory, which necessitate further theoretical work. The same applies to social science.

Comparative analysis can also examine the effects of political structures on citizens' political behavior. For example, does the nature of a nation's electoral system affect people's voting behavior? Or, does the structure of political institutions affect the patterns of political participation? Each nation represents a "natural experiment" wherein general theories of political behavior can be tested in a different political context.

Finally, even if we are interested only in a single nation, comparative research is still very valuable. An old Hebrew riddle expresses this idea: "*Question:* Who first discovered water? *Answer:* I don't know, but it wasn't a fish." Immersing oneself in a single environment makes it harder to recognize the characteristics of that environment. It is difficult to understand what is unique and distinctive about American political behavior, for example, by studying only American politics. Indeed, many students of American politics may be surprised to learn that the United States is often the atypical case in cross-national comparisons. American public opinion and political processes are unique in many ways, but we perceive this only by rising above the waters.

Choosing Nations to Compare

To balance our needs for comparison and attention to national differences, I focus on politics in four nations: the United States, Great Britain, the Federal Republic of Germany (FRG), and France.[2] I chose these nations for several reasons. By many standards, these are the major powers among the Western democracies. Their population, size, economy, military strength, and political influence earn them leadership positions in international circles. The actions of any of these nations can have significant consequences for all the others.

These nations also highlight the major differences in the structure of democratic politics (see table 1.1). For example, Great Britain has a pure parliamentary system of government. The popularly elected House of Commons selects the prime minister to head the executive branch. This produces a fusion of legislative and executive power, because the same party and the same group of elites direct both branches of government. In contrast, American government has a presidential system, with extensive checks and balances to maintain a separation of legislative and executive power. French politics has a modified presidential system. The public directly elects both the president and the National Assembly, which selects the premier to head the administration of government. Germany has a parliamentary system, with the popularly elected Bundestag selecting the chancellor as head of the executive branch. However,

Germany also has a strong federal structure and a separation of powers that is uncommon for a parliamentary government. These contrasting institutional forms should influence citizen politics in each nation (Lijphart 2012; Powell 2000).

Table 1.1	Comparing Political Systems			
NATIONAL CHARACTERISTIC	**UNITED STATES**	**GREAT BRITAIN**	**GERMANY**	**FRANCE**
Population (in millions)	313.8	63.0	81.3	65.6
Gross domestic product/capita	$49,000	$36,600	$38,400	$35,600
Political regime established	1789	Seventeenth century	1949	1958
State form	Republic	Constitutional monarchy	Republic	Republic
Government structure	Presidential	Parliamentary	Modified parliamentary	Modified presidential
Chief executive	President	Prime minister	Chancellor	President
Method of selection	Direct election	Elected by Parliament	Elected by Parliament	Direct election
Legislature	Bicameral	Bicameral	Bicameral	Bicameral
Lower house	House of Representatives	House of Commons	Bundestag	National Assembly
Upper house	Senate	House of Lords	Bundesrat	Senate
Power of upper house	Equal	Weaker	Equal on state issues	Weaker
Electoral System				
Lower house	Single-member districts	Single-member districts	Proportional representation and single-member districts	Single-member districts
Upper house	Statewide elections	Inheritance and appointment	Appointed by states	Appointed by communes
Major parties	Democrats Republicans	Labour Liberal Democrats Conservatives	Left Party (Linke) Greens Social Democrats Free Democrats Christian Democrats (CDU/CSU)	Communists Socialists Greens MoDem/ UDF Gaullists (UPM) National Front

Source: Compiled by author; population and GNP statistics are from the *CIA World Factbook, 2012.*

Electoral systems are equally diverse. Great Britain and the United States select the members of their national legislatures from single-member districts, where a plurality is sufficient for election. Germany uses a hybrid system for Bundestag elections; half the deputies are elected from single-member districts and half are selected from party lists. The French electoral system is based on deputies winning a majority in single-member districts, with a second ballot (*tour*) if no candidate receives a majority on the first ballot. Several studies have shown that such institutional arrangements can affect electoral outcomes (Dalton and Anderson 2011; Powell 2000; Taagepera and Shugart 1989).

The party systems of these four nations also vary. Party competition in the United States is usually limited to the Democratic and Republican parties. Both are broad "catchall" parties that combine diverse political groups into weakly structured electoral coalitions. In contrast, most European political parties are hierarchically organized and controlled by the party leadership. Candidates are elected primarily because of their party labels and not because of their personal attributes; most party deputies vote as a bloc in the legislature. Party options are also more diverse in Europe. British voters can select from at least three major parties; Germans have five major parties in the Bundestag. French party politics is synonymous with diversity and political polarization. Dozens of parties run in elections, and a large number win seats in parliament. France, a nation of perpetual political effervescence, provides the spice of comparative politics.

The contrasts across nations take on an added dimension because of German unification. Western Germans developed the characteristics of a stable, advanced industrial democracy. In contrast, the residents of the former East Germany, like most of the rest of Eastern Europe, are still learning about the democratic process. Furthermore, when possible, I broaden the cross-national comparisons to include a range other advanced industrial democracies.

A New Style of Citizen Politics

The findings of this book can best be described by asking you to do a thought experiment: If you are a student, think back to what politics must have been like several decades ago—when your grandparents were your age. The Constitution has not really changed since then, the institutions of government are basically the same, and the Democrats and Republicans still contend in elections. But, as I argue in this book, the people and politics have changed—and this has transformed the democratic process.

The changing nature of citizen political behavior derives from the socioeconomic transformation of the Western societies over the past fifty years. These countries are developing a set of characteristics that collectively represent a new form of *advanced industrial* or *postindustrial* society (Inglehart 1977, 1990; Crouch 1999). These changes are summarized in figure 1.1.

Figure 1.1 The New Citizen Politics

Modernizing social conditions create an advanced industrial society where citizens' skills and values change, and this produces a new style of citizen politics.

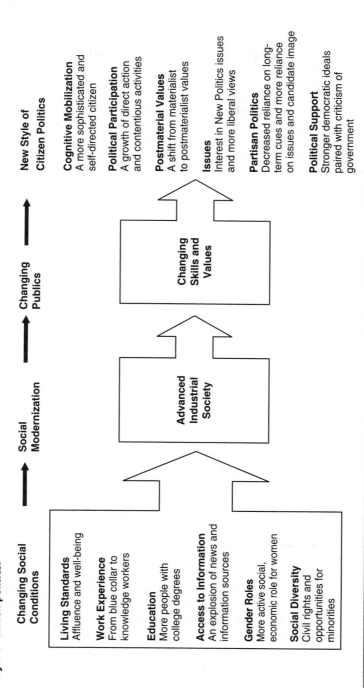

Changing Social Conditions → Social Modernization → Changing Publics → Changing Skills and Values → New Style of Citizen Politics

Changing Social Conditions

Living Standards
Affluence and well-being

Work Experience
From blue collar to knowledge workers

Education
More people with college degrees

Access to Information
An explosion of news and information sources

Gender Roles
More active social, economic role for women

Social Diversity
Civil rights and opportunities for minorities

Advanced Industrial Society

Changing Skills and Values

New Style of Citizen Politics

Cognitive Mobilization
A more sophisticated and self-directed citizen

Political Participation
A growth of direct action and contentious activities

Postmaterial Values
A shift from materialist to postmaterialist values

Issues
Interest in New Politics issues and more liberal views

Partisan Politics
Decreased reliance on long-term cues and more reliance on issues and candidate image

Political Support
Stronger democratic ideals paired with criticism of government

The most dramatic changes involve economic conditions. An unprecedented expansion of economic well-being occurred in the second half of the twentieth century. The economies of Western Europe and North America grew at phenomenal rates in the post–World War II decades. For example, analysts describe the astonishing expansion of the West German economy as the *Wirtschaftswunder* (Economic Miracle). Average income levels in our four nations are several times greater than at any time in prewar history. By most economic standards, these four nations rank among the most affluent nations of the world—and the most affluent in human history. The current recession may distract our attention from the basic changes in economic conditions during the past fifty years.

A restructured labor force is another major social change. The number of people employed in agriculture has decreased dramatically in most Western nations, and industrial employment has remained stable or declined. At the same time, employment in the service sector has increased markedly. In addition, because of the expansion of national and local governments, public employment now constitutes a significant share of the labor force. Richard Florida (2003) provocatively argued that a new creative class—individuals who create and utilize knowledge—are a vanguard for social and cultural change. Only a minority of jobs in today's economy existed in your grandparent's time. Moreover, social mobility and different career experiences change individual values and their outlooks on life. A blue-collar industrial worker on an assembly line, for instance, has a much different life experience than a computer programmer at Google—and this should affect their values.

Advanced industrialism also changes the context of the workplace and the residential neighborhood. Urbanization alters life expectations and lifestyles. It brings an increasing separation of the home from the workplace, a greater diversity of occupations and interests, an expanded range of career opportunities, and more geographic and social mobility. With these trends come changes in the forms of social interaction, as communal forms of organization are replaced by voluntary associations, which are less institutionalized and more spontaneous. Communities are becoming less bounded; individuals are involved in increasingly complex and competing social networks that divide their loyalties; and ties to institutions are becoming more fluid.

Educational opportunities also have expanded rapidly over the past several decades. If your grandparents went to school in 1950 or before, most ended their studies with a high school education or less. Access to education steadily increased as minimal education standards were raised and university enrollments skyrocketed. Today, more than three-quarters of American youth and about half of college-age European youth had some form of tertiary schooling. This trend has fundamentally changed the educational composition of contemporary mass publics.

Citizen access to political information has also dramatically increased. The electronic media, especially television, have experienced exceptional growth, and access to other information sources, such as books and magazines, have grown. Even more revolutionary is the rapid development of electronic information processing: computers, the Internet, blogs, Twitter, and related technologies. It seems like any piece of information is only a Google away. Again, the information environment of today and that of the 1950s–60s almost bear no comparison. Information is no longer a scarce commodity. Indeed, the contemporary information problem is how to adapt to life in cyberspace, managing an ever-growing volume of sophisticated knowledge.

One of the most basic changes involves the social, economic, and political status of women and minority groups. As noted later in the chapter, the social and political roles of women have been transformed from a restrictive and nonpolitical role to active participants in society and politics. For instance, Britain, Germany, and several other European nations have had a woman head of government; the 2007 French presidential election included a woman as the candidate of the Socialist Party. Before 1945, French women were not even allowed to vote. Similarly, legal and social limitations on the rights and opportunities of racial and ethnic groups have diminished—most dramatically in the United States but also in Europe. Once "the public" was defined as white men (sometimes only property owners), and now the definition of citizenship is more inclusive.

Western governments have also expanded their involvement in society. Government is increasingly responsible for protecting and managing society and the economy. Many European societies have extensive welfare programs, in which a network of generous social programs protects the individual against economic or medical hardship. Unemployment, illness, and similar problems still occur, but under the welfare state, their consequences are less dire than in the past. In addition, most people now see the government as responsible for protecting the environment, ensuring social rights, enabling lifestyle choices, and a host of other new obligations.

Despite these past trends, many political analysts ask whether these patterns can continue. Everywhere, it seems, there has been a retrenchment in government social programs. Increased international economic competition in a globalized economy has created new economic strains within these nations. Elation about the end of the Cold War and the development of new democracies is tempered by worries about growing nationalism, international terrorism, ethnic conflict, and new financial burdens. The Great Recession of 2008 deepened these concerns. In some established democracies, there are real worries that economic problems will revive reactionary political groups.

Admittedly, the miraculous economic growth rates of the post–World War II period now seem like distant history, especially in the wake of the 2008 Great Recession. Yet, the transformation of advanced industrial democracies involves more than simply the politics of affluence. Changes in occupational and social structures are continuing, and with them an alteration in life conditions and lifestyles. Expanded educational opportunities represent an enduring trait of modern societies. The information revolution is continuing—in fact, it is growing at an amazing rate. Advanced industrial societies are dramatically different from their 1950s predecessors. My expectation is that change will continue, albeit at a slower rate in the decades ahead.

This book maintains that one result of these social trends is the development of a new style of citizen politics. Our premise is that as the socioeconomic characteristics of these nations change, the characteristics of the public change as well. More educational opportunities mean a growth in political skills and resources, producing the most sophisticated publics in the history of democracies. Changing economic conditions redefine citizens' issue interests. The weakening of social networks and institutional loyalties is associated with the decline of traditional political alignments and voting patterns. Contemporary publics and democratic politics have been dramatically transformed over the past several decades.

The parts of this new style of citizen politics are not always, or necessarily, linked together. Some parts may be transitory; others may be coincidental. Nevertheless, several traits coexist for the present, defining a new pattern of citizen political behavior. This book systematically describes this new pattern of political thought and action. Figure 1.1 summarizes this causal process with the new patterns of citizen politics listed on the right of the figure.

One aspect of the new citizen politics is political engagement (chapters 2–4). Expanding political skills and resources should increase the cognitive sophistication of the citizenry. In addition, many people are placing greater emphasis on participating in political and economic decision making. Participation in elections is the most common form of political action—but voting is declining in most countries. However, protest, citizen action groups, boycotts, and direct forms of action are increasing. People are less likely to be passive subjects and more likely to demand a say in the decisions affecting their lives. The new style of citizen politics reflects a more active involvement in the democratic process.

Another broad area of change involves the values and attitudes of the public (chapters 5–6). Industrial societies aimed at providing affluence and economic security. The success of advanced industrialism fulfills many basic economic needs for a sizable sector of society. Thus, some people are shifting their concerns to new political goals (Inglehart 1990, 2008). Several of these new issues are common to advanced industrial democracies: social equality, environmental protection, the dangers of nuclear energy, gender equality, and human rights. In some instances, historic conditions focus these general concerns on specific national problems—for example, racial equality in the United States, regional conflicts in Britain, or center–periphery differences in France. Many of these issues are now loosely connected into an alternative political agenda that is another element of the new style of citizen politics.

Partisan politics is also changing (chapters 7–11). Comparative electoral research used to emphasize the stability of democratic party systems. This situation has changed. There is increased fragmentation and volatility of these party systems. Declining class differences in voting behavior reflect the general erosion in the social bases of voting. In most nations the public's identification with political parties and affect toward parties has decreased. These patterns have produced a partial *dealignment* of contemporary party systems (Dalton 2012a; Dalton and Wattenberg 2000).

These trends are at least partially the result of the addition of new issues to the political agenda and the difficulties of the established parties to respond to these issues. New parties have arisen across the face of Europe—ranging from green parties to new right parties. An even more novel Pirate Party has emerged in several nations where the established parties have not addressed young people's concerns about Internet privacy and file sharing. New political movements seek access to the Democratic and Republican parties in the United States. The changing characteristics of contemporary publics also increase party volatility. Unsophisticated voters once relied on social-group cues and partisan cues to make their political decisions. Because of the dramatic spread of education and information sources, more people can now deal with the complexities of politics and make their own political decisions. Consequently, issues and other short-term factors are more important as influences on voting choices. The new style of citizen politics features a more issue-oriented and candidate-oriented electorate.

Finally, attitudes toward government represent a new paradox for democracy (chapter 12). New issues have joined the agenda; the democratic process has become more inclusive; and the government has generally improved the quality of life—but at the same time, people have become more critical of government. The conflict over new issues and new participation patterns may offer a partial explanation of these trends. In addition, emerging value priorities that stress self-actualization and autonomy may stimulate skepticism of elite-controlled hierarchical organizations (such as bureaucracies, political parties, and large interest groups).

One thing you quickly learn about political science is that serious researchers can reach different conclusions based on similar evidence. Many other authors question this book's basic premise of political change. In reviewing European public opinion trends, for example, Dieter Fuchs and Hans-Dieter Klingemann concluded, "The hypotheses we tested are based on the premise that a fundamental change had taken place in the relationship between citizens and the state, provoking a challenge to representative democracy . . . [but] the postulated fundamental change in the citizens' relationship with the state largely did *not* occur" (1995, 429). Begin your reading from this skeptical position, and then see if the evidence supports it.

My own sense is that this is an exciting time to study public opinion because so much is changing. The puzzle for researchers, students, and citizens is to understand how democracy functions in this new context. This new style of citizen politics creates strains for the political systems of advanced industrial democracies. Protests, social movements, partisan volatility, and political skepticism are disrupting the traditional political order. Adjustment to new issue concerns and new patterns of citizen participation may be a difficult process. More people now take democratic ideals seriously, and they expect political systems to live up to those ideals. Democracy isn't an end state, but an evolutionary process. Thus, the new style of citizen politics is a sign of vitality and an opportunity for these societies to make further progress toward their democratic goals.

Suggested Readings

Baker, Wayne. 2004. *America's Crisis of Values: Reality and Perception*. Princeton: Princeton University Press.

Dalton, Russell, and Hans-Dieter Klingemann, eds. 2007. *Oxford Handbook of Political Behavior*. Oxford, UK: Oxford University Press.

Florida, Richard. 2002. *The Rise of the Creative Class: And How It's Transforming Work, Leisure, Community and Everyday Life*. New York: Perseus Books.

Inglehart, Ronald. 1990. *Culture Shift in Advanced Industrial Societies*. Princeton: Princeton University Press.

Notes

1. See appendix A for information on the major public opinion surveys used in this book. Neither these archives nor the original collectors of the surveys bears responsibility for the analyses presented here.
2. For a brief review of these nations, see Powell, Dalton, and Strom (2011). More detailed national studies are found in Norton (2010) for Britain, Conradt (2008) for Germany, and Safran (2008) for France.

Part One

Politics and the Public

2 The Nature of Mass Beliefs

The *Los Angeles Times* ran an article about a public opinion survey testing Americans' knowledge of pop culture versus politics.[1] The survey found that more people could name two of Snow White's seven dwarfs than could name two members of the U.S. Supreme Court. More Americans knew the name of the British author of the Harry Potter books than the name of Britain's prime minister. More people knew the names of the Three Stooges than the names of the three branches of the U.S. government.

This article and many more like it illustrate a continuing debate about the political abilities of democratic publics—their level of knowledge, understanding, and interest in politics. For voters to make meaningful decisions, they must know something about the issues and understand the available options. People also need sufficient knowledge of how the political system works if they want to influence the actions of government. In short, for democratic politics to be purposeful, the citizens must have at least a basic level of political skills.

Studying the public's level of sophistication also improves our understanding of the public opinion data presented in this book. With what depth of knowledge and conviction are opinions held? Do responses to public opinion surveys represent reasoned assessments of the issues or the snap judgments of individuals faced by an interviewer on their doorsteps? It is common to hear the public labeled as uninformed (especially when public opinion conflicts with the speaker's own views). Conversely, the public cannot be wiser than when it supports one's position. Can we judge the merits of either position based on the empirical evidence from public opinion surveys?

Debates about the public's political abilities are one of the major controversies in political behavior research. This controversy involves assumptions about what level of sophistication is required for democracies to fulfill their political ideals as well as differences in evaluating the evidence of whether the public fulfills these assumptions.

| Internet Resource |

Compare your level of political knowledge to that of the American public:

http://pewresearch.org/politicalquiz

The Supercitizen

Political theorists have long maintained that democracy is workable only when the public has a high degree of political information and sophistication. John Stuart Mill, John Locke, Alexis de Tocqueville, and other writers saw these public traits as requirements for a successful democracy. Most theorists also claimed that people should support the political system and share a commitment to democratic ideals such as pluralism, free expression, and minority rights (see chapter 12). Otherwise, misguided or unscrupulous elites might manipulate an uninformed and unsophisticated public. In a sense, these theorists posited a supercitizen model: for democracy to survive, the public must be a paragon of civic virtue.

This ideal of the democratic supercitizen is often illustrated by examples drawn from a popular lore about the sophistication of Americans.[2] Tocqueville (1966) praised the civic and political involvement of Americans when he described the United States in the nineteenth century. Voters in early America supposedly yearned for the stimulating political debates of election campaigns and flocked to political rallies in great numbers. New England town hall meetings became a legendary example of the American political spirit. Even on the frontier, there was a common lore that conversations around the general store's cracker barrel displayed a deep interest in politics.

History painted a less positive picture of the public in many European nations. In contrast to America, the right to vote came late to most Europeans, often delayed until the beginning of the twentieth century. The aristocratic institutions and deferential traditions of British politics limited public participation beyond the act of voting and severely restricted the size of the eligible electorate. In France, the excesses of the French Revolution raised doubts about the features of mass participation. The instability of the French political system supposedly produced a sense of "incivism" (lack of civic engagement), leading people to avoid political discussions and involvement.

Germany was the most graphic example of what might happen when the public lacks democratic norms. Under the authoritarian governments that ruled during the Second Empire (1871–1918), people were taught to be seen and not heard. The democratic Weimar Republic (1919–33) was a brief and turbulent interlude in Germany's nondemocratic history, but the frailty of democratic norms contributed to that system's demise and the rise of Hitler's Third Reich in 1933. Because a strong democratic culture eventually developed in the postwar Federal Republic, German democracy has flourished. These historical experiences strengthened the belief that a sophisticated, involved, and democratic public is necessary for democracy to succeed.

The Unsophisticated Citizen

The start of scientific public opinion surveying in the 1950s and 1960s provided the first opportunity to move beyond the insights of philosophers and social commentators. It was finally possible to test the lofty theorizing about the democratic citizen against reality. The public itself was directly consulted.

In contrast to the classic images celebrated in democratic theory, public opinion surveys presented an unflattering picture of the American public. Political sophistication seemed to fall far short of the supercitizen model. Most people's political interest and involvement barely extended beyond casting an occasional vote in elections. Furthermore, Americans apparently brought little understanding to their participation in politics. It was not clear that people based their voting decisions on rational evaluations of the candidates and their issue positions. Instead, habitual group loyalties and personalistic considerations seemed to shape the election choices of most voters. The seminal work in the area summarized these findings as follows:

> Our data reveal that certain requirements commonly assumed for the successful operation of democracy are not met by the behavior of the "average" citizen. . . . Many vote without real involvement in the election. . . . The citizen is not highly informed on the details of the campaign. . . . In any rigorous or narrow sense, the voters are not highly rational. (Berelson, Lazarsfeld, and McPhee 1954, 307–10)

The landmark study *The American Voter* (Campbell et al. 1960) supported these early findings by documenting a lack of political sophistication and ideological understanding by the American electorate.

In an influential essay on mass belief systems, Philip Converse (1964) spelled out the criteria for measuring political sophistication. As modeled in figure 2.1, Converse said there should be a basic *structure* at the core of individual political beliefs. An ideological framework such as liberalism or conservatism presumably provides this structure, at least at higher levels of sophistication. In addition, there should be *constraint* between issue positions. Constraint means a strong agreement between one's core beliefs and specific issue positions. A person who is liberal on one issue is expected to be liberal on others, and opinions on one issue should be ideologically (or at least logically) consistent with other beliefs. Finally, Converse said that issue opinions should be relatively *stable* over time so that voters held enduring beliefs that guided their behavior. The overall result should be a tightly structured system of beliefs like that depicted in the figure.

In testing this model, Converse concluded that most Americans fell short on these criteria. First, most people did not judge political phenomena in

Figure 2.1	Model of a Structured Belief System

Early research claimed that issue positions should be interconnected and linked to core values for citizens to make consistent and reasonable choices.

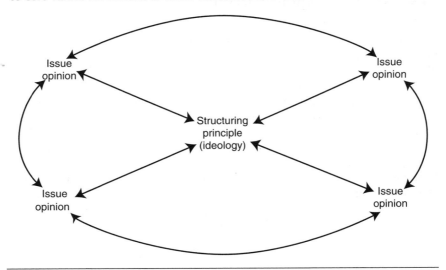

ideological terms, such as liberalism/conservatism or capitalism/socialism. People were generally unfamiliar with terms such as *liberal* or *conservative*, and barely a tenth of Americans used ideological concepts to structure their belief systems. Second, Converse found only a weak relationship between issues that seemingly were connected. For example, people who felt taxes were too high nevertheless favored increased spending for many specific government programs. Third, issue beliefs were not stable over time; many people seemed to change their opinions randomly across elections. The lack of structure, constraint, and stability led Converse (1970) to conclude that public opinion researchers are often studying "nonattitudes"—that is, many people apparently do not have informed opinions even on issues of long-standing political concern.

In *The American Voter,* Angus Campbell and his colleagues declared that the electorate "is almost completely unable to judge the rationality of government actions; knowing little of the particular policies and what has led to them, the mass electorate isn't able either to appraise its goals or the appropriateness of the means chosen to secure these goals" (1960, 543). Other studies soon showed that many people could not name their elected representatives, were unfamiliar with the institutions of government, and did not understand the mechanics of the political process.

The image of the American voter had fallen to a new low, and recent research claims that little has changed (for example, Lewis-Beck et al. 2008;

Caplan 2007). Several studies maintain that political information has not improved over time and may be decreasing because young people are becoming less interested and informed about politics (Delli Carpini and Keeter 1996; Wattenberg 2011a, ch. 3). A recent study thus asks the provocative question:

> Voters don't know very much, aren't aware of how little they know; aren't particularly proficient at getting the information they need, and can't remember the information once they've learned it. The problem is made worse by politicians and interest groups that actively hide information, by issues that are often complex enough to stymie the experts, and by the vast number of important issues. . . . How can democracy possibly be successful when it relies on the choices of voters who know so little? (Oppenheimer and Edwards 2012, 32–33)

The image of the unsophisticated citizen seemed equally applicable to West Europeans. Looking beyond election turnout, political involvement in Europe was often lower than in the United States (Almond and Verba 1963; Verba, Nie, and Kim 1978). Europeans also lacked well-formed opinions on the pressing issues of the day (Converse and Pierce 1986, ch. 7; Butler and Stokes 1969). For instance, 60 percent of British in the 1960s did not recognize the terms *Left* and *Right* as they applied to politics. And the telltale signs of nonattitudes—weak linkages between opinions on related issues and high opinion instability over time—were apparent.

Other research raised doubts about the public's commitment to political tolerance and other values underlying the democratic process (Stouffer 1955; McClosky and Brill 1983; Barnum and Sullivan 1989). People supported democratic ideals in the abstract, but not when applied to political groups they disliked, such as communists, Nazis, atheists, and political nonconformists. Again, the empirical reality apparently fell short of the democratic ideal.

Elitist Theory of Democracy

Having found that most people apparently fail to meet the requirements of classic democratic theory, political scientists faced a paradox: most individuals are not "good" democratic citizens, and yet democracies such as the United States and Great Britain have existed for generations. Gradually, scholars developed an *elitist theory of democracy* to interpret these survey findings in a positive light (Berelson et al. 1954, 313–23; Almond and Verba 1963, ch. 15).

This elitist theory turned the supposed limitations of the public into a strength of democracy. It held that politics might prove unworkable if every person were active on every issue at all times. Images of the centrifugal forces that destroyed the Weimar Republic were still fresh and generated concerns about the possible effects of excessive participation. These authors suggest that the model citizen "is not the active citizen; he is the potentially active citizen" (Almond and Verba 1963, 347). In other words, people must believe that they can influence the government and become active if the issue is sufficiently important. Few will realize this potential, however. The balance between action and potential action presumably ensures that political elites have enough freedom to make necessary decisions while keeping the public interest in mind.

Another element of this elitist theory stresses the heterogeneity of the public. "Some people are and should be highly interested in politics, but not everyone is or needs to be" (Berelson et al. 1954, 315). From this perspective, the responsiveness of the political system is secured by a core of active citizens and political elites, leaving the rest of the public blissfully uninformed and uninvolved. The mix between involved and indifferent voters supposedly ensures both the stability and flexibility of democratic systems.

The elitist theory of democracy is drawn from the realities of political life—or at least from the hard evidence of survey research. It is, however, a very undemocratic theory of democracy. The theory maintains that "the democratic citizen . . . must be active, yet passive; involved, yet not too involved; influential, yet deferential" (Almond and Verba 1963, 478–79). The values and goals of democracy are at least partially obscured by a mountain of survey data.

Accepting this new creed, some analysts advocated an extreme version of this model, implying that the rise in citizen activism undemocratic and politically destabilizing. As Thomas Dye and Harmon Ziegler (1970, 328) bluntly claimed,

> The survival of democracy depends upon the commitment of elites to democratic ideals rather than upon broad support for democracy by the masses. Political apathy and nonparticipation among the masses contribute to the survival of democracy. Fortunately for democracy, the antidemocratic masses are generally more apathetic than elites.

If a supportive and quiescent public ensures a smoothly functioning political system, then isn't it virtually the duty of the individual to remain uninvolved? Hurray for sitting on the couch and watching TV! In fact, when the public began to challenge political elites during the turbulent 1960s and 1970s, some political scientists cautioned that democracy required a public of followers who would not question political elites too extensively (Crozier, Huntington, and Watanuki 1975). They argued that too much democracy could threaten the democratic process. More recently, Fareed Zakaria, who hosts a Sunday morning CNN talk show, argued that we suffer from too much democracy (Zakaria 2003).

I believe that the elitist theory overlooks the complexities of the democratic process and takes an unsophisticated view of the evidence. For example, this theory ignores the inconsistencies that also exist among political elites. Members of the U.S. Congress routinely endorse formal budget limits and then act to circumvent these same limits in the next piece of legislation; in one vote they endorse strict measures to control crime, in the next they refuse to ban assault weapons.[3] Such inconsistencies in elite behavior are treated as examples of the complexity of politics, but the same patterns in public opinion are considered signs of limited sophistication. In addition, the elitist critique of the public's abilities has been challenged on both normative and empirical grounds.[4] The picture of the public's abilities isn't nearly as bleak as that painted by the elitist theory of democracy. Indeed, Arthur Lupia (2007) provocatively argued that the elitism of researchers contributes to their negative image of the public. As our scientific knowledge has increased, so, too, has our understanding of how people make political decisions.

Political Sophistication Reconsidered

I base my challenge to past descriptions of an unsophisticated public on several points. Profound social and political changes in the advanced industrial democracies have increased the public's political abilities. In addition, research has enriched our understanding of how people think about political matters. Each point deserves attention.

Cognitive Mobilization

Even if the public of the 1950s (and earlier) had limited political skills and resources, contemporary publics are different. A process of "cognitive mobilization" has raised the public's overall level of political sophistication (Dalton 2012a; Inglehart 1990). This process has two separate parts: the ability to acquire political information and the ability to process political information.

A generation or two earlier, the average citizen had limited access to information. In the past, one could read newspapers or magazines, but this could be demanding, especially for a public with limited education. Particularly in Europe, daily newspapers were of uneven quality and news coverage, and many mass newspapers were little more than scandal sheets. Information also arrived days or even weeks after the actual events. Today, the supply and variety of political news is nearly unlimited; this is a relatively recent development.

The expansion of the mass media, especially television, is the clearest example of this change (Norris 2000; Prior 2007). In 1950 television was still a novelty for most Americans and a luxury for most Europeans. Television sets were in only half of American homes, in fewer than 10 percent of homes in Great Britain and France, and in fewer than 5 percent of those in West Germany. The expansion of television ownership over the next two decades produced a growing reliance on television as a source of political information. In the 1952 U.S. elections, 51 percent of the electorate used television news as an information source. By 1960 the number had risen to a plateau of about 90 percent. In 1961 only 50 percent of the West German public depended on television for political information, but by 1974 the Germans had also reached the 90 percent level. British and French trends present similar patterns.

As television viewership increased, so too did the amount of political information provided by the medium. The now-standard American nightly half-hour national news program began only in 1963. Since then, technology and viewer interest have increased the proportion of television programming devoted to news and political affairs. Today, news reporting is instantaneous and done on a worldwide scale. Most Americans have access to news on a 24/7 basis: CNN, FOX, MSNBC, C-SPAN, and other cable channels create a rich media environment. Markus Prior (2007) shows that the expansion of media choice has raised the total consumption of political information, but also has increased the inequality in political information between the most and least interested. Those who are interested can find 24-hour news; those who are not interested watch *The Simpsons* during the news hour.

In addition to information from television, many people read newspapers and magazines, hear news on the radio, use the Internet, join online discussion groups, or learn about politics from their friends. Although many political scientists are critical of "soft news" programs, such as talk shows or Jon Stewart and *The Daily Show,* these programs also can be valuable sources of information (Baum and Jamison 2005). People have access to an array of information that would have been unimaginable a generation ago. The increases in the quantity and quality of political information provided by the media should improve political awareness.

Similar trends exist in most advanced industrial democracies. Cable and satellite channels are expanding the available options, ranging from the national networks to those of neighboring nations to a host of news and government information programs. The media's political role has also increased. For example, until the 1964 election the British government prohibited the BBC from carrying election news during the campaign period. Now television coverage is a central part of most modern campaigns (Norris et al. 1999). Equally dramatic and important, especially for younger citizens, is the rise of Internet-based news sources in the past decade or so.

Table 2.1 presents the use of various information sources to learn about current events.[5] As many other studies have shown, television news is the most heavily used source of information—cited by about 90 percent of the public in each of the four nations. It is significant that the second most commonly used information source is conversation with friends and colleagues. People are social animals, and we search out information from our friends. While other mass media sources—newspapers and printed magazines—are falling in circulation, there is a remarkable increase in the use of the Internet as an information source. Two-thirds of Americans say they regularly rely on the Internet, and this source is now the most commonly used among the young (Pew 2012a).

| Table 2.1 | Information Sources |

Television remains the most common information source, but Internet use is increasing especially in the United States.

	UNITED STATES	GREAT BRITAIN	FRANCE	GERMANY
Television/radio news	87	93	95	96
TV/radio in-depth reports	62	63	67	66
Friends and colleagues	82	83	77	87
Internet	67	49	37	48
Newspapers	64	72	62	85
Magazines	44	48	48	51
Books	32	42	33	37

Source: World Values Survey (2006–08). The question asked about weekly use separately for each information source; the figure presents the percentage who have used each source.

Political scientists are divided on whether the expansion of television (and now the Internet) as an information source is a boon or a curse for the democratic process (for example, Prior 2007; Norris 2000). Some scholars argue that television tends to trivialize information, emphasizing entertainment and drama over substance and creating a negative climate of opinion. The Internet is awash with unedited misinformation, as well as a wealth of reliable information. Other researchers have an idyllic image of a former age and lament the decrease in newspaper readers, especially among the young. Some of these concerns are well founded. I believe, however, that the benefits of the new media age outweigh the limits. Television can create a better sense of the political process by allowing all of us to watch legislative deliberations, to see candidates as they campaign, and to experience history firsthand. Observing an important parliamentary debate on television or watching the presidential inauguration live puts citizens in direct contact with their government and gives them a better understanding of how democracy works. The Internet provides access to an abundance of information not imagined except in early *Star Trek* episodes. Television, the Internet, and other modern information sources have great positive and negative potential, and the objective of democratic polities should be to maximize the positive benefits and minimize the negatives.

A provocative sign of the changing information climate comes from a study of opinion-holding on foreign policy matters. Matthew Baum (2003) found more public attentiveness and opinion-holding toward the 1991 Persian Gulf War than for either Vietnam or Korea at a similar stage of these conflicts.

Many people learned about politics from traditional sources, such as newspapers and network television news, but in today's new information age others learn from "soft news" programs, from the Internet, from their friends, or other sources. This is the new information age in which we live.

In addition to the media or friendship networks, a good deal of politically relevant information is available from our daily life experiences. Governments now have a large role in society, and how well or poorly they perform provides important political information. For example, if the economy is doing well, voters are apt to support the incumbents. Similarly, government runs most schools, sets health standards, administers family and social programs, protects the environment, and provides for our transportation needs. When a commuter notes that highways are deteriorating (or being improved) or parents note improvements (or deterioration) in their children's schools, these are significant political facts. We live in an information-rich environment, and politically relevant information is easily available.

Equally important, the expansion of information sources has been paralleled by the public's greater ability to process political information. A process of *cognitive mobilization* means that more people now have the resources and skills necessary to deal with the complexities of politics and to reach their own political decisions. Expanded access to political information provides an opportunity to the citizenry, but this abundance of news may be only a noisy cacophony unless one can process the information. Therefore, it is also necessary for the public to develop political skills.

The most visible change in political skills is the level of education. Advanced industrial societies require a more educated and technically sophisticated electorate, and modern affluence has expanded educational opportunities (see chapter 1). Consequently, the change in educational level from the 1950s to today is amazing. In 1952 nearly two-thirds of Americans had less than a high school diploma, and only a tenth had some college education. In 2012 roughly two-thirds have some college education. Parallel changes are transforming European publics. In postwar West Germany the number of people with only primary schooling exceeded those with a secondary school diploma (*Mittlere Reife*) by about five to one. Today, the number of better-educated Germans is twice as large as the lesser-educated.

The relationship between years of schooling and political sophistication is not one to one, but research shows that education is linked to a person's level of political knowledge, interest, and sophistication (Nie, Junn, and Stehlik-Barry 1996; Sniderman, Brody, and Tetlock 1991). Even more provocatively, social scientists have found that the average citizen's IQ has risen steadily over the past century in virtually all nations where long-term data are available (Flynn 2007; Pinker 2011, 650–60). The average American in 2010 had an IQ that was 18 points higher than that of the average American in 1950! We are getting smarter, according to this evidence. This rise is due to many factors, such as improving diets and health, but a major factor has been the expansion of education and the framework for thinking about the world.

In political terms, Samuel Popkin (1991, 36) suggested that rising educational levels also increase the breadth of citizens' political interests, even if they do not raise overall levels of political knowledge or issue constraint by the same amount. A doubling of the public's educational level may not double the level of political sophistication, but some increase should occur. In the long history of democracies, contemporary electorates are clearly the most educated, which should contribute toward making a more sophisticated electorate and a new style of citizen politics.

Another related societal change involves the social and political status of women. In the 1950s, a significant proportion of women had been raised before women received their voting rights (France delayed enfranchisement of women until 1945). Many women were at the borders of politics, by choice or social norms (see chapter 6). Even in public opinion surveys in the 1950s, women often referred interviewers to their husbands or expressed less interest in politics (Converse 2007, 311–12). This has changed dramatically over time, with women increasing their education levels at faster rates than men and voting at higher rates than men. This process increased the cognitive mobilization for this half of the public. In the United States, the incorporation of African Americans into politics and society was equally transforming for these citizens.

Philip Converse (1972, 1990) wrote that political attention is a more important indicator of the public's political skills than education. Reflecting and reinforcing the general trend of cognitive mobilization, political interest has increased in our four core nations over the past half-century (see figure 2.2).[6] Campaign interest may vary from election to election, but has generally trended upward. Political interest has grown most steadily in the Federal Republic of Germany, partly because of cognitive mobilization and partly because of the nation's resocialization to democracy. People in Britain, France, and most Western democracies now follow politics more closely (Vassallo 2011, 38–42). Americans' interest in campaigns has erratically followed a slight upward trend, with some variation depending on the intensity of the presidential election. Contemporary publics are generally more interested in politics than earlier generations.

Rational Choice versus Reasonable Choice

In the decades since the first public opinion surveys generated their negative images of the public, we have learned a great deal about how people process information and make political (and nonpolitical) decisions. This research has stripped away the idealized standards of classic democratic theory and the rationalizations of elitist democratic theory.

Instead of expecting fully informed, sophisticated, *rational choices*, which probably seldom occur in most aspects of our lives, researchers focused on how people make *reasonable choices* in most instances. People make political choices on a regular basis, whether those decisions involve voting in an

Figure 2.2	Political Interest

Political interest has generally increased over time.

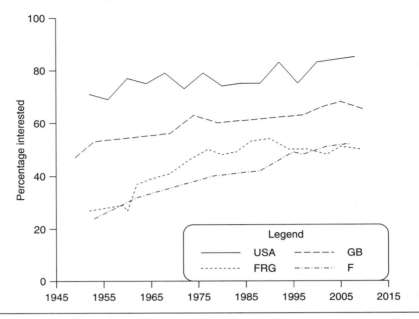

Sources: United States, 1952–2008, American National Election Studies; Great Britain, 1949–53, Gallup (1976a), 1963–79, British Election Studies, 1997–2011 British Social Attitudes Survey; West Germany, 1952–2009, surveys of the Institut für Demoskopie, Allensbach; France, 1953 and 1978, Charlot (1980), 1962, Gallup (1976b), 1978–2007, French Election Studies.

election, donating funds to a political group, or participating in a political discussion. Few people meet the ideal expectations of democratic theorists in rationally evaluating all the information that might go into such choices, but people are nevertheless making real political choices. Shaun Bowler and Todd Donovan (1998, 30) suggest that this finding leads to a different way to think about the citizens' role: "Voters, to use an analogy, may know very little about the workings of the internal combustion engine, but they do know how to drive. And while we might say that early voting studies focused on voter ignorance of the engine, the newer studies pay more attention to the ability to drive."

Cognitive research has described how people make choices in their lives, and this research begins with a different view of political information. There is too much information in the world for people to retain all they experience. The *Economist* recently reported that an average person reads around 10 megabytes (MB) worth of material a day; hears 400MB a day, and sees one MB of information every second! Human memory is limited, and most information—about our lives, our community, politics, and other life experiences—isn't retained. So, just as political scientists decry the public's limited knowledge about politics, economists say people need to know more about economics, natural scientists lament our limited knowledge of science, and geographers point to voids in our knowledge of the world.[7] But, to acquire "full information" is a daunting task, especially for politics, which is often secondary to immediate life concerns.[8] Almost all decisions in life are based on partial information, and so research on human behavior should focus on how people make reasonable choices with incomplete information.

Issue Publics. Cognitive research highlights several methods that citizens may use to make reasonable choices with incomplete information (Oppenheimer and Edwards 2012, chs. 7–8). First, instead of following all issues, people concentrate their attention on a few topics of personal interest. The total electorate is divided into several partially overlapping *issue publics* (Converse 1964). Being part of an issue public implies that people devote attention to the issue and have more informed beliefs. Many farmers, for example, closely monitor government agricultural policy while paying scant attention to urban renewal programs. Parents of school-age children may be interested in education policy, while the elderly are interested in Social Security. The largest issue publics generally exist for topics of broad concern, such as economic policy, taxes, and basic social programs. At the other extreme, only a few people regularly follow issues of foreign aid, international trade, or agriculture. Very few citizens are interested in every issue, but most citizens are members of at least one issue public. To paraphrase Will Rogers, "Everybody is sophisticated, only on different subjects."

The concept of issue publics influences how we think about political sophistication. When people define politics according to their own interests, a surprising level of political sophistication often appears. David RePass (1971) documented a high level of rational issue voting when citizens identified their own issue interests. Similarly, research demonstrates that members of an issue public are more likely to follow media coverage of the issue, gather information on the issue, hold stable preferences, and use these preferences as a basis of voting choice (Hutchings 2003; Krosnick 1990; Feldman 1989). Therefore, low consistency in issue opinions and low stability in opinions over time do not mean that the electorate is unsophisticated; the alternative explanation is that not all citizens are interested in and try to keep informed on all issues.

Some political scientists view issue publics as a negative feature of politics because a proliferation of issue publics works against policymaking based on a broad, coherent ideological framework. The reason is that policy interests in one area are not judged against interests in other policy areas. Policy fragmentation is potentially problematic, but such criticism may be overstated. If people limit their issue interests, it doesn't mean that they fail to judge these issues using a broad political framework; different clusters of issue interests still may emanate from a common underlying set of values. In addition, Robert Lane (1962, 1973) pointed out the potential negative consequences of an overly structured belief system—for example, dogmatism and intolerance (also Dahl 1971). Indeed, some of the popular criticism of Congress focuses on the narrow, polarized opinions of party elites that undermine the potential to pass legislation with broad public appeal. In some instances, therefore, issue publics may benefit the democratic process.

Political Cognition. Political psychology studies provide a new understanding of political cognition. Research that focuses on the public's ability to recall specific information misses the way that people process information. More recent research suggests that rather than memorizing specific events or details, a more common cognitive process is to evaluate new information and update a running tally of whether a specific issue or candidate is liked or disliked (Lau and Redlawsk 2006; Schwarz and Bohner 2001; Lodge and McGraw 1995). For example, you are unlikely to recall all the information you heard about the health care reform enacted by the Obama administration, but this doesn't mean that you don't have views on the issue. Each time one reads a story or hears something from a friend, you update your general impression of whether this issue or a candidate is good or bad for people like you. So studies of the public's ability to recall specific information present only a partial picture of how much information citizens use to make political choices.

Political psychology research also maintains that belief systems are structured differently than previously assumed. Instead of viewing belief systems as closely interconnecting a diverse range of political attitudes, as Converse originally proposed, there is a vertical structure (or network) of beliefs within specific political domains, as illustrated in figure 2.3. An individual's basic values are linked to general political orientations; specific issue opinions are derived from one or more of these general orientations (Conover and Feldman 1984). For example, attitudes toward government programs assisting minorities might reflect orientations toward the role of government *and* attitudes toward minorities. At the same time, even if opinions on specific issues are strongly linked to broader political orientations, the relationships between specific issue opinions can be weak because issues may not be directly linked together. This model therefore lacks the direct linkage between opinions on different issues that is posited in the *American Voter* model (see figure 2.1).

Furthermore, the specific attitudes included within these structures may vary across individuals. Some people's beliefs will include only a narrow part of the structure of figure 2.3, such as the issues on the left of the figure. Other belief structures might include a different subset of issues and general orientations. Thus, this literature often identifies specific cognitive structures that are relevant for subsets of issues, such as foreign policy, racial policies, or candidate evaluations.[9] So, even if people are not sophisticated on all political topics, they may have logical and structured beliefs within specific domains that enable them to manage political decision making.

Figure 2.3	A Hierarchical Model of Beliefs

Current studies suggest that belief systems are not tightly constrained but provide a loose structure for linking issues of salience to individual

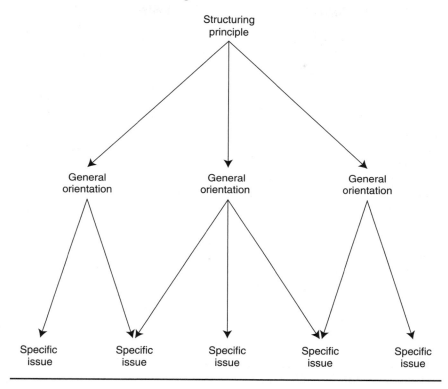

Heuristics. A third aspect of reasonable choice is that people use "shortcuts" or "heuristics" to simplify decision making (Sniderman, Brody, and Tetlock 1991; Lupia and McCubbins 1998; Barker and Hansen 2005; Lau and Redlawsk 2006; Lupia 2007). Samuel Popkin (1991, 218) writes that "the use of information shortcuts is . . . an inescapable fact of life, and will occur no matter how educated we are, how much information we have, and how much thinking we do." A heuristic provides political cues about how people like oneself might view political issues or parties at election time and is a shortcut to collecting and processing information.

People can turn to a wide variety of heuristics or cue-givers. Social groups are a common source of political cues (see chapter 8). Many policy issues involve conflicts among class, religious, ethnic, or other social groupings. One's ties or feelings toward a social group can be a guidepost in dealing with policy questions. French steelworkers, for example, might prefer larger social welfare programs because the labor union suggests it will benefit workers like themselves, and they vote for a leftist party that the union endorses (and that presumably represents the workers' interests). In contrast, a Bavarian Catholic might follow her pastor's advice to support government aid for religious schools and vote for the Christian Social Union candidate. Group references are also a common basis of party evaluation. When social conflicts are salient, and the parties take clear positions on these conflicts, then social characteristics can provide effective cues for following politics. People may not explain their policy preferences with sophisticated ideological arguments or reference to specific legislative proposals, but overall they still are making reasonable political choices.

Partisanship is an even more powerful heuristic than social group cues (see chapter 9). Many people early in their lives develop an enduring attachment to a political party that they believe best represents their views. Parties are central participants in democratic politics, so most political phenomena can be judged in reference to the parties. Because most elections involve a choice among parties, party attachments obviously can simplify voting choices. In Western Europe, where parties act as cohesive units, party voting is an effective and efficient shortcut for voting choice. The heterogeneity of American parties lessens the policy value of party voting, but the complexity of American elections makes party a valuable voting cue when one must decide on a long list of federal, state, and local candidates. Partisanship can also shape evaluations of political leaders and new political issues. If voters are unsure about an issue, party cues can suggest where their interests lie. If you are watching a member of Congress on television, you can predict what she will say depending on whether there is a D or R after her name. An issue supported by one's party is more likely to benefit oneself, while the policies of the opposition party are suspect. In sum, because of its heuristic value, party identification frequently is viewed as the central thread connecting the citizen and the political process.

Left/Right (or liberal/conservative) orientations are another potential source of political cues. Most people do not express sophisticated ideological views, but they still can locate themselves within a broad ideological family (Jacoby 1991; Fuchs and Klingemann 1989). A Left/Right orientation provides a framework for evaluating political objects. When an individual describes a candidate as too liberal or another as too conservative, he or she is using a shortcut to learn about the candidates' views on specific issues and evaluate them on this basis.

Some people may rely on the media for political cues. Newspapers list their editorial endorsements before elections and give editorial advice on the issues of the day. Watching FOX or MSNBC gives one cues about how Republicans or Democrats think about issues, just as reading a Labour- or Conservative-oriented newspaper in Britain provides clear political cues. Similarly, the endorsements of social groups, political groups, and respected elected officials can be an effective heuristic. If one is an environmentalist, and the Sierra Club endorses an issue, this provides valuable cues about the content of the issue. Other people turn to their family or friends for political advice, or they learn about political choices from coworkers. Indeed, the world is full of political cues that individuals may choose. Experiments by Arthur Lupia and Mathew McCubbins (1998) demonstrated that when individuals gain information from a trusted political source, they can make reasonable choices that reflect their self-interest.

Table 2.2 illustrates some of the diverse criteria that are used in making political judgments. The Political Action project (Barnes, Kaase, et al. 1979) asked people in the United States, Britain and Germany to describe the good and bad points of two major political parties in their country. Only a small percentage actively employed ideological concepts in judging the parties. This doesn't mean, however, that the remaining individuals are devoid of political judgments. About 40 percent of the Americans, British, and Germans evaluated the parties according to social group alignments. Even more people judged the parties by their organization and political competence. Nearly half of the responses cited specific policy criteria. The broadest and most frequently used criteria—judging parties by the nature of the times—evaluates parties by how well the economy and nation are faring. Just as President Ronald Reagan suggested that voters ask if they are better off than four years ago, this can be a meaningful basis of evaluation. I calculated a rough approximation of these categories for the 2004 American National Election Study and the 1994 German Media Study, and both show the continuing diversity of party images.[10]

Table 2.2	Party Evaluations				
People use diverse criteria in evaluating parties; few are ideologues but they judge parties in terms of group ties, their leaders, and their policy positions.					
CRITERIA FOR JUDGING PARTIES	UNITED STATES 1975	2004	GREAT BRITAIN 1974	WEST GERMANY 1974	1994
Ideological concepts	21	20	21	34	14
Social groups	40	37	41	45	42
Party organizations and competence	49	48	35	66	69
Policy concepts	45	43	46	53	51
Nature of the times	64	28	59	86	—
Political figures	40	11	18	38	32
Intrinsic values/ other	46	40	65	49	41
No content	14	22	18	6	21
Total	319	249	303	377	270

Sources: Political Action Study, 1974–75; 2004 American National Election Study; 1994 Klingemann German Media Study.

Note: Totals exceed 100 percent because multiple responses were possible; the later timepoints for the United States and Germany are estimates because the coding system was not fully consistent with the earlier survey.

Some researchers remain skeptical of the ability of heuristics to match the standards of "rational" decision making. Michael Delli Carpini and Scott Keeter (1996), for example, note that heuristics can sometimes give incorrect guidance and are subject to elite manipulation (also see Popkin and Dimock 1999; Kuklinski and Peyton 2007). In contrast, experiments by Richard Lau and David Redlawsk (2006) and Lupia and McCubbins (1998) are much more positive about the value of heuristics in reaching desired outcomes. So the debate continues. The reasonable choice perspective argues that people are making pretty good choices—not perfect choices.

The Wisdom of Democratic Choice

Are pretty good choices enough for democracy to be successful? We should be skeptical about setting our democratic expectations too low. However, other features of democracy tend to lessen the potential problem of making only reasonable choices.

Although skeptics might cite an individual election result as an example of the failure of mass publics, democracy is an ongoing process. Sometimes electorates do make poor choices or make decisions based on what turn out to be mistaken impressions. But all human activity is subject to this imperfection. One of the counterbalancing forces in democracy is that decisions are not permanent. If a politician doesn't perform, he or she can be voted out at the next election. If parties demonstrate that they are not trustworthy to follow their election promises, their support may fade in future elections. Indeed, experimental research shows that repeated experience playing a game improves the decisions that individuals make (Lupia and McCubbins 1998) and increases the reliance on heuristics (Lau and Redlawsk 2006, 242–44). Democracy succeeds not because it doesn't make mistakes, but because it is a dynamic system that has the ability to correct mistakes. Some might even say that voters display a greater ability to make such retrospective judgments and change their vote choices than do elected politicians who hold their views more persistently even in the face of a changing political context.

Perhaps even more important, elections are a *collective decision* of the entire electorate, and we should judge democracy by its collective outcomes rather than the individual choices that make up these outcomes. The collective decisions of elections are often better than the individual judgments of any single individual because they cumulate the information and the knowledge of the whole community. Some voters might be biased in one direction, and some in the opposite direction; some evaluate one political issue, and others use completely different criteria. When cumulated together, however, the total information brought to the collective decision improves the outcome over any single individual, even if fully "rational." James Surowiecki's *The Wisdom of Crowds* (2004) is full of fascinating examples of how collective decisions can be better than those of the individuals who contributed to the decision—ranging from guesses about how many jelly beans are in a jar to who should be president. Similarly, studies demonstrate a close fit between the collective preferences of the public and subsequent changes in public policy (see chapter 11 in this book). Collective decision making through elections is another explanation for why democracies can be effective even when some people have limited information and engagement.

Politics and the Public

We began by asking what democracy expects of its citizens and whether contemporary publics meet these expectations. Political theorists and democratic elitists set very high expectations: people should be fully informed in order to make rationally calculated political decisions. Some of those skeptical of the public's abilities remain skeptical today (Kinder 2007; Converse 2007; Cf. Oppenheimer and Edwards 2012; Lupia 2007). Democratic electorates will never meet these ideal theoretical expectations, which leads to claims that their shortfall undermines the democratic process. Few human beings can match these lofty expectations, even among political science professors.

But democracy has endured for more than two centuries, and a democratization wave has spread across the world since the early 1990s. It therefore makes little sense to argue that democracy requires an ideal that is never met. This conclusion doesn't mean we have given up on democratic publics by lowering our expectations. Instead, it recognizes that people bring their life experiences and knowledge to their political decisions, but in different ways than we initially presumed. Even Thomas Jefferson, who was a sophisticated political thinker, valued the basic abilities of the common citizen: "State a moral case to a ploughman and a professor. The former will decide it as well and often better than the latter because he has not been led astray by artificial rules."[11] If Jefferson thought a ploughman could make decisions as well as a professor, then perhaps democracy isn't at risk (a good topic to debate with a professor).

Think of this problem in personal terms. When you buy a car or a new flat panel television, or make a political decision, you seldom have the full information of an expert in automobiles, electronics, or politics. In addition, even experts will disagree on which is the best car, TV, or candidate. Some consumers will follow a rational choice model of conscious and detailed evaluation of the alternatives. They will read *Consumer Reports* and do research as if they were preparing for a bar exam. But most of us will find other means of balancing the costs and benefits of decision making to yield a reasonable choice based on our needs.

How do people make reasonable choices when it comes to politics? This chapter maintains that people can rely on various methods to make their decisions. Many people focus their attention on a few issues of particular interest rather than trying to master all the issues. The electorate, therefore, is composed of overlapping issue publics, each judging government action on different policies.

The sources of information and the bases of evaluation also vary within the public. Some citizens, but only a minority of them, judge politics by a broad ideological framework. Many more people use political cues, such as social groups or party attachments, to guide their behavior. By limiting their issue interests and relying on information shortcuts, the average voter can balance the costs and benefits of political involvement and still make reasonable political decisions. Perhaps the best description comes from Jon Krosnick (1990, 82), who argues that people are inevitably "cognitive misers" who find shortcuts or heuristics to make satisficing political choices rather than seeking a complete array of relevant information.[12]

Several studies show the diversity of decision-making processes within the public. Research demonstrates that cognitively mobilized individuals more often use ideological criteria or issue positions in making political choices; the less educated more often use group references or other political cues to make their decisions (Dalton 2012a; Sniderman et al. 1991). In both cases the decisions may broadly reflect the individuals' interests. Similarly, Arthur Lupia (1994) studied voting on insurance initiatives in California and found that a small attentive public was well informed on the initiatives and made choices appropriate for their expressed interests. In addition, many voters used group cues—such as which proposals were supported by Ralph Nader and which by the insurance industry—that also led to rational voting choices. This is pluralistic decision making in practice.

This pluralistic model has several implications for our study of public opinion. We should not interpret unstable or inconsistent issue opinions as evidence that voters lack any attitudes. Survey questions are imprecise; the public's issue interests are specialized; and a complex mix of beliefs may be related to a single issue. In addition, we must be sensitive to the diversity and complexity of mass politics. Simple models of political behavior that assume a homogeneous electorate may be theoretically elegant and empirically parsimonious—yet also unrealistic. Recognizing that people function based on diverse criteria and motivations, we should try to model this diversity, instead of adopting overly generalized theories of citizen politics. Finally, we must not underestimate the potential for change. As this chapter documents, citizens of the four nations examined in this book have fundamentally changed during the postwar period. Public opinion reflects a dynamic process, and we should avoid static views of an unchanging (or unchangeable) public.

At the same time, we should not be guilty of overestimating the sophistication of the citizenry. At times the public holds ill-advised or ill-informed opinions, and some citizens will remain ignorant of all political matters. Such is the imperfect nature of human behavior. Few individuals deserve the rating of fully sophisticated ideologues. The important lesson isn't to ignore or belittle the varied criteria citizens actually use in dealing with politics. Moreover, when voters make a poor decision, or conditions change, they can make new choices at the next election.

The ultimate question, then, isn't whether the public meets the maximum ideological standards of classic democratic theory, but whether the public has a sufficient basis for rational political action. Phrased in these terms, and based on the evidence presented in this chapter, I am optimistic about the political abilities of contemporary publics.

Suggested Readings

Converse, Philip. 1964. The nature of belief systems in mass publics. In *Ideology and Discontent,* ed. David Apter. New York: Free Press.

Delli Carpini, Michael, and Scott Keeter. 1996. *What Americans Know about Politics and Why It Matters.* New Haven: Yale University Press.

Friedman, Jeffrey, and Shterna Friedman, eds. 2012. *The Nature of Belief Systems Reconsidered.* London: Routledge.

Norris, Pippa. 2000. *Virtuous Circle: Political Communications in Postindustrial Societies.* Cambridge, UK: Cambridge University Press.

Oppenheimer, Danny, and Mike Edwards. 2012. *Democracy Despite Itself: Why a System That Shouldn't Work at All Works So Well.* Cambridge, MA: MIT Press.

Popkin, Samuel. 1994. *The Reasoning Voter,* 2nd ed. Chicago: University of Chicago Press.

Prior, Markus. 2007. *Post-Broadcast Democracy: How Media Choice Increases Inequality in Political Involvement and Polarizes Elections.* New York: Cambridge University Press.

Sniderman, Paul, Richard Brody, and Philip Tetlock. 1991. *Reasoning and Choice.* New York: Cambridge University Press.

Notes

1. "We know Bart, but Homer is Greek to us," *Los Angeles Times,* August 15, 2006, A14.
2. There were, of course, dissenting voices. Walter Bagehot (1978), Joseph Schumpeter (1943), and Walter Lippmann (1922) were highly critical of the average citizen, claiming people fell far short of the theoretical ideal.
3. For example, a candidate in the 2006 Texas gubernatorial election pointed out that the Texas legislature once unanimously passed a motion honoring the Boston strangler. A legislator sponsored the bill to demonstrate that his colleagues voted on bills without reading them. For other examples of elite inconsistencies, see Arnold (1990).

4. One source of debate has been methodological, focusing on how sophistication is measured. For a discussion of these points, see Kuklinski and Peyton (2007). Other research has questioned the evidence that elites are more politically tolerant than the general public (Jackman 1972; Sniderman et al. 1991).

5. The question asked about the sources people use "to learn about what's going on in the country and in the world." Although not explicitly limited to politics, the results are similar to those of questions that ask about sources of political information specifically (Dalton 2008, ch. 2).

6. The British, German, and French questions measure general interest in politics, and the questions differ across nations. The American question asked about interest in campaigns. Because of the differences in question wordings, the absolute levels of political interest should not be compared across nations; for such comparisons, see Jennings and van Deth (1989).

7. Critics of the public's level of knowledge often ignore parallel findings among elite groups. For example, Michael Zimmerman (1990, 1991) found that newspaper editors and elected politicians displayed limited knowledge about historical and scientific facts.

8. To the surprise of some political science professors, politics is only one part of people's lives. When the 2006–08 World Values Survey asked Americans what was very important in their lives, politics came at the end of the list: family (95 percent), friends (60 percent), religion (47 percent), leisure (38 percent), work (33 percent), and politics (16 percent). Similarly, politics was mentioned by 12 percent of the French, 10 percent of the Germans, and 9 percent of the British.

9. This literature is quite diverse in its applications (for example, Sniderman, Brody, and Kuklinski 1984; Peffley and Hurwitz 1985; Miller, Wattenberg, and Malanchuk 1986; Hurwitz and Peffley 1987).

10. The time comparisons are inexact because different coding procedures were used in the more recent studies, but they illustrate the general patterns that would likely emerge. The ideologue and nature of the times categories are drawn from Lewis-Beck et al. (2008, ch. 10), and I coded the other responses from the ANES master codes. The German results are based on reanalysis of Klingemann (1998) data.

11. Quoted in Surowiecki (2004), 267.

12. The public's reliance on various decision-making shortcuts—satisficing behavior—is common to decision makers in business and government (Cyert and March 1963). Nevertheless, democratic elitists denigrate the public when they adopt this model for political choices.

3

How We Participate

D emocracy should be a celebration by an involved public. People should be politically active because it's through public discussion, deliberation, and involvement that societal goals should be defined and carried out. Without public involvement in the process, democracy loses both its legitimacy and its guiding force. When Germans take the time to cast informed votes, British electors canvass their neighbors, the French protest, or Americans e-mail their president, the democratic process is at work. The global spread of democratization has brought these freedoms to millions of people. The jubilation that accompanied the first democratic elections in Eastern Europe and the expansion of democracy across the globe attest to the value that people place on these freedoms.

However, some political observers now claim that people in advanced industrial societies are becoming apathetic about their democratic rights. Socioeconomic development and the growth of cognitive mobilization should have increased political participation. Instead, turnout in elections is trending downward in the United States and many other democracies. Robert Putnam (2000) has warned that general civic engagement has decreased to dangerously low levels in America. John Hibbing and Elisabeth Theiss-Morse go a step further and claim, "The last thing people want is to be more involved in political decision making: They do not want to make political decisions themselves; they do not want to provide much input to those who are assigned to make these decisions; and they would rather not know all the details of the decision-making process" (also see Patterson 2003; Wattenberg 2002). A recent report by the American Political Science Association sees an ominous problem in these developments:

> American democracy is at risk. The risk comes not from some external threat but from disturbing internal trends: an erosion of the activities and capacities of citizenship. Americans have turned away from politics and the public sphere in large numbers, leaving our civic life impoverished. Citizens participate in public affairs less frequently, with less knowledge and enthusiasm, in fewer venues, and less equally than is healthy for a vibrant democratic polity. (Macedo et al. 2005, 1)

Can the situation really be this bad? Is decreasing participation placing democracy at risk?

Another set of researchers claim that participation is not decreasing; rather it's shifting from elections to nonelectoral forms of action (Dalton 2009a; Zukin et al., 2006). Ronald Inglehart (1997, 307) says, "One frequently hears references to growing apathy on the part of the public. . . . These allegations of apathy are misleading: mass publics *are* deserting the old-line oligarchical political organizations that mobilized them in the modernization era—but they are becoming more active in a wide range of elite-challenging forms of political action." These new forms of direct action include participation in public interests groups, political consumerism, Internet activism, and contentious activities.

This chapter looks at political action in its various forms: voting, campaigns, direct contacting, group activities, protest, and other forms of contentious action. Chapter 4 then examines the factors that influence political involvement across these various forms of action.

Modes of Participation

Democracy means popular rule. So how do you rule? Think for a moment about what you would do if you wanted to influence the government on a policy that was important to you. We often equate political participation with the act of voting. But if you consider political influence from the citizen's perspective, you will realize that participation is not limited to voting, nor is voting necessarily the most effective means of affecting public policy. Instead of waiting several years until the next election gives you a chance to vote for a candidate who supports your position—if there is such a candidate—you might contact government officials, work with others who share your interests, or find other ways to advocate your cause now. In short, democratic participation can take many forms.

Sidney Verba and his colleagues (Verba and Nie 1972; Verba, Nie, and Kim 1978) identified four general types of political action (and I added the last two):

- Voting
- Campaign activity
- Contacting officials directly
- Communal activity (working with a group in the community)

- Protest and other forms of contentious politics
- Internet activism (visiting websites, sending e-mails, forwarding e-petitions)

These researchers found that most people do not use these activities interchangeably, as analysts once assumed. Instead, people tend to focus on activities that match their motivations and goals. Specific kinds of activities frequently cluster together, and a person who performs one act from a particular cluster is likely to perform other acts from the same cluster but not necessarily activities from another cluster. Verba and Nie labeled these clusters of activities *modes of democratic participation.*

These participation modes require different things from participants and differ in the nature of their influence (table 3.1). Verba, Nie, and Kim (1978) classified the participation modes in terms of several criteria: (1) whether the act conveys information about the individual's political preferences and/or applies pressure for compliance, (2) the potential degree of conflict involved, (3) the amount of effort required, and (4) the amount of cooperation with others required.

Voting, for example, is a high-pressure activity because it selects government officials, but its policy focus is imprecise because an election involves many issues. Many people will vote for a party or candidate even if they disagree on some issues. Voting also is a reasonably simple act that requires little initiative or cooperation with others. By comparison, campaign activity makes greater demands on a person's time and motivation. Campaign work can also be more policy focused than the simple act of voting because

Table 3.1	Modes of Political Activity

Political activities differ in their characteristics and influence on government.

MODE OF ACTIVITY	TYPE OF INFLUENCE	CONFLICT	EFFORT REQUIRED	COOPERATION WITH OTHERS
Voting	High pressure/low information	Partisan conflict	Little	Little
Campaign activity	High pressure/low to high information	Partisan conflict	Some	Some or much
Direct contacting	Low pressure/high information	Varies	Very high	Little
Communal activity	Low to high pressure/high information	Varies	Some or much	Some or much
Protest	High pressure/high information	Very conflictual	Some or much	Some or much

Source: Verba, Nie, and Kim (1978, 55), with modifications.

individuals can choose which candidates to support. Or, an individual may contact the government directly by writing a letter, speaking with a government official, or sending an e-mail. Sometimes contacting is for a particular reason—to have a pothole fixed or request other government services—and other times it can concern broad policy questions. Participation in community groups, or communal activity, may require even more effort by the individual, and it produces a qualitatively different form of input. Citizen groups can control both the methods of action and the policy focus of their activities. Contentious politics, or protest politics, not only expands the repertoire of participation; it also represents a style of action that differs from other forms of activity. Protest can focus on specific issues or policy goals—from protecting whales to protesting the policies of a local government—and can convey a high level of political information with real political force. The Tea Party movement and Occupy Wall Street are recent American examples of protest in action. Internet activism is still developing and can take many forms. It's used to organize and share information with like-minded people, much like communal activity. It's also a form of contacting or even protest. *The point is that the different modes of political participation aren't equal:* they involve different types of individuals and exert different kinds of influence on the political process.

Cross-national participation studies generally describe participation modes that are very similar to those found by Verba and his colleagues.[1] This chapter discusses each of these participation modes: their characteristics, the level of activity, and how participation patterns are changing over time.

Voting

Nothing quite epitomizes democracy as much as voting in elections. It's a collective activity to go to the polls, stand with your fellow citizens, and make your voting choice. The counting of ballots and predictions of election outcomes—all accompanied by expert commentary on television—is democracy in action. And in the end, a new government is selected by the people.

The franchise to vote has gradually expanded over the past century and a half. The United States was one of the first nations to begin liberalizing suffrage laws; by 1850 virtually the entire white adult male population in the United States was enfranchised. Voting rights expanded more slowly in Western Europe, which lacked the populist tradition of the United States. European social groups were more sharply polarized than in the United States, and conservatives were hesitant to enfranchise a working class that might vote them out of office. A socialist movement pressed for the political equality of the working class, but mass suffrage often was delayed until war or revolution disrupted the conservative political order. French adult males gained voting rights with the formation of the Third Republic in 1870. Britain limited its election rolls until early in the 1900s through residency and financial restrictions on voting and by allowing multiple votes by business owners and university graduates. (You got two votes if you had a university degree!) Electoral reforms following World War I granted equal voting rights to virtually all British males. In Germany, true democratic elections with universal mass suffrage began with the creation of the Weimar Republic in 1919.

During the twentieth century, governments gradually extended suffrage to the rest of the adult population. Government first acknowledged women's right to vote in Britain (1918), followed by Germany (1919) and the United States (1920). France lagged behind most of Western Europe, enfranchising women only in 1945. The Voting Rights Act of 1965 removed most of the remaining formal restrictions on the voting participation of American blacks. Finally, in the 1970s all four nations lowered the voting age to eighteen.

Table 3.2	Levels of Turnout

Turnout is decreasing in most democracies.

	1950s	1960s	1970s	1980s	1990s	2000s	CHANGE SINCE 1960s
Australia	83	84	85	83	82	83	−1
Austria	89	90	88	87	77	76	−14
Belgium	88	87	88	89	84	86	−1
Canada	70	72	68	67	60	56	−16
Denmark	78	87	86	85	82	83	−4
Finland	76	85	82	79	70	69	−16
France	71	67	67	64	61	45	−22
Germany (West)	84	83	86	79	74	70	−13
Great Britain	79	74	74	73	72	59	−15
Greece	—	—	83	86	85	84	
Iceland	91	89	89	90	87	86	−3
Ireland	74	74	82	76	70	67	−7
Italy	93	94	94	93	90	82	−12
Japan	74	71	72	71	67	63	−8
Netherlands	88	90	85	81	73	77	−13
New Zealand	91	84	83	86	79	76	−8
Norway	78	83	80	83	76	75	−8
Portugal	—	—	87	81	75	67	—
Spain	—	—	76	76	79	77	—
Sweden	77	83	87	86	81	79	−4
Switzerland	61	53	61	40	36	38	−15
United States	59	62	54	52	53	57	−5
19–nation average	79	80	80	77	72	70	−10

Source: Institute for Democracy and Electoral Assistance, http://www.idea.int.

Note: Turnout figures are based on voting-age public (VAP) in parliamentary elections; for the United States, we used presidential election turnout. Australia and Belgium have strict enforcement of compulsory voting. The nineteen-nation average is based on the nations available since the 1950s.

The right to vote now extends to virtually the entire adult population in the established democracies. There are, however, distinct national differences in the rates of voting. Table 3.2 displays voting turnout rates for twenty-three established democracies from the 1950s to the early 2000s. Turnout is calculated as a percentage of the eligible voting age public, rather than of registered voters, in order to compensate for different registration rules across nations. The table shows large cross-national differences in the levels of turnout. In the United States and Switzerland, only about half of the voting age population (or less) votes in national elections. Voting rates are higher in most European nations where three-quarters of the public (or more) casts a ballot in several nations.

The other significant pattern in table 3.2 is the trend in turnout rates over time (Franklin 2004; Wattenberg 2002; Curtice 2012). A comparison of the 1960s (after postwar consolidation) and the 2000s for the nineteen nations with a complete time series shows that fourteen have experienced turnout declines of 5 percent or more (including Britain, France, Germany, and the United States), and none had significantly increased turnout. The first elections of the twenty-first century have seen a general continuation of the downward trend. Turnout in Britain dropped from 69 percent of the voting age public in 1997 to 61 percent in 2010; French turnout plummeted from 60 percent in 1997 to 42 percent in 2012. German turnout decreased 11 percent between 1998 and 2009. On average, turnout has dropped about 10 percentage points for the nineteen democracies where one can compare the present to the 1960s.

Several factors apparently contribute to the decline in voting turnout. Researchers argue that younger generations are disengaged from electoral politics, and lowering the voting age has therefore diminished participation rates (Franklin 2004; Wattenberg 2002). Decreasing trust in government and attachment to political parties has undoubtedly contributed to these trends as well (see chapter 9 and figure 4.1). It's ironic that as the number of voting opportunities has increased in most nations, the average turnout in elections has decreased. Citizens complain about "voter fatigue," even though the opportunities to vote remain quite limited in most nations.

Another set of factors explains cross-national differences in turnout levels. Turnout in the United States is significantly lower than in most other nations. Some analysts cite these statistics as evidence of the American electorate's limited political involvement (and, by implication, limited political abilities). A more complex set of factors—including voter registration systems and other electoral procedures—explain transatlantic differences in turnout (Wattenberg 2002; Franklin 2004). Most Europeans are automatically enrolled as registered voters, which the government updates. In contrast, Americans must register themselves, and many eligible citizens fail to do so.[2] By many estimates, participation in American elections would increase by several percentage points if the United States adopted the European system of registration (Blais 2000). The scheduling of most European elections on weekends also encourages turnout, because more voters can find the time to visit the polls. In addition, most European electoral systems are based on proportional representation, rather than plurality-based single-member districts as in the United States. Proportional representation stimulates turnout because parties receive legislative seats as a direct function of their share of the popular vote. In Germany, for example, if a small party gets 5 percent of the vote it gets 5 percent of the seats in Parliament. Some nations, including Australia and Belgium, require that people vote or face government fines. Political competition and sharp ideological cleavages between parties also encourages turnout. When European voters go to the polls, they are deciding whether their country will be run by parties with socialist, green, conservative, ethnic, or even religious programs. These sharp party differences encourage higher voting rates. The number of party choices, the competitiveness of elections, and the structure of legislative power in a system all affect turnout (Powell 1986; Kittilson and Anderson 2011).

The United States also differs from most other democracies because people vote on a very large number of choices. The typical European voter may have only three or four elections in a four-year period, but many Americans face a dozen or more separate elections over the same time span. Furthermore, Americans face choices for a much wider range of political offices at each election. Only one house of the bicameral national legislature is directly elected in Britain, Germany, and France; the French president is one of the few directly elected European heads of state. Local, regional, and even national elections in Europe normally consist of casting a single ballot for a single office. The extensive list of elected offices and long ballots common to American elections are unknown in Western Europe. Finally, Britain, France, and Germany use the referendum and initiative only sparingly.

Instead of counting the total number of people who vote in national elections, an alternative measure of participation is the *amount of electing* being done by the public (Dalton and Gray 2003). When the context of American elections is considered, the amount of electing is actually quite high:

> No country can approach the United States in the frequency and variety of elections, and thus in the amount of electing. No other country elects its lower house as often as every two years, or its president as frequently as every four years. No other country popularly elects its state governors and town mayors, or has as wide a variety of nonrepresentative offices (judges, sheriffs, attorneys general, city treasurers, and so on) subject to election. Only one other country (Switzerland) can compete in the number and variety of local referendums, and only two (Belgium and Turkey) hold party "primaries" in most parts of the country. Even if differences in turnout rates are taken into account, American citizens do not necessarily vote less often than other nationalities; most probably, they do more voting. (Crewe 1981, 262)

A simple comparison of the experiences of a typical European and American voter highlights this difference in the amount of electing: between 2008 and 2012, a resident of Oxford, England, could have voted four times, while a resident of Irvine, California, could have cast about forty votes in 2012 alone.[3]

Turnout rates in national elections are therefore a poor measure of the public's overall political involvement because the structure of institutions and the electoral rules strongly influence turnout. In addition, the simple quantity of voting must be judged by the quality of this activity. Verba, Nie, and Kim (1978, ch. 3) describe voting as a high-pressure activity because elections choose government officials. However, election results produce only limited information on the public's specific policy preferences because elections involve many different issues. Did a party win because of a specific policy it advocated, giving it a mandate to enact that policy, or did it win despite this one policy position? In addition, the infrequent opportunity to vote for a prepackaged candidate or party is a limited tool of political influence. Voter influence may increase when elections include a wide range of political offices and include referendums. Still, it's difficult to treat elections as mandates on specific policies because voters make their judgments based on broad packages of programs. Consequently, many people vote because of a sense of civic duty or as an expression of partisan support rather than as a major means to influence policy.

The limited policy content of voting led some critics to claim that by focusing mass participation on voting alone, parties and political elites are actually trying to limit citizen influence in order to protect their privileged position in the policy process (Piven and Cloward 2000). Even if this skepticism is deserved, voting remains an important aspect of democratic politics, as much for its symbolic value as for its instrumental influence on policy. Voting is one activity that binds the individual to the political system and legitimizes the rest of the democratic process. It's a good way to start participation, but it should not end there. Yet, the decline in voting turnout seems to confirm the claim that participation is waning in contemporary democracies.

Campaign Activity

As the election approaches, the booths start appearing at the Saturday morning markets across Germany. Party supporters are there to share information with people at the market, give them a brochure about the party's policies, and convince them of the importance of voting. There is something reassuring about democracy to see booths for the Linke, Greens, Social Democrats, Christian Democrats, and other parties set up between the vegetable stands and the van selling wurst.

These experiences are examples of why political campaigns are often described as "retail politics." This is where candidates and their supporters "sell" their programs to the voters. They are in town squares and go door to door to talk to prospective voters and leave campaign materials. Supporters may also contribute to a favorite party or candidate, staff a phone bank, or attend campaign meetings. Sometimes people try to persuade a spouse, friend, or coworker to vote a particular way.

Volunteering for a campaign extends electoral participation beyond the act of voting. Fewer people routinely participate in campaigns because this activity is more demanding than merely casting a vote. Campaign work requires more initiative, and there is greater need to coordinate participation with others (see table 3.1). Along with the additional effort, however, campaign activity can give a person more influence and convey more policy information than voting. Campaign work is important to parties and candidates, and candidates generally are more sensitive to, and aware of, the policy interests of their activists (Whiteley and Seyd 2002).

Campaign activities can take many forms, depending on the context of electioneering in the nation. In the United States, campaigns are now largely media events, and popular involvement in organized campaign activities is modest (see figure 3.1). Few Americans work for a party or candidate, attend party or campaign meetings, or display a campaign button or sticker. (The top panel of table 3.4 shows that U.S. levels of campaign activity are higher than those of the three European nations.[4])

The rate of campaign activities has ebbed and flowed since the 1950s without a clear trend. If anything, participation has grown a bit in the 2000s, defying claims that campaign activity is eroding.[5] Today, the most frequent campaign activities involve individualistic forms of participation: giving money to a campaign, displaying a button, or trying to persuade others how to vote. Equally important, new forms of campaign activity have developed with the Internet. Instead of posting a candidate's sign in one's yard, it's becoming increasingly common to "friend" or post comments about a candidate on one's Facebook page. About 6 percent of Americans

| Figure 3.1 | American Campaign Activity |

Traditional forms of campaign activity dipped in the 1980–90s but have grown since then.

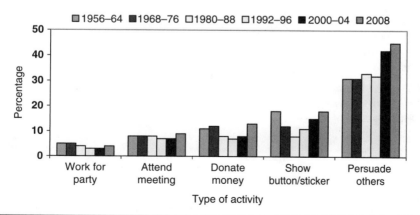

Source: American National Election Study 1956–2008.

contributed online to a campaign in 2008, and an increasing amount of campaign discussion occurs online (A. Smith et al. 2009). Adding these new forms of action to figure 3.1 would significantly increase the levels of campaign involvement in the past decade.

British elections differ from American elections in several ways. British elections do not follow a regular time schedule; instead, the prime minister may dissolve Parliament and call for new elections at almost any time during a legislative term. Therefore, elections are often quickly organized, and the campaigns are brief, averaging little more than a month. In addition, British parties depend on a pool of formal party members for much of the campaign work; they attend political rallies, canvass the constituency during the campaign, and contact potential voters on Election Day (Whiteley and Seyd 2002; Whiteley 2012). Beyond the core of party members, participation in most campaign activities is limited (see table 3.3). The decline in party membership has contributed to a general decrease in organized campaign activity over time. In the 1964 election, parties claimed more than 3 million members, but in the 2010 election this had dropped to a few hundred thousand.

Germany's democratic development after World War II increased citizen involvement in campaigns and most other aspects of politics. Membership in the political parties grew from the 1950s until the 1980s, and

Table 3.3   British Campaign Activity

Party membership and party organized activities have decreased, but the British still follow the campaign.

	1964	1966	1970	1974	1983	1987	1997	2005	2010
Discussed election with friends	—	—	—	—	—	—	—	46	45
Work for party or candidate	8	2	2	2	2	2	—	—	—
Attend meeting (indoors)	8	7	5	5	3	4	4	2	3
Attend meeting (outdoors)	8	3	6	4	—	—	7	—	—
Display poster	—	—	10	9	12	10	9	—	—
Visited a party's website	—	—	—	—	—	—	—	6	13
Party member	14	—	10	—	7	9	4	4	4
Read electoral address	46	49	53	51	49	49	62	56	50

Sources: 1964–97: British Gallup Poll; 2005–10: British Social Attitudes Survey; party membership data for all years: British Election Studies.

participation in campaigns also grew. Eleven percent of the public attended a campaign meeting in the 1961 election; by 1976 this figure had nearly doubled (20 percent). Beginning in the 1970s popular displays of party support also became a visible aspect of campaigns. Since the 1980s, however, formal party membership and overall campaign participation has dropped off (Gabriel, Keil, and Kerrouche 2012; Koch, Wasmer, and Schmidt 2001).

Still, many Germans are engaged in campaigns in some way, and I have noted that their turnout is much higher than in the United States.[6] In the 2002 Bundestag election, almost a third tried to convince another person how to vote, and a modest number were otherwise involved in the campaign (table 3.4). And again, more people are turning to the Internet to get campaign information (up to a fifth of the public in 2009) or to share information on the campaign.

Table 3.4	Comparing Participation across Nations			
Americans tend to be more politically active than Europeans—except for voting.				
	UNITED STATES	GREAT BRITAIN	FRANCE	GERMANY
Active in national campaign				
Tried to persuade others	44	18	29	28
Participated in campaign	30	13	7	6
Contacted by party/ candidate	47	33	7	13
Contacting				
Contacted government official last 5 years	28	19	12	13
Communal activity				
Worked with others in community last 5 years	35	13	20	26
Protesting				
Signed a petition last year*	35	34	21	35
Boycotted a product last year*	24	23	29	34
Attended protest last 5 years	6	7	24	12
Participated in demonstration last year*	6	2	17	6
Internet				
Joined Internet forum*	6	2	4	2

Sources: Comparative Study of Electoral Systems for national elections (2004 in United States, 2005 in Britain, 2002 in France and Germany); items marked with an asterisk are from 2004 International Social Survey Program.

There is less systematic evidence on participation trends in France (Vassallo 2010; Gabriel, Keil, and Kerrouche 2012). Formal party membership has declined as in most other European democracies. Attendance at campaign meetings, public displays of party support, and other campaign activities seem to vary with the intensity of the election and between legislative and presidential elections. Table 3.4 shows that French participation in the 2002 presidential election was comparable to German participation in 2002. French interest in the 2007 elections was even higher; nearly a third of the public said they tried to influence someone on how to vote and a seventh attended a meeting (Vedel 2011).

There is some evidence suggesting that campaign activity is generally decreasing in the established democracies (Dalton and Wattenberg 2000, ch. 3). Fewer people now attend political rallies, work for a party or candidate, or actively participate in election campaigns. But rather than decline, this may be a sign of how campaigns are changing. The media's expanding electoral role may decrease campaign activity because it lessens the importance of party-organized rallies and canvassing designed to inform the public. The candidates spend their time orchestrating "walkabouts" to generate stories for the evening television news; and televised preelection debates are becoming common. The party-organized activities that once marked election campaigns—mass rallies and in-person contacting—are now less frequent.

The current evidence is incomplete and ambiguous. Many individuals are still drawn to the excitement and competition of elections, but campaign participation now is more often individualistic, such as a display of party support or discussing the elections with friends. In addition, our long-term trends focus on traditional forms of campaign activity, and the rise of online activity may compensate for some of the decline in traditional participation. In short, the *level* of campaign activity may be changing as well as the *nature* of the public's involvement.

Direct Contacting

Janelly Fourtou is a member of the European Parliament, representing a French political party. One day she got a package from a public interest group in Austria. The Parliament was debating new copyright and Internet usage laws for Europe, and there was considerable interest in this legislation. Receiving a package was not unusual because politicians regularly get mail from their constituents. The contents, however, were unusual—the package contained two pig ears, artistically carved from a dead pig and mounted in a frame suitable for display. The ears were part of the Big Brother Award that the Austrian group gave to Fourtou as the "worst" MEP on copyright and intellectual property issues. The pig ears generated press coverage for the interest group and their cause and focused attention on Fourtou's voting record.

One of the most direct ways for people to express support or opposition to new legislation is to write their representatives or e-mail them, preferably without pig ears. Or one can go to a city council or school board meeting, talk to a representative in person, or write a letter to the local newspaper. About a fifth of the American public directly contacted government officials in the 1960s. This number almost doubled by the end of the 1980s, and it has increased since then (Verba, Scholzman, and Brady 1995, ch. 3; Dalton 2009a, ch. 4). Moreover, the advent of e-mail has made contacting politicians even easier and made it simpler for political groups to mobilize their supporters to write. Congressional mail statistics, especially e-mail messages, show a sharp increase in communications from constituents.

Contacting has also become more common in European nations (Pattie, Seyd, and Whiteley 2004, ch. 3; Koch, Wasmer, and Schmidt 2001). The level of contacting now rivals campaign activity (except voting). The second panel of table 3.4 shows the percentage of the public who had contacted a politician or government official during the previous five years. A full 28 percent of Americans, 19 percent of the British, 12 percent of Germans, and 12 percent of the French answered affirmatively.

The level of direct contacting is important for several reasons. Contacting can expand the potential influence of the public, perhaps even more than campaign activity. Contacting can occur when, where, and how the citizen thinks it will be most effective—rather than waiting several years for the next election. This high information activity allows people to signal their policy preferences. Direct contacting also seems to be increasing, which contrasts with the decline in electoral participation. Finally, direct contacting requires a significant level of political skill and motivation by the individual, so this implies an engaged citizenry. It's therefore a sign that people are involved in politics but may be changing how they participate.

Communal Activity

The essence of grassroots democracy is when people get together to collectively address their needs. Community activity often involves group efforts to deal with social or community problems, ranging from school issues to improving the roads to protecting the local environment. From the PTA to local neighborhood committees, this is democracy in action. Such autonomous group action defines the civil society that theorists from Thomas Jefferson to the present have considered a foundation of democracy. Tocqueville, for example, saw such group activity as a distinctive feature of American democracy:

> The political activity that pervades the United States must be seen to be understood. No sooner do you set foot upon American ground than you are stunned by a kind of tumult; . . . here the people of one quarter of a town are meeting to decide upon the building of a church;

there the election of a representative is going on; a little farther, the delegates of a district are hastening to the town in order to consult upon some local improvements; in another place, the laborers of a village quit their plows to deliberate upon a project of a road or a public school. . . . To take a hand in the regulation of society and to discuss it is [the] biggest concern and, so to speak, the only pleasure an American knows. (Tocqueville 1966, 249–50)

This mode is distinct from campaigns because communal activity occurs largely outside of the regularized, institutional setting of elections and lacks a partisan focus. In addition, a relatively high level of political sophistication and initiative is required of communal activists (see table 3.1). People define their own issue interests, the methods of influencing policymakers, and the timing of influence. The issue may be as broad as aid to Africa or as narrow as the policies of the local school district—and people, not elites, decide. Control over the framework of participation means that communal activities can convey more information and exert more political pressure than the public's restricted participation in campaigns. In short, group activity shifts control of participation to the public and thereby increases their political influence.

Political scientists are intensely debating whether participation in citizen groups is following the same downward spiral as election turnout. In a provocative series of analyses, Robert Putnam (2000) claimed that Americans are "bowling alone." He found that participation in social and civic groups ranging from the Elks and the PTA to bowling leagues dropped off markedly since the 1970s. Putnam noted that such groups taught skills and norms that spurred democratic political involvement, and he argued that the decline of such associations has decreased political involvement. He documented a drop in the number of Americans who attend a public meeting on town or school affairs, who belong to a "better government" group, or who serve on a committee for a local organization. Instead, too many of us are sitting at home in front of our television sets, computer monitors, or X-boxes.

Putnam's critics maintain that he is studying the "old" forms of group activity—that contemporary publics aren't joining social clubs but participating in self-help groups, neighborhood associations, and issue-oriented organizations such as environmental groups and the women's movement (Skocpol and Fiorina 1999). In fact, Putnam gave examples of these new forms of action when he listed the range of social activities held in one California church:

The weekly calendar of the Crystal Cathedral . . . included sessions devoted to Women in the Marketplace, Conquering Compulsive Behaviors, Career Builders' Workshop, Stretch and Walk Time for Women, Cancer Conquerors, Positive Christian Singles, Gamblers Anonymous, Women Who Love Too Much, Overeaters Anonymous, and Friday Night Live. (Putnam 2000, 66)

These new forms of social organization aren't tapped by membership in the traditional social institutions such as fraternal groups or civic clubs. In addition, group participation can include the new style of public interest groups, such as environmental advocacy, women's issues, human rights groups, or consumer protection.

The unstructured nature of communal activities makes it difficult to measure participation levels accurately or to compare levels across nations. Still, citizens in all four nations in our study are engaged in communal activities to a significant degree. Group-based participation has long been a distinctive aspect of American political culture, where membership in social groups often exceeds that in other democracies. The percentage of Americans participating in community groups increased from 30 percent in 1967 to 34 percent in 1987, and 38 percent in 2000.[7] The World Values Survey found that American membership in civic associations, environmental groups, women's groups, or peace groups increased from 6 percent in 1980, to 18 percent in 1990 and 33 percent in 1999 (figure 3.2).

Figure 3.2 | Public Interest Groups

Group membership is increasing over time.

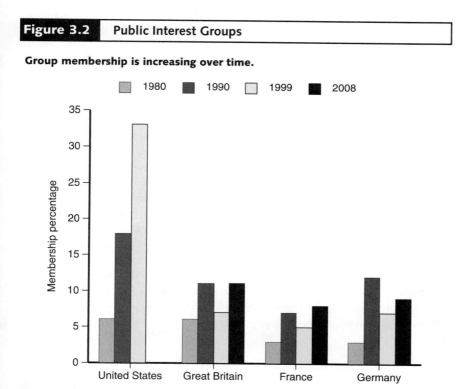

Sources: 1980–81 World Values Survey; 1990–93 World Values Survey; 1999–2002 World Values Survey/European Values Survey; 2008 European Values Survey.

Note: Figure entries are the percentages of individuals who belong to a civic association, environmental group, women's group, or peace group in each nation.

European political norms traditionally placed less emphasis on group activities, and the structure of European political systems didn't encourage direct citizen contact with government officials. But communal activity has apparently grown in these democracies as well. British participation in social groups and other forms of nonelectoral participation has grown (Curtice and Seyd 2002; Whiteley 2012), and the World Values Survey/European Values Survey finds a general upward trend in civic association membership from 1980 to 2008 (figure 3.2). As one example, the membership in the three largest British environmental groups increased from a few hundred thousand in the mid-1970s to more than 5 million today (Rootes 2007). Communal activity also has increased in Germany, and they coined a new term to describe these groups (*Bürgerinitiativen*) (Offe and Fuchs 2002). Only 3 percent of Germans claimed to belong to a civic association or political group in 1980s; this figure bumped up to 12 percent in 1990, and was still 9 percent in 2008. By most accounts, communal activity is more limited in France. Tocqueville, for example, contrasted American social cooperation with the individualism of the French political culture. Even in France, however, these surveys track an increase in civic group membership over time (Keil 2012).

The third panel in table 3.4 compares the level of community activity across a larger set of democracies. Working together on community issues can obviously take a variety of forms—from working with the PTA to a local environmental group—but this is the nature of communal activity. Collective action is highest in the United States, where 35 percent participated in community activities; 13 percent to 26 percent of the three European publics had worked with others. In fact, communal activity is roughly as common as working on an election campaign.

Putnam identified important changes in the American political process, but I am not convinced that his findings mean that political involvement of all sorts is declining, or that the patterns he described for the United States apply to other democracies. Especially within the three European nations we examine, participation in social and civic groups has increased, introducing more direct citizen involvement in the political process.[8] (Furthermore, many of the factors that Putnam uses to explain the American trends have also occurred in Europe, but apparently without the same effects; see Putnam 2002.) Even if Americans are less likely to participate in electoral politics, engagement in informal groups, social movements, and community initiatives has grown. In summary, communal activity reinforces the view that political participation is continuing in contemporary democracies.

Protest and Contentious Action

Historically, protest and contentious actions arose from feelings of frustration and deprivation. Concentrated among the socially disadvantaged, repressed minorities, or groups alienated from the established political order, protest was an outlet for those who lacked access through conventional channels. A graphic illustration was the democratic revolution that spread through Eastern Europe, East Asia, South Africa, and other democratizing nations in the late 1980s and early 1990s. Occupy Wall Street protests and demonstrations in European capitals over the financial impact of the Great Recession are examples of discontent leading to collective action.

The nature of protest is, however, changing in advanced industrial democracies (Barnes, Kaase, et al. 1979; Norris 2002). Protest has broadened from the disadvantaged to include a wider spectrum of society. Gray Panthers protest for senior citizen rights, consumers activists monitor industry, environmentalists call attention to ecological problems, and citizen groups of all types are proliferating. In the past, protests often challenged the legitimacy of political institutions. Protests in advanced industrial democracies seldom seek to overthrow the established political order; after all, the affluent and well-educated participants are some of the primary beneficiaries of this order. Instead, reformism has replaced revolutionary fervor. Modern protest is typically a planned and organized activity in which groups consciously orchestrate their activities to occur when the timing will most benefit their cause. It takes a lot of people to organize a "spontaneous" demonstration. For many people, protest is just another political resource for mobilizing public opinion and influencing policymakers. Scholars once considered protest as different from conventional forms of political participation, but it now appears to be an extension of conventional politics by other means.

Table 3.5 describes the levels of protest activity across several established democracies. The column on the left ranks nations according to the percentage who have signed a petition—a modest and common form of protest, and a conventional part of politics. The act of signing a petition is routine for a large share of the public in most established democracies. The petition has a long and venerable heritage in British and American politics, and political groups of every orientation use it. One can hardly enter a Walmart in the United States or a Marks & Spencer in Britain without being asked to sign a petition. Most Americans, Britons, French, and Germans have signed a petition, and this activity is commonplace in most other nations as well.

A more telling test of the public's willingness to transcend conventional political bounds is participation in the two challenging acts summarized in the right-hand column of table 3.5. More than two-fifths of the French have participated in at least one of these two activities. This finding verifies our earlier description of the French as avoiding conventional politics and relishing protest. In addition, its cultural tradition enshrines France's revolutionary history. In just the single year following the 2007 French survey, truckers blockaded gas stations and fisherman disrupted shipping on the Dover Strait to protest fuel prices, protestors disrupted the Olympic torch relay to protest Chinese human rights violations, Greenpeace climbed the Eiffel Tower in an anti-nuclear demonstration, public sector workers and students protested against government budget cuts, transport workers went on strike against a plan to increase retirement age, farmers protested the low price of milk subsidies, and a demonstration by winemakers for more government aid turned violent in the wine country. French protest knows few social bounds.

Table 3.5	Protest Activity		

Levels of protest now rival more conventional forms of political action.

SIGNED A PETITION		PARTICIPATED IN A CHALLENGING ACT	
Sweden	82	France	48
Australia	79	Denmark	40
Norway	73	Italy	37
Canada	73	Spain	37
United States	70	Switzerland	35
France	68	Norway	35
Denmark	67	Canada	32
Britain	66	Belgium	31
Switzerland	65	Australia	26
Japan	60	Sweden	30
Belgium	59	Germany	29
Germany	57	Finland	28
Finland	54	Netherlands	26
Ireland	54	United States	25
Netherlands	53	Britain	20
Austria	49	Austria	19
Italy	51	Ireland	19
Spain	41	Portugal	17
Portugal	27	Japan	12

Sources: 2006–08 World Values Survey for United States, Australia, Canada, and Japan; 2008 European Values Survey for European nations.

Note: Entries in the second column are the percentages who have participated either in a lawful protest or a boycott.

Most other nations display a modest level of protest, involving 20 to 30 percent of the public in at least one of these activities. A third of Germans and a quarter of Americans and Britons have participated in one of these activities, as protest is an accepted form of action by groups ranging from neighborhood associations to advocates for the environment. Mediterranean and Scandinavian nations are near the top of this ranking, while the Japanese show a marked aversion to protest activities. Protest is obviously separate from harsh living conditions when the affluent Danes, the Norwegians, and the Swiss are high in protest activity. It's notable that Britain and the United States rank lower in challenging activities than in signing petitions. I return to this point later in the chapter.

One caveat: protest activity in table 3.5 appears very common because the question asked whether the respondent had "ever done" the activity. By comparison, the fourth panel in table 3.4 presents contentious actions over specific time periods. Still, nearly a third of these publics said that in the previous year they had signed a petition or attended a protest. The increase in contentious politics is greater if we expand the definition of protest to include political consumerism: buying or boycotting a product for a political reason. This form of protest is often missing from earlier participation studies (Stolle, Hooghe, and Micheletti 2005). Roughly a quarter of American, British, and French respondents said they had boycotted a product for political reasons in the previous twelve months, and this number rises to a third among Germans (table 3.4). Other studies find that *buy*cotting—purchasing a product for political reasons—is even more common.

Although most people in established democracies participate in some form of contentious action, if only by signing a petition, some researchers claim that protest participation is declining. Certainly the media seem to find protest less newsworthy than a decade or two ago. But because the usage of protest politics has spread within society, the overall level of protest has generally risen. Table 3.6 tracks the development of protest activity over time for our four core nations. Because the surveys start with 1974, they do not show the initial growth of protest activity that occurred during the 1960s. It's still clear that protest grew in most established democracies over the last quarter of the twentieth century (Inglehart 1997, ch. 8; Norris 2002, ch. 10). Using participation in lawful demonstrations as one example, in the thirty-plus years since the first survey, this activity increased by 6 percent in the United States, 9 percent in Britain, 12 percent in Germany, and 20 percent in France. Although the rate of increase has apparently slowed, protest activity is now more common than some other conventional forms of action.

The growth of contentious politics probably reflects a general increase in small actions over neighborhood issues, schools, government programs, and other specific concerns, rather than a just few large-scale movements (such as antiwar protests or Occupy Wall Street protests). In addition, the creation of citizen lobbies, environmental groups, consumer advocacy groups, and other nongovernmental organizations (NGOs) provides an institutional basis for organizing protests. These new public interest groups are changing the style of citizen politics. Protest is becoming a common political activity, and the era of protest politics is not passing.

These time trends may also explain why the United States ranks relatively low in recent cross-national comparisons (see table 3.5). Americans had high levels of protest in the first systematic cross-national studies done in the 1970s (Barnes, Kaase, et al. 1979)—perhaps because this survey followed the decade of civil rights and anti-Vietnam protests—and participation has gradually increased since then. But protest has grown even more rapidly in Great Britain, France, Germany, and several other established democracies.

Table 3.6 Protesting over Time

Protest activity has increased over the past three decades.

	UNITED STATES					GREAT BRITAIN					WEST GERMANY					FRANCE			
	1975	1981	1990	1999	2007	1974	1981	1990	1999	2009	1974	1981	1990	1999	2008	1981	1990	1999	2008
Sign a petition	58	61	70	81	62	22	63	75	81	66	30	46	55	47	57	44	51	68	68
Participate in lawful demonstrations	11	12	15	21	17	6	10	13	13	15	9	14	25	22	26	26	31	39	46
Join in boycott	14	14	17	25	22	5	7	14	17	14	4	7	9	10	13	11	11	13	16
Participate in unofficial strike	2	3	4	6	—	5	7	8	9	7	1	2	2	2	4	10	9	12	12
Occupy building	2	2	2	4	—	1	2	2	2	2	*	1	1	1	3	7	7	9	9
Damage property	1	1	—	—	—	1	2	—	—	—	*	1	—	—	—	1	—	—	—
Engage in personal violence	1	2	—	—	—	*	1	—	—	—	*	1	—	—	—	1	—	—	—

Sources: 1974–75 Political Action Study; 1981–83, 1990–93, 1999–2002 World Values Surveys; 1999–2002 European Values Survey; 2006–08 World Values Survey for United States and 2008 European Values Survey for other nations.

Note: Table entries are the percentages of individuals who say they have done the activity. An asterisk denotes fewer than 1 percent; a dash indicates that the question was not asked in this study.

American participation hasn't declined, but protest has grown at a faster rate in other democracies and is overtaking U.S. activity levels.

Although I have generally spoken about protest in positive terms, the dark side of protest occurs when people engage in violent behavior. Abortion clinic bombings, the 2006 riots and car burnings in Paris suburbs, and the violent activities of terrorists in America and Europe are fundamentally different from democratic protest and go far beyond the tolerable bounds of politics. The early surveys in table 3.5 show that although protest is widely accepted, the number who participates in violent activities is minimal. In 1981, for example, 44 percent of the French public had signed a petition and 26 percent had participated in a lawful demonstration, but only 1 percent had damaged property or engaged in personal violence. Contemporary democratic citizens want to protest the actions of their government, not destroy them.

Wired Activism

January 18, 2012, was the biggest day of online protest in the English world in history (Wortham 2012). The U.S. Congress was considering two pieces of legislation that would regulate information flows on the Internet. Many individuals and groups saw this legislation as a threat to privacy and free access to the Web, and became active. More than 25,000 blogs on the popular platform WordPress chose to go black to support the cause, and 12,500 others added a "Stop Censorship" ribbon to their sites. There were apps to fax an opposition letter to members of Congress. Millions of tweets discussed and criticized the legislation. Google and Wikipedia "went dark" for the day; Google said 4.5 million people signed its online petition to Congress, voicing displeasure at the legislation. Mark Zuckerberg called for better legislation on his Facebook site and got hundreds of thousands of likes on his post. Social media were used to organize live protests against the legislation. Both bills stopped their progress through Congress because of these protests and public response.

The Internet has created a new way for people to carry on traditional political activities: to connect with others, to gather and share information, and to attempt to influence the political process (Coleman and Shane 2012; Schlozman, Verba, and Brady 2012; Chadwick 2006). E-mails are now the most common and rapidly growing form of communications from constituents to members of the U.S. Congress. Candidate websites were unheard of in the 1992 U.S. elections, but today they are a standard and expanding feature of electoral politics in America and Europe. A 2008 survey found that 19 percent of Americans had signed an online petition, 18 percent had contacted a government official by e-mail, and 6 percent had donated money to a candidate or party online (A. Smith et al. 2009). The blogosphere is a still newer source of political information and commentary that potentially empowers individuals as rivals to the established media. The Internet can support online political activism. The same 2008 survey found that 11 percent of Americans had participated in an online political discussion and 10 percent had posted comments online about a political issue. Some governments are even experimenting with Internet voting (Alvarez and Hall 2008) and California allowed online voter registration in 2012.

In addition, the Internet is creating political opportunities that had not previously existed. The most dramatic example of change was Barack Obama's 2008 and 2012 presidential campaigns. The e-mail addresses of those who attended early campaign events created a database the campaign used to recruit volunteers and contributions. The campaign created a social networking site in 2008, MyBo, where Obama supporters could meet online, discuss the campaign, and coordinate their activities. Facebook affinity tags replaced yard signs in these campaigns, and YouTube videos became important conduits of campaign information. The online funding efforts of the Obama campaign achieved unprecedented success. President Obama had almost 15 million followers at the start of 2012. A wide range of political groups, parties, and interest groups use the Internet to disseminate information. Moveon.org now boasts more than 5 million members and a long list of other political efforts organized through the website. The Tea Party movement used the Internet to communicate and coordinate their activities with great success in the 2010 elections. The Internet is becoming an important method of political communication and mobilization across the political spectrum.

Various evidence points to the increased importance of online activism in other democracies. For instance, online participation in British elections grew from 13 percent of the public in 2005 to 31 percent in 2010 (Park et al., 2011). In 2004 Internet activism through joining a political forum was most common among Americans (6 percent), and this activity has undoubtedly spread in all four nations since then (see table 3.4). Broader measures of Internet activism (including circulating e-petitions and forwarding e-mails) suggest that these activities match or exceed the percentage of individuals who had donated money to any political group, worked for a party or candidate, or protested over the same time period. The numbers are still modest, and the uses are still growing, but the Internet is adding to the tools of political activism, especially among the young.

Changing Publics and Political Participation

On the popular television program, *Mythbusters,* the hosts scientifically test various urban myths and pronounce them as confirmed or busted. In a sense, I have tested two myths in this chapter. I began with the "myth" that political participation has been decreasing, which imperils the vitality of contemporary democracies. Indeed, there is an apparent paradox: rising levels of education, increased media consumption, and the other aspects of social modernization described in chapter 1 should increase political participation. Nevertheless, turnout in elections, and possibly campaign activity, has declined in most advanced industrial democracies. Richard Brody (1978) referred to this situation as "the puzzle of political participation." Why is electoral participation decreasing, if the public's political skills and resources are increasing?

This is a puzzle with many possible explanations. Some research suggests that declining turnout in the United States is due to political organizations' weakening ability to mobilize individuals into action (Rosenstone and Hansen 1993). In most established democracies, the political parties are now less active in bringing individuals to the polls and getting the public involved in campaigns. Growing social isolation and the decline of community are other explanations (Putnam 2000; Teixeira 1992, ch. 2). Although these arguments carry some weight, they are partially circular in their logic: people are less active in partisan politics because fewer people (and organizations) are mobilizing them to be involved. Moreover, if electoral activity is generally decreasing across nations, this observation leads us to ask why political organizations are generally less engaging.

To understand the trends in participation we must recognize the full impact of social modernization and other social and technological developments on contemporary politics. Greater political sophistication does not necessarily imply a growth in all forms of political activism; instead, rising sophistication levels may change the *nature* of participation. For example, high turnout levels in the past often reflected the efforts and skills of political groups to get out the vote rather than the public's concern about the election. Moreover, citizen input through voting is limited by the institutionalized structure of elections, which narrows (and blurs) the choice of policy options and limits the frequency of public input. A French environmental group bluntly stated its disdain for elections with a slogan borrowed from the May Revolts of 1968: *Élections—piège à cons* (Elections—trap for idiots). A sophisticated and cognitively mobilized public places less dependence on voting and campaign activity as the primary means of influencing the government.

The public's growing political skills and resources have increased participation in activities that extend beyond voting; these activities are citizen initiated, less constrained, more policy oriented, and directly linked to government. New forms of "creative participation" are pushing the boundaries of how we can become politically engaged—from political swarms to blogging to using market pressures (Micheletti and McFarland 2011). Participation in citizen lobbies, single-issue groups, and citizen action movements is rising in nearly all advanced industrial democracies. Issue-based contacting of political elites has significantly increased, and new forms of political consumerism are expanding the boundaries of political action. Indeed, the range of different activities in table 3.4 is impressive evidence of the diversity of contemporary political activism, and even this listing is incomplete. My rough calculation is that the overall levels of political activity in America have risen by about a third compared to the mid-1960s. It is possible that participation rates will stabilize or grow more slowly in the future—because social modernization and cognitive mobilization are growing more slowly than in the past—but contemporary publics are more engaged than their predecessors. In short, the first myth of decreasing participation is busted. Scholars who focused on electoral participation did not consider the full range of possible activities. Instead of disengagement, *people are now involved in more forms of political action.*

A second myth is the belief that Americans' engagement in politics is lower than most other nations. Voting turnout is lower in the United States, and nearly all European nations have higher turnout rates. This is a truism we all recognize. But Americans are highly active in campaigns, contacting, communal activity, and contentious politics. Europeans frequently vote in national elections, but they generally participate less in nonelectoral forms of political action. If we look beyond the electoral arena, America remains a participatory society. This myth is busted.

What are the practical implications of these patterns? These results mean that contemporary democracies are experiencing changes in the style of political action, and not simply a decline in political engagement. The new style of citizen politics seeks to place more control over political activity in the hands of the citizenry. These nonelectoral forms of participation also likely increase public pressure on political elites through lobbying activities, contentious action, and the mobilization of public opinion. Citizen participation is becoming linked to citizen influence.

The changes in the style of citizen participation require that governments adapt to these new patterns of action if citizen input is to be maximized and used more effectively. This means that governments should undertake institutional reform, and progress so far has been mixed (Coleman and Blumler 2009; G. Smith 2009; Cain, Dalton, and Scarrow 2003). There are many ways that democracies can become even more democratic. However, bureaucracies are often loath to open up the administrative process, and elected leaders strain to retain their autonomy. Internet activism also has the potential to transform the nature of the relationship between citizens and their government, which is not always embraced by politicians who are hesitant to change. Perhaps some government officials repeat the myth that people are not interested in politics to shelter themselves from reform. But democracy makes progress by adapting, and that is what is needed now.

As a last point, these new forms of action also make greater demands on the participants, and this may affect who participates and potential inequalities of representation. This latter point depends on who participates in the various forms of political action.

Suggested Readings

Anduiza, Eva, Michael Jensen, and Laia Jorba, eds. 2012. *Digital Media and Political Engagement Worldwide: A Comparative Study.* Cambridge, UK: Cambridge University Press.

Chadwick, Andrew. 2006. *Internet Politics: States, Citizens, and New Communication Technologies*. Oxford, UK: Oxford University Press.

DeBardeleben, Joan, and Jon Pammett, eds. 2009. *Activating the Citizen: Dilemmas of Participation in Europe and Canada*. London: Palgrave Macmillan.

Gabriel, Oscar, Silke Keil, and Eric Kerrouche, eds. 2012. *Political Participation in France and Germany*. Colchester, UK: ECPR Press.

Micheletti, Michele, and Andrew McFarland, eds. 2011. *Creative Participation: Responsibility-Taking in the Political World*. Boulder, CO: Paradigm.

Pattie, Charles, Patrick Seyd, and Paul Whiteley. 2004. *Citizenship in Britain: Values, Participation, and Democracy*. New York: Cambridge University Press.

Putnam, Robert. 2000. *Bowling Alone: The Collapse and Renewal of American Community*. New York: Simon and Schuster.

Vassallo, Francesca. 2010. *France, Social Capital and Political Activism*. New York: Palgrave Macmillan.

Wattenberg, Martin. 2002. *Where Have All the Voters Gone?* Cambridge, MA: Harvard University Press.

———. 2011. *Is Voting for Young People?* 3rd ed. New York: Longman.

Whiteley, Paul. 2012. *Political Participation in Britain: The Decline and Revival of Civic Culture*. New York: Palgrave Macmillan.

Zukin, Cliff, et al. 2006. *A New Engagement? Political Participation, Civic Life, and the Changing American Citizen*. New York: Oxford University Press.

Notes

1. Parry, Moyser, and Day (1992) show that contentious participation is another mode of British participation; Pattie, Seyd, and Whiteley (2004) found three dimensions of individual actions: consumerism, contributing, and elections; contacting; and protest. Teorell, Torcal, and Montero (2007) identified five modes of participation in Europe. Also see Claggett and Pollack (2006).
2. McDonald and Popkin (2001) show that a growing percentage of noneligible adults (noncitizens or those with criminal records) have lowered statistics on U.S. voting rates. This gap has also increased over time. Turnout in 2008, for example, was about 5 percent higher if noneligibles are excluded. See: http://elections.gmu.edu/voter_turnout.htm
3. The British voting opportunities included local council and county elections, the 2010 House of Commons election, and the 2009 European

Parliament election. The American voter's opportunities included primary and general elections in 2012: three votes in the primary for federal offices and two for state offices (these five offices were filled in the general election), one judicial election, one for the county board of education, one county supervisor, three community college board members, three members of the Irvine school district, the mayor of Irvine, three Irvine city council members, and twenty-six initiatives or referendums.

4. America's high campaign involvement partially reflects the decentralized structure of American elections, and the long list of candidates and campaign issues that appear on the ballot. In 1997, for example, the U.S. Census Bureau estimated that there were more than 500,000 elected officials in the United States, each of whom called on friends, neighbors, and donors to support his or her candidacy at election time (and the same for the losing candidates). In contrast, I estimate that there are only about 25,000 elected officials in Britain and an equally small number in Germany.

The British results in the table are from the CSES postelection module; comparable questions in the full 2005 British Election Study show substantially higher levels of activity.

5. Putnam (2000, ch. 2) and Macedo et al. (2005) rely on commercial polls, which show general declines in participation in the United States. Because academic surveys have better sampling and interviewing methods, I emphasize the findings from these surveys (Dalton 2009a, ch. 4).

6. Studies comparing Eastern and Western Germany find that easterners lag a bit behind on party and campaign involvement but have comparable levels of political interest and discussion (van Deth 2001).

7. Verba, Schlozman, and Brady (1995, 72) compared the first two time points; the third is from the 2000 Social Capital Survey: http://www.cfsv .org/communitysurvey/index.html.

8. Admittedly, much of the evidence for Europe is incomplete because few surveys in the 1960–70s devoted extensive attention to political participation, and more recent surveys typically use different question wording making comparisons over time more difficult. Systematic survey evidence generally begins in the 1980s or early 1990s, at which time much of the effects of social modernization on participation would have already happened.

4 Who Participates?

Political participants come in many shapes and sizes. Virginia R. has been a poll worker in Lawrence, Kansas, at every U.S. election since 1952 (except for the 2006 primary that she missed while having triple bypass heart surgery). Alix is a sixteen-year-old living in Northern California who is too young to vote, but she switched shampoos because of animal testing, will not buy clothes made by child labor, and yells at people who litter. Klaus R. is a lifelong member of the German Christian Democrats and regularly staffs the party's election booth in his hometown square. Sophie C. is a twenty-one-year-old film student who marched with thousands of other French students in 2006 to protest a new labor law affecting youth employment.

The question of who participates is as important as the question of how many people participate. First, if participation influences policy results, then the pattern of who participates determines which citizens are communicating with policymakers and which interests are not being represented. Second, the characteristics of participants partially define the meaning of political activism. Are people who are dissatisfied with the status quo more active or do they withdraw from politics? Whether the dissatisfied or satisfied participate more casts a different light on how one interprets participation. Finally, comparing the correlates of action across nations and participation modes shows how the politics of each nation can shape citizen choices on how to participate.

The Civic Voluntarism Model

Is it rational to be politically active? According to rational choice theorists, the decision to participate can be considered irrational (Downs 1957). Participation takes time and resources. For example, voting requires not just the time to cast the ballot but also the time to follow the campaign and make one's voting choices. But then, our single vote is diluted by the votes of thousands or millions of others. Rational choice theory would suggest that we should all stay home, because participation takes more effort than the likely impact of the effort. In addition, even if participation does have

---

Internet Resource

Visit the Initiative and Referendum Institute for information on the use of referendums in the United States and other democracies:

http://www.iandrinstitute.org

---

an effect, people could be "free riders" and reap the benefits of cleaner air, safer highways, or better schools by relying on the efforts of active citizens. Fortunately, most citizens look beyond narrow self-interested calculations and participate because of their desire to be active and influence the policies that affect their lives. Political participation is a social and psychological decision as much as a rational choice calculation.

Sidney Verba, Kay Schlozman, and Henry Brady (1995) summarized previous social-psychological theories of why people participate in terms of the "civic voluntarism model." In their terms, *people participate because they can, they want to, or someone asked them.* This means that three main factors influence the decision to participate:

- The personal resources of the person
- Political attitudes that encourage participation
- Connections to groups or people who ask one to participate

Under the first factor, political scientists claim that social status (for example, education and income) provides resources that facilitate political action. Higher-status individuals, especially the better educated, are more likely to have the time, the money, the access to political information, and the ability to become politically involved. So widespread is this notion that social status is sometimes described as the "standard model" of political participation (Verba and Nie 1972, ch. 8).

We can add a few other personal characteristics to this list. Participation also varies by age. For many young people, politics comes second to more immediate concerns, such as school, dating, and beginning a career. As individuals age, however, they take on social and economic responsibilities that increase their motivation to follow politics: they become taxpayers and homeowners, their own children enter public schools, and they may begin to draw benefits from government programs. Consequently, political engagement typically increases with age, although generational experiences also affect participation (Campbell 2006; Dalton 2009a). In addition, men are often more politically active than women (Norris 2002; Schlozman, Burns, and Verba 1994). Differences in political resources may explain part of this gender gap, and societal norms that traditionally socialized women to be less politically engaged are another factor.

A second set of potential predictors includes attitudes that motivate people to participate. Beliefs about the citizen's role and the nature of political action may influence participation patterns (Dalton 2009a, ch. 4; Pattie, Seyd, and Whiteley 2004). People often vote because they believe this is a duty of citizenship, even if their vote is mixed with millions of others. A sense of political efficacy—the feeling that one's actions can affect the political process—also may stimulate action. Conversely, political cynicism may lead to political apathy and withdrawal: if one cannot affect the political process, why bother to try? Researchers debate the causal role of political dissatisfaction. On the one hand, satisfaction with government may increase support for the political process and encourage participation. On the other hand, dissatisfaction may stimulate activity to change public policy. Although scholars disagree on the impact of dissatisfaction, they agree that it is an important factor to consider.

Partisanship and ideology are other potential influences on participation. Are liberals more likely to vote than conservatives? Do ideological groups differ in their likelihood of protesting? If participation influences policymakers and the government, then whether activists are drawn equally across ideological or partisan camps has important implications for the representativeness of the democratic process. Participation that is heavily concentrated among ideological extremists may also distort the policy process.

The third set of potential predictors is group-based forces. Some group influences may be psychological, such as attachment to one's preferred political party. A sense of party identification motivates people to vote or participate in campaigns as a display of party support. Conversely, people with weak or nonexistent party bonds are less concerned with elections and are less likely to participate.

Participation in social groups can also increase political action (Verba, Schlozman, and Brady 1995; Putnam 2000; Vassallo 2010). Experience in a social club or volunteer organization develops skills and orientations that carry over to politics, and certain groups actively encourage their members to be politically active. Even running the bingo game or bake sale at church teaches skills that can be applied to political activism. Social groups also provide a useful touchstone for judging whether participation is a worthwhile activity (Uhlaner 1989). Therefore, participation in nonpolitical groups may stimulate political involvement.

Who Votes?

Voting is the most common political activity, and I begin by considering which factors influence who is likely to vote. I also use voting to introduce some of the variables in the civic voluntarism model. Because resources provide the *standard model* of participation, I start with this category. Education taps personal resources that are strongly related to turnout. The better educated should be more likely to vote because they have a stronger sense of civic duty and possess the resources to follow political campaigns and to be politically active. Figure 4.1 displays the levels of turnout as a function of education in the four core nations.

In all four democracies the better educated vote more than the least edu-cated.[1] Education-based differences in turnout are greater among Americans than Europeans because the complexity of the U.S. registration and electoral system means that educational skills help in navigating the electoral pro-cess. In addition, Labour/Social Democratic parties mobilize less-educated working-class voters in Europe, which may explain the uptick in turnout among the least educated group in Germany and France. The hurdles to voting are also lower in these European countries because of the registration system and the nature of elections (see chapter 3).

Age also affects voting rates. As a starting point, research suggests that political involvement increases as people age, assume family and career responsibilities, and become integrated into their communities. This is generally known as the "life cycle model" of participation (Verba and Nie 1972; Schlozman, Verba, and Brady 2012). However, several schol-ars claim that the decreasing electoral engagement among the younger generation is producing a general decline in electoral participation (Wat-tenberg 2011a; Franklin 2004; Putnam 2000). Such results have given rise to a chorus of older political experts on both sides of the Atlantic who write about the supposed ignorance, indifference, and apolitical orientation of youth today (Damon 2001; Bauerlein 2008; Twenge and Campbell 2010). Frankly, I am skeptical of this blanket indictment of the

| Figure 4.1 | Education and Voting |

The better-educated are more likely to vote, especially in the United States.

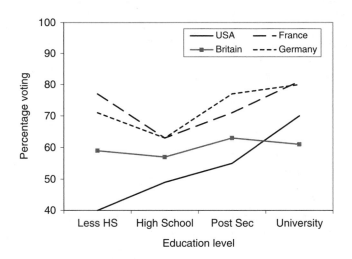

Source: Comparative Study of Electoral Systems (module II).

young. Although it is clear that young people vote less often than in the past, we might withhold a final judgment until we compare voting with participation in other types of activity.

Figure 4.2 shows that voting turnout is significantly higher among older citizens. Indeed, the age gap in turnout has widened over time (Wattenberg 2011a). Fewer than half of Americans under age twenty-four voted in the 2004 election, but turnout averaged more than two-thirds among those over age forty-five. Even with the enthusiasm for Barack Obama among youth in 2008, the same basic age difference persists. The three European electorates show a similar age pattern.

If elections influence politics, then the differential turnout by age has real implications. As one example, if American youth—with their greater preference for the Democratic Party—had voted at rates equal to their elders in the 2000 and 2004 elections, the Democratic presidential candidate would have won both elections. In addition, when older citizens vote, their participation makes politicians more sensitive to their needs and less responsive to the issue interests of young people who don't vote. In short, who votes has real consequences for electoral outcomes and the content of politics.

Education and age are only two of the factors in the civic voluntarism model. I could examine each trait by itself, but many of them are interrelated. For example, education levels are related to political norms and social group

Figure 4.2	Age and Voting

Turnout in elections systematically increases with age in all four nations.

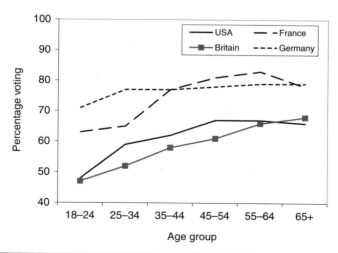

Source: Comparative Study of Electoral Systems (module II).

activity, and age groups systematically differ in their education levels and presumably in their norms and values.

Therefore, to determine the separate influence of each factor and the explanatory power of the civic voluntarism model, I combined seven different variables into a basic statistical analysis predicting political participation:

- Education
- Age
- Gender
- Political efficacy
- Left/Right attitudes
- Political party attachments and
- Membership in union or business group

The first three tap the resources and social characteristics described by the model. The next two—political efficacy and Left/Right position—represent attitudinal elements. The last two variables—party attachments and group membership—indicate possible group influences on participation.

Figure 4.3 shows the influence of each predictor on the decision to vote; this methodology is described in appendix B of this book.[2] The coefficients from the statistical analysis show the importance of each variable, while controlling for the other variables. For example, do gender differences still exist after simultaneously considering the educational and attitudinal differences between men and women? The thicker the arrow in the figure, the stronger the influence of the variable.

As just shown, education is strongly related to turnout. In all three European nations, the better educated are more likely to vote. Differences in education level are even more pronounced in the United States (coefficient $\beta = .13$) because of the complexity of the registration and electoral system.

The second set of predictors is political motivations. Feelings of political efficacy exert a modest impact in each nation; those who feel that they can influence politics are more likely to vote. The differences in turnout between Left and Right voters are negligible. In this most common of political activities, the ideological bias in participation is minimal because both sides mobilize their supporters to vote, which is how it should be.

The third set of causes is group effects. Because elections are partisan contests, those who identify strongly with a party are more likely to show up at the polls (and presumably cast a ballot for their own party). Partisans are like sports fans, and those who feel a strong identity with the team are most likely to show up on game day (see chapter 9). Thus, the strength of partisan ties is a significant predictor of turnout. Another organizational

| Figure 4.3 | Predicting Voting Turnout |

Education and party attachments are the most important predictors of voter turnout in the United States, with modest differences in other democracies.

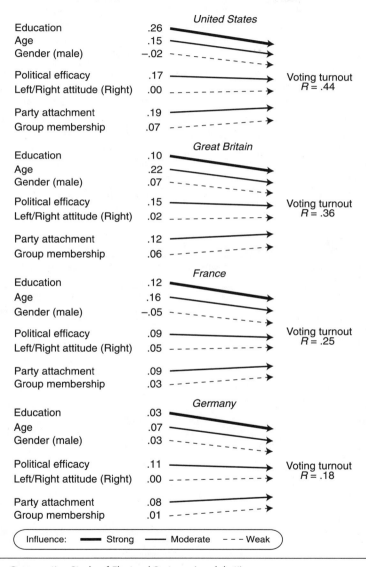

Source: Comparative Study of Electoral Systems (module II).

Note: Figure entries are standardized coefficients from a multiple regression analyses. See note 2 for a description of how to interpret regression coefficients.

influence, group membership, shows a weak influence on turnout, perhaps because the question in the survey is too simple.[3]

Campaign Activity

If you have worked on an election campaign—canvassing door to door, staffing a phone bank, or even just stuffing envelopes—you know how demanding this form of political action can be. As discussed in chapter 3, campaign activity requires substantial individual initiative and is a more partisan activity than voting. The patterns of campaign activity should reflect these differences.

I combined two types of campaign activism into a single measure.[4] Then I used our seven predictors to explain campaign activism. Table 4.1 presents analyses similar to those in figure 4.3, now presented in tabular form. Because campaign work is an intensely partisan activity, partisan ties exert an even stronger force than for voting turnout. Most of the partisanship coefficients for campaign activity in table 4.1 are more than double their effects for voter turnout. These differences are quite large: 72 percent of

Table 4.1	Predicting Campaign Activity			
Party attachment is the strongest predictor of campaign activity, and other factors are secondary.				
PREDICTORS	UNITED STATES	GREAT BRITAIN	FRANCE	GERMANY
Resources				
Education	.09	.06	−.02	.09
Age	−.11*	.08	.00	.10*
Gender (male)	.02	.10	.07	.13*
Motivations				
Political efficacy	.11*	.10*	.09	.11*
Left/Right position (Right)	−.05	−.01	−.08	.01
Group factors				
Party attachment	.27*	.34*	.18*	.24*
Group membership	.07	.04	.10*	.09
R	.37	.44	.29	.37

Source: Comparative Study of Electoral Systems (module II).

Note: Table entries are standardized coefficients from multiple regression analyses. Statistically significant effects ($p < .05$) are denoted by an asterisk. See note 2 and appendix A, the statistical primer, for a description of how to interpret regression coefficients.

strong partisans in the United States did at least one campaign activity in 2004, compared to only 31 percent of nonpartisans.

Older people tend to be more involved in campaigns, even while holding constant the other factors. This age pattern in campaign activity is smaller than for voting and in the United States was actually reversed in 2004. Education differences are also smaller than for voting turnout, even though campaign activity is a more demanding form of action.

Is there a gender gap? For both voting and campaign activity, gender differences in participation are small. For campaign activity, women tend to be more active once other factors are controlled. These small differences are actually a positive sign: changing gender norms are reducing the participation gap between men and women.

Finally, people who feel their input makes a difference are more likely to become active in a campaign. And, because both sides work to mobilize their supporters, ideological differences in campaign activity are small and unsystematic.

Direct Contacting

Direct contact differs from electoral activity because it requires that citizens take the initiative. I recently heard about an unusual example. Sylvia lives in Orange County, California, and is very interested in politics. On Monday, Wednesday, and Friday she gets up at 6:00 a.m. to call the White House in Washington, D.C., and give them her input on the issues of the day. On Tuesday and Thursday she calls her representatives in the House or Senate to share her opinions. When she has time, she sends them all letters as well. Sylvia is unusual in many ways, but she is a super-citizen when it comes to contacting.

Contacting officials can take different forms, it can range from the taxpayer writing city hall about garbage collection to calling the office of a member of Congress to protest federal policy. It can be done as an individual or as a collective effort of people working together. In all of these instances, contacting requires substantial individual initiative and significant political skills to identify the appropriate government official and cogently state one's case.

Consequently, resources are important for contacting (table 4.2). Education has some of its strongest effects in predicting contacting. The coefficient for the United States, for example, is the strongest across all the different types of activity. Contacting is also more common among older people, presumably because they have greater needs and more experience in working with government.

As one moves away from electoral politics, however, the impact of partisanship weakens. Partisans are politically engaged and therefore more likely to contact politicians, but these effects are weaker than for voting or campaign activity.

Table 4.2	Predicting Direct Contacting			
Education and group membership are strong predictors of contacting.				
PREDICTORS	**UNITED STATES**	**GREAT BRITAIN**	**FRANCE**	**GERMANY**
Resources				
Education	.26*	.12*	.07*	.15*
Age	.14*	.16*	.08	.06
Gender (male)	.05	.00	.12*	.07
Motivations				
Political efficacy	.06	.03	.03	.02
Left/Right position (Right)	−.03	−.04	.05	.00
Group factors				
Party attachment	.10*	.14*	.07	.16*
Group membership	.02	.09*	.10*	.11*
R	.33	.28	.22	.28

Source: Comparative Study of Electoral Systems (module II).

Note: Table entries are standardized coefficients from multiple regression analyses. Statistically significant effects ($p < .05$) are denoted by an asterisk. See note 2 and appendix A, the statistical primer, for a description of how to interpret regression coefficients.

Because social groups can organize contacting—through chain letters, e-mail campaigns, or newsletters encouraging members to act—there are modest group influences on contacting. This illustrates Verba, Schlozman, and Brady's dictum that people often participate because they have been asked.

Communal Activity

Neighbors working together on a common project is a central part of democratic politics in America and is growing in importance in European democracies. We see this in local political groups, large national issue groups, and a variety of ways that people get together to work for a common cause. This is Tocqueville's image of small-scale democratic politics. But when these groups assemble, who is in the room?

Group activity often requires considerable initiative and sophistication from the participants. Table 4.3 shows that the better educated are significantly more likely to participate in communal activities in three of the four nations.

Equally interesting is a nonrelationship in the table. Although the young are systematically less involved in voting, there is no systematic age pattern in communal activity once other factors are taken into account. In fact, in

| Table 4.3 | Predicting Communal Activity |

Group membership has its strongest effect for communal activity, and partisans also tend to be active.

PREDICTORS	UNITED STATES	GREAT BRITAIN	FRANCE	GERMANY
Resources				
Education	.16*	.10*	−.02	.05
Age	−.04	.02	−.01	.05
Gender (male)	−.05	.02	.09*	.06
Motivations				
Political efficacy	.01	.04	.10	.04
Left/Right position (Right)	.01	−.05	−.15	−.01
Group factors				
Party attachment	.09*	.17*	.08	.14*
Group membership	.04	.14*	.15*	.12*
R	.21	.29	.29	.25

Source: Comparative Study of Electoral Systems (module II).

Note: Table entries are standardized coefficients from multiple regression analyses. Statistically significant effects ($p < .05$) are denoted by an asterisk. See note 2 and appendix A, the statistical primer, for a description of how to interpret regression coefficients.

the United States and in Britain the young are slightly more active once one controls for the other possible predictors. Young people may not be engaged in electoral politics, but they find ways to participate through other venues, such as group activity.

Working with a group is distinct from voting and campaign activity because communal participation is generally not a partisan activity. Participants may be drawn to group efforts precisely because they are distinct from party politics. Table 4.3 shows that partisanship has less impact on communal participation than on voting or campaign activities. Social group membership helps to mobilize individuals to participate in collective efforts, and this factor has its strongest effect for communal activity.

Who Protests?

Why do citizens protest? If you have attended a protest, why did you go? Every protester has an individual explanation for his or her action. A commitment to an issue stimulates some people to act. General opposition to the government leads other protestors into action. Still others are caught up in the excitement and sense of comradeship that protests produce, or they simply accompany a friend who invites them to come. Social scientists have tried to systematize these individual motivations to explain the general sources of protest activity.

In contrast to other forms of political participation, protest is often described as an "unconventional" form of action that can be stimulated by feelings of frustration and political alienation. Political analysts from Aristotle to Karl Marx saw personal dissatisfaction and the striving for better conditions as the root cause of protests and political violence. More modern social scientists have echoed and quantified these themes (Gurr 1970). This view implies that political dissatisfaction should predict protest activity. Indirectly, the theory suggests that protest should be more common among lower-status individuals, minorities, and other groups who feel deprived or dissatisfied.

In contrast, other researchers argue that protest in contemporary democracies has become an extension of conventional politics by other means (Norris 2002; Inglehart 1990). Protest is another political method (like voting, campaign activity, or communal activity) that individuals may use in pursuing their goals (see chapter 3). From this perspective, certain elements of the civic voluntarism model may also apply to protest. In contrast to the deprivation explanation, the civic voluntarism model implies that protest should be higher among the better educated and politically sophisticated—those who have the political skills and resources to engage in these activities. Involvement in social groups may also provide resources and experiences that encourage activities such as signing a petition, protesting, or joining a boycott. Research routinely shows that the young are more likely to protest; protest also more often involves men, although this pattern may be changing with a narrowing of gender roles.

Protest is often seen as a tool for liberals who want to challenge the political establishment, but it may have broadened across the political spectrum in modern societies. For example, chapter 3 discussed the diversity of protest in France, and there is a similar growth of "enraged citizens" (*Wutbürger* in Germany).[5] Feelings of political efficacy may also encourage protest. And last, if protest is becoming a planned, organized activity, social groups and their members may be more active protesters.

Table 4.4 presents the analyses of protest activity.[6] I added a question on satisfaction with government performance to the seven-factor model in order to test the dissatisfaction thesis. Dissatisfaction with the government encourages protest in all four nations, but the effects are modest in the United States and negligible in France and Germany.[7] Furthermore, the pattern of other predictors undercuts the dissatisfaction explanation. For example, the willingness to protest is more common among the better educated, even though less-educated and lower-income citizens are generally more dissatisfied. There is also a consistent, albeit weak, tendency for protest to be more common among those who feel efficacious about politics.

In short, protest isn't primarily an outlet for the alienated and deprived; often, it is just the opposite. Protestors are dissatisfied, but dissatisfaction

| Table 4.4 | Predicting Protest Activity |

Protest is more common among the young and better educated and among those dissatisfied with the government's performance.

PREDICTORS	UNITED STATES	GREAT BRITAIN	FRANCE	GERMANY
Resources				
Education	.14*	.08	.03	.14*
Age	−.05	−.06	−.16*	−.08
Gender (male)	−.03	.00	.04	.00
Motivations				
Dissatisfied with government performance	.08	.08	.16*	.11*
Political efficacy	.03	.02	.05	.04
Left/Right position (Right)	−.10*	−.17*	−.20*	−.13*
Group factors				
Party attachment	.05	.12*	.11*	.11*
Group membership	.11*	.15*	.04	.05
R	.26	.28	.37	.28

Source: Comparative Study of Electoral Systems (module II).

Note: Table entries are standardized coefficients from multiple regression analyses. Statistically significant effects ($p < .05$) are denoted by an asterisk. See note 2 and appendix A, the statistical primer, for a description of how to interpret regression coefficients.

alone is not enough to produce protest. Protest more often follows the expectations from the civic voluntarism model. Protesters are people who have the ability to organize and participate in political activities of all forms, including protest. The clearest evidence of this finding is the tendency in all four nations for the better educated to engage in protest.

In one important area, the correlates of protest differ from conventional electoral activity. Voting and campaign participation routinely increase with age, as family and social responsibilities heighten the relevance of politics. In contrast, protest is the domain of the young. In the United States, 11 percent of those under age twenty-five reported participation in a protest in the previous five years, compared to only 3 percent among those over age sixty-five.

Political scientists offer different interpretations of this age pattern. On the one hand, age differences may reflect life cycle differences in protest. Youth is a period of enthusiasm and rebellion, which may encourage protesting and other such activities. Young people also may have more opportunities to protest because of their free time and concentration in university settings. This explanation would predict that an individual's protest activity should decline with age. On the other hand, age differences may represent a pattern of generational change in participation styles. That is, today's young people protest, not because of their youth, but because their generation has adopted a new style of action. Higher levels of education and political sophistication and changing citizenship norms encourage direct action techniques among the young. If this is true, younger generations will remain more assertive even as they get older. Moreover, protest is but one example of a general pattern of greater use of contentious politics, direct action, and political consumerism among the young (Dalton 2009a, ch. 4; Zukin et al. 2006).

Although groups on the Left and Right both use protest, the willingness to engage in these activities is more common among leftists. These effects are stronger than the ideological biases in conventional forms of political action, and they are consistent even though two nations—Great Britain and Germany—were headed by leftist governments at the time of the surveys. Protest politics is still disproportionately the domain of the Left.

Internet Activism

The Internet offers a new means of political access and activity that can span many types of participation (see chapter 3). People can contact government officials, forward Internet petitions, and use the Internet to support contentious forms of action. In addition, the Internet has special potential in bringing together like-minded individuals in a community, or in a virtual community.

The 2005 Citizens, Involvement, Democracy (CID) survey asked about three types of Internet activism: visiting political websites, forwarding political e-mails, or participating in online political activities.[8] A fifth of the American public had done at least one of these activities in the previous year.

What results should one expect from a survey of Internet activism? Figure 4.4 shows that—no surprise—Internet activism is more common among the young than older people. In addition, there are strong signs that Internet activism builds on the general civic voluntarism model. The strongest predictor of wired activism is higher levels of education, and those who belong to more social groups are also more likely to use the Internet as a political tool. Similarly, those who believe that politicians care what they think are more likely to participate in online activity. These results are only from the United States, but I suspect similar patterns would appear in other established democracies. The Internet seems to broaden the repertoire of political action for the young, as well as providing an additional form of action for those who are already likely to participate.

Comparing the Correlates of Different Activities

At the beginning of this chapter, I stated that who participates does matter because it shows which parts of society are expressing their political views and therefore what interests are influencing public policymaking. In addition, who votes (and doesn't vote) can affect the outcome.

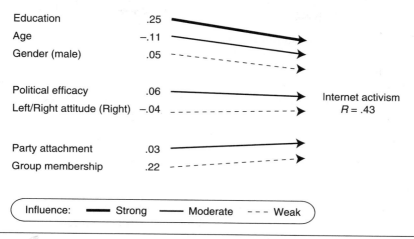

Figure 4.4 | **Predicting Internet Activism**

Education and group ties are the most important factors in predicting the Internet activism of Americans.

Education	.25
Age	−.11
Gender (male)	.05
Political efficacy	.06
Left/Right attitude (Right)	−.04
Party attachment	.03
Group membership	.22

Internet activism
R = .43

Influence: ━━ Strong ── Moderate - - - Weak

Source: Citizens, Involvement, Democracy survey, Georgetown University, 2005.

Note: Figure entries are standardized coefficients from a multiple regression analyses. See note 2 for a description of how to interpret regression coefficients.

Our analyses repeatedly show the importance of individual resources in spurring activity. The growing complexity and technical nature of contemporary issues require that citizens are sophisticated about the world of politics. Participation in virtually all forms of action is higher among the better educated, those with higher income, and other social status resources.

Consequently, democracies may be experiencing a growing social status bias in citizen participation and influence, which runs counter to democratic ideals (Schlozman, Verba, and Brady 2012; Marien, Hooghe, and Quintelier 2010; Bartels 2010). These social status biases are significant for voting in elections, which select government officials. The potential is even greater for nonelectoral participation where there is no "one person, one vote" limit. Working-class parties may mobilize the less educated to vote, but it is harder to mobilize these same individuals to write a letter to their representative or participate in community activities. Thus, an unexpected consequence of the changing patterns of political activism may be an increase in the participation gap between lower-status and higher-status individuals.

Disparities in education levels are often greater in the United States than in the other nations. Educational disparities in U.S. electoral turnout are far greater than in Britain, France, or Germany. The same pattern occurs for other forms of political action. Too large a gap in participation rates

between social strata means that certain groups in America are not participating in the democratic process, and this gap is smaller in most European
democracies. The weakness of labor unions and the absence of a working-
class party to mobilize participation, when coupled with the restrictive registration requirements of the American electoral system, create a serious
participation gap between social groups in the United States. The size of
the participation gap shows the need to find a way to equalize the involvement of all social groups in American politics. This matter is so important
that Schlozman, Verba, and Brady (2012) stress that unequal political voice
represents the broken promise of American democracy. The solution to this
inequality problem is to find means to raise the participation levels of lower-
status groups, not to limit the activity of the better educated. Political leaders must facilitate participation by a broader spectrum of the public and
lower the remaining barriers to participation.[9]

We also highlighted the commonly expressed concern over the political
disengagement of the young. Several well-respected political scientists argue
that the young are dropping out of politics and that democracy is at risk as a
result (Macedo et al. 2006; Wattenberg 2011a). Robert Putnam (2000), for
example, holds that the slow, steady, and ineluctable replacement of older
civic generations by Generations X and Y is a central reason for the erosion
of social engagement in America. An even stronger statement comes from a
2006 study of civic life in America: "Each year, the grim reaper steals away
one of the most civic slices of America—the last members of the 'Greatest
Generation.' This is a cold generational calculus that we cannot reverse until
younger Americans become as engaged as their grandparents" (National
Conference on Citizenship 2006, 8). What a cold-hearted description of
American youth—but is it accurate?

This chapter's broader view of political participation suggests that these
indictments of the young are overstated. Young people in Western democracies are not dropping out of politics; rather, they are changing their style of
action. Their participation in electoral politics is declining, but age groups
participate almost equally in communal activities, and the young are more
active in direct action methods such as protest, political consumerism, voluntarism, and Internet activism (Dalton 2009a; A. Smith 2009; Henn, Weinstein, and Wring 2002). Cliff Zukin and his colleagues recently examined
the full repertoire of political action among the young, and they rejected the
general claim of youth disengagement: "First and foremost, simple claims
that today's youth . . . are apathetic and disengaged from civic live are simply wrong (Zukin et al. 2006, 189). Wattenberg tried to minimize the participation of the young in these domains, but his own data run counter to his
claims. He found that American youth volunteer more than their parents at
the same age and are similarly more likely to petition, demonstrate, or boycott (Wattenberg 2011a, 152, 165).[10] In summary, it is too simple to claim
that the young are systematically less politically active than their parents at
the same age—today's youth are active, but not in the same ways as their

parents or grandparents. Moreover, I would expect the activism of today's youth to further increase through the life cycle and perhaps change in form.

Political attitudes also vary in influence. Political efficacy motivates electoral participation, but seems less important for other forms of political action. For protest, both leftist attitudes and dissatisfaction with government spur participation—but protest is more common among those with the resources to be active. Left/Right ideology has minimal impact on other forms of action, including Internet-based activism.

Finally, group ties are an important influence on participation. Feelings of party attachments are most important for electoral participation, because this is where partisans can come out to support "their team." Partisan effects are significant, but weaker, for contacting and communal activity. In addition, group membership generally encourages all forms of political action, especially communal activity where participation often is based on a group. The characteristics of each mode of action are apparent in the factors that shape who participates.

Participation and the Democratic Process

Several scholars argue that citizen involvement in society and politics is waning, and that this trend has serious and dangerous consequences for democracy (Putnam 2000; Macedo et al. 2005; Wolfe 2006). The evidence presented in chapters 3 and 4 questions this conclusion. Overall, political involvement isn't generally decreasing in advanced industrial societies. Instead, *the forms of political action are changing.* The old forms of political participation—voting, party work, and campaign activity—are in decline, while participation in citizen-initiated and policy-oriented activities is increasing. This trend is even more apparent when adding new forms of action to the mix, such as political consumerism and Internet activism. In the United States the total amount of political activity may have grown by as much as a third since the benchmark Verba and Nie survey in the late 1960s.

Increases in nonelectoral activities are especially significant because they place greater control over the locus and focus of participation in the hands of the citizenry. Political input isn't limited to the issues and institutionalized channels determined by elites. Instead, a single individual, or a group of people, can organize around a specific issue and select the timing and method of influencing policymakers. These direct action techniques also are high-information and high-pressure activities. They therefore serve some of the participation demands of an increasingly educated and politically sophisticated public, far more so than voting and campaign activities (Cain, Dalton, and Scarrow 2003, ch. 12).

Democratic societies should seek to expand citizen participation in the political process and thereby increase popular control of government. Therefore, increases in communal action, protest, and other citizen-initiated activities should generally be welcomed. This changing pattern of action is an important element of the new style of citizen politics. At the same time, it presents new challenges to contemporary democracies, such as the growing social status bias in who participates. New forms of influence for the cognitively mobilized should not ignore the needs to represent everyone in the political process.

In addition, the new forms of political action such as contacting and even citizen interest groups tend to be more individualistic, replacing the collective actions of election and party work. Atomistic participation may decrease attention to the collective needs of society and make it more difficult to balance individual interests and societal interests. Many individuals (and groups) will participate to maximize their own specific interests while downplaying society's collective interests. The solution is to construct new methods of aggregating political interests to balance the expansion of interest articulation that has already occurred.

Direct action methods pose another challenge to contemporary democracies. By their very nature, direct action techniques disrupt the status quo. These activities occasionally challenge the established institutions and procedures of contemporary democracies. The potential for disruption has led some critics to ask whether rapidly expanding citizen participation, especially in protest activities, is placing too many demands on political systems. Policy cannot be made in the streets, they argue. Efficient and effective policymaking requires a deliberative process, in which government officials have some latitude in their decisions. A politicized public with intense policy-focused minorities lobbying for their special interests would strain the political consensus that is a requisite of democratic politics. Indeed, just as citizen demands for influence are rising, a survey of Washington political elites suggests that those who make and implement policy doubt the abilities of the American public.[11]

Some writers therefore argue that it is possible to have too much of a good thing—political participation. Some even cite the evidence accompanying the elitist theory of democracy as a basis for this position (see chapter 2). Citizen activism must be balanced against the needs for government efficiency and rational policy planning, they contend, and the expansion of participation in recent years may have upset this balance, leading to problems of governability in Western democracies. These arguments were commonplace in the 1980s, and I believe that even after the democratization wave of the 1990s there are still too many people who would limit the rights of others.

Those who caution about an excess of participation display a disregard for the democratic goals they profess to defend; they seem to have more in common with the former regimes of Eastern Europe than with real democratic principles. An editor of *The Economist* noted the irony of worrying about the excesses of democracy while simultaneously celebrating the fall of communism:

> The democracies must therefore apply to themselves the argument they used to direct against the communists. As people get richer and better educated, a democrat would admonishingly tell a communist,

they will no longer be willing to let a handful of men in the Politburo take all the decisions that govern a country's life. The same must now be said, with adjustment for scale, about the workings of democracy. As the old differences of wealth, education and social condition blur, it will be increasingly hard to go on persuading people that most of them are fit only to put a tick on a ballot paper every few years, and that the handful of men and women they thereby send to parliament must be left to take all the other decisions. (Beedham 1993, 6)

Contemporary calls for direct citizen action are not antidemocratic behavior. Typically, they are attempts by ordinary people to pressure the political system to be responsive to public opinion. Furthermore, very few people subscribe to the extreme forms of violent action that might threaten a democratic system.

I favor a Jeffersonian view of the democratic process. The logic of democratic politics is that expanding political involvement also can expand citizens' understanding of politics. People learn about the responsibilities of governing and the choices facing society by becoming involved—and that makes them better citizens. And research shows that participation increases the public's knowledge about politics (Parry, Moyser, and Day 1992, ch. 13). In the long run, involving the public can make better citizens and better politics.

Ironically, active citizens also may become more critical of politicians and the political process (Parry, Moyser, and Day 1992, ch. 13). The educational aspects of participation can lead to further challenges to the political status quo. But one hopes that a responsive political system could build positive experiences with the democratic process and make progress by addressing the demands of a critical public.

Contemporary democracies clearly face important challenges, and their future depends on the nature of the response. That response should not be to push back the clock in an attempt to recreate images of politics from a bygone age—a politics that probably never existed. Democracies must adapt to survive, ideally by maximizing the advantages of greater citizen participation while minimizing the disadvantages. The experience of the past several years suggests that we are following this course. Institutions are changing to encourage citizen access (Cain, Dalton, and Scarrow 2003; A. Smith 2009), and politicians and bureaucrats are becoming more comfortable with an expanded form of democracy. Democracy is most threatened when we fail to take the democratic creed literally and deal creatively with the challenges posed by the new style of citizen politics.

Suggested Readings

Cain, Bruce, Russell Dalton, and Susan Scarrow, eds. 2003. *Democracy Transformed? Expanding Political Access in Advanced Industrial Democracies.* Oxford, UK: Oxford University Press.

Campbell, David. 2006. *Why We Vote: How Schools and Communities Shape Our Civic Life*. Princeton: Princeton University Press.

Conway, M. Margaret. 2000. *Political Participation in the United States*. 3rd ed. Washington, DC: CQ Press.

Dalton, Russell. 2009. *The Good Citizen: How Young People Are Reshaping American Politics*. Rev. ed. Washington, DC: CQ Press.

Deth, Jan van, José Ramón Montero, and Anders Westholm, eds. 2007. *Citizenship and Involvement in European Democracies: A Comparative Analysis*. London: Routledge.

Gabriel, Oscar, and Silke Keil, eds. 2012. *Society and Democracy in Europe*. London: Routledge.

Schlozman, Kay, Sidney Verba, and Henry Brady. 2012. *The Unheavenly Chorus: Unequal Political Voice and the Broken Promise of American Democracy*. Princeton: Princeton University Press.

Stolle, Dietlind, and Michele Micheletti. 2013. *Political Consumerism: Global Responsibility in Action*. Cambridge, UK: Cambridge University Press.

Verba, Sidney, and Norman Nie. 1972. *Participation in America*. New York: Harper and Row.

Verba, Sidney, Kay Schlozman, and Henry Brady. 1995. *Voice and Equality: Civic Voluntarism in American Politics*. Cambridge, MA: Harvard University Press.

Zukin, Cliff, et al. 2006. *A New Engagement? Political Participation, Civic Life, and the Changing American Citizen*. New York: Oxford University Press.

Notes

1. Surveys typically overestimate the percentage of the public who vote. Partly this is self-selection among those who agree to be interviewed, and partly some nonvoters claim to have voted. Therefore, we weighted the turnout percentages so that the aggregate total in the survey matches the reported turnout among the voting age population in the election. Figures 4.1 and 4.2 are based on these weighted statistics.
2. The statistical primer (appendix A) provides a guide for interpreting regression results and other statistics in this volume. The results in figure 4.1 are from multiple regression analyses; the standardized regression coefficients (ß) measure the impact of each variable, while statistically controlling for the effects of the other variables in the model. We interpret coefficients of .10 or less as a weak relationship, .10–.20 as a modest relationship, and .20 or larger as a strong relationship.

I use the Comparative Study of Electoral Systems (CSES) to estimate influences on voting in each nation (and other modes of participation in this chapter). The CSES includes the 2004 U.S. elections, the 2005 British elections, the 2002 German elections, and the 2002 French presidential elections.

3. The Comparative Study of Electoral Systems asked about membership in unions, business association, farmer associations, and professional associations. It did not include other forms of group activity, and it did not assess whether respondents were passive or active members.

4. Campaign activity combines whether the respondent worked for a party or candidate in the campaign and whether they tried to persuade others how to vote.

5. The German Language Society designated *Wutbürger* as the word of the year in 2010 because of the spread of citizen protests on a wide variety of topics.

6. The survey asked whether the respondent had participated in the activity in the past five years.

7. I used the question of whether the respondent was satisfied with the government's performance on the most important issue facing the nation. There are essentially the same results if I use satisfaction with the working of the democratic process.

8. The CID conducted in-person interviews with a random sample of Americans in 2005. The three Internet-related items are discussed in chapter 3. Figure 4.4 tries to replicate the analyses of other participation modes with similar questions from the CID. The largest difference is that the index of group membership includes potential membership in almost two dozen social groups, and this likely increases the importance of this factor in comparison to the CSES results. The survey and other information are available from the project website: http://www.uscidsurvey.org.

9. Thus it is troublesome to see partisan elites in the United States attempt to restrict voting rights under the guise of limiting voting fraud (Alter 2012).

10. Furthermore, Wattenberg overlooks the intermixing of generational and life cycle effects in many of his tables. And he does not examine Internet-based participation where age patterns are even more distinct and run counter to his generational decline thesis.

11. The Pew Research Center (1998) surveyed members of Congress, top presidential appointees, and members of the Senior Executive Service. Among members of Congress, just 31 percent think Americans know enough about issues to make wise decisions about public policy. Even fewer presidential appointees (13 percent) and senior civil servants (14 percent) feel this way.

Part Two
Political Orientations

5 Values in Change

The Fall 2010 Eurobarometer Survey asked citizens of the European Union what values were most important to them. This is a profound question because it asks people to identify the values that presumably shape their attitudes, their behaviors, and their lives. You might think for a minute about what you would say. Our values tell us what is important to us and society. They provide the reference standard for making our decisions. We structure our lives and make our choices based on what we value, whether it is a career, a marriage partner, or something as trivial as which movie to watch on Saturday night.

Politics often involves human values. When people answered the Eurobarometer survey, they listed human rights, peace, and respect for human life as the three most important values to them personally (democracy was fourth). Values identify what people think are—or should be—the goals of society and the political system. Shared values help define the norms of a political and social system, while the clash between alternative values creates a basis for competition over public policies to reflect these different values. Should welfare programs stress economic efficiency or empathy for the families in need? Should attitudes toward stem cell research reflect moral views about when life begins or concern for those suffering from disease? In a real sense, politics regularly involves conflicts over values.

The new style of citizen politics occurs in part because a growing number of people are changing their basic value priorities. Compared to a generation or two ago, contemporary societies display major changes in social norms: hierarchical relationships and deference to authority are giving way to self-expression, decentralization, and a desire to participate in the decisions affecting one's life. Previous chapters have described how participatory norms are stimulating greater political involvement, but the consequences of value change are much broader. The new values affect attitudes toward work, lifestyle, and the individual's role in society.

The definition of societal goals and the meaning of "success" are also changing. Until recently, many Americans and Europeans measured success almost solely in economic terms: a large house, two cars in the garage, and other signs of affluence. The late Malcolm Forbes once said that life was a

─────┤ **Internet Resource** ├────────────────────────────────────

Visit the World Values Survey website for information on this global survey of values:

http://www.worldvaluessurvey.org

contest, and the winner was the person who accumulated the most possessions before he or she died (he is dead now). In other industrial democracies the threshold for economic success might have been lower, but material concerns were equally important.

Once affluence became widespread, however, many people realized that bigger isn't necessarily better. The desire for economic growth is now tempered by a concern for improving the quality of life. Interest in protecting the environment has spread throughout advanced industrial societies. Instead of just income, careers are measured by the feeling of accomplishment and the freedom they offer. Social relations and acceptance of diversity are additional examples of values in change. Progress on racial, sexual, and religious equalities are transforming American and European societies. Even after experiencing the Great Recession of 2008, these societal changes have largely endured.

Evidence of value change is all around us, if we but look. We think in the present, however, and so the magnitude of these changes isn't always appreciated. You can get a sense of these changes by comparing contemporary American lifestyles to the images of American life depicted on vintage television reruns from the 1950s and 1960s. TV series such as *Leave It to Beaver* and *The Brady Bunch* reflect the values of a bygone era. How well would the Cleavers or the Bradys adjust to a world transformed by gender equality, the new sexual morality, racial desegregation, rap music, tattoos, and alternative lifestyles? Imagine June Cleaver hanging out with the *Desperate Housewives* or the Bradys as neighbors on *Modern Family*.

This chapter first examines the evidence that values are systematically changing in advanced industrial societies and then turns to the implications of value change for these nations.

The Nature of Value Change

Our values provide the standards that guide our attitudes and behaviors. Some people may place a high priority on freedom, equality, and social harmony and favor policies that strengthen these values. Others may stress independence, social recognition, and ambition in guiding their actions.

Many personal and political decisions involve making choices between valued goals that lie on opposite sides of a given situation. One situation may create a choice between independence and obedience or between polite evasiveness and blunt sincerity. A national policy may present conflicts between the goals of world peace and national security or between economic growth and protecting nature.

People develop a general framework for making these decisions by arranging values in terms of their personal importance. Behavior may appear inconsistent and illogical (see chapter 2) unless we consider the values of each person and how they apply these values in specific situations. To one citizen, the issue of immigration reform taps values of social equality and human rights; to another, it concerns obeying the law and protecting their livelihood. Both perspectives are reasonable, and attitudes toward immigration are determined by how people weigh these conflicting values.

Value systems should include the salient goals that guide human behavior. Milton Rokeach (1973) developed an inventory of eighteen instrumental values dealing with the methods of achieving desired goals and eighteen terminal values defining preferred end-state goals. As the evidence of the public's shifting values became apparent, social scientists have offered several theories of how contemporary values are changing (for example, Schwartz 2012; Flanagan and Lee 2003; Schwartz and Bardi 2001).

The most influential research is Ronald Inglehart's theory of value change in advanced industrial societies (Inglehart 1977, 1990, 2008). Inglehart bases his value change theory on two premises. First, he suggests a *scarcity hypothesis:* individuals "place the greatest value on those things that are in relatively short supply" (1981, 881). That is, when some valued object is difficult to obtain, its worth is magnified. If the supply increases to meet the demand, then people take the object for granted and shift their attention to things that are still scarce. Water is a precious commodity during a drought, but when normal rains return, the concern over water evaporates. This general argument can be applied to other items valued by society.

Second, Inglehart presents a *socialization hypothesis:* "To a large extent, one's value priorities reflect the conditions that prevailed during one's pre-adult years" (1981, 881). These formative conditions include both the situation in one's family and broader political and socioeconomic conditions. Value change may continue after this formative period as people move through the life cycle or are exposed to new experiences. But Inglehart assumes that later learning must overcome the inertia of preexisting orientations.

The combination of both hypotheses—scarcity and socialization— produces a general model of value change. People initially form their basic values early in life and emphasize the goals that are in short supply during this formative period. Once these values priorities develop, they generally endure through later changes in personal and social conditions.

Chapter 1 described how advanced industrial societies have unprecedented affluence, higher levels of education, expanding information opportunities, extensive social welfare systems, and other traits that changed dramatically during the later twentieth century. I have linked these trends to the growing sophistication, cognitive mobilization, and participation of modern publics. In addition, Inglehart maintains that these social forces are changing the public's basic value priorities. As the relative scarcity of valued objects changes, this trend produces parallel changes in what the public values most.

To generalize the scarcity hypothesis into a broader model, Inglehart drew on the work of Abraham Maslow (1954), who produced a hierarchical ordering of human goals.[1] Maslow suggested that people are first driven to fulfill basic sustenance needs—water, food, and shelter. When these needs are met, they continue searching until enough material goods are acquired to attain a comfortable margin of economic security. Having accomplished this goal, people may turn to higher-order needs, such as the need for belonging, self-esteem, participation, self-actualization, and the fulfillment of aesthetic and intellectual potential. Thus, social conditions generally predict the broad values emphasized by the public.

The television show *Survivor* presents the Maslovian value hierarchy in practice. Once the group of relatively affluent people reaches the island, the quality-of-life concerns they may have emphasized at home are overtaken by the need to survive. The aspiring actor from Hollywood is suddenly unconcerned with appearances and worried about how much rice is left for his or her tribe. Their priorities shift toward subsistence needs: finding water, ensuring that they have enough rice for the day, and maybe even hunting rats for additional protein. This is Maslow as Robinson Caruso.

Inglehart applied the logic of Maslow's value hierarchy to political issues (see figure 5.1). Many political issues, such as economic security, law and order, and national defense, tap sustenance and safety needs. Inglehart describes these as *material* values. In a time of depression or civil unrest, for example, security and sustenance needs necessarily receive maximum attention. If a society can make significant progress in addressing these needs, attention can then shift toward higher-order values, reflected in issues such as individual freedom, self-expression, and participation. Inglehart labels these *postmaterial* values.

Inglehart maintained that a material/postmaterial dimension is the primary value change occurring in advanced industrial democracies. In his more recent writings, Inglehart describes this pattern as the shift from survival values to self-expressive values (Inglehart 1997; Inglehart and Welzel 2005; Welzel 2013). In another book, I found a similar shift toward engaged citizenship norms among the American public (Dalton 2009a).[2] The broad nature of these value changes leads others to describe the process as a transition from "Old Politics" values of economic growth, security, and traditional lifestyles to "New Politics" values of individual freedom, social equality, and the quality of life. One sign of the significance of this concept is the large number of studies that examine the postmaterial phenomenon (see the extensive literature cited in van Deth and Scarbrough 1995).

There are two major challenges to Inglehart's theory of value change. First, several studies have questioned whether socioeconomic conditions are linked to citizen values as Inglehart predicts. Harold Clarke and Nitish

Figure 5.1	Maslovian Value Hierarchy

Societal development moves from sustenance to safety needs to postmaterial values.

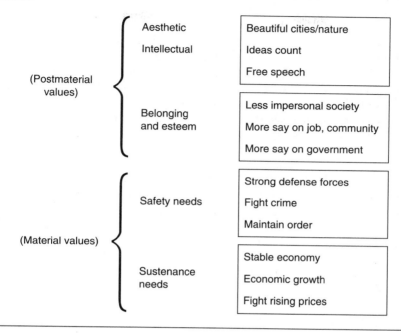

Source: Inglehart, Ronald; *The Silent Revolution.* © 1977 Princeton University Press, 2005 Renewed PUP. Reprinted with permission by Princeton University Press.

Dutt (1991; Clarke et al. 1999) demonstrated that Inglehart's simple value index is closely related to the ebb and flow of economic conditions, instead of consistently reflecting the conditions of earlier formative environments. Raymond Duch and Michael Taylor (1993, 1994) also questioned whether formative conditions are the principal determinants of values (see the response in Abramson and Inglehart 1995). In large part, I see these critiques as questions about the measurement of values, such as whether one's educational level primarily represents formative conditions or present social position. This critique does, however, highlight the point that values are dependent on formative conditions *and* present circumstances.

A second critique asks about the content of changing values. Scott Flanagan (1982, 1987; Flanagan and Lee 2003) argued that values are shifting along at least two dimensions: one that involves a shift from material to noneconomic values, and a second that involves a shift from authoritarian to libertarian values. And recently, Shalom Schwartz described human values in terms of dimensions of social change and self/self-transcendent values that extend beyond the framework proposed by Inglehart (Schwartz and Bardi 2001).

In his latest work on global value comparisons, Inglehart presents a more differentiated view of changing values (Inglehart and Welzel 2005). He distinguishes between a dimension of survival to self-expressive values, and a dimension of traditional to secular/rational values. Societies are changing in multiple ways that tap different parts of people's value systems. Steven Pinker (2011) similarly describes how the "civilization process" has changed social norms in established democracies, which has dramatically decreased violence of all sorts and transformed living conditions for women, minorities, and the disadvantaged. This is clearly an area where further research is warranted. But Inglehart's framework generally overlaps with the value dimensions that other researchers have suggested. And regardless of how we conceptualize this process, there is general agreement that the value priorities of modern publics are different from previous generations.

Materialists and Postmaterialists

Most people attach positive worth to material *and* postmaterial goals. The average person favors economic growth and a clean environment, social stability and individual freedom. Politics, however, often involves a conflict between these goals. Therefore, rather than study one set of values in isolation from another, research asks which goals take priority in the public's mind when values come in conflict.

Surveys use various ways to measure values. Because values are deeply held feelings, they are difficult to tap with a simple opinion survey question. In addition, researchers debate whether we should measure values in terms of personal life conditions or phrased as political goals.

Following Inglehart's model of the Maslovian value hierarchy, the 2005–08 World Values Survey (WVS) assessed value priorities by asking respondents to rank the importance of twelve political goals. Because all goals are potentially important, they were allowed to choose only six from this set. Table 5.1 presents the top priorities of American, British, French, and German citizens across these items.

Most people on both sides of the Atlantic cited material goals as their first priority. Americans most often emphasized economic growth, a stable economy, and crime prevention. In a major change since the previous WVS, Americans' emphasis on a strong defense increased from 18 percent to 61 percent, apparently reflecting the terrorist attacks on September 11, 2001, and the continuing war on jihadist terrorism. Europeans stress the same top three material goals but give decidedly less attention to defense.

I used the choices made among these items to create a single index of the relative weight given to postmaterial goals.[3] Materialists place high priority on the six economic and security goals, while postmaterialists stress one of the postmaterial goals in table 5.1. The cross-national percentages of postmaterialists on this twelve-item index over time appear in table 5.2.

In the early 1970s postmaterialists were a relatively small minority in every nation. On the twelve-item index, only 13 percent of West Germans and 18 percent of Britons scored high on the postmaterial scale. The proportion

Table 5.1	Value Priorities			
People cite a mix of materialist and postmaterialist issues as most important.				
	UNITED STATES	GREAT BRITAIN	FRANCE	GERMANY
High level of economic growth (M)	67	66	68	82
A stable economy (M)	67	61	51	72
More say in work/community (PM)	49	71	72	74
Fight against crime (M)	63	69	50	32
Protect free speech (PM)	59	55	49	38
Maintain order in nation (M)	47	58	48	42
More say in government (PM)	54	56	42	57
More humane society (PM)	37	36	60	52
Fight rising prices (M)	36	26	59	57
Make cities/country beautiful (PM)	28	26	36	23
Ideas count more than money (PM)	29	28	37	37
A strong defense (M)	61	28	18	10

Source: 2006–08 World Values Survey.

Note: Table entries are the percentage of respondents listing the item as first or second choice among items presented in sets of four. Missing data were included in the calculation of percentages.

M = material value; PM = postmaterial value

of materialists was even larger with Inglehart's four-item index (1977; 1990). The larger number of materialists was not surprising because the conditions fostering postmaterial value change were still developing. In historical perspective, advanced industrial societies are a relatively recent phenomenon.

By the 1990s the proportion of postmaterialists had increased in each nation where long-term trends are available. More time points are available for the four-item postmaterial index. These trends show a general shift toward postmaterial values for a large set of advanced industrial societies (Inglehart and Welzel 2005, ch. 4; Inglehart 2008). Data from 2006–07 for our four core nations show a clear increase in the percentage of postmaterialists since 1973. The percentage of postmaterialists increased by half in Britain, France, and western Germany over this time span. In summary, large proportions of the public in advanced industrial societies—often a third—now give priority to postmaterial goals. Because many individuals favor both kinds of values, the number of people exclusively preferring material goals is also a minority in most nations. Since the mid-1970s critics have claimed that postmaterialism is a "sunshine" issue that will fade with the next economic downturn or period of political uncertainty. In the 1970s the Organization of the Petroleum Exporting Countries (OPEC) increases in oil prices stimulated global recessions that some claimed would end the

Table 5.2	Becoming Postmaterialist			

The percentage of postmaterialists is generally increasing in advanced industrial societies.

COUNTRY	1973	1990	1999	2007
Belgium	38	38	—	—
Canada	—	29	30	—
Denmark	19	32	—	—
France	33	27	—	35
Germany (West)	13	36	43	30
Great Britain	18	19	—	25
Ireland	15	23	—	—
Italy	16	33	—	—
Japan	—	31	28	—
Netherlands	35	39	—	—
Norway	—	17	20	26
Spain	—	37	29	—
Sweden	—	31	29	—
United States	24	21	23	—

Sources: 1973 European Communities Study; for first U.S. time point: 1974 Political Action Study; 1990–91 World Values Survey; 1998–2002 World Values Survey; for 1999 German time point: 1995–98 World Values Survey; 2005–08 World Values Survey.

Note: Figure entries are the percentages placing a higher priority on postmaterial goals, using the twelve-item values index in table 5.1. See note 3 on scale construction. Dashes indicate the question was not asked.

liberalism of the 1960s. The 1980s were heralded as the "me" decade. The 1990s were years of economic strains in Germany, Japan, and many other nations. Despite these potential countertrends, the trends we have presented document the growth of postmaterial values over time.

Still, many skeptics believe that postmaterial values will quickly fade if real economic problems emerge. A natural experiment occurred with the Great Recession of 2008 and the severe economic problems in America and Europe. If Inglehart is correct, value priorities should largely endure because they are set early in life and reflect a combination of social factors in addition to economic condition. If postmaterialism is a sunshine issue, there should be a marked decline of postmaterial values after 2008.

New evidence is available from the 2010 International Social Survey Program (ISSP) survey that repeated the postmaterial values battery from the 2000 ISSP. The percentage of postmaterialists is essentially unchanged in the United States, Britain, and Germany—even though the 2000 survey followed a period of substantial economic growth and the 2010 survey followed an economic recession.[4] We expect that the pace of value change will continue in the future, albeit at a slower pace because the rate of social change has slowed. Nevertheless, this evolutionary change in values has transformed the nature of citizen politics.

How Values Change

How do we know that support for postmaterial goals really reflects the social modernization of advanced industrial societies? At first, the evidence was tentative. With time, however, the evidence of postmaterial value change has grown. The trends cited in table 5.2 provide one sort of evidence.

The most telling evidence supporting the postmaterial thesis comes by testing the two parts of Inglehart's value change theory. The scarcity hypothesis predicts that the socioeconomic conditions of a nation are related to the priorities of its citizens. The socialization hypothesis predicts that values become set early in life. Therefore, the overall values of a society reflect the conditions decades earlier, when values were being formed.

We can test the first hypothesis by comparing national levels of postmaterial values to the socioeconomic conditions of each nation. If scarcity breeds materialist concerns, then these concerns should be more common in nations with lower living standards. Conversely, the affluence of advanced industrial societies should increase support for postmaterial goals. In addition, according to the socialization hypothesis, these effects should occur with a time lag. So the best predictor of public values should be national conditions a generation earlier, when the current public's values were forming.

Figure 5.2 shows a clear relationship between national affluence (GNP per capita in 1980) and the distribution of material/postmaterial values in 2005–08 for thirty-five nations where we have both measures.[5] Postmaterialists are generally most common in nations (including the core nations in this book) that had relatively high living standards during the formative years of the average adult. In contrast, there are fewer postmaterialists in poor nations, such as India, China, and Indonesia. One should note that these relationships exist even ignoring economic changes—for the better or the worse—in the twenty-five years between measuring GDP and surveying citizen values.[6]

The figure also describes a curved relationship between economic conditions and value change. The greatest value shift occurs during the transition from a subsistence economy to an industrial society, such as that found in postwar Western Europe. Once this level of affluence is achieved, further improvements in living standards produce progressively smaller changes in values, which implies that value change will continue at a slower rate in the future. Furthermore, this same cross-national pattern has appeared across the several editions of this book with updated survey data—this is an enduring empirical pattern.

Another test of the postmaterial theory involves the socialization hypothesis. Older generations, reared in the years before World War II, grew up in a period of widespread uncertainty. These people suffered through the Great

| Figure 5.2 | Affluence and Postmaterialism |

The relative percentage of postmaterialists increases with national affluence.

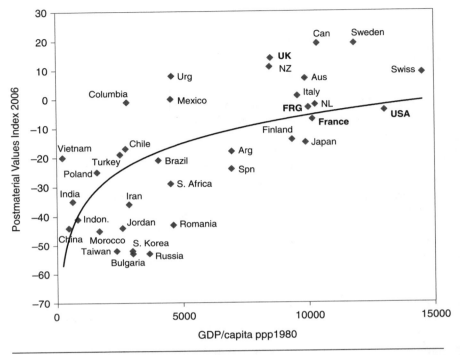

Sources: Four-item Postmaterial Index from 2006–08 World Values Survey; GNP per capita (purchasing price parity) in 1980 from World Bank, World Development Indicators 2001 (*N* = 35 countries).

Depression of the 1930s and endured two world wars and the social and economic traumas that accompanied these events. Given these conditions, older generations in most Western democracies should have been socialized into a greater concern with material goals: economic growth, economic security, domestic order, and social and military security. These values should also persist over time, even if social conditions have improved dramatically.

Conversely, younger generations in Europe and North America grew up in a period of unprecedented affluence and security. Present-day living standards are typically several times higher than before World War II. The expansion of the welfare state now protects most people from most major economic risks. Postwar generations also have a broader worldview, reflecting their higher educational levels, greater exposure to political information, and more diverse cultural experiences. Furthermore, most Europeans have experienced the longest period without a major war in modern European history. Under these conditions, the material concerns that preoccupied prewar generations should diminish in urgency, and younger generations should shift their attention toward postmaterial goals.

Furthermore, Inglehart's socialization hypothesis predicts that values formed during adolescence should persist through the life span. That is, different age groups should retain the mark of their formative generational experiences even if family or societal conditions change. Older Europeans should still stress security concerns today even if their present lifestyles reflect a high level of affluence. Younger generations socialized in the conditions of relative affluence should retain their greater concern for postmaterial values even as they age and assume greater family and economic responsibilities.

A crucial test of the value change thesis tracks the value priorities of generations over time. Figure 5.3 describes the values of several European generations from 1974 until 2008, using Inglehart's four-item value index.[7] The oldest generation—those born between 1885 and 1909 (who were ages sixty-five to eighty-eight in 1974)—is located near the bottom of the figure. In 1974 the proportion of materialists in this generation outweighs postmaterialists by nearly 50 percent. In contrast, in 1974, the youngest generation—those born between 1940 and 1954—is almost evenly balanced between material and postmaterial values.

Not only is the relative ranking of generations important evidence in support of Inglehart's theory, but so is the persistence of this pattern. The level of values fluctuates over time in response to random sampling variation and the sensitivity of the four-item values index to inflation levels (a methodological imperfection in the simple four-item measure).[8] Most important, the generational gaps in value orientations remain fairly constant over time— as seen in the parallel movement of each generation—although all cohorts are moving through the life cycle. The youngest age group from 1974 has reached middle age by the 2000s, but their average level of material/postmaterial values doesn't change significantly between 1974 and 2008. Life cycle experiences normally modify, but do not replace, the early learning of value priorities. And the Millennial generation was first apparent in the 2008 survey; it was the most postmaterialist of all generations.

The size of the generational differences in values across nations provides further support for the value change thesis. West Germany, for example, has experienced tremendous socioeconomic change during the twentieth century. Consequently, the value differences between the youngest and oldest German cohorts are larger than for many other nations. In nations that experienced less socioeconomic change during the same period, age groups should display smaller differences in their values. Abramson and Inglehart (1995, 134) showed that there is a strong relationship between rates of economic growth and the size of the age gap in value priorities. Large social changes produce large changes in values.[9]

Education is another indirect measure of an individual's economic conditions during the formative years because access to higher education often reflects the family's social status.[10] In addition, education may affect values

| Figure 5.3 | Generations and Postmaterialism |

The relative percentage of postmaterialists is higher in younger generations.

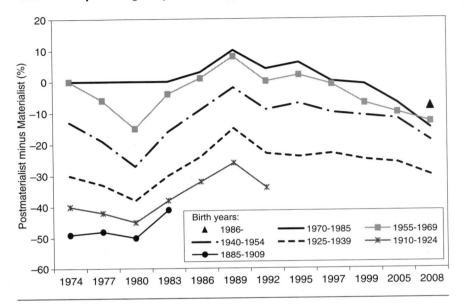

Source: Eurobarometers, 1974–2008.

Note: The data are based on a combined weighted sample of Eurobarometer surveys carried out in six nations (Belgium, France, Great Britain, Italy, the Netherlands, and West Germany). The total sample size is more than 400,000 respondents. The values in the figure are the percentages of postmaterialists minus the percentages of materialists, aggregated for six generational groups. Where available, surveys across three-year periods were combined to provide more reliable results.

because of the content of learning. Contemporary Western educational systems generally stress the values of participation, self-expression, intellectual understanding, and other postmaterial goals. The liberal orientation of the modern university milieu may encourage a broadening of social perspectives. And finally, the effects of education overlap with those of generation; the young are better educated than the old.

Results from the 2005–08 World Values Survey (not shown) find that the better educated are more postmaterialist in all four core nations. For example, in France only 25 percent of the group with the least education is postmaterialist, compared to 56 percent among those with at least some university education.

The concentration of postmaterial values among the young and better educated gives added significance to these orientations. If Inglehart's theory (and figure 5.3) is correct, the percentage of postmaterialists should gradually increase over time, as older materialist generations are replaced by younger, more postmaterialist generations.[11] This point is important because postmaterialists are more active in politics than materialists, and the political influence of postmaterialists is greater than their numbers imply. Indeed, among the group of future elites—university-educated youth—postmaterial values predominate. As these individuals succeed into positions of economic, social, and political leadership, the impact of changing values should strengthen. Value change appears to be an ongoing process.

The Consequences of Value Change

Postmaterialists are only a minority of the population in most advanced industrial democracies, but their impact is already apparent, extending beyond politics to all aspects of society. Indeed, one of the most impressive aspects of Inglehart's book *Culture Shift in Advanced Industrial Society* (1990) is the range of phenomena he links to postmaterialism.

In the Workplace. These new value orientations fuel demands for a flexible work environment that better accommodates individual needs. Rigid, hierarchical, assembly-line systems of production are being challenged by worker participation (codetermination), quality circles, and flexible working hours. The 2008 European Values Survey found that instead of stressing good pay and job security as important characteristics of a job, postmaterialists emphasize goals such as having the opportunity to use initiative, a job at which they learn something and where they have a say in important decisions. Many business analysts bemoan the decline of the work ethic, but it is more accurate to say that the work ethic is shifting to a new set of goals. Think of the work style at Google instead of the GM assembly line.

Social Relations. Postmaterial values are also changing authority patterns in society. Neil Nevitte (1996, 2013) shows that deference to authority is generally waning: bosses, Army officers, university professors, and political leaders all decry the decline in deference to their authority. The postmaterial credo is that an individual earns authority, rather than having it bestowed by a position. Parents today, especially the postmaterialists, are stressing greater independence as they educate their children. The public's behavior in many aspects of social and political life is becoming more self-directed. This increasing independence is reflected in the declining brand-name loyalty among consumers and in the decline of political party loyalty among voters. In short, contemporary lifestyles reflect a demand for greater freedom and individuality, which appears in fashion, consumer tastes, social behavior, and interpersonal relations.

Moral Standards. The process of value change includes religious values and sexual mores (Inglehart 1997; Norris and Inglehart 2011). Materialists are more likely to hold traditional restrictive attitudes toward religious and moral issues, such as extramarital sex, abortion, and homosexuality. In contrast, postmaterialists are more tolerant of individual choice and alternative life styles. Thus through the process of value change, social norms on these issues have steadily shifted over the past several decades (see chapter 6).

The Issue Agenda. Postmaterialists champion a new set of political issues—environmental quality, sustainable energy, gender equality, and multiculturalism—that the political establishment had often overlooked. Debates in Washington about global warming, the safety of nuclear plants, and gender equality have close parallels in the capitals of Europe. Proponents of these issues have similar characteristics: they are young, better educated, and postmaterialist (Rohrschneider, Miles, and Peffley 2013).

Some of the most telling evidence comes from a study of legislation in the U.S. Congress by Jeffrey Berry, who found that a majority of the congressional agenda was concerned with material issues in 1963, but that by 1991 the emphasis had shifted to a predominately postmaterial agenda (Berry 1999, chs. 4–5). Inglehart (1995) tracked a sharp increase in the attention that political parties devote to environmental issues over time. At present and for the foreseeable future, politics in most advanced industrial societies will address a mix of material and postmaterial issues.

Participation. Value change also affects political participation. Postmaterial values stimulate direct involvement in the decisions affecting one's life—whether at school, in the workplace, or in the political process. In all three European nations in the 2005–08 WVS, postmaterialists generally were more likely than materialists to be interested in politics and say that politics is important in their lives.

The activist orientation of postmaterialists adds to the puzzle of participation noted in chapter 2: If postmaterialism stimulates political action, why are voting and some other forms of participation declining? Our answer reinforces the argument that the style of political action is changing in advanced industrial democracies. The participatory orientation of postmaterialists doesn't affect all participation modes equally. Voting turnout is often lower among postmaterialists because most established parties have not fully embraced postmaterial issues. In addition, postmaterialists are skeptical of formal hierarchical procedures and organizations, such as elections and most political parties.

Instead, postmaterialist are more likely to participate in citizen initiatives, protests, and other forms of direct action. The 2005–08 WVS found that postmaterialists are more likely than materialists to participate in protest (see figure 5.4). These activities provide postmaterialists with a more direct influence on politics, which matches their value orientations. Most postmaterialists also possess the political skills to carry out these more demanding forms of political action. As noted in chapters 3 and 4, along with increasing levels of citizen involvement has come a change in the form of political participation.

Inevitably, changes in value priorities and the style of participation contribute to public pressure for reforms of democratic institutions and processes. Postmaterialists advocate a greater use of initiative and referendum,

Figure 5.4	Postmaterialism and Protest

The percentages who have either participated in a lawful demonstration or a boycott is higher among postmaterialists.

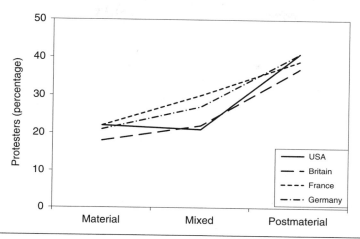

Source: 2005–08 World Values Survey.

the opening up of administrative processes, and the expansion of the legal rights of citizen groups. A recent example comes from the 2011 British Social Attitudes survey that found most people favored directly elected mayors and police commissioners, and even larger numbers believed in wider use or referendums (Curtice and Seyd 2002). Public interest groups have accelerated this process of increased access and transparency of government. Political parties are also searching for new ways to involve citizens more directly in party decisions such as the selection of candidates. As a consequence, the last quarter of the twentieth century experienced a quiet revolution in transforming the democratic process to increase citizen access (Cain, Dalton, and Scarrow 2003; A. Smith 2009).

Social Change and Value Change

When I was an undergraduate student, I remember when some of my friends at UCLA interviewed for what were considered plum jobs at IBM. The understanding was that you had to have a suit with a white shirt at the interview, because IBMers only wore white shirts. If you were hired, you should be open to being sent wherever the company needed you and doing whatever was needed. In return, IBM would provide a good income and security to its employees.

Today, the plum jobs are at places like Google or Lucas Films (ILM). Casual dress is the norm, and offices are filled with diversions besides a desk and paperwork. As one journalist recently wrote, "If your ideal work-space includes a slide, a games room, a 'chill-out' aquarium and plenty of free food then you had better get your CV into Google" (Wakefield 2008). The 20 percent rule at Google encourages employees to spend a fifth of their time on independent projects of personal interest. It isn't that Google employees don't care about money; they follow the stock prices of their Google portfolio and enjoy good salaries. But there is more to life than just the paycheck.

These two examples illustrate how value change is affecting contemporary societies. The best description might be that there is a growing diversity in citizen values. More people still give primary attention to material goals, and the socioeconomic issues deriving from these values will continue to dominate political debate for decades to come. The persistence of material values should not be overlooked.

At the same time, postmaterial values are becoming more common. A sizable proportion of the public wants to balance economic growth with a cleaner environment. Many people value the opportunity to participate in the decisions affecting their lives more than they value job security. And an even larger group of people now want a mix of material and postmaterial goals.

The current mix of values sometimes makes it difficult for political analysts and politicians to know what the public wants. For nearly every example of the persistence of traditional material values, a counterexample reflects post-material values. For almost every citizen lobbying a local town council to stimulate the economy, another worries that growth will mean a loss of green space or a diminution in the quality of life. The diversity of values marks a major change in the nature of citizen politics: political debates again involve definition of goals and not just means to reach consensual goals.

This process of value change has several consequences for contemporary politics, as we have noted in this chapter. The issues of political debate are shifting. Concerns about environmental protection, individual freedom, social equality, participation, and the quality of life have been *added* to the traditional political agenda of economic and security issues. As noted, value change also reshapes the patterns of political participation and increases pressures for democratic reform. Politics is changing as a result of the public's shifting value priorities.

Only a few skeptics still doubt that value priorities are changing among Western publics; the evidence of change is now quite apparent. It is more difficult to anticipate the many consequences of these new values. By monitoring these trends, however, we may get a preview of the nature of citizen politics in advanced industrial democracies.

Suggested Readings

Dalton, Russell. 2009. *The Good Citizen: How the Young Are Reshaping American Politics*. Rev. ed. Washington, DC: CQ Press.

Inglehart, Ronald. 1990. *Culture Shift in Advanced Industrial Society.* Princeton: Princeton University Press.

Inglehart, Ronald, and Christian Welzel. 2005. *Modernization, Cultural Change, and Democracy: The Human Development Sequence.* New York: Cambridge University Press.

Nevitte, Neil. *The Decline of Deference.* 1996. Petersborough, CAN: Broadview.

Pinker, Steven. 2011. *The Better Angels of our Nature: Why Violence Has Declined.* New York: Viking.

van Deth, Jan, and Elinor Scarbrough, eds. 1995. *The Impact of Values.* New York: Oxford University Press.

Welzel, Christian. 2013. *Freedom Rising.* New York: Cambridge University Press.

Notes

1. Inglehart's early work was closely linked to the Maslovian value hierarchy, but Maslow is less prominent in his recent research. As Inglehart has broadened his research beyond advanced industrial societies, he has examined how social modernization affects affluent and developing nations.
2. Inglehart's postmaterial values battery is included in the data supplement (appendix B) to this book.
3. We counted the number of material goals mentioned minus the number of postmaterial goals; entries in table 5.2 are the percentages that place a higher priority on postmaterial goals. This table uses a different method from Inglehart's standard twelve-item index so that we can begin the trend with the 1970s surveys that used a different question format.
   Several of the analyses in this chapter use a four-item subset of the twelve items to construct a material/postmaterial values index (Inglehart 1990, ch. 2). The four-item index is that it is a narrow measure of basic human values, but in some surveys it is the only index available.
4. The percentage with postmaterial values in the two ISSP surveys is as follows:

Nation	2000	2010
United States	19	18
Britain	11	12
West Germany	28	31

5. We use 1980 GDP/capita (purchasing price parity) to approximate the period when values were being formed for many of the adults surveyed around 2005. See earlier editions of this text for comparable analyses for earlier time periods.

6. There is a strong relationship ($r = .72$) between GNP/capita in 1980 and values in 2005. Also see Abramson and Inglehart (1995).

7. Figure 5.3 is based on the combined results of samples from six nations: Great Britain, West Germany, France, Italy, Belgium, and the Netherlands. The results were combined to produce age group samples large enough to estimate values precisely. For additional discussion of generational effects, see Abramson and Inglehart (1995) and Inglehart (2008).

8. One limitation of the Inglehart index is that it attempts to measure basic values using specific political issues. It is not surprising that the four-item index is sensitive to inflation rates because one of the items taps concern about rising prices (Clarke and Dutt 1991; Clarke et al. 1999). A broader measure of values, such as the twelve-item index or the social priorities question of Flanagan (1982), would be less susceptible to these measurement problems.

9. These patterns also imply that age differences in postmaterial values will narrow in more recent surveys, because the older pre–WWII generations are leaving the electorate and they were most distinct in holding materialist priorities. Contemporary publics are increasingly composed of those raised in advanced industrial societies.

10. Raymond Duch and Michael Taylor (1993) used multivariate analysis to argue that formative conditions do not influence current value priorities. Abramson and Inglehart (1995) challenged this interpretation, arguing that Duch and Taylor's results were distorted by the selection of time points and they misinterpreted the meaning of educational effects. I believe that the evidence of generational change is predominant, and that educational effects are another measure of formative life conditions, especially in Europe.

11. Even during this brief time span, generational turnover contributes to a postmaterial trend (Abramson and Inglehart 1995). In 1970 the pre–World War I generation was about 16 percent of the West German public; by 1980 this group was about 5 percent. By 2008 the pre–WWII generation also had essentially left the electorate, and was replaced by young Germans socialized in the post–World War II era.

6 Issues and Ideological Orientations

obert Kagan (2003) coined a phrase that is frequently used to describe the supposed political differences between Americans and Europeans: "Americans are from Mars, and Europeans are from Venus." Kagan was primarily referring to the contrasting orientations toward defense among NATO members on both sides of the Atlantic. Americans seemed more willing to use force to resolve international disputes, while Europeans favored diplomacy and international peace keeping. But the sentence also captured a sense of economic and political differences. Americans were seen as leaning toward individualism, a small state, and market-based competition, while some European leaders criticized this "elbow society" as too harsh compared to the social welfare states in Europe. Moral and ethical orientations also appeared to divide Americans from many Europeans.

Some of the Europeans' feelings were exacerbated by tensions over the 2003 Iraq invasion and the social policies of the George W. Bush administration, but such claims of trans-Atlantic differences are common among political analysts before and after Bush's tenure. The basic claim is that the policy goals of Americans differ systematically from most Europeans because of contrasting historical forces and political cultures. We explore this idea in this chapter by comparing the issue opinions of Americans and Europeans, with a special attention on how these opinions may have changed over time as a result of social modernization.

Issues are the everyday currency of politics. Issue opinions identify the public's preferences for government action and their expectations for the political process. Political parties are distinguished by their issue positions, and elections provide a means for the public to select between competing issue programs. As people become more sophisticated and involved in politics, issue opinions should have a stronger influence on voting choice and the policy process. Indeed, issues are what politics is about.

Issue opinions also represent the translation of broad value orientations into specific political concerns. Issues are partly determined by the values examined in the previous chapter as well as by other factors: cues from political

---| **Internet Resource** |---

The International Social Survey Program (ISSP) website has additional information on these surveys:

http://www.issp.org

---

elites, the flow of political events, and the specific political context. A person may favor the principle of equal rights for all citizens, but his or her attitudes toward legislation on voting rights, job discrimination, and affirmative action may spring from a mix of values and practical concerns. Consequently, issue opinions are more changeable and varied than broad value orientations.

Another important characteristic of issues is that people focus their attention on a few areas—they are members of one or several "issue publics" (see chapter 2). Some people are especially concerned with education policy; others are more interested in foreign affairs, civil rights, environmental protection, or immigration. In general, only a minority of the public is interested and informed on any specific issue, although most people are members of at least one issue public. Members of an issue public are relatively well informed about their issue and generally follow the news about that issue.

Issue opinions are a dynamic part of politics, and the theme of changing popular values also applies to policy issues. In some areas, contemporary publics are obviously more liberal than their predecessors. The issues of women's rights, environmental protection, social equality, and individual lifestyles were highly divisive or even unrecognized a few decades ago, but a fairly solid consensus now exists on these issues. In other areas, people remain divided on their opinions. Support for tax revolts, neoconservative revival, "family values," and restricting immigration suggests that conservative values have not lost their appeal for many people. This chapter describes the issue opinions of Western publics and highlights, where possible, the trends in these opinions.

Domestic Policy Opinions

At one time, domestic policy was synonymous with economic matters, and economic issues still rank at the top of the public's political agenda at most elections. But the number of salient domestic issues has grown, and many people are now concerned with issues such as social equality, environmental protection, and immigration. This section provides an overview of the wide range of domestic policy concerns.

Socioeconomic Issues and the State

One of the most enduring debates in Western democracies involves the question of the government's role in society and the economy, especially the provision of basic social needs.

A prime example is the set of government-backed social insurance programs that most governments administer (such as Social Security in the United States or government health care programs in Europe). Social programs protect people from economic calamities caused by illness, unemployment, disability, or other hardships. In some nations, the government's economic involvement includes public ownership of major industries and active efforts to manage the economy.

Labor unions have historically favored the extension of government social policy as a way to improve the life chances of the average person. Business leaders and members of the middle class frequently oppose these policies as an unnecessary government intrusion and a potential drag on the economy. At stake isn't only the question of government involvement in society but also the desirability of certain social goals and the distribution of political influence between labor and business. To a large extent, the terms *liberal* and *conservative* have been linked to one's position on these questions. These issues are a major source of political competition in most elections.

Debates on the role of government seem to ebb and flow with the condition of the economy and social needs. In the 1980s, conservative politicians on both sides of the Atlantic championed a populist revolt against big government: slowing the growth of government, privatizing government-owned businesses or government-run programs, and reducing government social programs. The 2008 recession stimulated new debates, such as criticisms of President Barack Obama's 2009 stimulus package or debates about the role of the state in France's 2012 elections.

Support for the principle of big government also ebbs and flows. The Gallup surveys show that in the 1950s fewer than half of the American public felt they were paying an unfair amount of taxes; from the early 1980s to the late 1990s, about two-thirds believed their share of taxes was too high; since 2000 about equal numbers have claimed that taxes were too high as said they were about right. These divided opinions fuel popular opposition to tax policy and new government programs among Americans, and the Republican Party has appealed to these antitax sentiments as a basis of its electoral support.

Signs of the variations in opinion also appear among Europeans. British public opinion surveys showed an increasing criticism of big government beginning in the late 1970s that fueled Prime Minister Margaret Thatcher's program of privatization of government-owned enterprises and a general attempt to reduce the scope of British government. Chancellor Helmut Kohl's government pursued similar policies in Germany during the 1980s. But then the pendulum swung back. British Prime Minister Tony Blair's Labour government pursued modest liberal reforms starting in the late 1990s, and the SPD–Green coalition won in 1998 in a backlash to Kohl's conservative policies. Now many European governments have again changed course in elections after the 2008 recession. The government's role in the economy is an enduring issue facing contemporary democracies; a good summary of public opinion's role is provided by Soroka and Wlezien (2010). They describe public opinion as a thermostat: when government gets too hot in one direction or too cold in another, then the public readjusts to have a policy balance they prefer.

Despite the electoral dynamics of this issue, public opinion surveys show that many people believe that government is responsible for promoting individual well-being and guaranteeing the social needs in several areas. Table 6.1 displays the percentages of citizens who think the government is "definitely responsible" for dealing with specific social problems. The French have very high expectations of government: more than half believe the government is definitely responsible for providing health care, ensuring a decent standard of living for the elderly, and maintaining strict environmental laws, reducing income inequality, and even providing aid to college students. Such attitudes are consistent with the French traditions of social solidarity and social protection guaranteed by government programs.

Table 6.1 What Should Government Do?

Americans, British, and Germans are similar in their overall expectations for government responsibilities, with the French most likely to favor an activist government.

OPINION	UNITED STATES	GREAT BRITAIN	FRANCE	GERMANY
Provide health care for sick	55	71	58	55
Provide decent living standard for the elderly	56	60	52	48
Establish and maintain strict environmental laws	61	48	72	47
Give aid to needy college students	55	34	56	40
Keep prices under control	45	32	48	36
Provide job for everyone who wants one	16	17	33	35
Reduce income differences between rich and poor	27	27	53	34
Provide housing for those who need it	32	25	37	22
Provide a decent living standard for the unemployed	16	11	18	19
Provide industry with help	28	29	30	20
Average	39	35	46	36

Source: 2006 International Social Survey Program.

Note: Table entries are the percentages who say that each area should definitely be government's responsibility. Missing data were excluded from the calculation of percentages.

British attitudes toward government became more conservative in the late 1970s, more liberal with the Blair administration, and then more skeptical of government since the late 1990s. The table shows the modest proportions citing these policy areas as essential government responsibilities, a significant drop-off from the previous ISSP survey in 1996 (also see Whiteley 2012, ch. 2; Edlund 2009). Similarly, Germans are now more cautious in holding the government responsible in various policy areas, which is a change from earlier periods. However, residents of the former East Germany expect more of government.

The stereotype of Americans favoring small government and limited social consciousness isn't supported by this evidence because their support for government responsibility isn't notably different from the British and Germans. In part, this may be another example of the thermostat model; after the conservatism of the Bush administration more Americans favored liberal policy programs, including the provision of health care—which led to democratic victories in the 2006 election and then again in 2008 and 2012.[1] However, more recent media polls suggest some retrenchment of these sentiments as concerns about the scale of government activity under the Obama administration have grown. It is probably the case that Americans generally lean toward a smaller government than the Europeans, but the differences were modest in 2006.

Another way to gauge public expectations of government is to ask about spending preferences in various policy areas. Table 6.2 displays the percentages of Americans who favor more government spending in a policy area minus those who want to spend less. Since the surveys span from the 1970s to the 2010s, I have combined results by decade. (A positive number means that those favoring more spending exceeded those wanting a cut by this percentage.) There is a long-term consensus in favor of increased government spending on education, crime prevention, health care, preventing drug addiction, and environmental protection. Only welfare, the space program, and foreign aid are consistently identified as candidates for budget cuts. Moreover, although specific spending priorities change over time, the average preference for increased government spending listed across the bottom of the table has varied surprisingly little across eight administrations.

If one looks more closely at the annual surveys combined in the table, Americans' priorities for spending on specific programs respond to changes in the federal budget and the political context in a manner consistent with the thermostat model of public opinion and public policy (Soroka and Wlezien 2010; Page and Shapiro 1992). For example, as the George W. Bush administration was attempting to cut government spending, the American public wanted more money spent on these programs in 2002. In fact, support for greater government spending hit a high point in 2006 and 2008. Then, with the expansionary spending of the Obama administration, and a Tea Party backlash, public support for government spending decreased in the 2010 survey, which rebounded back up to the long-term average by 2012.

Table 6.2	U.S. Spending Preferences					
Americans lean toward more spending on a variety of social policies, while favoring cuts in welfare, defense, the space program, and foreign aid.						
PRIORITY	1970s	1980s	1990s	2000s	2010	2012
Halting rising crime rate	63	66	64	54	51	53
Protecting the nation's health	57	57	63	71	44	50
Dealing with drug addiction	54	58	53	50	46	46
Protecting the environment	49	50	56	57	45	47
Improving the educational system	42	56	66	68	67	67
Solving problems of big cities	34	31	43	34	23	26
Improving the condition of blacks	5	15	18	20	16	23
The military and defense	−9	−6	−19	−3	−8	−8
Welfare	−37	−24	−35	−17	−19	−24
Space exploration program	−48	−28	−34	−25	−21	−10
Foreign aid	−71	−67	−66	−52	−51	−55
Average	13	19	19	22	18	20

Source: NORC General Social Survey, combines surveys from various years in each decade.

Note: Table entries are the percentages saying "too little" being spent on the problem minus the percentages saying "too much."

Support for spending more on specific policy programs such as health care, environmental protection, education, housing, and social services is widespread among Europeans as well (see table 6.3). The British favor increased spending in most areas, especially on policies identified with the welfare state. Germans display modest support for higher spending, but this attitude must be seen in the context of already large public expenditures and the economic uncertainties accompanying German unification. And in contrast to popular expectations, Americans in 2006 were more likely than Europeans to favor increased government spending on various government programs, despite their reservations about the scope of government.[2]

The contrast between the general skepticism about government and the endorsement of higher spending on specific areas reflects a common contradiction in public opinion. The motto for government is clear: tax less and spend more. This is widely described as the combination of ideological conservatism and programmatic liberalism (Ellis and Stimson 2012). Americans

| Table 6.3 | Cross-National Spending Preferences |

In 2006 Americans were in favor of more public spending than were European publics; generally there are more areas where people want to spend more than where they want to spend less.

OPINION	UNITED STATES	GREAT BRITAIN	FRANCE	GERMANY
Education	80	71	53	80
Health	75	79	50	60
Police and law enforcement	49	58	19	37
Old-age pensions	58	70	39	46
Environment	40	53	44	27
Unemployment benefits	21	−28	−28	15
Culture and arts	−5	−35	−25	−18
Military and defense	12	6	−40	−44
Average	40	35	14	24

Source: 2006 International Social Survey Program.

Note: Table entries are the percentages saying "too little" being spent on the problem minus the percentages saying "too much." Missing data were excluded from the calculation of percentages.

and Europeans continue to demonstrate an ambiguous mix of support for and opposition to government action.

The most accurate description of popular attitudes toward government might be that citizens are now critical of "big" government, but they also are accustomed to, and depend on, the policies of the modern state. When people confront the choice between cutting taxes and maintaining government services, many surveys find that people are conflicted—they want both. The mix of opinions limits initiatives for dramatic increases in public spending as well as cuts in public spending. This is the quandary that leads governments to borrow funds to pay for public policies, delaying the day of reckoning to the future.

Race and Equality

The world is getting smaller, and Western societies are becoming more racially and ethnically diverse. After generations of dormancy, the demand for civil rights and racial equality inflamed American politics beginning in the 1960s. For most of the next two decades, the civil rights issue preoccupied the attention of many Americans and became a major source of political conflict. Race and ethnicity continue to be central in American politics, for the success of the civil rights movement among African Americans has encouraged similar activity among Hispanics, Asian Americans, and other minorities.

Europe is also now confronting issues of racial tolerance and minority rights as immigration has increased the diversity of these societies. Decolonialization by Great Britain and France created a steady inflow of minority immigrants from former colonies. Labor force shortages led the West Germans to invite "guest workers" from less-developed Mediterranean countries to work in German factories. The number of immigrants and asylum seekers increased dramatically during the 1990s. Nonwhites now account for 5 percent to 10 percent of the population in these three nations, and as much as a quarter of the workforce in some cities. Moreover, the recent wave of immigrants has introduced greater cultural differences, and greater political tensions, as these newcomers often differ from the indigenous populations in race, religion, and social status.

Despite government efforts to address these issues, backlashes against minorities persist. Tensions between French and North Africans have occasionally erupted into violence in southern France, and the National Front Party espouses antiforeigner policies. Immigrants and minority groups staged massive urban protests and violence in France in 2005 and 2006. German unification produced a surge of violence against foreigners, the emergence of the xenophobic Republikaner Party, and eventually a tightening of German immigration and asylum laws. Perhaps the most dramatic example was the emergence of the List Pim Fortuyn in the Netherlands, headed by an otherwise liberal gay activist who was extremely critical of the presence of Muslim fundamentalists in Dutch society.

Although racial and ethnic conflicts are still part of contemporary politics, the trends in racial attitudes document a massive change in the beliefs of Americans. In the 1940s a majority of white Americans openly endorsed racial segregation of education, housing, transportation, and employment (see figure 6.1). The values of freedom, equality, and justice that constitute the American creed didn't apply to blacks. A phenomenal growth in support for racial integration occurred during the next four decades, however, as integration of housing, education, and employment won widespread endorsement. A dramatic sign of how things have changed is Barack Obama's victory in the 2008 and 2012 presidential elections.

As racial integration became accepted, the politics of race broadened to include a new set of issues—affirmative action, government social programs, and equity standards—that now divide the American public (Bobo et al. 2012). Several policies aimed at redressing racial inequality—affirmative action policies (such as school busing and preferential treatment) and racial quotas—are opposed by a majority of white Americans (Schuman et al. 1997). Many political analysts claim that these divided opinions are signs of a new racism. Based on an innovative set of survey experiments, Paul Sniderman and Thomas Piazza (1993) showed that that although a minority of Americans still harbor racial prejudice, the contemporary clash over racial policies is more often attributable to broader ideological conflicts over the scope of government, beliefs about equality, and other political values.

European attitudes toward racial and ethnic minorities seem to reflect a similar mix of two factors (Sniderman et al. 2001; Sniderman and

| Figure 6.1 | Racial Integration in America |

Support for racial integration is nearly universal today, but it was opposed by a majority of Americans until the 1960s.

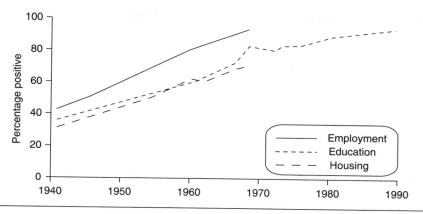

Sources: Adapted from Smith and Sheatsley 1984, and updated from Schuman et al. 1997.

Note: Figure entries are the percentages favoring integration in each area.

Hagendoorn 2007). One factor is prejudice toward individuals of a different race or religion—although such sentiments appear among only a minority of Europeans. The other factor is a clash of interests or goals that is analogous to class, regional, or other social interests. For example, middle-class people can disagree with policies to benefit farmers without being prejudiced against farmers. Genuine prejudice is difficult to address or correct, but differences in interests are open to reconciliation and compromise. The mix of factors is important in judging the potential resolution of these issues.

Perhaps the best way to compare tolerance of racial/ethnic diversity across nations is to focus on attitudes toward immigrants (Schain 2008; Alba, Schmidt, and Wasmer 2003). Table 6.4 describes attitudes toward immigrants and immigration issues across all four core nations.[3] The upper panel in the table shows attitudes toward immigration: the majority of Europeans favor strict limits or prohibition of immigration and Americans are only slightly more open. A large majority of Europeans also favor an assimilation policy, whereby immigrants assume the values of their new country rather than maintaining their culture and customs. Americans are about equally divided on this topic, which likely reflects our immigrant heritage. The majority in all four nations favors stronger actions to exclude illegal immigrants, which has generated recent political debates and policy reforms in all four nations.

| Table 6.4 | Attitudes toward Immigrants |

Americans are somewhat more tolerant of immigrants, but all four publics display some negativity.

OPINION	UNITED STATES	GREAT BRITAIN	FRANCE	GERMANY
Attitudes toward Immigration				
Anyone can come	12	4	6	5
Come if there are jobs	45	34	34	33
Strict limits	39	49	50	56
Prohibit immigration	4	13	10	7
Illegal Immigration				
Stronger action to exclude illegals	69	83	70	84
Multicultural versus Assimilation of Immigrants				
Minorities preserve traditions	48	27	27	36
Should assimilate	52	73	73	64
Positive Attitudes toward Immigrants				
Immigrants good for economy	47	22	31	27
Immigrants bring new ideas	59	34	39	55
Immigrants (don't) take jobs away	57	54	73	58
Average	54	37	48	47

Sources: 1999–2002 European Values Survey/World Values Survey; 2003 International Social Survey Program.

Note: Table entries are the percentages agreeing with each statement. Missing data were excluded from the calculation of percentages.

At the same time, tolerance toward immigrants is apparent in other survey items in the lower half of the table. Sizeable minorities in each nation feel immigrants are good for the economy and bring new ideas and traditions (these questions also include a neutral response, so the majority doesn't necessarily reject this position). A majority in each nation says that immigrants don't take jobs away or is neutral on this issue. Overall, averaged across all three items, Americans are again slightly more supportive of immigrants than are the European publics. The juxtaposition of abstract support for the principles of equality and tolerance and the fears over concrete issues raised by immigration makes this question so difficult for Americans and Europeans.

Although the climate of opinion now accepts more racial and ethnic diversity, one must be cautious not to overlook the real problems that persist. Support for the principle of equality coexists with the remnants of segregation in the United States; racial conflict can still flare up in Brixton, Marseilles, or Berlin. Problems of housing segregation, unequal education, and job discrimination are real. Public opinion alone isn't sufficient to resolve these problems, and some survey respondents undoubtedly overstate their tolerance level. Still, the shift of social norms toward support of racial equality makes these problems easier to address than when discrimination was openly practiced and condoned.

Gender Issues

Another social issue concerns equality between men and women. Throughout history, traditional gender roles were deeply entrenched on both sides of the Atlantic. American women faced limited career opportunities, and German housewives were expected to devote their efforts to *Kinder, Kirche, und Küche* (children, church, and kitchen). France didn't recognize women's right to vote until 1945. The status of women in Great Britain and other advanced industrial societies was also constrained.

These attitudes underwent a profound change in the latter half of the twentieth century (Campbell and Mardsen 2012). The women's movement grew in the United States and in Europe (Banaszak, Beckwith, and Rucht 2003). These groups, along with individual women, raised society's consciousness about the different treatment of men and women. As political action led to legislation equalizing the rights of both sexes, the public at large became more sensitive to gender issues, and social norms gradually changed.

Most Americans now express belief in equal opportunities for men and women. One long-time survey question asks about approval of a married woman working if she has a husband to support her, by implication condoning the norm that married women belong at home (see figure 6.2). In 1938,

---

Figure 6.2	Women's Equality in America

A majority of Americans did not favor women working or a woman as president until the 1960s.

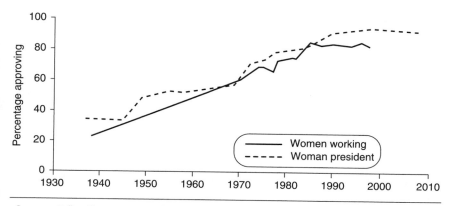

Sources: Gallup Organization, 1938–75; General Social Survey, 1972–2008.

when this question was first asked, only 22 percent of Americans approved of a woman working in these circumstances; this figure had increased to 80 percent or more by the end of the 1990s. Gallup data show that in 1936 only 31 percent of Americans said they would vote for a woman as president; by the mid-1990s this figure had risen above 90 percent. The political advance of women in a single generation has been amazing. Margaret Thatcher was Britain's first woman prime minister in 1979, Angela Merkel became Germany's first woman chancellor in 2005, and the political successes of Hillary Clinton in the United States and Ségolène Royal in France mark just how much has changed.

Table 6.5 provides further evidence on how Americans and Europeans think about gender-related issues (also see Inglehart and Norris 2003; Braun and Scott 2009). The first two items on gender equality are a good example of these changing attitudes. Large majorities now disagree with the proposition that men have first right to employment or to a university education. And as norms of equality have become nearly universal, the gender gap in these sentiments has narrowed.

One striking pattern involves images of whether politics and business are predominately male roles. Longitudinal data showed that these were once common among Americans (figure 6.2). Today, large majorities reject the idea that men are better than women in politics or business. The most common response is that both genders are equally capable. This is quite a shift from public opinion a generation or two ago. Although women remain underrepresented in the top stratum of political officials, old stereotypes of politics as an exclusively male domain have eroded. And even if these

Table 6.5   Attitudes toward Gender Equality

Most people favor gender equality in the workplace and politics.

OPINION	UNITED STATES	GREAT BRITAIN	FRANCE	GERMANY
Gender Equality				
Men have more right to a job (Disagree)	93	84	82	81
University education is more important for boy (Disagree)	92	93	93	84
Political/Economic Role				
Men are better political leaders (Disagree)	75	80	79	81
Men are better business executives (Disagree)	83	83	86	83

Source: 2005–08 World Values Survey.

Note: Table entries are the percentages who agree (or disagree) with each statement.

expressed opinions are not fully matched by the reality of actions, the changes in political norms are having real effects on the status of women.

In one sense, it is amazing that gender roles formed over millennia have shifted so rapidly. At the same time, this transformation is incomplete. For example, European surveys show that most men still believe that women are primarily responsible for housework and that women have primary child-raising responsibilities (Scott, Braun, and Alwin 1998). Other surveys find that many working women believe their situations are worse than men's in regard to wages, promotion prospects, job opportunities, and job security. Ultimately, the legacy of the women's movement may be the creation of a choice for women—both work and family are now accepted options—instead of limitation to a single role.

Environmental Protection

Environmental quality is frequently cited as an example of postmaterial concerns in advanced industrial democracies. In the 1960s a few very visible ecological crises stimulated environmental concerns, which have since then persisted and expanded. Separate issues were linked together into environmental programs; citizen groups mobilized in support of environmental issues; and new green parties formed in several nations (Rootes 1999). There gradually developed a public awareness of how human activity and economic development could harm the natural environment, reduce the quality of life, and threaten the sustainability of human progress.

The broadest sign of public concern is interest in the host of environmental issues that have reached public consciousness. Global warming, the ozone hole, and biodiversity have become global concerns (Dunlap 2008). And locally, people are more conscious about the quality of their environment and ways to protect the quality of life and conserve natural resources. This interest in environmental issues translates into support for environmental protection; contemporary publics broadly support government actions to protect the environment.

Table 6.6 presents several measures of environmental attitudes from the 2010 International Social Survey Program. The two items in the top panel show that majorities in each nation say they are concerned about environmental issues. Similarly, most Americans, French and Germans (and a plurality of the British) reject the view that other things are more important than the environment. But espousing support for the environment in a survey is a cost-free endorsement. To minimize lip service support for the environment, the survey also asked people to balance their environmental beliefs against the potential economic costs of environmental protection. The results in the middle panel of table 6.6 show that roughly a third of these publics claim they would give up part of their income, pay higher taxes, or cut their living standards to prevent pollution. Roughly another third disagrees, and a third holds a neutral position.

Table 6.6	Thinking Green			

There is substantial support for environmental protection.

OPINION	UNITED STATES	GREAT BRITAIN	FRANCE	GERMANY
Interest				
Concerned about the environment	65	56	63	61
More important things than environment (Disagree)	54	43	57	61
Trade-Off Questions				
Would pay higher prices to protect environment	47	27	29	37
Would pay higher taxes to prevent pollution	34	23	15	22
Would cut living standard to protect environment	36	22	38	39
Nuclear Power				
Nuclear power is very dangerous	46	39	46	70

Source: 2010 International Social Survey Program.

Note: Table entries are the percentages who agree with each statement. Missing data were excluded from the calculation of percentages.

Nuclear power is an especially contentious environmental issue. It has stimulated intense environmental protests in all four of our core nations and entered the election platforms of several parties. When the Greens entered the German government in 1998, one of their priorities was to phase out Germany's nuclear power stations. In the wake of the Japanese nuclear disaster at Fukashima in March 2010, Chancellor Merkel called for the closure of all nuclear facilities in Germany. The bottom row of the table shows that a large majority of Germans and a plurality of Americans, British, and French consider nuclear power very dangerous.

Despite evidence such as this, almost since the blossoming of the environmental movement in the mid-1970s, there have been persistent predictions of the death of environmentalism (for example, Nordhaus and Shellenberger 2007). There is some evidence from the International Social Survey Program (ISSP) timeseries and other polls that public concern for the environment peaked around the mid-1980s and has declined since then. Some of the decline is because policy reforms have cleaned up the air and water and addressed other pressing environmental concerns. In addition, when economic times are difficult, there is some moderation of environmental concerns. For instance, the General Social Survey (GSS) found that between 2008 and 2010 there was a 10 percent decline in the percentage of Americans who want the government to spend more on the environment—but this rebounded slightly by 2012.

Today, the environment is a significant part of the political agenda in advanced industrial democracies. Many people are interested in environmental issues and say they are willing to sacrifice financially to improve the environment. And recycling and conservation actions have increased during the past two decades.[4] Furthermore, these concerns reflect more than just a growing awareness of the hidden health and economic costs of pollution. Environmentalism is often linked to postmaterial values and reflects the processes of value change that are part of the new style of citizen politics.

Social and Moral Issues

Some issues are old and new at the same time. In the late 1960s and early 1970s, young people began to question traditional values involving sex and lifestyle choices. These questions tested the extent of individual freedom on matters such as premarital sex, abortion, divorce, homosexuality, and pornography. These issues entered the political debate in a variety of ways, often spawning counter-movements from religious and conservative members of society. Pro-choice groups stimulated pro-life replies; advocates of gay rights evoked a conservative reaction.

These issues are often linked to the values of the New Politics, but they also tap traditional religious values because of their moral content (Norris and Inglehart 2011). Social issues such as abortion or homosexuality involve some people's basic moral principles of right and wrong. Religious and secular values are typically an important influence on these opinions. People often find it is difficult to compromise on social issues because their opinions are bound up in who they are. The issue publics for social policy questions often are larger than might otherwise be expected. The active interest groups on social issues are normally religious organizations and Christian Democratic parties, not labor unions and business groups.

Table 6.7 presents public opinion data on several social and moral issues. In the past, traditional value orientations led many people to be highly critical of divorce; scandal, dishonor, and religious isolation often accompanied the divorce decree. Table 6.7 presents a different picture: large majorities in our four countries now believe that divorce is sometimes justified. As attitudes toward divorce have become more tolerant, nearly all Western democracies have changed their laws to remove the limits on divorce and provisions discriminating against women. Similarly, majorities in all four nations now express some tolerance of prostitution and euthanasia.

Perhaps even more striking is the broad tolerance of homosexuality, which was once seen as a form of social deviance. A few decades ago, few gays or lesbians believed they could openly acknowledge their orientation. Bullying and social stigma accompanied a homosexual life, and most Christian religions considered it a moral failing. But today a majority in all four nations says that homosexuality is sometimes justified.

The dramatic change in public values is evident from trend data in figure 6.3. In the early 1980s, about half of Europeans and only a third of Americans expressed some tolerance of homosexuals. Tolerance grew fairly

Table 6.7	Moral Issues and Religious Values

There is a liberal majority on many moral issues even though many people still have strong religious identities.

OPINION	UNITED STATES	GREAT BRITAIN	FRANCE	GERMANY
Divorce is sometimes justified	94	89	94	93
Homosexuality is sometimes justified	67	75	80	83
Prostitution is sometimes justified	57	53	58	72
Euthanasia is sometimes justified	78	81	91	77
Abortion Attitudes				
Abortion is sometimes justified	74	75	87	80
Abortion is not at all wrong:				
If child may have birth defect	52	61	82	54
If parents are poor	29	35	51	17
Religious Attitudes				
I am a religious person	72	48	43	37
God is important in my life	83	42	36	33
Religious attitudes average	78	45	40	35

Sources: United States, 2005–08 World Values Survey; European nations, 2008 European Values Survey; abortion is not wrong items: 2008 International Social Survey Program.

Note: Table entries are the percentages who agree with each statement. Missing data were excluded from the calculation of percentages.

steadily to the levels described in the table 6.7 (also see Dalton 2009a, ch. 5; Anderson and Fetner 2008). One possible explanation is that this reflects the secularization of these societies—but the change in attitudes was too large and to quick. The think line in the figure displays the percentage considering themselves religious averaged across the four nations; this has declined, but only slightly (also see Höllinger and Haller 2009). Rather, people have decoupled their broader sense of religious values from the specific examples presented in table 6.7. One can now have a religious identity and still accept practices that were once consider sacrilegious.

Another often intense debate involves abortion. Abortion policies have been the subject of major legislative or judicial action in the United States, Germany, and several other European nations. Today, most people believe that abortion is sometimes justified, such as when the health of the mother is at risk. Fewer people approve of abortion when it is based on economic factors. Despite the dramatic ebbs and flows in public events on abortion, there doesn't appear to be a strong trend in these attitudes over time.

The findings in this section lead to two broad conclusions. First, Americans are generally more conservative than Europeans on social and moral issues. This pattern is likely the result of national differences in religious feelings.

Figure 6.3	Tolerance toward Homosexuals

The percentage saying homosexuality is sometimes justified has grown substantially since the early 1980s.

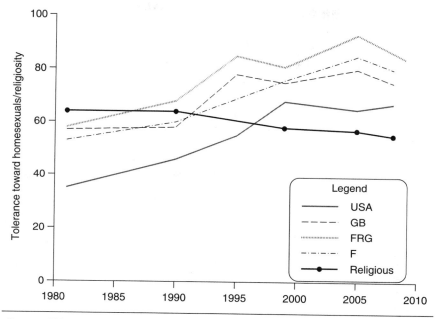

Sources: 1981–2008 World Values Survey; 2008 European Values Survey for European Nations.

Note: Figure entries are the percentage in each nation saying homosexuality is justified and the four-nation average in the percentage saying they are religious.

Despite the affluence, high mobility rates, and social diversity of its citizens, the United States is among the most religious of Western societies. American church attendance and religious feelings are among the highest in the world. About three-quarters of Americans say they consider themselves religious, and four-fifths say God is important in their lives. Fewer than half of Europeans share these same opinions.[5]

Second, public opinion has generally become more tolerant on most social issues as the social modernization and secularization have transformed these societies. Long-term opinion series for all four core nations show a gradual liberalization of attitudes toward sexual relations and homosexuality.

A decline of religious attachments and values partially explains longitudinal trends on social and moral issues. Church attendance has decreased and religious attachments have weakened (see chapter 8).[6] A more secular public sees humankind in a different light. Furthermore, there has been a shift in norms even within many churches, depicting a greater tolerance for individual choice. Because we attribute these trends to general processes of social modernization, we expect these trends to continue.

The change in values has mixed effects on these issues. The decline in religiosity may prompt greater tolerance of abortion and homosexuality. At the same time, weakening religious attachments are probably linked to declining respect for and acceptance of authority as well changes in moral and ethical standards.

Foreign Policy Opinions

Foreign policy is an issue that follows the trends in international events (Eichenberg 2007). After decades of silent conflict during the Cold War, the collapse of the Soviet Union dramatically reshaped the international order. The democratic revolution that spread throughout Eastern Europe altered these political systems and international relations in fundamental ways. Then, just as a new stability was emerging, the 2001 terrorist attacks on the World Trade Center, the war in Afghanistan beginning in 2001, the 2003 American overthrow of Saddam Hussein's regime in Iraq, the 2004 Madrid bombings, and the 2005 London bombings transformed the international landscape. The world is changing rapidly, and governments and people are unsure about what lies ahead and what policies governments should follow.

Typically, fewer people follow foreign policy compared to the issue publics for many domestic policy areas. But international events often bring opinions into focus at least for a while. This section describes contemporary foreign policy opinions in several areas.

Conflict

Although the Cold War is over, the world can still be a brutish place. Regional and local conflicts—such as those in Sudan and Syria—threaten individual and international security. Yet the end of the Cold War has transformed peace and conflict issues in the current world. Potential conflict between the United States and Russia is no longer the central theme of international relations; public attention has shifted toward other sources of international conflict.

Even after the end of the Cold War, the acceptance of conflict in the international system is still widespread (table 6.8). For example, three-quarters of Americans say that war is sometimes necessary to obtain justice, which seems to support Kagan's description at the start of this chapter about the orientation of Americans. But this simple description does not hold up under closer scrutiny. First, an equivalent percentage of the British share these views, even though the French and Germans are much less supportive. Second, when one discusses specific potential sources of conflict or the use of military force, the patterns between Americans and Europeans often overlap rather than being distinct. For instance, the French are hesitant to say war is sometimes necessary—but then 60 percent would support military action to prevent Iran from acquiring nuclear weapons and approve of military intervention in Libya. Only the Germans are consistently hesitant about the use of military force; in other nations it depends on the circumstances and national interests. Europeans are more willing to take action in their region, while Americans are more concerned about China. Kagan's Mars versus Venus dichotomy is too simple.

Cooperation

The other side of foreign policy is international cooperation. One of the most striking changes in the past several decades has been a growing

Table 6.8	Foreign Policy Opinions

Foreign policy opinions vary depending on international conditions; favorable opinion in one situation is often counterbalanced by negative opinions in another.

OPINION	UNITED STATES	GREAT BRITAIN	FRANCE	GERMANY
International Conflict				
War is sometimes necessary	75	74	28	28
Concern about Iranian nuclear weapons	76	72	76	75
Military action to prevent Iranian nuclear weapons	54	43	60	39
Approve of intervention in Libya	59	53	60	39
China is a military threat	47	35	29	33
International Cooperation				
United States and Europe have common values	71	64	68	66
Common values with China	53	41	32	18
Favorable opinion of the United States	83	78	58	72
Favorable opinion of the European Union	65	58	59	74
Favorable opinion of Russia	48	48	56	50
Favorable opinion of China	42	53	35	52
International Institutions				
NATO is essential	62	69	60	58
EU is a good thing	—	45	61	69
Confidence in United Nations	34	45	56	39

Sources: 2010 and 2011 Transatlantic Trends Surveys (http://trends.gmfus.org); the last item is from the 2005–08 World Values Survey.

Note: Table entries are the percentages agreeing with each item.

institutionalization of international cooperation and a globalization of economic systems. These relationships are especially dense between America and Europe—despite occasional spats among allies. The middle panel of table 6.8 shows that large majorities in all four nations agree that the United States and Europe share common values. Americans are about as favorable about the European Union (EU) as the three EU members are about the United States.

However, there are still tensions in international relations. For example, barely half of the public in all four nations have favorable opinions about Russia. This is an improvement from the Cold War era, but not a solid foundation for international cooperation. Favorable opinions are also limited for China. Most Europeans do not see that they share common values, and only a bare minority of Americans have these opinions. The full German Marshall Fund (GMF) survey provides several examples of how China is seen as a growing economic and military rival by nations on both sides of the Atlantic.

International Institutions

Another element of foreign policy is attitudes toward international organizations. The bottom panel of table 6.8 shows that belief in the essentiality of NATO remains high in all four nations, even though the end of the Cold War has lessened the rationale for NATO. Trends from the GMF surveys suggest that support for NATO has not followed a systematic trend since the end of the Soviet Union in 1991. There is also substantial support for the European Union among its member states, although these opinions are likely to be more fluid as Europe now struggles with the economic recession, the Euro, and the fallout from these problems.[7] The bottom-most entry in the table depicts limited confidence in the United Nations, but this is lower than the support levels found in most other surveys. Typically, the United Nations receives more favorable ratings—even in the United States, where conservative politicians have long denounced the United Nations.

In summary, we are living in a period in which international relations are in flux, and new threats to world order have appeared. Although it is too early to discern the exact shape that foreign policy opinions will take in this new context, it appears that Western publics are broadening their perspectives and thinking about foreign policy in more cooperative and international terms.

Left/Right Orientations

People are now interested in a wider range of issues than just socioeconomic concerns, and so a general assessment of overall political positions must consider a range of issues. The rate of social change across various issues is uneven: preferences for social spending have fluctuated, support for social equality has grown rapidly over time, and attitudes toward abortion have been more stable. In addition, the salient political controversies change over time.

In the United States the intense racial issues of the 1960s—school desegregation, open housing, and public accommodations—now register overwhelmingly liberal responses, but new racial issues—quotas, affirmative action programs, and family assistance policies—divide the public. This change represents progress in the development of racial tolerance, but racial policy remains politically contentious. One of the major points we have (re)learned from recent political trends is that new issues of conflict inevitably replace old resolved issues.

One way we can generalize about the overall political leanings of Western publics is to examine broad political orientations that encapsulate specific issues. Political scientists frequently measure these orientations in terms of Left/Right attitudes (Inglehart 1990; Dalton, Farrell, and McAllister 2011, chs. 4–5). Political issues are often discussed or summarized in terms of Left/Right or liberal/conservative philosophies. Republicans attack what they call the "loony Left," while Democrats rail against the "reactionary Right." These labels provide reference points that help voters interpret and evaluate political activities.

People's ability to identify themselves in Left/Right terms doesn't imply that they possess a sophisticated conceptual framework or theoretical dogma. For many people, Left/Right attitudes summarize their positions on the political issues of greatest personal concern. These issues can vary within and across nations. So Left/Right is a sort of "super-issue" that summarizes current political positions.

Opinion surveys regularly ask people to place themselves on a 10-point scale, extending from "Left" to "Right." In almost all nations, this produces a bell-curve-like distribution of responses. For our four core nations, for example, 49 percent of these publics position themselves at the middle two positions on the Left/Right scale. About 9 percent take the two most leftist positions, and 5 percent at the two most rightist positions.

The average placement of the public varies systematically across nations. Figure 6.4 plots the average Left/Right position for twenty-one nations. The United States is one of the more conservative nations in overall Left/Right terms; in fact, few advanced industrial democracies are farther to the right. The Unites States' Left/Right placement reaffirms the impression derived from many of the specific issue areas examined in this chapter. The average Briton is located at almost the center of the scale. Germany moved to the Left during the 2000s, and also at the liberal pole are Mediterranean nations—France and Spain—that have significant leftist traditions.

There is considerable debate on whether people are becoming more liberal or conservative over time. James Stimson and his colleagues argue that there have been large ebbs and flows in liberal/conservative identities among Americans and the British during the past several decades (Ellis and Stimson 2012; Erikson, MacKuen, and Stimson 2002; Bartle, Avellaneda, and Stimson 2011). Figure 6.4 suggests that between 1981 and 2005–08 many more nations moved in a significant leftward direction and few moved rightward. However, the most reliable evidence in the United

Figure 6.4	National Left/Right Positions

National traditions and current politics determine the public's average position on the Left/Right Scale.

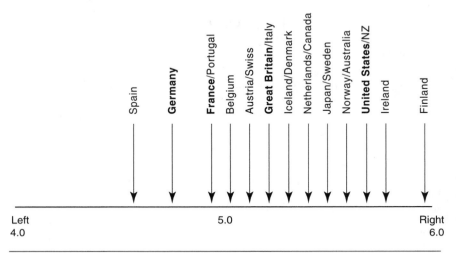

Left	5.0	Right
4.0		6.0

Sources: 2008 European Values Survey for European nations; 2005–08 World Values Survey for non-European nations.

Note: The Left/Right Scale was coded (1) Left to (10) Right; the figure presents the national mean score.

States comes from the General Social Survey, which has regularly monitored these orientations since 1974. The GSS finds only minor fluctuations over a thirty-six-year period until 2010.[8] Other national trends show varied patterns.

More meaningful, however, is to consider that the content of Left and Right orientations reflects the issues of salience to the public, and this content changes over time. The meaning of the terms also varies across age and political groups (Fuchs and Klingemann 1989; Dalton, Farrell, and McAllister 2011, ch. 4). For older citizens, these terms are often linked to socioeconomic issues: *Left* shows support for social programs, working-class interests, and the influence of labor unions; *Right* is identified with limited government, support for middle-class interests, and the influence of the business sector. Among the young, the New Politics issues of environmental protection, social equality, and lifestyle freedoms are added to socioeconomic interests. For the young, the term *Left* can mean opposition to nuclear energy, support for sexual equality, internationalism, or endorsement of social programs.

Therefore, it is difficult to speak in simple terms of whether contemporary publics are becoming more liberal or conservative in Left/Right attitudes.

There are political tides that move in one direction or the other for a period of time. Underlying these cycles, however, it appears that the meaning of *Left* and *Right* in political discourse has changed in the long term as social modernization has transformed the issues of debate.

Public Opinion and Political Change

Today, more people are interested in more issues. Opinions on socioeconomic issues were once the predominant concern of voters and political elites; one could realistically describe political competition in terms of a single overarching policy area, such as the New Deal in the United States or capitalist/socialist conflicts in Europe. Now the public's issue interests have diversified. Socioeconomic matters still attract widespread attention, but social equality, environmental protection, social morals, immigration, and foreign policy also capture the interest of many people. And because issue opinions are changeable, some of the patterns in this chapter have undoubtedly changed in reaction to recent events—but we won't know which until there is a new survey.

The expansion of the boundaries of politics to include these new issues has several implications for politics today. Governments have increased the scope of their activity and must worry not only about economic policy but also whether the environment is clean, personal life choices are tolerated, and other issues. The expansion of the government's role has rekindled ongoing debates about the appropriate scope of government, although the policy content of the current debate is much different from earlier debates about the economic role of the state.

The proliferation of issue publics also changes the nature of political representation and decision making. Issue publics try to maximize representation on their issues, but the proliferation of such focused interests increases the complexity of the governing process. A majority of (differing) voters want government to spend more on (differing) specific programs; a majority also wants government to tax them less. Policymakers get mixed signals from the public and have no method (or perhaps no motivation) to resolve these conflicts systematically. Government responses to the demands of one issue public often conflict with the demands of another. Policy proliferation can lead to issue-by-issue decisions rather than broad programmatic planning. One of the challenges facing contemporary governments is how to adapt the democratic process to this different pattern of interest demands.

What can we say about the overall political orientations of contemporary publics? Journalists and social commentators frequently refer to a liberal or conservative mood sweeping a nation. The early 1960s and early 1970s supposedly were a time of radical change and liberal ascendance. Similarly, discussions of a new conservative mood in Western democracies became commonplace in the 1980s, exemplified by the electoral strength of U.S. president Ronald Reagan, Thatcher, Kohl, and French president

Jacques Chirac. Bill Clinton's presidential victory in 1992 was called a signal of a new era, but just two years later the Republicans won a majority in Congress, which was followed by Clinton's reelection in 1996. There were similar claims that George W. Bush's reelection in 2004 created a new Republican majority, but then Republicans lost both the House and Senate to the Democrats in 2006, and Obama won the presidency in 2008. This was quickly followed by Republican gains in the 2010 midterm elections and then Obama's reelection in 2012.

Tested against public opinion data, generalizations about shifts from right to left based on election outcomes are difficult to substantiate. The counterculture movement of the 1960–70s, the conservative revival of the 1980s, and the liberal trend of the 1990–2000s were not as widespread as the media suggested. The visible public actions of political groups can distort our perception of the broader currents of public opinion.[9] Furthermore, there are many issues of potential interest to the public, and not all of them move in a consistent direction over time.

Still, some general trends emerge from our findings. One apparent trend has been the shift toward what might be termed *libertarian attitudes*. Contemporary publics are becoming more tolerant of individual diversity and are interested in protecting individual freedoms. This applies to the rights of minorities and women as well as to a general acceptance of individual freedom in social relations. These trends appear in attitudes toward social equality, moral issues, and the quality of life. Paralleling these changes is a decline in respect for authority and concern about social order.

The counter-evidence is *socioeconomic attitudes*. Uneasiness over the excessive cost and bureaucracy of government is now commonplace (even if people favor greater government spending on a wide variety of programs). The end of socialism and the retrenchment of the welfare state in the West have made it impossible for the Left to attain its traditional goals of state control of the economy and full guarantees of basic social needs. There has been a conservative shift on many the socioeconomic issues. The 2008 recession strengthened these trends.

In a period of increasing issue proliferation, such conflicting trends are not surprising. A gradual liberalization of political values on social issues can coexist with a conservative tilt on socioeconomic matters. But even this generalization would be difficult to sustain because the meaning of such ideological labels has changed as part of the process of issue proliferation. No longer does liberalism stand for the creation of social programs, the nationalization of industry, and peaceful coexistence with the communist world—it may just as well mean protection of a clean environment or women's rights legislation. No longer does conservatism represent the prohibition of government social programs or the defeat of the Soviet Empire—it may instead mean limits on immigration or supporting family policies.

The content of contemporary political debate is therefore difficult to compare to the political conflicts of the New Deal era of the 1930s or even those of the Great Society of the 1960s. Perhaps this shift in the content of the political debate is what most directly shows how advanced industrial societies are progressing politically in the new millennium.

Suggested Readings

Alba, Richard, Peter Schmidt, and Martina Wasmer, eds. 2003. *Germans or Foreigners? Attitudes toward Ethnic Minorities in Post-reunification Germany.* New York: Palgrave Macmillan.

Bardes, Barbara, and Robert Oldendick. 2012. *Public Opinion: Measuring the American Mind.* 4th ed. Lanham, MD: Rowman and Littlefield.

Ellis, Christopher, and James Stimson. 2012. *Ideology in America.* New York: Cambridge University Press.

Haller, Max, Roger Jowell, and Tom Smith, eds. 2009. *The International Social Survey Programme, 1984–2009.* London: Routledge.

Inglehart, Ronald, and Pippa Norris. 2003. *A Rising Tide: Gender Equality and Cultural Change around the World.* New York: Cambridge University Press.

Jowell, Roger, et al., eds. 1998. *British—and European—Social Attitudes: The 15th Report.* Brookfield, VT: Ashgate.

Marsden, Peter, ed. 2012. *Social Trends in American Life.* Princeton: Princeton University Press.

Niedermayer, Oskar, and Richard Sinnott, eds. 1995. *Public Opinion and International Governance.* New York: Oxford University Press.

Norris, Pippa, and Ronald Inglehart. 2011. *Sacred and Secular: Religion and Politics Worldwide.* 2nd ed. New York: Cambridge University Press.

Schuman, Howard, et al. 1997. *Racial Attitudes in America: Trends and Interpretations.* Rev. ed. Cambridge, MA: Harvard University Press.

Sniderman, Paul, et al. 2000. *The Outsider: Prejudice and Politics in Italy.* Princeton: Princeton University Press.

Notes

1. In 2006 Americans' belief that these policies were a definite government responsibility averaged 39 percent; in 1996 the average was only 26 percent.
2. However, the American General Social Survey finds that pro-spending feelings hit a high point in 2006, and by 2010 returned to more typical levels.
3. The results in table 6.4 are based on the entire public. It would be even more informative to compare the opinions across racial/ethnic groups within each nation.

4. The 2010 International Social Survey found that 80 percent of Germans said they "always" sort their trash for recycling, as do 78 percent of the French, 73 percent of Britons, and 40 percent of Americans; sizeable minorities engage in other conservation behaviors.
5. Opinion differences within Germany reflect the legacy of the two German states. The 2008 European Values Survey finds that 56 percent of respondents from West Germany consider themselves religious, but only 18 percent of respondents from East Germany do so.
6. Most advanced industrial societies have experienced a long-term trend toward secularization. Church enrollment has dropped off in most nations, as have other forms of involvement in churches (Norris and Inglehart 2011, ch. 4).
7. The European Union has an extensive program of polling public opinion. See the resources at http://ec.europa.eu/public_opinion/index_en.htm.
8. For instance, the GSS shows virtually no relationship between the year of the survey and average liberal/conservative positions ($r = .03$). In 1974 there were 30 percent liberals, 40 percent moderates, and 30 percent conservatives. In 2010 there were 29 percent liberals, 38 percent moderates, and 34 percent conservatives. These percentages also change very little from survey to survey (typically within the range of sampling error) and show little sign of the large shift in moods that Ellis and Stimson find (2012, ch. 4).
9. Elections provide a poor indicator of ideological trends because elections reflect the positions of parties and candidates relative to the electorate but not the overall distribution of opinion on any specific issue. A party that moves too far left can lose votes, as can one that moves too far right. Furthermore, the combination of issues in an election makes it difficult to make simple estimations of the voters' intentions on specific policies.

Part Three
The Electoral Connection

7   Elections and Political Parties

If you travel through France at election time, it is an interesting experience. For an American it is a surprise to see election posters touting the Communist Party (not something I often see in Orange County). On the next street corner might be a poster for the extreme right National Front, with Marine Le Pen saying "Oui, la France." Nicolas Sarkozy of the Union for a Popular Movement (UMP) might look down on you from the next billboard, as he advocates a strong France while gazing off into the horizon. Across the street could be a banner for the Socialists, or the Greens, or the Democratic Movement. Elections in France offer voters a diverse range of choices, and more than a dozen parties won seats in Parliament after the 2012 elections.

Elections are the foundation of democratic politics. Elections are one of the few ways that a society can reach a collective decision on what the whole public prefers. The choice between (or among) parties aggregates the preferences of individual voters, thereby converting public opinion into decisions on who governs and their policies. Other forms of citizen participation may influence government policymaking, but they lack these representative qualities. Elections determine who manages the affairs of government and makes public policy. The selection of leaders—along with the ability to "throw the rascals out" at the next election—is the public's penultimate power. Political elites may not always deliver what they promise, but the selection of a government produces popular control over these elites.

In virtually every functioning democracy, political parties are the core of electoral process (Dalton, Farrell, and McAllister 2011). Parties define the choices available to voters. Candidates in most European nations are selected by the parties and elected as party representatives, not as individuals. Open primaries and independent legislators as exist in the United States are virtually unknown in Europe. A large proportion of Europeans (including the Germans) vote directly for party lists rather than for individual candidates.

| Internet Resource |

Visit the Political Compass website to take a short political quiz and see where you would be located in a 2-D political space in the United States or Britain:

http://www.politicalcompass.org

Political parties also direct the content of election campaigns and often rely on formal party members as their main campaign workers. Party programs help define the issues that are discussed during a campaign (Klingemann et al. 2006). In many European nations, the parties and not individual candidates control campaign advertising.

Once in government, parties control the policymaking process. Leadership of the executive branch and the organization of the legislative branch are decided based on party majorities. The parties' control is often absolute, as in the parliamentary systems of Europe, where representatives from the same party vote as a bloc. American parties are less united and less decisive, but even here parties actively structure the legislative process. Because of the centrality of political parties in the democratic process, political scientists describe many European political systems as examples of "responsible party government."

Consequently, the chapters in this section focus on parties and elections to understand the workings of democratic representation. A well-known political scientist, E. E. Schattschneider (1942, 1), concluded that "modern democracy is unthinkable save in terms of political parties." James Bryce (1921, 119) said, "Parties are inevitable. No one has shown how representative government could be worked without them." Many contemporary political scientists share these views.

This chapter summarizes the history and social bases of contemporary party systems. We present a framework for understanding the party options available to voters, as well as the characteristics of the major parties as political organizations and agents of representative democracy.

The History of Party Systems

It is often said that if political parties did not exist, they would have to be invented in order for democracy to function. And when representative democracy first developed in the United States in the late 1700s, political parties as we know them today did not exist. But soon political factions became political parties. And when democracy emerged in Europe, parties were central to this development.

We often think of each election in terms of the issues of the day. But across elections, parties normally take consistent positions that reflect their historical roots based in either an ideology or a connection with enduring social interests. Many voters repeatedly support the same party for the same reasons. The current Democratic tendencies of American Catholics, for example, result from their class position when they first emigrated to America and the manner in which Catholics were integrated into society and politics. The Republican leanings of Cuban Americans reflect their unique historical experiences, which link them to the Republican Party, while Mexican Americans tend to vote Democratic.

Seymour Martin Lipset and Stein Rokkan (1967) wrote that modern party systems broadly reflect the historical patterns of national and socioeconomic development. Table 7.1 summarizes their analyses and outlines the voting implications of this framework. Lipset and Rokkan said that two successive revolutions in the modernization of Western societies—the *National Revolution* and the *Industrial Revolution*—created social group divisions that still structure partisan competition today. Although their discussion dealt primarily with Western Europe, the approach is relevant to other Western democracies, including the United States.

The National Revolution meant the building of unified nation states during the eighteenth and nineteenth centuries in Europe. The National Revolution spawned two sets of competing social groups (social cleavages) that are shown in the middle column of table 7.1. The *center/periphery* cleavage pitted the dominant national culture against ethnic, linguistic, or religious minorities in the peripheral regions. For example, were Alsatians to become Germans or French? Was Scotland a separate nation or a region within Britain? The diverse state histories within the United States generated similar tensions between regional cultures, eventually leading to a civil war. This cleavage is visible today in regional differences in politics: between the English and the Welsh and the English and the Scots, between Bretons and the Parisian center, between the "Free State of Bavaria" and the Federal Republic of Germany, between the old Federal Republic and the new German states in the East, and between the distinct regional orientations in the United States.

The National Revolution also formalized *church/state* conflict, which cast the centralizing, standardizing, and mobilizing forces of the national

Table 7.1	The Development of Party Systems	
How historical developments produced distinct alignments of voter groups.		
HISTORIC ERA	**CLEAVAGE**	**VOTING GROUPS**
National Revolution	Center/periphery	Region
	Church/state	Religious denomination
		Religious/secular
Industrial Revolution	Land/industry	Urban/rural
	Owners/workers	Middle/working class
Postindustrial Revolution	Cultural values	Material/postmaterial

Source: Author.

government against the traditional values of the Catholic Church. As governments challenged the church's role, the church often tried to protect its status by resisting the government or creating political groups to represent its interests. Protestants often allied themselves with nationalist forces in the struggle for national autonomy. Contemporary divisions between religious denominations and between secular and religious groups continue these earlier social divisions.

The Industrial Revolution in the nineteenth century generated two additional social cleavages (table 7.1). The *land/industry* cleavage pitted rural and farming interests against the economic concerns of a rising industrial class. The barons of industry challenged the landed gentry of Britain and agrarian interests in the United States; the Ruhr industrialists contested the power of the Prussian Junkers. This cleavage continues in contemporary conflicts between rural and urban interests.

As industrialization progressed, a second cleavage developed between owners and workers within the industrial sector. This cleavage reflected class conflict between the working class and the middle class composed of business owners and the self-employed. The struggle for legitimacy and representation by the working-class movement often generated intense political conflict. Today, this cleavage appears in the competition between labor unions and business associations and more generally between members of the working class and the middle class.

These historical events may seem very distant from contemporary party politics, but Lipset and Rokkan (1967) claimed that a connection exists for party systems of the twentieth century. These four cleavages define major sources of social conflict existing within most democracies. Social groups related to these cleavages—such as farmer associations or labor unions—participated in the political process even before the extension of the voting franchise. When voting rights were granted to most Europeans around the turn of the twentieth century, the structure of group competition was already in place. New voters followed these group cues in supporting a political party linked to their group interests. The Conservative Party in Britain, for example, was the representative of the middle-class establishment, while the Labour Party catered to the interests of the working class. The working class in France and Germany supported the Communist and Socialist Parties. The American party system developed more gradually because the voting franchise was granted earlier and social groups were less polarized. But the modern U.S. party system continues to reflect cleavages from the Civil War and the Great Depression. The Democratic Party, for example, still draws upon the New Deal coalition that formed its base in the 1930s.

The formation of mass political parties thus institutionalized the existing group alignments, creating the framework for modern party systems. Once voters formed party loyalties, and interest groups established party ties, these links became self-perpetuating. At each election, parties turned to the same social groups for their core support, and most members of these groups habitually supported the same party. In one of the most often cited conclusions of comparative politics, Lipset and Rokkan stated that "the party systems of the 1960s reflect, with but few significant exceptions, the cleavage structures of the 1920s" (1967, 50).

Early electoral research substantiated Lipset and Rokkan's claims. Regional voting patterns from the early twentieth century appeared in recent election returns. Survey research found that social cleavages, especially class and religion, strongly influenced people's votes. For example, Richard Rose's (1969) comparative study of voting patterns in the 1960s found that voting choices were clearly related to the cleavages that Lipset and Rokkan described.

Just as this theme of partisan stability was becoming the conventional wisdom, dramatic changes began to affect these party systems starting in the 1970s. The established parties faced new demands and challenges, and evidence of partisan change mounted (Dalton, Flanagan, and Beck 1984). New parties emerged to compete in elections, and some of the established parties fragmented. The evidence of more fluid and dynamic party politics has grown during the subsequent decades.

The current fluidity of party systems is partially due to a weakening of the social group relationship that Lipset and Rokkan described. Chapter 8 demonstrates how traditional social divisions have less ability to predict voting choices. Because of this erosion in traditional social group–based politics, voting choices became more fluid. Partisan volatility increased at the aggregate and individual levels. Popular attachments to political parties weakened (see chapter 9). The major research question shifted from explaining the persistence of historical patterns to explaining the growing instability of party systems.

While several unique national circumstances contributed to this instability, one important factor was the Postindustrial Revolution that brought new postmaterial issues onto the political stage (see table 7.1 and chapter 5). New issues entered the political agenda: environmental protection, social equality, nuclear energy, gender equality, and alternative lifestyles. Some voters demanded more opportunities for participation in the decisions affecting their lives and pressed for a further democratization of society. Once these trends began, they provoked a conservative response that opposed the liberalization of social norms and other postmaterial issues. Sometimes this backlash has led to a reassertion of traditional value conflicts based on religion or other historic social cleavages. These new postmaterial conflicts are now another important aspect of contemporary politics.

Because the established parties were often tentative in their responses to these new demands, new parties formed in many nations to specifically represent these viewpoints. The first wave included environmental parties, such as the Green parties in Germany and France or Left-libertarian parties (Mueller-Rommel and Poguntke 2002; Burchell 2002). This was followed by a counterwave of New Right parties, such as the National Front in France and the Republikaner in Germany (Mudde 2007; Norris 2005). It is unclear whether these parties reflect temporary responses to modern issues or a more permanent realignment of political conflict. American history is full of third-party movements that were eventually incorporated into the established parties. The present partisan instability in these democracies could be just another case of this recurring pattern.

Party systems are in a state of flux, and it is difficult to determine how fundamental and long lasting these changes will be. It is clear, however, that the new political conflicts of advanced industrial societies have contributed to this fluidity. While we wait for history to determine the significance of these trends, we can look more closely at the political alignments that now exist in the United States, Britain, Germany, and France.

Four Contemporary Party Systems

The major political parties in our four core nations come in all shapes and sizes.[1] They vary in their vote shares, structure, and governmental experience, as well as in their political orientation.[2]

As table 7.2 shows, the American party system is atypical in many ways. Members of Congress are selected from single member districts, which encourages the development of a two-party system of Democrats and Republicans because only the largest vote-getter in each district is elected. A party system based on only two parties is rare; most democracies have more parties competing in elections, and multiparty coalitions are necessary to form a government majority. In the United States, in contrast, power shifts back and forth between the two major parties. The Republicans' dramatic breakthrough in the 1994 congressional elections ended forty years of Democratic rule. Since then, the election victories have been fairly evenly divided between the parties. The fluctuation in congressional vote totals over time is relatively small, averaging less than a 3 percent vote change between elections.

Presidential election results are usually more varied than congressional elections. Lyndon Johnson won in a huge Democratic landslide in 1964, and Ronald Reagan won an equally impressive Republican majority in 1984. The presidential elections of 2000 and 2004 demonstrated the rough balance between the parties. Obama's 2008 victory was partially a public repudiation of the presidency of George W. Bush and the attraction of a charismatic candidate, and then he was reelected in 2012. Presidential elections are heavily influenced by the individual candidates as well the broader party programs. Therefore, our cross-national analyses of voting use American congressional elections, because these elections are more similar to Western European parliamentary contests.

Another distinctive aspect of the American political system is the decentralized nature of party organizations. Because of the federal system of American government, instead of one Democratic Party (or Republican Party) there are really fifty—one in each state. National party meetings are something like medieval gatherings of feudal states rather than the assembly

Table 7.2	Party Characteristics

Party systems vary in the number of parties and their political characteristics.

PARTY	YEAR FOUNDED	LEGISLATIVE ELECTION		PARTY STRUCTURE	YEARS IN GOVERNMENT (1977–2012)
		VOTE %	SEATS		
United States (2012)					
Democrats (U.S. Dem)	1832	49.1	201	Decentralized	19
Republicans (U.S. Rep)	1856	48.1	234	Decentralized	16
Great Britain (2010)					
Labour (Lab)	1900	29.0	258	Centralized	12
Liberal Democrats (LibDem)	1987	23.0	62	Decentralized	3
Conservatives (Con)	1830	36.1	306	Mixed	13
Scottish National Party (SNP)	1934	1.7	6	Mixed	
Plaid Cymru (PCy)	1925	.6	3	—	0
Other parties		9.6	16	Mixed	0
Germany (2009)					
Linke	1990	11.9	76	Centralized	0
Social Democrats (SPD)	1863	23.0	146	Centralized	12
Greens (Grüne)	1980	10.7	68	Decentralized	8
Free Democrats (FDP)	1948	14.6	93	Decentralized	23
Christian Democrats (CDU/CSU)	1950	33.8	249	Mixed	21
Republikaner/ NPD	1983	1.9	0	Mixed	0

(Continued)

Table 7.2	(Continued)				
		LEGISLATIVE ELECTION			
PARTY	YEAR FOUNDED	VOTE %	SEATS	PARTY STRUCTURE	YEARS IN GOVERNMENT (1977–2012)
France (2012)					
Communist Party (PCF)	1920	1.1	10	Centralized	5
Socialists (PS)	1905	40.9	280	Centralized	13
Left Radicals (PRG)	1972	2.3	12	—	0
Greens (Verts)	1978	3.6	17	Decentralized	5
Democratic Movement (MoDem)	2007	1.8	3	Mixed	0
Union for Popular Movement (UMP)	1947	38.0	194	Mixed	24
New Center (formerly UDF)	1978	2.5	11	Mixed	24
National Front (FN)	1972	3.7	2	Personalistic	0
Other parties		6.1	48		

Source: Compiled by the author; election statistics from Election World database on Wikipedia.

of a unitary organization. The presidential nominating conventions are not controlled and directed by the national party but are taken over every four years by the personnel of the winning candidates. Even in Congress, American legislators historically have been more likely to cross party lines when voting on legislation than are parliamentarians in disciplined party systems.

Great Britain presents a different partisan pattern—often described as a two-and-a-half-party system. The Labour Party is the major force on the left, and the Conservative Party is the representative of the right. Each of these major parties routinely receives between 35 percent and 45 percent of the national vote. The smaller Liberal Democratic Party, located near the center of the political spectrum, normally garners 15 percent to 20 percent.[3]

The diversity of the British party system has grown since the 1970s. Regional movements strengthened the nationalist parties in Scotland (Scottish Nationalist Party; SNP) and Wales (Plaid Cymru; PCy), and the development of regional parliaments in the 1990s reinforced these parties. At the end of the 1980s, the Liberal Party was reformed as the Liberal Democrats, combining traditional conservatism on economic issues with more liberal policies on social issues. Other minor parties have periodically won significant vote shares, especially in the European Parliament elections, which are proportional representation elections. The 2010 election produced an unusual result; neither Labour nor the Conservatives had a majority of seats for the first time in nearly seventy years. This produced a multiparty government of Conservatives and Liberals.

The British parties are much more highly organized and centralized than the American parties. Britain, like most other democracies, lacks a primary system to select candidates, as in the United States; the national parties work with the formal party members in each constituency to select candidates and determine the strategies of election campaigns. Once elected, members of Parliament (MPs) are party loyalists in policy debates and in their parliamentary votes.

Another feature of parliamentary systems is the emphasis on the party rather than on individual politicians. British voters do not cast a vote for the chief executive (the prime minister) the way Americans vote for president. Under its parliamentary system, the party group that controls Parliament elects the prime minister, who heads the executive branch. Other party deputies in Parliament simultaneously hold jobs in the executive branch as ministers or junior ministers. Even when it comes to electing a local district representative, British voters choose a party, often without knowing much about the candidates who represents the parties in the district. The British political system follows a model of strong party government.

The German party system is even more diverse. The electoral system is based on proportional representation (PR): a party's share of the votes ultimately determines its share of the seats in Parliament.[4] As a result, Germany has a multiparty system, with two major parties and several smaller parties. The Christian Democrats (CDU/CSU) are the major conservative party. Reflecting regional traditions, the CDU runs in fifteen German states and the Christian Social Union (CSU) exists only in Bavaria. The Social Democrats (SPD) are the major leftist party. A multiparty system means that all German governments are a coalition of parties. The CDU/CSU government for the first two decades of the Federal Republic (1949–69), 1982 to 1998, and now since the 2005 election. The SPD controlled coalition governments from 1969 until 1982, 1998 to 2005, and was part of the grand coalition with the CDU/CSU (2005–09).

The small Free Democratic Party (FDP) is the oldest of the smaller parties. It captures between 5 percent and 10 percent of the vote and has been a junior coalition partner in governments headed by both the CDU/CSU and the SPD. The Greens emerged on the partisan stage in the 1980s as an advocate of New Politics causes. For example, when they were part of the 1998–2005 SPD/Green government they initiated many new green policies.

German unification in 1990 further changed the political landscape, adding millions of new voters from the East. The Party of Democratic Socialism (PDS) was the successor to the Communist Party of the German Democratic

Republic. In 2005 the PDS allied itself with a group of former SPD and leftists in the West and evolved into the new Linke Party. The party won seventy-six seats in the 2009 elections. Germany has several small parties on the extreme right, such as the Republikaner, and the National Democratic Party, that advocate nationalist and antiforeigner sentiments. None of them has won seats in the national Parliament, but their presence affects the country's political debate. There is also speculation that the new Pirate Party, which formed around the issue of Internet privacy, may win seats in the 2013 parliamentary elections.

The German political system emphasizes the role of political parties to a greater degree than does the U.S. system. Parties control the candidate selection process. In Bundestag elections, the voter casts two votes. The first vote (*Erststimme*) is for a district candidate who is nominated by a small group of official party members or by a committee appointed by the membership (not through a primary election). The second vote (*Zweitstimme*) is directly for a party, which determines half the Bundestag deputies from lists created by the parties. The government finances the parties' election campaigns, and access to media election advertising is allocated to the parties rather than the candidates. Government funding for the parties continues between elections to help them perform their educational functions as prescribed in the constitution. Parties organize the activities of Parliament and the majority selects the chancellor to head the executive branch. Therefore, it is not surprising to hear Germany sometimes described as a system of "party government."

France has an even more highly fragmented multiparty system. The two-tour electoral system allows many parties to run for office and win seats. Instead of one party on the left, there are several: the Communist Party (PC), the Socialist Party (PS), and various smaller extreme leftist parties. Instead of one major party on the right, there are several: the Union for a Popular Movement (UMP, formerly the Rally for the Republic, or RPR), represents the Gaullist tradition. The Democratic Movement (MoDem) is the successor to the Union for French Democracy (UDF); it has a center-right position. During the 1980s the National Front (FN) emerged as an extreme right-wing party that attracts nationalist voters and those opposed to foreign immigrants. The party was originally led by a retired French general, but now his telegenic daughter is party leader. An environmental party was born in the early 1980s. It is now called the Greens (*Verts*) and attracts some support from young, postmaterial voters. Added to this mix are miscellaneous small centrist or extremist parties. After the 2012 election, more than a dozen party groups are represented in the Parliament, and many more ran for office.

The electoral history of the Fifth Republic is one of party change and electoral volatility. The Gaullists were originally the major party on the right and participated in conservative governments for the first two decades of the Fifth Republic. The tide shifted to the left and the Socialists won the presidency and a legislative majority in the 1981 elections. The conservatives controlled the Parliament from 1986 to 1988, and then a leftist majority reestablished itself. The conservatives swept the parliamentary elections of 1993, and then a Socialist/Green/PCF majority formed after the 1997 elections. A conservative majority won the 2002 legislative elections and control of Parliament and presidency in 2007, only to be replaced by a Socialist president and National Assembly majority in 2012. Along the way, a variety of smaller parties have come (and gone). In short, the French party system is exceptionally fluid.

It is difficult to describe the French system as an example of responsible party government. On the one hand, the French party system gives voters greater ideological choice than is available to American, British, or German voters. The parties exert their influence over the political campaigns and the activities of the parliament. On the other hand, the fragmentation of the party system often requires coalition politics, wherein several parties must negotiate and compromise on their programs. This process weakens the chain of party responsibility that exists in the British or German governments. Moreover, it is often the party leader, rather than the national party organization, who defines a party's goals and strategies. In addition, the number and names of parties are continually changing.[5] The French party system could be characterized as a party system in continual transition.

The Structure of Political Alignments

Most political parties are still focused on the traditional political conflicts and issues described by Lipset and Rokkan—which we can describe as the Old Politics cleavage that pits the Old Left coalition against the Old Right. Lipset and Rokkan considered social class to be the primary factor of the Old Politics cleavage because economic and class-based issues formed the identity of many parties. The Old Left represented by many social democratic or labor parties identifies itself with the working class and labor unions, as well as with secular groups and urban interests. The Old Right is synonymous with business interests and the middle class. When political issues tap the concerns of the Old Politics cleavage—for example, wages, employment programs, or social security programs—class characteristics are strongly related to voting preferences.

Another element of the Old Politics is conflict over religious or moral issues. Many Western democracies still face conflicts over the relationship between church and state. Sometimes this cleavage separates Catholics and Protestants who have different views on these matters. At other times, the cleavage divides secular and religious voters. Indeed, several European party systems feature Christian or Christian Democratic parties as major actors on the right.

The New Politics dimension involves conflict over issues such as environmental quality, alternative lifestyles, minority rights, social equality, and other postmaterial issues (Kriesi et al. 2008; Kitschelt 1994). On one side of this cleavage are proponents of these issues, the New Left that is largely comprised by Green and social liberal parties. On the other side are citizens who feel threatened by these issues, the New Right, such as the French National Front or the small extreme parties in other nations.

The Old Politics cleavage is likely to remain the primary basis of partisan conflict in most advanced industrial democracies for the near future. The New Politics dimension is significantly affecting these party systems, however, because it can cut across the established Old Politics cleavage. Despite their economic differences, labor unions and business interests typically support nuclear energy. Farmers and students sometimes join together to oppose large development projects that may threaten the environment. Fundamentalist blue-collar and white-collar workers both oppose challenges to their moral code. The emergence of New Left and New Right interests may restructure social group alignments and party coalitions in new ways. In sum, the simple dichotomy between Old Left and Old Right no longer adequately describes patterns of political competition. The contemporary political space is now better described by at least two dimensions (or more).[6]

We can illustrate the separation of the Old Politics and New Politics cleavages with examples drawn from the United States. For much of the past century, the Old Politics cleavages structured party competition in the U.S. party system. The New Deal coalition created by President Franklin Roosevelt in the 1930s determined the social bases of party support: the Democratic Party and its working-class supporters against the Republicans and big business. The formal separation of church and state muted religious differences in America.

Beginning in the 1960–70s, student protesters, the women's movement, and other groups challenged the symbols of the political establishment. Herbert Weisberg and Jerold Rusk (1970) described how this cultural conflict generated a new cleavage, as represented by dissident Democratic presidential candidates such as George McGovern and Gary Hart in the 1980s. These researchers found, however, that Democrats and Republicans were not clearly aligned on New Politics issues, which divided parties internally rather than separating them politically.

The policies of the Reagan and George H. W. Bush administrations (1981–93) stimulated a convergence of Old Politics and New Politics alignments. The Reagan administration's taxing and spending priorities sharply favored business and the more affluent sectors of society, which reinforced ties between business interests and the Republican Party. Furthermore, the Reagan administration pursued a conservative social agenda and developed political links to fundamentalist Christian groups.

The Reagan–Bush administrations also clarified party positions on the New Politics agenda. The Republican Party previously had supported some environmental issues; President Richard Nixon created the Environmental Protection Agency and introduced a variety of environmental legislation. However, the Reagan–Bush administrations were critical of the environmental movement and thwarted further environmental reform. In addition, these two administrations were openly antagonistic toward feminist groups. The abortion issue became a litmus test of Republican values in the appointment of federal judges and the selection of candidates.

As the Republicans grew more critical of the New Politics agenda, the Democrats became advocates of these same causes. The Democrats supported environmental reform and stronger environmental protection standards. Bill Clinton (1993–2001) attempted to unite the old constituency of labor unions and the new constituency of environmentalists and feminists. Al Gore focused on environmental issues in his bid for the presidency in 2000.

Meanwhile, the Republican Party united its traditional middle-class and business supporters with its new voters among cultural conservatives. George W. Bush moved even further to strengthen the conservative identity of the Republican Party, especially on social issues such as abortion, stem cell research, and gay rights. Since 1980 the American party system has experienced a clear polarization of the political parties.

We can illustrate the current social and partisan alignments with data from the 2008 American National Election Study. The survey asked respondents whether they felt close or distant to a set of sociopolitical groups and the political parties.[7] I used a statistical analysis method to map the sociopolitical space as perceived by Americans.[8] When there is a strong similarity in how people evaluate two groups, they are located near each other in the space. When people evaluate groups in dissimilar terms, the groups are positioned a distance apart. Figure 7.1 charts the political map that voters use to place themselves in relation to social groups and political parties.

The figure depicts the American sociopolitical space in 2008. The traditional Left/Right cleavage of the Old Politics is quite evident as the horizontal dimension in the figure. Barack Obama is located at the left, along with his running mate, Joe Biden. Both politicians are seen as closest to the labor unions among all the groups in the figure. In contrast, John McCain is located at the right end of the continuum, with Sarah Palin even further to the right. The nearest groups to the Republican standard bearers are big business and Christian fundamentalists. This horizontal Left/Right dimension reflects the polarization of parties and their leaders, and the continuing relevance of the class cleavage to partisan politics.

The figure also maps the position of other groups in this space. New Left groups, including feminists and environmentalists, are seen as closer to Obama and the Democrats. The positioning of these New Left groups near the Democrats, and the Christian fundamentalists near the Republicans, may indicate the integration of cultural issues into American party politics.[9] Thus, the vertical dimension in this space contrasts attitudes toward gays, feminists and liberals at one end versus Christian fundamentalists (and Catholics) at the other. Gays and lesbian rights has become the current marker for cultural clashes on moral issues—and it shows in this figure. And interestingly, the ethnic and racial groups that lean toward the Democrats

Figure 7.1	The Sociopolitical Space

In addition to traditional economic Left/Right dimension, there is a cultural dimension to group alignments.

Source: 2008 American National Election Study.

Note: The figure presents a mapping of groups in the political space; similarly evaluated groups are located near each other, and dissimilar groups are at a greater distance in the space. The map is based on multidimensional scaling of thermometer scores (see note 8).

along the horizontal dimension lean toward the conservatives on the cultural dimensions.

Comparable maps of the sociopolitical space in Britain, Germany, and France are not available, but other evidence suggests similar patterns exist in these nations. For example, Hanspeter Kriesi and his colleagues (2008) examined the political spaces in several European nations based on issue questions in election studies and their coding of the parties' campaign statements. They argue that the political space is increasingly defined by a traditional Left–Right economic dimension and sociocultural dimension defined by attitudes toward immigrants, European integration, environmentalism, and cultural liberalism. They further maintain that the cultural dimension is becoming more important than the traditional economic dimension as a basis of party differentiation and voting choice. Equally intriguing, Kriesi et al. link the sociocultural dimension to the effects of globalization, such as increased immigration into Europe because of economic globalization.

Another way to compare the relative positions of political parties is to ask academic experts to position the parties in their nation along a set of policy dimensions (Benoit and Laver 2006). The party positions can then be compared across nations and across issues.

Figure 7.2 presents party positions in the early 2000s on two policies: maintaining social spending versus tax cuts as a measure of the socioeconomic issues of the Old Politics, and environmental protection versus economic growth as a measure of New Politics issues. The dots in the figure represent individual parties in each of the eighteen established democracies in the Benoit/Laver study. The major parties in our four nations are denoted by the parties' initials in the figure (see table 7.1).[10]

Figure 7.2	Economics and the Environment

Party positions on services and taxes are only partially linked to their environmental positions, especially for leftist parties.

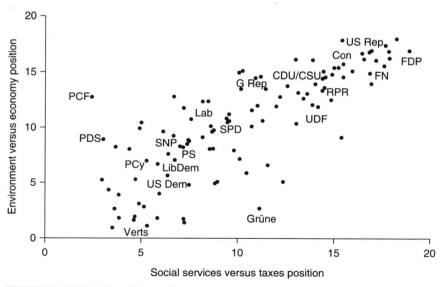

Source: Party positions from Benoit and Laver (2006); parties from eighteen advanced industrial democracies are included in the figure.

Note: The figure presents the position of political parties on both policy dimensions as determined by a panel of experts. Party abbreviations are listed in table 7.2.

The horizontal axis in the figure locates parties on the social spending versus tax cut issue as an example of the traditional Old Politics alignment.[11] The furthest left party is the French Communist Party (PCF) and the post-Communist PDS in Germany, which strongly favor raising taxes to increase social services. At the opposite end of the Old Politics dimension are parties that favor reducing social services to cut taxes, such as the British Conservatives and the American Republican Party.

The vertical dimension displays a party's position on protecting the environment versus supporting economic growth even at a cost to the environment—a New Politics cleavage. The French Greens (*Verts*) and German Greens (*Grünen*) are strong advocates of the former position. In contrast, the opposition includes a diverse mix of liberal parties (PCF and British Labour) and conservative parties (the CDU/CSU, British Conservatives, and U.S. Republicans).

This figure thus illustrates the diversity of party choice in each system (Dalton 2009b). The French party system offers a wide spread of parties, from the Greens to the Front National, with a range parties in between or holding a different mix of positions. The German party system also covers a wide span of this political space, from the PDS to the FDP, with the Greens advocating a distinct environmental option. The fluidity of contemporary party systems is perhaps best illustrated by the British parties. In the late 1990s Tony Blair consciously moved the Labour Party to the ideological center to attract more voters, and his efforts are apparent by the party's location in the figure. The Labour Party was outflanked on both the Old Left and New Left by the Liberal Democrats, as well as the Scottish National Party and Plaid Cymru. A generation ago (and perhaps since the 2010 election), the British party system would have displayed sharp polarization along the social spending/tax cut dimension, with Labourites at one pole, Conservatives at the other, and Liberals in the middle.

The two American parties display a wide separation in this political space. Experts position the Democrats as favoring more social services and more strongly supporting the environment than the major leftist parties in Britain, France, and Germany. Conversely, the Republicans are perceived as one of the most conservative parties on both dimensions and are located at the upper right of the figure. I suspect this polarization is an overstatement, reflecting the growth in party differentiation during the preceding decade and heightened political tensions between parties starting during the George W. Bush administration. With only two parties, there is a tendency to locate one at one pole and the other at the opposite end. American political parties have become more distinct, but perhaps not as much as suggested by the figure.[12]

In addition to economic and environmental policies, social or moral issues also divide parties. These issues reflect the persistence political influence of religion that is often expressed in terms of gender rights and lifestyle choices; they also tap the libertarian tendency of postmaterialists. Therefore, we mapped party positions with services versus tax cuts on the horizontal axis and positions on social policies on the vertical axis (figure 7.3). The social policy dimension taps positions on issues such as abortion, homosexuality, and euthanasia.[13] Parties have the same position on the social services/tax cut dimension as in figure 7.2, but now one sees a different alignment on the social policy dimension. Parties of the economic left also hold fairly liberal positions on social issues, clustering at the bottom left of the figure. However, social issues create divisions within economically conservative parties. For example, the German FDP is strongly conservative on the economic dimension but distinctly liberal on social policy issues. So-called New Right parties, such as the German Republikaner and French National Front, hold distinctly conservative views on the social issues, even to the right of the German Christian Democrats. So just as environmentalism causes divisions among the economic left, social policy issues cause divisions within the economic right.

The experts again see a stark policy separation between Democrats and Republicans in the United States. They view the Democrats as holding a

| Figure 7.3 | Economics and Social Policy |

Party positions on services versus taxes are only partially linked to their position on social policies, especially for rightist parties.

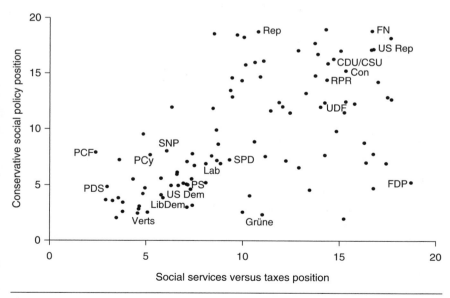

Source: Party positions from Benoit and Laver (2006); parties from eighteen advanced industrial democracies are included in the figure.

Note: The figure presents the position of political parties on both policy dimensions as determined by a panel of experts. Party abbreviations are listed in table 7.2.

liberal position on social issues such as abortion and homosexual rights. Conversely, the Republicans have become more conservative on social issues since the 1980s, and especially during the George W. Bush administration. This party cleavage also appears in figure 7.1, in which the public locates the Christian fundamentalists as closer to McCain and Palin. In the United States, the alignment of the two parties is now similar on both Old Politics and New Politics dimensions.

If Old Politics issues, such as government social spending, were the only source of electoral competition, then Lipset and Rokkan would still be correct in describing contemporary party systems in terms of the cleavages of the 1920s. The class-based Left/Right party alignment that historically structured partisan politics remains clearly visible in political experts' positioning of the contemporary parties on the social services versus tax cut dimension.

The content of the political agenda, however, now includes New Politics issues that can produce a different party alignment. For instance, the German Greens are a strong advocate for environmental causes and are located at the far left end of this continuum (see figure 7.2). The Social Democrats are closer to the conservative CDU/CSU on the environmental dimension than they are to the Greens. The environmental dimension separates the Greens and other New Left parties from *all* the other parties.

In addition, social issues (such as homosexual rights), and controversies over immigration and international issues (such as globalization, international trade, or conflict in the Middle East) introduce more variability into party alignments (Benoit and Laver 2006). Instead of a single Old Politics cleavage to structure electoral competition, parties are asked to take positions on potentially contradictory issues, which generate greater complexity and fluidity to contemporary electoral politics. The mix of these old and new dimensions fuels the current processes of electoral change in these nations.

Party Systems Today

Germany is about the last place you would expect to find pirates, but in 2009 a newly formed Pirate Party ran in the Bundestag elections and received 2 percent of the vote. In 2011 the Pirates garnered 8.9 percent of the vote in Berlin elections and elected fifteen deputies into the Berlin Senate. By the end of 2012, they held seats in four state parliaments, and they seemed on course to enter the Bundestag after the 2013 elections. Suddenly there are a lot of Germans sporting eye patches and growling "Argh."

The German Pirate Party follows the course first set by the Pirate Party in Sweden (Miegel and Olsson 2008). In the mid-2000s the Swedish government began to take action against websites that facilitated BitTorrent file sharing of music, video, and other files, especially *Pirate Bay*. This led to the formation of the Swedish and German Pirate Parties in 2006. The Pirates advocate open file sharing on the Internet, protection of privacy on the Web, reforms of copyright and patent laws to reflect the new information age, more transparency in government, and a set of other issues.[14]

On a small scale, the Pirate's experience reflects the points made in this chapter. The development of the Internet and new technology—like the earlier social changes described by Lipset and Rokkan—created new issues of privacy and the applicability of patent and copyright laws. A distinct group of people is interested in these issues—mostly young, better-educated computer users—but the established parties were unresponsive. To have an impact on the political debate, a cadre of young techies felt it was necessary to form a political party and participate in the electoral process. (As Green parties had learned in the 1980s, it was much easier to influence policymaking if you could participate as a political party.) The Pirate Party remains on the fringes of German and Swedish politics, but they are affecting discussions of these issues and prodded the other parties to address their positions. The German party has also introduced an intriguing new tool of online deliberative democracy (LiquidFeedback) to engage their members in discussing issues and guiding party leaders. Like other political parties in the past, the Pirate parties formed to represent citizens in public debates, perhaps win seats in elections, and influence public policy.

This chapter has similarly described the foundations and characteristics of political parties across the four nations of this book. Most of the established political parties still represent the Old Politics divisions of class and religion. Even if these cleavages have become less salient, the political ties between social groups and political parties perpetuate this framework. Parties are, after all, still turning to the same interest groups and associations for the core of their support. Contemporary publics see rightist parties as linked to business interests (and sometimes church groups) and leftist parties as allied with the labor unions.

The New Politics cleavage is another important cleavage affecting political parties. Contemporary publics are developing postmaterial values that lead to new policy interests (chapters 5 and 6). Greens, social liberals, and other parties now represent New Politics concerns. These small parties draw their support from the young, the better educated, and postmaterialists—the groups that define the New Politics cleavage. In contrast, New Right parties in many Western nations advocate conservative social values, social order, and often a criticism of immigration and minority politics. In Europe, the issues of the European Union inject other controversies into elections and the party systems of these nations.

Some established parties are trying to combine Old Left and New Left issue appeals into a single program, although such a coalition is difficult to maintain because of contrasting interests. Unions that would be pleased with a socialist party's position on social services might be displeased by pro-environmental policies that would threaten employment. Similarly, some conservative parties have attempted to appeal to both Old Right groups on economic issues and New Right groups on social issues and have experienced the same tensions in pulling this coalition together.

Consequently, many established parties have been slow to formalize close ties to groups advocating these new issues, especially in Western Europe, where the Old Politics ties remain strong. Parties are naturally cautious about taking clear stands on a new dimension of conflict before the costs and benefits are clear.

The 2012 U.S. presidential election illustrated these multiple dimensions of electoral competition within and between the parties. Mitt Romney began the campaign with close ties to the fiscal conservatives in the Republican Party but limited support among many social conservatives. Social conservatives gravitated toward Rick Santorum and others. Ron Paul maintained a small but dedicated core of libertarian Republicans. Divisions also existed within the Democratic primaries in 2008. John Edwards and Hillary Clinton had strong ties to labor, and Hillary drew support from women's groups. Barack Obama appealed to younger postmaterial voters, minorities, and a politically cynical middle class. Electoral politics has fragmented into a fluid, multidimensional issue space that goes beyond the broad framework of Old Politics and New Politics cleavages, as seen in the Pirate Party example.

Because of the uncertainties facing the parties and the difficulties in integrating new political cleavages into the existing party systems, future partisan change is likely in most established democracies. Continuing changes in citizen values and issue interests mean that the potential for further partisan change is real.

Suggested Readings

Benoit, Kenneth, and Michael Laver. 2006. *Party Policy in Modern Democracies*. New York: Routledge.

Dalton, Russell, David Farrell, and Ian McAllister. 2011. *Political Parties and Democratic Linkage: How Parties Organize Democracy*. Oxford, UK: Oxford University Press.

Eijk, Cees van der, and Mark Franklin. 2009. *Elections and Voters*. London: Palgrave Macmillan.

Farrell, David. 2011. *Electoral Systems: A Comparative Introduction*. London: Palgrave Macmillan.

Kriesi, Hanspeter, et al. 2008. *West European Politics in the Age of Globalization*. Cambridge, UK: Cambridge University Press.

LeDuc, Lawrence, Richard Niemi, and Pippa Norris, eds. 2010. *Comparing Democracies 3: Elections and Voting in the 21st Century*. 3rd ed. Thousand Oaks, CA: Sage.

Lijphart, Arend. 2008. *Thinking about Democracy: Power Sharing and Majority Rule in Theory and Practice*. London: Routledge.

Luther, Richard, and Ferdinand Mueller-Rommel, eds. 2002. *Party Change in Europe*. Oxford, UK: Oxford University Press.

Webb, Paul, David Farrell, and Ian Holliday, eds. 2002. *Political Parties in Advanced Industrial Democracies*. Oxford, UK: Oxford University Press.

Notes

1. There are several good analytic studies of recent American elections (Abramson, Aldrich, and Rohde 2010), British elections (Clarke et al. 2008, 2012), German elections (Langenbacher 2010), and French elections (Cautres and Muxel 2011).
2. We calculated vote share based on the most recent national election: United States (2012), Britain (2010), Germany (2009), and France (2012). The computation of years in government is complicated by the separation of powers in the United States and France. We counted the number of years a party was part of the legislative majority between 1977 and 2012 as the most comparable cross-national statistic.
3. Because of the single-member-district electoral system, the Liberal Democrats are routinely disadvantaged in winning seats in Parliament. In 2010, for example, the party won 23 percent of the popular vote nationwide but only 8 percent of the seats in the House of Commons.
4. German electoral law requires that a party win 5 percent of the national vote on the second ballot, or three district seats, in order to share in the proportional distribution of Bundestag seats.
5. Only the communists have retained the same party name since the formation of the Fifth Republic in 1958. All other parties have undergone multiple name changes, fragmentation, or merger with other parties. For instance, in virtually every edition of this book the lineup of major French parties has changed.
6. Although this chapter presents new alignments in the two dimensions of the Old Politics and New Politics, it is more accurate to describe party systems as moving from simple structures of one or two dimensions to a fragmented structure of many dimensions.
7. These are the so-called feeling thermometer questions that measure positive and negative feelings toward each object. Respondents are given a thermometer-like scale to measure their "warmth" or "coldness" toward each group.
8. I used a multidimensional scaling program to estimate a sociopolitical space based on the feeling thermometers; I rotated the space so the Obama–McCain dimension was aligned horizontally in the scale. For earlier analyses of similar sociopolitical spaces, see Barnes, Kaase, et al. (1979); Inglehart (1984); and previous editions of this text.
9. Ideally, what is needed is a tracking of sociopolitical alignments over time to see if there has been a systematic change in the Democrats' and Republicans' electoral alliances.

10. The figure includes parties from Australia, Austria, Belgium, Britain, Canada, Denmark, Finland, France, Germany, Ireland, Italy, Japan, Netherlands, New Zealand, Norway, Spain, Sweden, and the United States. Instead of the new Democratic Movement we plot its predecessor, the Union for French Democracy, and we plot the German PDS as the predecessor of the Linke.

11. The services/taxes dimension ranges from (1) promotes raising taxes to increase public services, to (20) promotes cutting public services to cut taxes. The environment dimension ranges from (1) supports protection of the environment, even at the cost of economic growth, to (20) supports economic growth, even at the cost of damage to the environment.

12. See the voters' own left/right placement of the parties in chapter 10 (figure 10.2).

13. The social dimension ranges from (1) favors liberal policies on matters such as abortion, homosexuality, and euthanasia, to (20) opposes liberal policies on matters such as abortion, homosexuality, and euthanasia.

14. The unconventional party's unconventional platform is available online: https://wiki.piratenpartei.de/Parteiprogramm/en.

8 The Social Bases of Party Support

E lections attract attention from political scientists for several reasons. Obviously, democracy can't exist without free and fair elections. Elections also involve most of the public, so we can study how most people make political decisions. Voting provides an opportunity to determine how political attitudes influence behavior—the casting of a ballot. Because people are making a voting decision, choices are likely to be relatively well thought out, intelligible, and predictable. Elections are therefore a good setting for studying political thoughts and behavior beyond a simple response to a public opinion survey. If there is one political act that provides a window into the minds of citizens, it is voting.

In addition, voting behavior reflects the changing patterns of citizen politics described in this book. A different calculus of voting existed in the 1950s and 1960s, when most elections began with the outcomes already decided for most voters. A few decades ago, the large majority of voters relied on long-term predispositions derived from their social positions or partisan loyalties. This chapter and the next describe these predispositions. We also describe how these factors are weakening as influences on voting choice. In the new style of citizen politics, more voters make their decisions during campaigns based on their views of the candidates and issues of the day.

How people reach their voting choice tells us a great deal about how we should interpret elections—are these policy-centered debates or reliance on habitual loyalties? The reliance on social group cues also illustrates what social cleavages are important in a nation, and thus what elections are deciding—is a nation focused on economic issues or cultural issues? And the reliance on group characteristics provides valuable information on the quality of citizenship in contemporary democracies.

┤ **Internet Resource** ├

Visit the national election websites for data, resources, and bibliographies:

United States: http://www.electionstudies.org
Britain: http://www.bes2009–10.org
Germany: http://www.gles.eu/index.en.htm

The Social Group Model of Voting

The setting in Marienplatz, Munich's central town square, is always the same the weekend before the national elections. The various political parties have information booths to convince people to vote for their party. Labor union members and their families typically staff the booth for the Social Democratic Party. Members from Catholic auxiliary groups are common at the Christian Social Union booth. The Free Democratic Party is often represented by young professionals or older businesspeople. And the Greens typically have shaggy environmentalists handing out party information. If the Pirate Party runs in 2013, it will be interesting to see whether they have a booth staffed by young techies, or maybe just a touch screen. This linkage between social groups and political parties is a common feature of democratic elections.

From its beginnings, electoral research has stressed social group attachments as important influences on voting choice. Social groups represent the distinct social interests—such as between different class or religious groups—discussed in chapter 7, and elections are a way to resolve these different interests. One of the first empirical studies of American voting focused on the social bases of partisanship (Lazarsfeld, Berelson, and Gaudet 1948). This study found that the *Index of Political Predispositions*, based on social class, religion, and rural/urban residence, strongly predicted voting choice. Social stratification is greater in Europe than in the United States, producing sharper group differences in voting patterns. Class historically structured the British party system; class and religion are strong correlates of voting in France and Germany.

Social characteristics such as class and religion can influence a voter's electoral choice in several ways. First, one's social position often indicates his or her values and political beliefs. A French steelworker is more likely than a shopkeeper, for example, to favor an expansion of social services or government regulation of business. Opposition to liberal abortion laws is more likely among Christian fundamentalists than among the nonreligious. Social characteristics indirectly reflect the attitudinal differences between groups of voters and their perceptions of which party best represents their policy positions.

Second, a person's social characteristics reflect some of the political cues to which he or she is exposed. A British mineworker may hear about politics from his coworkers or other working-class neighbors and friends, and he receives political information from the union representative at work and from union publications at home. His working-class environment provides repeated cues on which policies will benefit people like him and which party best represents his interests; these cues inevitably convey a strong Labour Party bias. A Bavarian Catholic hears about political issues at weekly church services, from Catholic social groups, and from predominately conservative Catholic friends; this information generally encourages a favorable opinion of the Christian Social Union and its program.

Third, social groups can be important in orienting voters to political issues and providing information about politics. Even if they are not members of a labor union or regular churchgoers, the knowledge that unions favor one party and the Catholic Church another can help voters locate themselves in relation to the parties. Social networks and group–party ties provide cues that guide many people's political attitudes and voting choices.

Reliance on social group cues is an example of the "satisficing" decision-making model described in chapter 2. Social cues can narrow voters' choices to parties that are consistent with their social positions. Voters therefore face an election favoring the party (or parties) that historically supports the class or religious groups to which they belong, while excluding parties with unsupportive records. Political parties nurture such ties, communicating their group loyalties to the voters by calling themselves "Labour" or "Christian Democrats."

Many voters decide between competing parties based on cues that social groups provide—the endorsements of labor unions, business associations, religious groups, and the like—as well as the parties' appeals to these groups. In most cases, this process produces reasonable voting choices, even if the voter is not fully informed on all the relevant issues. When British industrial workers cast their votes for Labour because the party represents people like themselves, they are making a reasonable choice.

Reliance on social characteristics is a shortcut in making voting decisions. A very knowledgeable citizen is well prepared to make an informed voting choice and to justify this decision in issue-oriented and ideological terms. Social characteristics provide a simpler, although less certain, method of choosing which party represents one's interests. Still, when strong social group identities are matched with clear party positions on these social cleavages, as in most European nations, social characteristics can provide meaningful guides for voting choice.

Social Class and the Vote

In the 1960s a British political scientist penned the now well-known saying that "class is the basis of British party politics, all else is embellishment and detail." Class politics taps the essence of what we have described as the Old Politics—an economic conflict between the haves and the have-nots.

Class issues reflect the problems industrial societies face in reaching their economic and material goals: improving standards of living, providing economic security, and ensuring a just distribution of economic rewards. Issues such as unemployment, inflation, social services, tax policies, and government management of the economy reinforce class divisions.

Social scientists have probably devoted more attention to the relationship between social class and voting than to any other social characteristic. In theory, the class cleavage involves some of the most basic questions of power and politics that evolve from Marxist and capitalist views of societal development. Historically, one's position in the class structure has been a strong predictor of voting choice. Seymour Martin Lipset's early cross-national study of voting described the class cleavage as one of the most pervasive bases of party support:

> Even though many parties renounce the principle of class conflict or loyalty, an analysis of their appeals and their support suggests that they do represent the interests of different classes. On a world scale, the principal generalization that can be made is that parties are primarily based on either the lower classes or the middle and upper classes. (1981, 230)

Even modern elections are often framed in terms of potential "class warfare" or the 1 percent versus the 99 percent. Class conflict still seems important to party politics.

Research normally defines social class in terms of occupation. Following Karl Marx's writings, occupations are classified based on their relationship to the means of production. The bourgeoisie are the self-employed and the owners of capital; and the workers who sell their labor to live are the proletariat. This framework is then generalized to define two large social groupings: the middle class and the working class. Socialist and Communist parties initially formed to represent the interests of the working class; conservative parties, in turn, defend the interests of the middle class.

This Marxist dichotomy once defined the class cleavage, but the changing nature of advanced industrial societies has reshaped the class structure. The traditional bourgeoisie and proletariat have been joined by what is variously described as "new middle class," "white-collar workers," or the "salatariat": salaried white-collar employees and civil servants. Richard Florida (2003) identified a special subset of the new middle class as "knowledge workers," those who make their livelihood on the creation and use of information and are typically the vanguard for New Politics views. Other research distinguishes between employment in profit-making businesses versus government or nonprofit organizations. All these examples represent the transformation of labor structures away from the Marxist dichotomy. Daniel Bell (1973) defined a postindustrial society as one in which most of the labor force holds positions in "new middle-class" positions; nearly all Western democracies met that definition by the 1980s.

The new middle class is an important addition to the class structure because it lacks a clear position in the traditional dichotomy between the working class and the bourgeoisie. The separation of management from capital ownership, the expansion of the service sector, and the growth of government (and nonprofit) employment creates a social stratum that does not conform to Marxist class analysis. The new middle class does not own capital as the old middle class did, and it differs in lifestyle from traditional blue-collar workers. Members of the new middle class seem relatively less interested in the economic conflicts of the Old Politics and relatively more attuned to the New Politics issues (see chapters 5 and 6). Consequently, the political identity of the new middle class differs from both the bourgeoisie and the proletariat. This leads to the question of how class groups vote in elections today.

Table 8.1 presents the voting preferences of these social classes in the most recent election for which we have data.[1] Historical class alignments persist in each nation. The working class gives disproportionate support to leftist parties, ranging from 48 percent voting for Labour in the 2010 British election to 58 percent voting Social Democratic (SPD), Greens, or Linke in the 2009 German election. At the other extreme, the old middle class is the bastion of support for conservative parties. But what is most striking is the changing shape of the labor force. Blue-collar workers were once a majority, but the development of a service economy and the de-industrialization produced by globalization has severely shrunk the size of the working class.

Today, the new middle class is now the largest group of voters and, more important, has ambiguous partisan preferences. It is normally located between the working class and the self-employed in its Left/Right voting preferences and disproportionately supports parties that represent a New Politics ideology, such as Green or New Left parties. The new middle class is a major contributor to the changing political alignments of advanced industrial democracies.[2]

Although social class can still influence voting choice, the impact of class cues has generally decreased since the mid-twentieth century (Knutsen 2006; Oskarson 2005). Figure 8.1 presents the long-term pattern of class voting. The figure presents the Alford index of class voting, which is the simple difference between the percentage of the working class voting for the Left and the percentage of the middle class (old and new) voting for the Left.[3]

The general trend in figure 8.1 is obvious: class differences have declined. The Alford index decreased dramatically in Britain and Germany during the past fifty years. The gap in leftist support between the working class and middle class was once 40 percent, but now it barely registers in double digits. Class voting follows an irregular decline in U.S. congressional elections; in recent elections the gap has been virtually non-existent despite the rhetoric of class conflict. Michael Lewis-Beck and his colleagues (2008, ch. 12) show that the erosion of class voting also occurs in U.S. presidential elections. Social class had a modest impact on

| Table 8.1 | Class and Vote |

Working-class voters still lean to the Left and old middle-class voters lean to the Right.

	WORKING CLASS	NEW MIDDLE CLASS	SELF-EMPLOYED
United States (2004)			
Democrats	56	55	48
Republicans	44	45	52
Total	100	100	100
Great Britain (2010)			
Labour	48	31	22
Liberal Democrats	14	25	26
Conservatives	27	37	47
Other parties	11	7	5
Total	100	100	100
France (2007)			
PCF	4	5	4
Socialists	40	39	17
Greens	7	7	4
MoDem	4	11	11
UMP	40	38	59
National Front	4	1	4
Total	99	101	99
Germany (2009)			
Linke	16	13	10
Greens	12	18	15
SPD	30	22	11
FDP	15	17	31
CDU/CSU	27	30	33
Total	100	100	100

Sources: United States, 2004 American National Election Study because ANES had not released occupation for 2008; Great Britain, 2010 British Election Study (Comparative Study of Electoral Systems [CSES]); France, 2007 Election Study (CSES); Germany, 2009 German Election Study (CSES).

Note: U.S. data are based on congressional vote; German data are for East and West electorates combined. Social class is based on occupation of the respondent.

voting during the French Fourth Republic (1946–58), but the turbulent events accompanying the formation of the Fifth Republic—including the creation of a broad-based Gaullist Party—abruptly lowered class voting

Figure 8.1	Class Voting Trends

The gap in Left/Right voting between the working class and middle class has narrowed substantially over time.

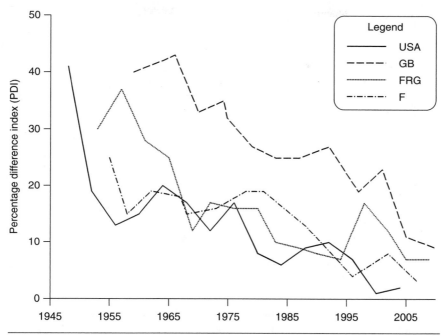

Sources: United States, 1948–2004, American National Election Studies (2008 occupation variable not yet coded by ANES); Great Britain, 1955, Heath et al. (1985); 1959, Civic Culture study; 1964–2010, British Election Studies; Germany, 1953–2009, German Elections Studies (Western Germany only, 1990–2005); France, 1955, MacRae (1967, 257); 1958, Converse and Dupeux survey; 1962, IFOP survey; 1967, Converse and Pierce survey; 1968, Inglehart survey; 1973–88, Eurobarometer; 1996 and 2002 ISSP, 2007 French Election Study.

Note: Figure entries are the Alford Class Voting index, that is, the percentage of the working class preferring a leftist party minus the percentage of the middle class voting for the Left. U.S. data are based on congressional elections, except for 1948, which is based on presidential vote.

in 1958. Since then class voting has generally trended downward in parliamentary and presidential elections (Boy and Mayer 1993; Lewis-Beck, Nadeau, and Bèlanger 2012).

Despite the evidence that class voting differences have narrowed, some researchers argue that new class alignments in advanced industrial societies are perpetuating class voting in new ways (see review in Knutsen 2006; Evans 1999, 2000; Manza and Brooks 1999; Wright 1997). Some scholars propose a class categorization that adds notions of job autonomy and authority relationships into traditional class criteria such as income level and manual labor. Others have created class categories that reflect new social contexts, such as the middle-class salatariat or affluent blue-collar workers. Researchers also explore criteria other than employment as potential new bases of cleavage, such as education separating the information-rich, technologically sophisticated voter from the information-poor, unskilled voter. Others maintain that conflicts between the public and private sectors are supplanting traditional class conflicts. And there are methodological debates on the statistics to measure class voting.

This reconceptualization of social class implies that social cues now function in more complex and differentiated ways than in the past. This is partially correct. Still, the empirical reality remains: even these new class frameworks have only a modest value in explaining how citizens vote. Harold Clarke and his colleagues (2004, ch. 3) used three different ways to estimate class voting in Britain from the 1960s to the 2001 election: all three methods trace a very similar downward trend. Other large cross-national studies showed that alternative statistical measures of class voting do not change these long-term trends across a large set of Western democracies (Nieuwbeerta 1995; Nieuwbeerta and de Graf 1999; Knutsen 2006).

Figure 8.2 presents a more elaborate measure of social class and places the current levels of class voting in our four nations in cross-national comparison. We examine the voting preferences of six class groups to allow for greater variation in the composition of the class structure.[4] The Cramer's V correlation measures the size of class voting differences among these class groups (see appendix A). Across six editions of *Citizen Politics*, we have followed the downward trend in class voting with such analyses. Today, class is only modestly related to vote choice. The greatest class polarization exists in Scandinavian countries, albeit at a lower level than in the past. Even with this more extensive measure of social class that includes multiple middle-class categories, the average level of class differences in these nations is quite modest (Cramer's V = .16).

In terms of our four core nations, British class differences once were fairly large, reflecting the importance of class interests in British politics—and the influence of class cues on voting. These differences have clearly moderated over time. Germany and France display modest levels of class voting, less than the cross-national average and smaller than in the past. Even with the heightened discussion of economic issues since the 2008 recession, the United States, Britain, France, and Germany all display modest class voting. In most elections the American two-party system blurs the influence of social class on voting choice, as both parties draw substantial parts of their support from across class lines.

Why Is Class Voting Decreasing?

David Butler and Donald Stokes (1969, 85–87) developed a framework to explain group-based voting that may help to identify the sources of declining

Figure 8.2	Class Voting Cross-Nationally

The correlation between social class and voting choice is now quite modest in most nations.

.30   Portugal

.20   Swiss
       Finland

       Norway/Sweden
       Netherlands/Austria
       Germany/Spain

       United States/Britain
       France
       New Zealand
       Ireland
       Japan/Iceland/Greece
.10   Australia

.00

Sources: United States, 2004 American National Election Study because ANES had not yet coded occupation for 2008; Comparative Study of Electoral Systems (module III); 2010 British Election Study.

Note: Figure entries are Cramer's V correlations measuring the relationship between social class and party preference.

class voting. They described group-based voting as a two-step process: voters are first linked to a social group, and then the group is linked to a political party. The combined strength of these two links determines the overall level of group-based voting. What has changed: the relationship between voters and class groupings or the relationship between class groupings and the political parties?

One possibility is that the changing class structure of contemporary societies may weaken the link between individuals and class groupings (Knutsen

2006, ch. 7). Members of the traditional social strata—industrial workers, farmers, and the self-employed—often remain integrated into class networks and remain distinct in their voting preferences. But the number of such voters has diminished, and labor unions have lost workers they might mobilize. The growth of the new middle class reduces the percentage of the public for whom traditional class ties are directly relevant.[5]

A general narrowing in the life conditions of social classes can also weaken the connection between individuals and their respective classes. On the one hand, spreading affluence leads to the *embourgeoisement* of some parts of the working class—some workers have incomes and living standards that overlap with those of the middle class. On the other hand, the expanding ranks of low-paid and low-status white-collar employees and the growth of white-collar unions are producing a *proletarianization* of part of the middle class. Fewer individuals now possess exclusively middle-class or working-class social characteristics, and the amount of class overlap has grown over time. In sum, a convergence of life conditions may contribute to the convergence of class voting patterns.

Social and occupational mobility also may weaken the link between individuals and traditional social classes. Each of the nations in this study has experienced a long-term decline in the number of farmers and blue-collar workers along with a rise in middle-class employment during the second half of the twentieth century. This social mobility means that an individual's ultimate social position is often different from that of his or her parents. Many farmers' children moved away from conservative political upbringings into unionized, working-class environments in the cities, just as many working-class children went from urban, leftist backgrounds into white-collar occupations that are traditionally conservative. Some socially mobile adults will change their class identity and voting behavior to conform to their new social contexts; others will not. This mix of social forces blurs traditional class alignments.

A second general explanation for the decline in class voting is the changing relationship between class groups and the political parties. During the latter half of the twentieth century, many leftist parties tried to broaden their electoral appeal to attract new middle-class voters. Socialist parties in Europe shed their Marxist programs and adopted more moderate domestic and foreign policy goals. Conservative parties also tempered their views and accepted the basic social programs proposed by the Left. Socialist parties vied for the votes of the new middle class, and conservative parties sought votes from the working class. Historical analyses of party programs show a general convergence of party positions on socioeconomic issues during the past half-century (Caul and Gray 2000). With smaller class-related differences in the parties' platforms, it seems only natural that class cues would become less important in guiding voting behavior.

Initially at least, this second theory appears to be a plausible explanation for the decline in class voting differences. However, various studies show that people still see distinct party differences in class leanings. A survey of political experts documented a clear awareness of the continuing party differences on the socioeconomic issues that underlie the class cleavage (Benoit and Laver 2006; also see chapter 7). Furthermore, Americans clearly perceive the partisan leanings of unions and business associations (figure 7.1). I earlier showed that social groups are often a basis of party evaluations (table 2.2). In short, it does not appear that people are unaware of the class voting cues that parties provide; instead, many voters are not simply relying on these cues.

In summary, the decline in class voting patterns is important for several reasons. First, it signals a change in the nature of political conflict. Even if elections still debate economic issues, these are not framed and evaluated in simple class terms (or nonclass issues have been added to the electoral mix). Parties that draw significant support across different social classes are less likely to advocate single-class interests if they enter the government. Second, these trends signal a change in how voters reach their decisions. The bonds linking voters to social classes are weakening, even while the political cues provided by traditional class groups (and parties) persist. Union members may understand that labor leaders want them to vote for leftist parties, but they are now more likely to make their own decisions. Other factors influence voting decisions. Third, social modernization implies that the long-term decline in class voting should continue.

Religion and the Vote

A person's religious identity inevitably shapes his or her values and political positions. The relationship between religion and parties arises from a centuries-old interplay of these two forces. As with the class cleavage, disagreements over religious issues structured conflict between different elite groups and defined the political alliances existing in the late nineteenth century. The political parties that formed during this period often allied themselves with specific religious interests: Catholic or Protestant, religious or secular. The party alignments at the start of the twentieth century institutionalized the religious cleavage, and many features of these party systems have endured to the present (Lipset and Rokkan 1967).

Early empirical research on voting behavior underscored the importance of the religious cleavage. Richard Rose and Derek Urwin's examination of the social bases of party support in sixteen Western democracies concluded that "religious divisions, not class, are the main social bases of parties in the Western world today" (1969, 12). Many contemporary political issues—abortion, homosexual rights, and moral standards—are often linked to religious values. And cultural conflicts and religious fundamentalism are reviving the importance of religion in the political world (Norris and Inglehart 2011; Putnam and Campbell 2010).

Measuring the impact of religious cues on voting behavior is more complex than the study of class voting. The class composition of most industrial democracies is similar, but their religious compositions are varied.

Britain is largely Protestant, and nearly two-thirds of the population is nominally Anglican. In contrast, about 80 percent of the French are baptized Catholics, and the Protestant and Muslim minorities are small. Germany has a mixed denominational system, with Lutheran Protestants slightly outnumbering Catholics. The United States lacks a dominant national religion and instead has significant numbers of Catholics, Reformation-era Protestants, Pietist Protestants, other Protestant and Christian groups, Jews, and the nonreligious.

In addition to the varied religious composition of nations, the partisan tendencies of religious denominations can vary. Catholics normally support parties on the Right, and Protestants normally support parties on the Left, but historical events have sometimes led to different religious alignments. For instance, Catholics in the United States and Britain have generally voted leftist because of historical experiences. In short, the voting cues provided by religious affiliation may differ across nations, in contrast to the consistent working-class/middle-class pattern.

As table 8.2 shows, the relationship between religious denomination and party support is often substantial, but each nation has a unique pattern. The historical conflict between the Catholic Church and the Liberal/Socialist parties still appears in Germany. The Christian Democratic Union (CDU/CSU) defends traditional values and the church's prerogatives. Consequently, a plurality (48 percent) of Catholics voted CDU/CSU in 2009, and this increased to 63 percent among Catholics who attend church weekly. In contrast, Protestants and the nonreligious give greater support to the leftist parties: SPD, Greens, and Linke.

The differences in voting behavior between French Catholics and non-Catholics are sizable. In 2007 only 26 percent of those without a religion favored conservative parties, compared to 55 percent among Catholics. But because the French public is overwhelmingly Catholic, the electoral impact of non-Catholics is modest.

In Britain, religious divisions follow another pattern. The Church of England historically allied itself with the political establishment, so Anglicans are more likely to vote for the Conservative Party. Catholics lean toward the Labour Party because of their minority status and the historical issue of Irish independence. Presbyterians usually support Labour and now the Scottish National Party (SNP).

Religious and moral conflicts are a recurring theme in American history (Wald 2003; Putnam and Campbell 2010); yet the formal separation of church and state moderates the impact of religion on partisan politics. Table 8.2 shows that the Reformation-era Protestant denominations (Anglicans, Calvinists, Lutherans, and so on) and Baptists predominately supported the Republican congressional candidates in 2008. These differences are modest, however, and may reflect factors other than religion per se. The slight Democratic leanings of American Catholics reflect the historical legacy of ethnic and class influences rather than explicitly religious values. Jewish Americans historically give disproportionate support to the Democrats, and they continued to do so in 2008.

| Table 8.2 | Religion and Vote |

Religious denomination influences voting preferences but in different ways across nations.

United States (2008)	No Religion	Catholic	Reformation Protestant	Baptist	Other Protestant	Jewish
Democrats	63	62	48	46	46	87
Republicans	37	38	52	54	54	13
Total	100	100	100	100	100	100

Great Britain (2010)	No Religion	Catholic	Anglican	Presbyterian
Labour	32	35	28	46
Liberal Democrats	27	24	17	14
Conservatives	32	35	48	18
Other parties	9	6	5	22
Total	100	100	100	100

France (2007)	No Religion	Catholic
PCF	11	3
Socialists	45	29
Greens	8	4
MoDem	10	9
UMP	24	53
National Front	2	2
Total	100	100

Germany (2009)	No Religion	Catholic	Protestant
Linke	25	6	10
Greens	13	7	16
SPD	24	21	27
FDP	14	18	16
CDU/CSU	25	48	31
Total	100	100	100

Sources: United States, 2008 American National Election Study; Great Britain, 2010 British Election Study; France, 2007 French Election Study (Comparative Study of Electoral Systems [CSES]); Germany, 2009 German Election Study (CSES).

Note: U.S. data are based on congressional vote; German data combines East and West electorates.

To see how our four core nations compare to other established democ-racies, the left side of figure 8.3 displays the levels of denomination-based voting across nations. Even in religiously divided societies, such as Germany, the Netherlands, and Switzerland, denominational differences are now quite modest. In essentially monodenominational societies, such as New Zealand, Finland, and Ireland, the correlation largely results from differences between religious voters (of all denominations) and those without any religious affilia-tion. The average correlation of religious denomination with party preferences is about the same as social class-based voting (Cramer's V = .16). In many nations religious matters are not explicitly discussed in elections, yet religion taps value orientations that provide a basis for voting choice for some citizens.

Figure 8.3	Religion and Vote Cross-Nationally

Religious denomination and church attendance have a modest influence on voting.

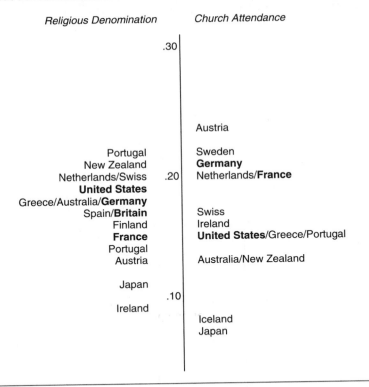

Religious Denomination	*Church Attendance*
.30	
	Austria
Portugal	Sweden
New Zealand	**Germany**
Netherlands/Swiss	.20	Netherlands/**France**
United States	
Greece/Australia/**Germany**	
Spain/**Britain**	Swiss
Finland	Ireland
France	**United States**/Greece/Portugal
Portugal	
Austria	Australia/New Zealand
Japan	
.10	
Ireland	
	Iceland
	Japan

Sources: Comparative Study of Electoral Systems (module III); 2010 British Election Study.

Note: Figure entries are Cramer's V correlations between religious denomination and vote choice on the Left, and church attendance and vote choice on the Right.

Another aspect of the religious cleavage is the influence of religiosity, such as church attendance or religious feelings separate from one's denomination. In predominately Catholic nations, such as France, this dimension represents a voter's integration into the Catholic culture. In mixed denominational systems, the secularization process has often stimulated an alliance between Protestants and Catholics in a joint defense of religious interests, and denominational differences are replaced by a secular/religious cleavage. In Germany the Christian Democratic Union unites active Catholics and Protestants against secular interests in society. In the United States, recent Republican Party candidates have actively sought the votes of religious conservatives of all denominations, even among social and ethnic groups that were traditionally affiliated with the Democratic Party.

Table 8.3 presents the relationship between religious involvement, measured by the frequency of attending religious services, and party preference. The voting gap between religious and nonreligious citizens is considerable in France and Germany (Lewis-Beck, Nadeau, and Bèlanger 2012; Elff and Rossteutscher 2011). Only 21 percent of French citizens who attended church weekly preferred the Socialist or Communist parties in 2007, compared to 61 percent among those who never went to church. Because of the Church of England's relationship to the government, religious conflicts have not been a major factor in British electoral politics since early in the twentieth century.

The role of religion in U.S. elections, especially in the most recent elections, has generated considerable discussion (Putnam and Campbell 2010; Layman 2001; Kohut et al. 2000). The Republican Party's appeal to Christian fundamentalists and the emphasis on cultural issues such as abortion and gay rights has seemingly brought religious issues to the fore. And yet, table 8.3 shows that frequent church attenders were only slightly more likely to vote for a Republican congressional candidate in 2008. Because of the many denominations and the complexity of religious attachments in America, it is an oversimplification to claim that religious beliefs exert a clear partisan influence in the United States. While white evangelicals may lean toward the Republican Party, very religious black and Hispanic voters support the Democrats. Many active Catholics support the Republican Party, but other active Catholics are lifelong Democrats.[6]

The right-hand side of figure 8.3 shows how nations compare in the impact of church attendance on voting choice. The secular/religious divide is often a stronger explanation of the vote than social class. In Sweden, for example, religion reflects continuing controversies over lifestyle issues, such as temperance and moral values. In other nations, the religious/secular cleavage is related to issues such as abortion, gay rights, or state support for religious schools (see chapter 6). Religion is a hidden agenda of politics, tapping differences in values and moral beliefs that might not be expressed in a campaign but nevertheless influence voter choices. Indeed, a variety of evidence indicates that moral or religious issues continue to divide the parties in many Western democracies.[7]

Table 8.3	Church Attendance and Vote		
Attending church regularly increases support for parties on the Right.			
	NEVER	OCCASIONALLY	WEEKLY
United States (2008)			
Democrats	58	61	44
Republicans	41	39	56
Total	100	100	100
Great Britain (2010)			
Labour	32	31	43
Liberal Democrats	24	17	17
Conservatives	35	44	34
Other parties	9	8	6
Total	100	100	100
France (2007)			
PCF	9	5	4
Socialists	52	34	17
Greens	10	5	2
MoDem	6	9	12
UMP	22	44	64
National Front	1	2	1
Total	100	99	101
Germany (2009)			
Linke	20	7	5
Greens	15	11	7
SPD	24	25	7
FDP	16	18	18
CDU/CSU	25	39	64
Total	100	100	101

Sources: United States, 2008 American National Election Study (CSES); Great Britain, 2010 British Election Study; France, 2007 French Election Study (CSES); Germany, 2009 German Election Study (CSES).

Note: U.S. data are based on congressional vote; German data are for East and West electorates combined.

Our analyses also underscore the diversity of religious voting patterns across the four core nations. Religious denomination and church attendance are somewhat related to voting preferences in Germany. The religious cleavage in France emphasizes the voting differences between practicing Catholics and the nonreligious. In Britain, we see only modest partisan differences by church attendance. The limited degree of religious voting in the United States illustrates the continued separation of church and state despite the attempts by some candidates to politicize religion. And in virtually all Western democracies the public is becoming more diverse in its religious orientations.

We might expect that social modernization would disrupt religious alignments in the same way it blurred social class lines. Changing lifestyles, and changing religious beliefs, have reduced involvement in church activities and lessened the church as a focus of social (and political) activities. Most Western nations display a steady decline in religious involvement over the past fifty years. In the Catholic nations of Europe, frequent church attendance has decreased by nearly half since the 1950s. Predominately Protestant countries, such as the United States and the nations of northern Europe, began with lower levels of church involvement but followed the same downward course. By definition, the trend toward secularization means that fewer voters are integrated into religious networks and exposed to the religious cues that can guide the vote.

At the same time, there are other reasons to expect the persistence of religious patterns in voting choice. As with social class, those who remain embedded in a distinct religious milieu may continue to use religion to guide their political choices. The rise of fundamentalist orientations among some church members may even intensify religious cues. In addition, many of the cultural issues debated in recent elections—abortion and gay rights in the United States or tensions with Muslim fundamentalists in Europe—may tap both religious values and postmaterial/material value cleavages. Some analysts argue that religiously based values stimulated the "culture wars" in American politics, which has overtaken class interests among some voters (Frank 2004; compare Bartels 2006). Thus, there is a continuing research debate on whether religious-based voting is waxing or waning in contemporary democracies (Knutsen 2004; Putnam and Campbell 2010; Layman 2001; Kohut et al. 2000).

To explore the possible decline in religious voting, figure 8.4 plots the correlation between religious denomination and voting preference across elections for our four core nations.[8] In the United States, the religious cleavage spiked with John F. Kennedy's candidacy in 1960 and debates on his Catholic faith. But other elections display weak religious voting with no clear trends. Despite the stress on religious voting blocs in recent American elections, there was a slight convergence in Protestant/Catholic voting in congressional elections before 2008. More refined measures of religion would show stronger correlations, but the impact of religion on citizens' voting choices is still muted compared to the rhetoric of campaigns and media commentary on American elections. Similarly, religious denomination has had only a minor impact on choices between the three main British parties. In recent elections the importance of religious denomination has reflected the increased support for the SNP among Presbyterians in Scotland.

The religious cleavage in western Germany has erratically trended downward since the 1960s, and in the East religious attachments are much weaker.[9] In 2009 the religious voting gap in Germany was less than half that of the 1961 election, despite the emergence of two new parties (Greens and Linke) that attract distinctly secular voters. Religion has had an enduring impact on voting preferences in France, with secular citizens supporting leftist parties and religious Catholics supporting conservative parties. By some measures religious voting has narrowed over time, but the evidence is not striking.

Figure 8.4	Religious Voting Trends

The impact of religious cues on vote are stable or decreasing.

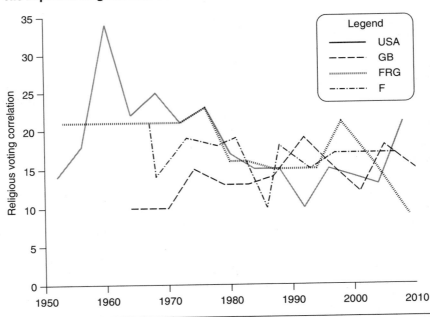

Legend
——— USA
- - - - GB
.... FRG
-·-·-·- F

Sources: United States, 1952–2008, American National Election Studies; Great Britain, 1964–2005, British Election Studies; France, 1967, Converse and Pierce survey; 1968, Inglehart survey; 1973–97, Eurobarometer; 2007, French Election Study (CSES); Germany, 1953–2009, German Elections Studies (Western Germany only, 1990–2009).

Note: Figure entries are the Cramer's V correlation between religious denomination and voting choice. U.S. results are based on congressional elections.

In summary, denominational differences may have narrowed slightly in some of these cases, but religion has not declined as sharply as we observed for class voting (for additional cross-national evidence see Knutsen 2004). I think these results occur because the pattern of decline for religion is more complex than for class voting. Comparisons of the voting patterns of religious denominations appear to be moderating slightly. People who attend services regularly remain well integrated into a religious network and maintain distinct voting patterns; however, there are fewer of these individuals today. In many cases, secular/religious divides are replacing denominational conflicts. By definition, however, secular voters do not turn to religious cues to make their electoral choices. Therefore, as the number of voters who rely on religious cues decreases, the ability of religious characteristics to explain voting outcomes is slowly weakening.

Other Social Group Differences

If you think of how you might define your social characteristics, class and religion are often central identities. But other traits can also be important. A French voter might be an active churchgoer as well as identify with her home region of Brittany and her current *arrondissement* in Paris, her family class traditions, her own career group, and—of course—her gender. All these factors might provide political cues.

For example, regional interests can shape party choice. The rhetoric of red and blue states illustrates the persistence of regional differences in the U.S. elections (Frank 2004; Fiorina 2005). Similarly, regional contrasts in Britain have widened as devolution strengthened regional identities in Scotland and Wales; and Germany unification created new east–west polarization. In most nations, however, region exerts only a modest influence on voting.[10] Similarly, urban/rural residence often reflects different life conditions, but this produces only modest differences in voting patterns.

Political analysts have focused increasing attention on the gender gap in voting. The available empirical evidence, however, suggests that gender differences are generally quite modest. The difference between men and women in Left/Right voting normally averages less than 10 percent (see note 10). Still, the impact of social modernization is apparent if we take a longer time frame. In many democracies the gender gap traditionally ran in the opposite direction from what we see today. Women historically favored parties of the Right. However, as feminism changed the political orientations of some younger women, male/female voting differences narrowed—and then reversed—with more women supporting parties of the Left (Inglehart and Norris 2003, ch. 4). Furthermore, significant voting differences begin to emerge if one combines gender and life status measures, such as employment status and childrearing (R. Campbell 2006).

Race and ethnicity are other possible social cleavages, and more so as established democracies become more diverse. There are sharp racial differences in partisan support within the American electorate, and these differences have widened over time (Abramson, Aldrich, and Rohde 2010). Eighty-five percent of African Americans—compared to 74 percent of Hispanics and 47 percent of white Americans—voted for Democrats for Congress in 2008, which is not much different from 2004. Ethnicity has the potential to become a highly polarized cleavage in Europe as well, because it often involves large differences in social conditions and strong feelings of group identity (Saggar 2007). Yet most European societies are relatively homogeneous in racial terms, which limits the impact of race/ethnicity as a predictor of vote choice. The racial/ethnic gap is largest in the United States (Cramer's V = .27) because it has a diverse population and clear party orientations; this gap is modest in Britain (.13 in 2010) and Germany (.14 in 2009). Because of France's official "color-blind" policy, race and ethnicity questions are not regularly asked in opinion surveys or in the national census.

These analyses lead to a general conclusion that sociological factors have a weak and declining influence on voting choice. The rate and timing of this decline varies across nations, but the result is the same (Knutsen 2004; Franklin, Mackie, and Valen 1992; compare Brooks, Nieuwbeerta, and Manza 2006). In party systems such as the United States and Canada, where social group–based voting was initially weak, the decline has occurred slowly. In other electoral systems—such as Germany, the Netherlands, and several Scandinavian nations—where sharp social divisions once structured the vote, the decline has been steady and dramatic. Franklin, Mackie, and Valen's (1992, 385) earlier comparisons across fourteen established democracies led them to conclude, "It is now quite apparent that almost all of the countries we have studied show a decline . . . in the ability of social cleavages to structure individual voting choice."

New Politics and the Vote

As traditional social group influences decrease in importance, the New Politics (or postmaterial) cleavage may produce a new partisan alignment. Environmental protection, gender equality, multiculturalism, and other social issues are not easily related to traditional class or religious alignments. Furthermore, New Politics issues attract the attention of the same people who are weakly integrated into the Old Politics cleavages: the young, the new middle class, the better educated, and the nonreligious.

Developing a new partisan cleavage is onerous. Groups must organize to represent New Politics interests and mobilize voter support, but the group bases of these issues are diffuse rather than concentrated in labor unions or churches, as with the Old Politics cleavages. The environmental and women's movements, for example, have multiple groups representing them, but they seldom speak with a single voice, and the voters' bonds to specific groups are weaker than to class and religious groups. Many established political parties are hesitant to identify themselves with New Politics issues because the parties are often internally divided on the issues and have a different political identity.

Despite these limiting factors, the potential voting impact of New Politics values has increased. Small Green or New Left parties now compete in many European democracies. In response, the established parties are gradually becoming more receptive to the political demands of New Politics groups. The inclusion of Green parties in the government coalitions in France (1997), Germany (1998), and other European nations signals how these parties are gaining voice and influence on policy.

Many voters also seem willing to base their choices on New Politics concerns (Knutsen and Kumlin 2005). Europeans also frequently express a willingness to vote for an environmental party; the potential electorate for a Green party rivals that of Socialist and Christian Democratic parties (Inglehart 1990, 266)! And as postmaterial parties have gained representation, populist-rightist parties have often emerged to challenge their views—the basis of a distinct new partisan cleavage.

We used the material/postmaterial values index (chapter 5) to see whether these values influence voting choices. Table 8.4 displays the relationship between postmaterial values and party preferences. In most instances, postmaterialists favor the Left, while materialists lean toward the Right. (The notable exception in the figure is the British Labour Party, which had lost its postmaterial support to the Liberals and minor parties.) The influence of changing values is especially clear for the New Left environmental parties in France and Germany. For example, 19 percent of German postmaterialists supported the Greens, compared to only 5 percent of materialists.

The overall size of these voting differences is considerable, often exceeding the Alford index scores for class or religious voting. The four-item postmaterialism index tends to understate the impact of these values (compared to the twelve-item index). Still, in the United States and Germany the gap in Left/Right support exceeded 30 percent.

Figure 8.5 compares the level of postmaterial values–based voting across advanced industrial democracies. These results are only a snapshot, and the surveys do not correspond with an election in progress. Still, we find that postmaterialism has a strong influence on party preferences in most established democracies. Postmaterial–based voting is significant in Germany and France, exceeding the influence of class voting (compare to figure 8.1). The increasing partisan debate over New Politics issues in the United States has apparently strengthened the influence of postmaterial values on party choice—which is in striking contrast to the modest voting effects for class and religion. Figure 8.5 also shows that the average correlation of postmaterial value priorities (Cramer's V = .19) now exceeds the weight of social class on voting choice (figure 8.1).

We expect that in contrast to the declining impact of social characteristics, postmaterial values should have generally increasing influence as these issues enter the political agenda and parties respond by offering policy choices.

Table 8.4	Postmaterial Values and Vote		

Postmaterialists support Green and New Left parties in Europe, the Democrats in the United States.

	MATERIALISTS	MIXED	POSTMATERIALISTS
United States			
Democrats	44	59	78
Republicans	56	41	22
Total	100	100	100
Great Britain			
Labour	35	29	24
Liberal Democrats	14	15	19
Conservatives	38	43	39
Other parties	13	14	17
Total	101	101	99
France			
PC/Extreme Left	10	14	20
Socialists	25	34	38
Greens	8	10	17
MoDem	7	14	16
RPR/UPM	45	26	9
National Front	6	2	1
Total	101	100	101
Germany			
PDS	3	5	7
Greens	2	6	12
SPD	36	33	44
FDP	1	4	3
CDU/CSU	59	51	35
Total	101	99	101

Sources: United States: 2005–08 World Values Survey; European nations, 2008 European Values Survey.

Note: Value priorities are measured with the four-item index (see chapter 5).

However, time series data on postmaterialism and voting choice are not as readily available as other social characteristics and vote. The postmaterial values index is not routinely included in national election study surveys, and

| **Figure 8.5** | Postmaterial Values and Vote Cross-Nationally |

Postmaterial values significantly influence party preferences in most established democracies.

.30

                    Spain/Italy

                    Switzerland/**United States**
                    Australia/**France**
          .20   Denmark/Finland/Ireland
                    Belgium/Sweden/Japan
                    Austria/Netherlands/**Germany**
                    Iceland

                    Ireland/New Zealand
                    Portugal

          .10   **Britain**
                    Canada

          .00

Sources: 2008 European Values Survey; World Values Survey for non-European nations.

Note: The figure displays Cramer's V correlations between the postmaterial values index and party preferences.

no longer is a regular feature of the Eurobarometer time series. To the extent that trend data are available, such as in the previous edition of this book, the evidence suggests that these values have a persisting or growing impact on voting choice (Knutsen and Kumlin 2005). Perhaps the best series is available for Germany (not shown), and these data show that the voting difference between materialists and postmaterialists in West Germany was modest in the early 1970s, increasing by the end of the 1990s (with a spike when the Greens first ran for Parliament in the early 1980s) and fluctuating from election to election since then.

It would be a mistake to assume that the growing electoral salience of New Politics issues means an inexorable increase in support for leftist parties. The Old Politics cleavages will remain as major influence on voting for some time. Furthermore, the partisan consequences of the New Politics depend on how parties respond to these issues. Environmentalism, for example, is not a Left or Right issue in the traditional Old Politics meaning of these terms; rather, the partisan effects of these issues depend on how the parties respond (see Dalton 2009b). In addition, as Green and other New Left parties have developed; New Right parties have challenged their issue positions. The major lesson is that public interests and party alignments are changing, and the contemporary party systems are affected by these trends.

The Transformation of Social Cleavages

Harold Clarke and his colleagues (2004) began their study of the 2001 British election with a vignette of two British voters that captures the spirit of this chapter:

> Jim Hill voted Labour in the 1955 general election. Jim worked as a welder . . . and made castings for the motor industry. He belonged to the Transport and General Workers' Union. He rented a house . . . from the local council. . . . Jim did not think much about politics— although he paid his union dues and occasionally talked politics with his mates in the local pub. Like most people he knew, Jim had always thought of himself as "Labour."
>
> Jim's granddaughter, Melanie, still lives today in the Midlands town where her grandfather spent his life, although the foundry where he worked closed in the early 1980s. She lives in her own terraced house, which she is buying with her partner, in an area where 40 percent of the population is Asian. After graduating from university in the early 1990s, she became a teacher. She left in 1996, disillusioned with work in the public sector, to become a customer services manager at a nearby airport. . . . In the 1997 general election, Melanie voted Labour. In 2001, she thought about not voting at all, but finally opted for the Liberal Democrats. (p. 1)

The transformation of social conditions between Jim Hill and Melanie Hill—and consequently the political choices of the Hill family across three generations—illustrates the social changes that have occurred in all advanced industrial democracies.

Throughout much of the twentieth century, the dominant social cleavage in most democracies separated working-class and middle-class parties. And then, social modernization weakened class alignments. Similarly, secularization is decreasing the influence of religion on voting behavior. These class and religious trends are often accompanied by a drop in the influence of regional, residential, and other social cleavages. (For a contrasting view see Brooks, Nieuwbeerta, and Manza 2006.)

Because of the tendency to view party systems as representing social group differences, one response to the erosion of group divisions has been to search for a possible new group basis of party alignment. Political scientists define a *partisan realignment* as a significant shift in the group basis of party coalitions, usually resulting in a shift in the relative size of the parties' vote shares.

Western party systems have undergone many realignments in which one system of group cleavages is replaced by another. Realignments have been a regular feature of American electoral history. For example, the 1930s New Deal realignment can be traced to the entry of large numbers of blue-collar workers, Catholics, and blacks into the Democratic Party coalition. Similar realignments have occurred in European party systems, such as the British Labour Party's rise in the early 1900s and the Gaullist realignment at the beginning of the French Fifth Republic.

Some analysts suggest that New Politics issues may provide the basis of a new partisan alignment. These issues are attractive to voters who are weakly integrated into traditional group alignments. Eventually, these interests may realign electorates and party systems. The growing partisan polarization along the New Politics value cleavage apparently supports this realignment thesis. Value priorities have become a more important influence on voting choice; new Green parties now represent these perspectives, and New Right parties challenge their positions.

I am not convinced that one should think of contemporary partisan politics in the same terms as past partisan realignments. Partisan realignment is normally based on clearly defined and highly cohesive social groups—such as union workers, church members, or farmers—that can develop institutional ties to the parties and provide clear voting cues to their members.

Today there are few social groupings comparable to labor unions or churches that might establish a New Politics realignment. Generational differences in support for New Politics parties might indicate an emerging New Politics cleavage, but age groups are a transitory basis for mobilizing voters because they are too loosely defined. Other potential group bases of voting cues, such as education or alternative class categorizations, so far remain speculative, without firm evidence of realigning effects.

Postmaterial values are related to partisan preferences, but values per se are unlikely to provide a basis for a new group–party alignment. Values define clusters of like-minded people, but one cannot identify a postmaterialist in the same way that class, religion, or region provides a basis of personal identity and group mobilization. Indeed, postmaterial values are antithetical to traditionally bureaucratic organizations such as unions and churches. Instead, a vast array of single-issue groups and causes represents New Politics concerns—from the women's movement to peace organizations to environmental advocates. And their opposition on the New Right is often equally fluid. In general, these groups are loosely organized with ill-defined memberships that wax and wane.

The lack of a cohesive social group as a basis for the New Politics cleavage highlights another aspect of the new style of citizen politics. The kinds of cleavages that divide modern electorates and the kinds of groups they represent are changing. Electoral politics is moving from cleavages defined by identities with fixed social groups to issue/value cleavages that are based on communities of like-minded people. Social groups may still represent some of the political interests of contemporary electorates, but *we are witnessing a transformation from social group cleavages to issue group cleavages.*

Consequently, the bases of electoral mobilization are becoming more individualized and focused on discrete issue publics. Interest mobilization along any political dimension—Old Politics or New Politics—will be characterized by more complex, overlapping, and cross-cutting associational networks; more fluid institutional loyalties; and looser organizational structures. Fewer citizens will use voting cues from external reference groups such as unions or churches. Economic and moral issues remain key elements of the political agenda. Labor union leaders will still support leftist parties, and labor union members will still perceive these cues, but it is now less likely that the rank-and-file workers will follow their leaders and support the leftist party. The fact is that fewer individuals are following such external cues, and this independence affects the breadth, effectiveness, and stability of any future partisan alignment.

The new style of citizen politics therefore should include more fluid voting patterns (Dalton 2012a). Partisan coalitions will lack the permanence of previous class and religious cleavages. Without clear social cues, voting choices will become a more demanding task for each voter and more dependent on the beliefs and values of each citizen.

Suggested Readings

Abramson, Paul, John Aldrich, and David Rohde. 2010. *Change and Continuity in the 2008 Elections.* Washington, DC: CQ Press.

Cautres, Bruno, and Anne Muxel, eds. 2011. *The New Voter in Western Europe: France and Beyond.* New York: Palgrave Macmillan.

Evans, Geoffrey, ed. 1999. *The End of Class Politics? Class Voting in Comparative Context.* New York: Oxford University Press.

Judis, John, and Ruy Teixeira. 2002. *The Emerging Democratic Majority.* New York: Scribner.

Knutsen, Oddborn. 2006. *Class Voting in Western Europe: A Comparative Longitudinal Study.* Lanham, MD: Lexington Books.

Langenbacher, Eric, ed. 2010. *Between Left and Right: The 2009 Bundestag Elections and the Transformation of the German Party System*. Brooklyn, NY: Berghahn.

Lewis-Beck, Richard Nadeau, and Éric Bèlanger. 2012. *Presidential Elections*. London: Palgrave Macmillan.

Manza, Jeff, and Clem Brooks. *Social Cleavages and Political Change*. 1999. New York and Oxford, UK: Oxford University Press.

Notes

1. Most U.S. voting studies analyze presidential elections, which reflect a different set of electoral forces than are normally found in European parliamentary elections. To ensure comparability of American and European results, the U.S. analyses in this chapter are based on U.S. House elections.

   Unfortunately, and inexplicably, even by March of 2013 the ANES had not coded occupation and other open-ended questions in the 2008 survey, so we present congressional voting results from 2004. In Britain we examine the percentage voting Labour (and Liberal Democrats in 2005 and 2010); in Germany, the percentage voting SPD of the two-party vote (SPD and CDU/CSU) before 1980, and leftist percentage (SPD, Greens, and Linke/PDS) in later elections; in France, the percentage voting for leftist parties (PC, Socialist, and other Left).

2. The relationship between class and vote is also generally stronger among older generations than among the young (Franklin, Mackie, and Valen 1992, ch. 19).

3. The analyses are based on western Germany from 1990 to 2005 to be comparable to earlier elections; starting in 2009 I include the eastern states. For a discussion of East/West differences in voting see (Dalton and Jou 2010).

4. I measured social class by the occupation of the respondent coded into the following categories: (1) white collar, (2) manual worker, (3) farmer, (4) self-employed, and (5) other occupations/no occupation.

5. In support of this interpretation, new middle-class voters have been a major source of electoral volatility in the United States (Abramson, Aldrich, and Rohde 2010) and European democracies (Knutsen 2006; Oskarson 2005).

6. Religion interacts with racial and class patterns in the United States. African Americans, for example, are very strong Democrats, but they also tend to be religious. Thus, many studies of religious voting examine only white voters, where religiosity generally leads to Republican Party preferences. The analyses here are based on the entire U.S. electorate, which displays weaker religious patterns.

7. Benoit and Laver (2006) show that political elites in most Western democracies still perceive significant party differences on issues such as pro-/anticlerical and the permissiveness of social policy (also see chapter 7). Similarly, chapter 7 found that Americans perceive fundamentalist Christian groups as closer to the Republican Party than to the Democratic Party.

8. See appendix A for interpretation of the Cramer's V correlation. The coding of religion and party is consistent over time and follows the categories in table 8.2. The U.S. results are based on a seven-category coding of denomination, except 1952–56 when only a four-category variable was available.

9. The long-term trends in voting differences between religious and nonreligious citizens are relatively stable over time (data not shown). The religious/secular gaps in France and Germany are substantial, with some evidence of decline in Germany. In the United States the gap between religious and nonreligious voters is limited. For instance, the religious/secular gap was 14 percent in 2008; this is similar to elections of the 1950s and 1960s, and less than half the level of religious differences in Germany and France.

10. The following Cramer's V correlations summarize the impact of these other social characteristics on vote based on the CSES surveys and 2010 British Election Survey:

Characteristic	United States	Britain	France	Germany
Region	.17	.20	.15	.12
Urban/Rural	—	—	.09	.09
Gender	.09	.05	.08	.13
Race/Ethnicity	.27	.13	—	.14

9 Partisanship and Voting

Several years ago I went with a group of American professors on a *Wissenschaftsreise* to observe the German national elections. As we traveled around the country, I talked to average Germans in pubs and marketplaces about who they would vote for and why. Very few people saw the parties in identical terms—talking with a student in a pub gave a different view of the issues and candidates than talking to a senior citizen. This resensitized me to the complexity and diversity of the factors that go into people's voting choices.

Our life as democratic citizens requires that we make periodic choices at elections. The early research on voting stressed the importance of heuristics—such as class and religious cues—in guiding electoral choice (chapters 7 and 8). There were frequent references to group interests in talking to German voters (for example, see table 2.2). However, in most discussions people described the political issues and candidate images that were influencing their voting choices. And these opinions were often distinct from group ties or the cues derived from group political statements.

This experience is reflected in contemporary electoral research that emphasizes the opinions and attitudes of voters as pivotal factors in their voting choices. People make judgments about which party best represents their interests, and these perceptions guide their behavior. As we discuss in this chapter and the next, attitudes toward the issues and candidates in an election are necessary elements in any realistic model of voting choice.

A Sociopsychological Model of Voting

Early research demonstrated the limits of the sociological group-based approach as an explanation for voting choices. Consequently, researchers developed voting models to include psychological factors, such as issues and attitudes, as influences on voting choice. A team of researchers at the

    ┤ **Internet Resource** ├

    Visit the Comparative Study of Electoral Systems website; the project surveys voters
    in dozens of nations:

    http://www.cses.org

University of Michigan first formalized a model combining both sociological and psychological influences on voting (Campbell et al. 1960, ch. 2).
This sociopsychological model describes the voting process in terms of a
funnel of causality (figure 9.1). The figure has many elements, but its basic
logic is fairly straightforward. At the wide mouth of the funnel on the left
side of the figure are the socioeconomic conditions that generate the basic
conflicts of interests within society: the economic structure, social divisions
such as religion or race, and regional alignments such as the North/South
division in the United States (see chapter 7). These factors structure the
party system, as represented by the arrows in the figure, but are distant
from the actual voting decisions of individual citizens.

| **Figure 9.1** | **Funnel of Causality** |

**This model shows how broad social forces gradually become focused and specific,
leading to voting choices.**

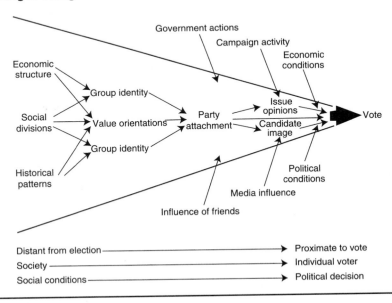

Source: Author.

As we move through the causal funnel, socioeconomic conditions influence group loyalties and basic value orientations (as signified by the arrows). For example, economic conditions may bond an individual to a social class, or regional identities may form in reaction to social and political inequalities. Social conditions are translated into attitudes that can more directly influence the person's political behavior.

The causal funnel narrows further as group identities and values shape more explicitly political attitudes. Angus Campbell and his colleagues (1960; 1966) explained individual voting decisions primarily in terms of three attitudes: party attachment, issue opinions, and candidate images. These attitudes are closest to the voting decision and therefore have a direct and very strong impact on the vote. In addition, the events of the campaign—media reports, campaign activity, economic and political conditions—influence the voter's issue opinions and candidate images.

Although the logic of the funnel of causality is simple by contemporary research standards, it was a major conceptual breakthrough for voting research. The model is still useful in organizing the factors that can influence voting choices. To understand voting, one has to recognize the causal relationship among the many factors involved.

- The factors on the left of the figure are temporally *distant* from the voting decision; the factors on the right are more *proximate* to voting choice.

- The wide end of the funnel represents broad *social conditions* that structure political conflict; attention shifts to explicitly more *political factors* as we move through the funnel.

- The factors on the left are *conditions of society*, and then groups; the factors on the right are considerations made by the *individual voter*.

In summary, the funnel of causality connects the various elements—either distant or proximate—that influence voting choices. Social characteristics are an important aspect of the voting process, but their primary influence is in forming broad political orientations and group identities. The voting impact of social characteristics is mostly mediated by attitudes closer to the voting decisions. In addition to group identities and values, attitudes reflect other stimuli such as friends, media, government actions, and the activities of the campaign. Each aspect of the voting process has a place in the funnel of causality, and we can understand each part in relation to the others.

In addition to the descriptive value of the model, the sociopsychological approach successfully predicts voting choices. Attitudes toward the parties, issues, and candidates of an election are psychologically close to the actual voting decisions and therefore are strongly related to this decision. In fact, the model can predict voting decisions more accurately than individuals can predict their own behavior in the months before the election (Campbell et al. 1960, 74)!

The sociopsychological model guides how we think about elections and how researchers analyze the voting process. This chapter examines partisan attachments as a central concept in the sociopsychological model of voting. We also discuss how party attachments have changed over time. The next chapter examines issue opinions and candidate images as additional parts of this model.

Partisan Attitudes

The sociopsychological model led us to focus on the specific issue opinions and candidate evaluations that determine voting choice. Yet, it soon became clear that partisan loyalties strongly influenced many of the specific political beliefs and behaviors of the citizenry. As one elderly Tallahassee voter once commented to me while we were waiting to vote, "I vote for the candidate and not the party. It just seems like the Democrats always choose the best candidate." Many voters begin each electoral season with their partisan predispositions already set. These partisan loyalties are a central part of an individual's belief system, serving as a source of political cues for other attitudes and behaviors.

The Michigan researchers described these partisan attachments as a sense of *party identification* (PID), similar to identifications with a social class, religious denomination, or other social group. Party identification is a long-term, affective, psychological identification with one's preferred political party (Campbell et al. 1960, chap. 6).[1] Party attachments are distinct from voting preferences, which explains why some Americans vote for the presidential candidate of one party while expressing loyalty to another party. Indeed, the conceptual independence of voting and party identification initially gives the latter its significance.[2]

The discovery of party identification is one of the most significant findings of public opinion research. Partisanship often serves as a core value for individual belief systems, as discussed in chapter 2. Partisanship is the ultimate heuristic, because it provides a reference structure for evaluating many new political stimuli—What position does "my" party take on this issue?—and making political choices. As seen in chapter 4, partisanship also stimulates participation in campaigns and elections. The developers of the concept emphasized the functional importance of partisanship for many aspects of political behavior:

> Few factors are of greater importance for our national elections than the lasting attachment of tens of millions of Americans to one of the parties. These loyalties establish a basic division of electoral strength within which the competition of particular campaigns takes place. And they are an important factor in ensuring the stability of the party

system itself. . . . The strength and direction of party identification are of central importance in accounting for attitude and behavior. (Campbell et al. 1960, 121)

Herbert Weisberg and Steve Greene (2003, 115) wrote, "Party identification is the linchpin of our modern understanding of electoral democracy, and it is likely to retain that crucial theoretical position."

After the description of PID in the United States, the concept was exported to other democracies. In several cases, researchers had problems finding an equivalent measure of partisanship in multiparty systems or in nations where the term *partisanship* holds different connotations for the voters (Budge, Crewe, and Farlie 1976). The concept of a partisan "independent" isn't as common in other nations as it is in the United States. Researchers couldn't simply translate the American PID question into French or German, and they had to find a functional equivalent for measuring partisan attachments.[3] Still, most election experts agree that voters hold some party allegiances that endure over time and strongly influence other opinions and behaviors (Holmberg 2007). Questions on party identification are now asked in the election studies of virtually all contemporary democracies.

The Learning of Partisanship

The significance of party identification for political behavior partially results from the early origins of these attachments. Socialization studies find that children develop basic partisan ties at a very early age, often during the primary school years (Hess and Torney 1967, 90). Children learn party loyalties before they can understand what the party labels stand for—a process similar to the development of many other group ties. These early party attachments then provide a reference structure for future political learning (which often reinforces early partisan biases).

The early life formation of party identities means that parents play a central role in the socialization of these values. The importance of the family can be seen by comparing the party identifications of parents and their children. A cross-national study interviewed parents and their children to compare their PIDs directly (table 9.1). There were relatively high levels of partisan agreement within American, British, and German families.[4] In the United States, 70 percent of Democratic parents have children who were also Democrats, and 54 percent of Republican parents have Republican offspring. Fewer than a sixth of the children favor the party in opposition to their parents. These levels of partisan agreement are similar to those found in a larger and more representative study of American adolescents (Jennings and Niemi 1973). British and German studies also show that the parents' party attachments are frequently re-created in their children's values (Zuckerman and Kroh 2006).

Parents successfully transmit their partisanship to their children because party loyalties are formed when parents are the dominant influence in a child's life. Parents commonly expose their children to partisan cues. Parties

Table 9.1	Parent–Child Agreement on Partisanship

Parents tend to raise children who share their partisanship.

	United States		
	Parental party preferences		
	Democrat	Republican	Independent
Child's party preference			
Democrat	70	25	40
Republican	10	54	20
Independent	20	21	40
Total	100	100	100
	Great Britain		
	Parental party preference		
	Labour	Liberal	Conservative	None
Child's party preference				
Labour	51	17	6	29
Liberal	8	39	11	6
Conservative	1	11	50	6
None	40	33	33	59
Total	100	100	100	100
	West Germany		
	Parental party preference		
	SPD	FDP	CDU/CSU	None
Child's party preference				
SPD	53	8	14	19
FDP	4	59	1	3
CDU/CSU	9	—	32	12
None	34	33	53	66
Total	100	100	100	100

Source: Political Action Surveys.

are visible and important political institutions, and political discussion frequently includes some partisan content. Consequently, it doesn't take long for a child to figure out his or her parents' partisan leanings from their reactions to television news and statements in family discussions. In addition, party attachments endure across elections, and children are exposed to relatively consistent cues on which party their parents prefer. For example, one of my university colleagues was openly proud that he had conditioned his preschool child to groan each time a specific former president appeared on television. Either through explicit reinforcement or subconscious internalization of parental values, many children adopt their parents' partisan preferences.

Once people establish party ties, later electoral experiences often follow these early predispositions. Democrats tend to vote for Democratic candidates; Republicans vote for Republicans. Electoral experience normally reinforces initial partisan tendencies because most citizens cast ballots for their preferred party. Morris Fiorina (1981) describes partisanship as a "running tally" of an individual's accumulated electoral experience. If early partisan leanings are reinforced by later voting experience, party ties strengthen over time. If voting experiences counteract partisanship, then these party loyalties may gradually erode (Niemi and Jennings 1991).

Accumulated experience of voting for the same party and the political agreement that leads to such partisan regularity thus strengthen partisan ties. Consequently, partisan loyalties generally become stronger with age—or, more precisely, with continued electoral support of the same party (Converse 1969, 1976).[5]

Figure 9.2 displays the percentage of party identifiers by age across our four core nations.[6] The percentage expressing a party identity increases with age as electoral learning builds on early life socialization. For instance, only 46 percent of the youngest American age group said they are close to any party, compared to 68 percent among the oldest age group. The same general age pattern is evident in the other three nations. The figure shows results only for western Germans, since easterners have not had a lifetime to accumulate party ties. And as one might expect, for every age group Germans in the East are less likely to have party ties than westerners. This gap in party ties is smallest among the young Germans who were raised in a democratic system in both West and East, and largest among seniors who grew up under different political systems (data not shown). Overall, the strength of partisanship shows a similar pattern of intensifying party bonds with age or with accumulated experience of supporting the same party.

Partisanship may change in reaction to later life experiences, but these ties are not easily altered once they have formed. Consequently, PID is one of the most stable political attitudes, far exceeding the stability of opinions on national issues such as race relations, economic programs, and foreign policy (Converse and Markus 1979). Further evidence of partisan stability comes from a panel study of high school seniors and their parents. M. Kent Jennings and Greg Markus (1984) found that 78 percent of American adults and 58 percent of adolescents held the same partisan ties in 1965 and 1973, spanning one of the most turbulent political periods in twentieth-century American history (also see Jennings, Stoker, and Bowers 2009).

Evidence from other nations mirrors this pattern. British party attachments are significantly more stable than other political beliefs (Schickler and Green 1997). On average, between 80 percent and 90 percent of the British public retain consistent party ties from one election to the next. Partisanship

| Figure 9.2 | Partisanship and Age |

The percentage feeling close to a party is higher among older citizens.

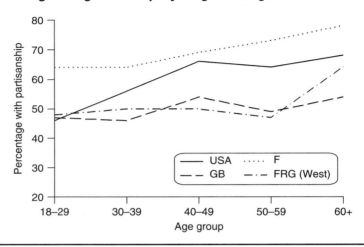

Sources: United States, American National Election Study (2008); Comparative Study of Electoral Systems (CSES): France (2007) and Germany (2009); 2010 British Election Study, CSES supplement.

Note: The CSES uses a comparably worded question on party closeness, and the United States presents the standard PID question.

is also a very stable political attitude in Germany (Zuckerman and Kroh 2006). Even the limited evidence for France shows considerable continuity in the partisan orientations of the French public, despite the substantial turbulence in the parties themselves (Converse and Pierce 1986, ch. 3).

We can see the relative constancy of partisan attachments by comparing the stability of partisanship and voting preferences (see table 9.2).[7] Reinterviews with the same American voters in 2000 and 2004 found that 95 percent had stable party identifications, while 81 percent had stable congressional party votes. Even when American voters switched parties between elections, most had stable partisanship (22 percent); only 4 percent changed their PID. Party preferences were also more stable than voting preferences in Great Britain and Germany. There is a greater tendency for partisanship and vote to go together in Europe; when vote changes, partisanship may follow (Holmberg 1994; LeDuc 1981). Because of their limited number of voting opportunities, Europeans are less likely to distinguish between long-term partisanship and current voting preferences. Still, partisanship is generally stable over time, even in the face of vote defections.

In sum, partisanship is a central element in an individual's belief system and a basis of political identity. These orientations are formed early in

Table 9.2	Interelection Partisan Change

Even when people shift their votes, they are likely to retain their same party identities.

	United States, 1972–1976	
	Vote	
Party identification	Stable	Variable
Stable	71	22
Variable	4	3
N= 539		

	Great Britain, 1970–1974	
	Vote	
Party identification	Stable	Variable
Stable	75	10
Variable	5	10
N= 795		

	West Germany, 1976	
	Vote	
Party identification	Stable	Variable
Stable	71	22
Variable	4	3
N= 707		

Sources: United States, 2000–04 American National Election Study Panel; Britain, 1992–97 British General Election Panel Survey; Germany, German Longitudinal Election Study, 2005–09 Panel.

life and may condition later life learning. It is therefore easy to see why partisanship occupies a central position in the sociopsychological model of voting choice.

The Impact of Partisanship

In sports, loyalty to a team helps fans know who to root for and which players to admire, and it motivates people to actively support their team. Such ties often develop early in life, and they endure through the ups and downs of the franchise. In my case, my attachment to the Dodgers strengthens with repeated trips to cheer on my team, even if it loses. (Chicago Cubs fans are an even better example.)

The same patterns apply to partisan attachment: parties help to make politics "user friendly." When the political parties take clear and consistent policy positions, the party label provides an information shortcut on how "people like me" should decide. Once voters decide which party generally represents their interests, this single piece of information can act as a perceptual screen—guiding how they view events, issues, and candidates. A policy advocated by one's party is more likely to meet with favor than one advocated by the other team.

Compared to social group cues such as class and religion, PID is a more valuable heuristic. Party cues are relevant to a broader range of phenomena because parties are so central to democratic politics. Issues and events frequently are presented to the public in partisan terms, as the parties take positions on the issues of the day or react to the statements of other political actors. When you see politicians giving interviews on TV, you can normally predict their views by whether there is a "D" or an "R" after their names. People vote for parties or party candidates at elections. Governments are managed by partisan teams. So, reliance on partisanship may be the ultimate example of the satisficing model of politics.

The *Washington Post* did an interesting experiment that shows the power of partisanship as a political cue (Morris 1995). The newspaper included a question on a fictitious government act in one of its opinion surveys. One form of the question referred to either President Bill Clinton's or the Republicans' position on the issue, and another form discussed the act without any partisan cues. They found that the number of people expressing an opinion on the act increased when a partisan cue was given. In addition, the cue-giving effects of partisanship were clear: Democrats were far more likely to oppose the fictitious act when told Clinton wanted repeal, and Republicans disproportionately opposed the act when told the Republicans in Congress wanted repeal.

Another example shows the power of PID to shape even nonpartisan opinions. Before the 2000 U.S. elections, the American National Election Study (ANES) asked the public to judge whether the national economy would improve or worsen over the next twelve months. With the Democrats in the White House, Democrats were more optimistic about the nation's economic future than Republicans by an 8 percent margin. After the election, with George W. Bush the apparent winner (although the election outcome was still in doubt), Republicans were more positive about the economy by a small margin. This reversal of the relationship between preelection and postelection surveys shows the power of partisanship to shape citizen perceptions of the political world. Partisanship has an even stronger influence on opinions that are more closely linked to the parties, such as evaluations of government performance and candidate images (Abramson, Aldrich, and Rohde 2010, ch. 8; Dalton 2012a, chs. 6–7). Partisans root for the players (candidates) on their team and save their catcalls for the opponents.

Party ties also mobilize people to become politically active (see chapter 4). Just like loyalty to a sports team, attachment to a political party encourages an individual to become active in the political process to support his or her side. The 2008 ANES found that turnout was 25 percent higher among strong partisans than among independents. In addition, strong partisans are more likely to try to influence others, to display campaign materials, to attend a rally, or to give money to a candidate during the campaign. Partisanship functions in a similar way in other established democracies. Strong partisans voted at a higher rate in the 2009 German Bundestag elections, and they were several times more likely to participate in campaign events and twice as likely to try to persuade others how to vote. Ninety-one percent of strong partisans believed it makes a difference who controls the German government, but only 47 percent of weak partisans and 33 percent of nonpartisans shared this conviction.

Party identifications also clearly affect voting choices. Partisanship means that a voter has a predisposition to support his or her preferred party. Philip Converse (1966) described partisanship as the basis for a "normal vote"—the vote expected when other factors in the election are evenly balanced. If other factors come into play, such as issue positions or candidate images, their influence can be measured by the change in preferences from initial partisan predispositions. For the unsophisticated voter, a long-term partisan loyalty and repeated experience with one's preferred party provides a clear and low-cost cue for voting. Even for the sophisticated citizen, a candidate's party affiliation normally signifies a policy program that serves as the basis for reasonable electoral choice.

Generally, there is a close relationship between PID and voting in parliamentary elections. In the 2007 French legislative elections, 81 percent of partisans voted for their party in the first tour. Similarly, in the 2002 Bundestag elections, a full 83 percent of German partisans voted for a district candidate from their own party, and 81 percent cast a party vote on the second ballot. The limited voting opportunities in most European nations tend to narrow the separation between partisanship and vote.

The American citizen, in contrast, "has to cope simultaneously with a vast collection of partisan candidates seeking a variety of offices at federal, state, and local levels; it is small wonder that he becomes conscious of a generalized belief about his ties to a party" (Butler and Stokes 1969, 43). The separation between attitudes and behavior is therefore most noticeable in American elections, especially when voters are asked to make a series of choices for local, state, and federal offices (Beck et al. 1992). In highly visible and politicized presidential elections, candidate images and issue appeals have the potential to counteract partisan preferences. The success of Republican presidential candidates from Ronald Reagan to George W. Bush, for example, occurred because they attracted defectors from the Democratic majority as well as independents. Even in the intense two-party contest of 2008, 8 percent of American partisans cast presidential votes contrary to their party identification, and 12 percent cast cross-party votes in the congressional election.

Similar diversity exists in France. The two-candidate runoff in French presidential elections is decided by the size of the vote the candidates can attract from parties other than their own (Lewis-Beck et al. 2012). Voting choices more closely conform to standing partisan preferences in French legislative elections.

In summary, partisanship is the ultimate heuristic because it:

- Creates a basis of political identity
- Provides cues for evaluating political events, candidates, and issues
- Mobilizes participation in campaigns and election turnout
- Provides cues on voting preferences
- Stabilizes voting patterns for the individual and the party system

Thus, partisan identification is the cornerstone to our understanding of how citizens manage the complexities of politics and make reasonable decisions at election time.

Partisan Dealignment

Because partisanship is so important for different aspects of citizen political behavior, it came as a surprise when researchers first noted that party ties seemed to be eroding in several advanced industrial democracies. Initial signs of partisanship decline appeared in the greater swing in election outcomes starting in the late 1970s. The weakening of social group–party linkages described in chapter 8 contributed to eroding partisanship which then increased interelection volatility. These patterns hinted that deeper party loyalties were weakening.

At first, it was difficult to be certain that partisanship was eroding when this trend was intermixed with the normal partisan changes between elections. Clear evidence of the weakening of party ties first became apparent in the United States (see figure 9.3). From the 1950s to the early 1960s, the percentage of party identifiers in the United States was a stable 70–75 percent of the public, and less than a quarter of the public claimed to be "independents." Partisan loyalties started to weaken after the 1964 election, and by the 1980s, more than a third of the electorate were nonpartisans. In the 1990s H. Ross Perot's candidacy pushed the percentage of partisans down still further. The percentage of partisans reached a new low (59 percent) in the 2000 election survey, and this level continued into the 2004 and 2008 elections. As the 2012 election approached, the percentage of partisans hit a historic low point (Dalton 2012a).

Several experts questioned the existence or significance of these trends in the United States. Bruce Keith and his colleagues (1992) doubted that the decrease in party identifiers was a meaningful change. Green, Palmquist, and Schickler (2002, 31) examined a variety of partisan behaviors in the ANES time series and concluded, "Partisanship is alive and well, and as far as we can tell, it is as influential for us as it was for our parents and grandparents." Other researchers claimed that the ability of partisan identities to

| **Figure 9.3** | **Where's the Party?** |

The percentage of party identifiers has been trending downward.

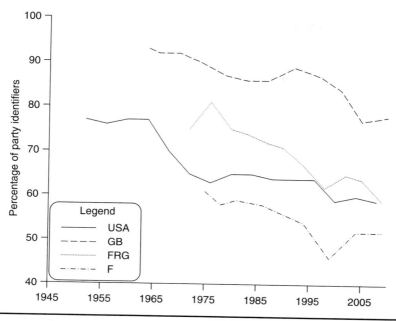

Sources: United States, 1952–2008, American National Election Studies; Great Britain, 1964–2010, British Election Studies; Germany, 1972–2009, German Elections Studies (Western Germany only 1990–2009); France, Eurobarometer Surveys (1975, 1978, 1981, 1986, 1988), European Election Studies (1994, 1999, 2004, and 2009).

predict presidential vote preferences had not significantly diminished over the five-decade series of the ANES (Miller and Shanks 1996; Bartels 2000). The significance of partisanship is so great that many doubted that these ties were really weakening.

The topic of partisanship is a good example of the value of cumulative research, and especially of comparative analysis. As the body of evidence has grown, adding more nations and more elections, it is now clear that a general pattern of partisan decline is broadly affecting advanced industrial democracies (Dalton 2012a; Dalton and Wattenberg 2000; Fiorina 2002; Clarke and Stewart 1998). Voters are not simply defecting from their preferred parties in one or two elections, or just in the United States. Instead, across a wide set of nations, the evidence shows an erosion in partisan loyalties—the same loyalties that electoral research emphasized as a core element in explaining citizen political behavior.

For example, an almost identical pattern of declining party ties occurred in Great Britain (figure 9.3). Because of the traditions of the British party system and the format of the British partisanship questionnaire, fewer Britons claim to be nonpartisans. In the 1964 British Election Study, 93 percent claimed a standing partisan preference; by the 2010 election the share of partisans had dropped to 78 percent. The strength of party attachments display an even clearer pattern: more than 40 percent of the British public were strong partisans during the late 1960s, but only 11 percent in the 2010 elections.

Germany initially deviated from the pattern of partisanship found in other advanced industrial democracies. Partisanship increased between 1961 and 1976, as West Germans developed commitments to the new postwar democratic party system (Baker, Dalton, and Hildebrandt 1981, ch. 8). In the late 1970s, however, the trend began moving in the opposite direction. Partisans were 81 percent of the public in 1976; by 2009 they accounted for 59 percent among westerners. Partisanship is even lower among easterners because they lack prior partisan experience and are just beginning to develop party attachments. During the 2009 election, 46 percent of eastern Germans claimed to lack party ties.

The series of comparable French survey data is much shorter and is drawn from the Eurobarometer and European Election Surveys. Beginning in the 1970s, the percentage of partisans slowly decreased, and then there was a marked dropoff at the end of the 1990s (also see Muxel 2011).

This weakening of partisanship is occurring in almost all advanced industrial democracies. Among the nineteen advanced industrial democracies for which I have long-term survey data, seventeen show a drop in the percentage of partisans (Dalton and Wattenberg 2000, ch. 2; Dalton 2012a, ch. 8). Furthermore, the *strength* of partisanship has decreased in all nineteen nations. In countries as diverse as Austria, Canada, Japan, New Zealand, and Sweden, the pattern is the same: the partisan attachments of the public have weakened during the past several decades.

Other evidence points to growing negativity toward parties as political institutions. Several cross-national surveys find that public confidence in political parties rates at the bottom of a list of diverse social and political institutions. Data from Britain, Canada, Germany, Sweden, and other nations demonstrate that contemporary publics are significantly less trusting of political parties than were a generation or two ago (Dalton and Weldon 2005; Norris 2011, ch. 4).

Advanced industrial democracies are experiencing a new period of *partisan dealignment,* which means that a significant portion of the public isn't developing party attachments and is often openly critical of political parties. Researchers first thought that dealignment was a temporary phase, as parties and politicians struggled with new problems that weakened their support in the short term (like a sports team on a losing streak). However, dealignment has become a continuing feature of contemporary politics. If PID is the most important attitude in electoral research, then dealignment should have major implications for all these nations.

The Consequences of Dealignment

Does it matter if fewer people now identify with a political party? It should, if our theories about the value of partisanship are correct. Because partisan ties are seen as so central to citizen politics, the erosion of these ties should have obvious and predicable effects on citizen politics. Indeed, the evidence of partisan dealignment is visible in a range of examples.

Partisanship binds people to a preferred party. As these ties weaken, so should partisan-centered voting. For example, people should become more likely to shift their party support between elections as they react to the flow of events rather than choose based on habitual party loyalties.[8] Recall estimates of voting choice show a growing volatility of the party vote between elections (figure 9.4). In both Britain and Germany, the percentage of the electorate who changed their vote between elections has grown by nearly two-thirds between the 1960s and recent elections. The analyses for the United States are more complicated; recall of congressional vote is not asked, so we must rely on presidential vote. The figure shows that the amount of vote switching in presidential elections is highly dependent on whether there is a viable third-party candidate or an incumbent running for reelection.

One by-product of this fluidity is the increased number of parties competing in elections and winning seats in parliaments (Dalton 2012a, ch. 9). More nonpartisans create more potential for new parties to emerge to capture their support, at least for an election or two and possibly longer. Nonpartisans are a potential base of support for new parties as diverse as the Pirates in Germany or the National Front in France.

Another specific example of party bonds is split-ticket voting, when voters support different parties on the same ballot. Only a few democracies, including Germany and the United States, have multiple offices on the ballot. There is strong evidence of a rise in split-ticket voting between the first and second ballots in German elections (Schoen 2000). About 10 percent split their votes in the 1960s, and now it is a third of voters. The evidence for the United States is more ambiguous. Split-ticket voting between the president and Congress is most strongly affected by the presence of a third-party presidential candidate on the ballot, and the realignment of party support in southern states. Consequently, there is no clear trend from the 1950s to the 2000s. Still, split-ticket voting appears to be a generally increasing in democracies that have multiple-party choices on the same ballot (Dalton and Wattenberg 2000, ch. 3).

Because partisanship also mobilizes people to participate in politics, it is no surprise that dealignment is paralleled by declining turnout in elections (see chapter 3). Nonpartisans are less likely to vote, and if there are more nonpartisans overall, then turnout decreases. Participation in campaign activities—going to meetings, working for candidates, and displaying party support—has also atrophied compared to other forms of action. If politics is like sports, then the decreasing number of habitual fans means that there are fewer to attend each game and participate in the sport of partisan politics.

Figure 9.4   Swing Voters

Switching party votes between elections is increasing in Britain and Germany, and fluctuations in U.S. presidential elections mostly reflect whether a third-party candidate is running.

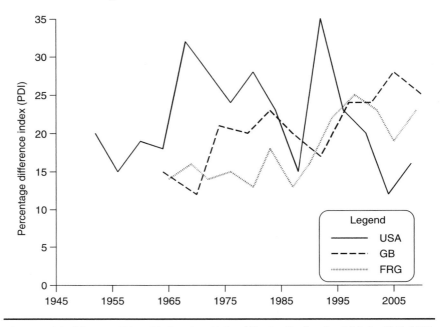

Sources: United States, 1952–2008, American National Election Studies; Great Britain, 1964–2010, British Election Studies; Germany, 1961–2009, German Elections Studies (Western Germany only, 1990–2009).

Note: Figure entries are the percentages voting in adjacent elections who change their party votes.

Finally, the decline in partisanship also changes how the public reaches its voting choices. As long-term party and social group cues are losing importance, the decision-making process shifts toward the issues and candidates of the campaign. As one sign of this shift, trend data show a systematic tendency for voters to make their decisions later in the campaign (Dalton 2012a, ch. 9). Campaigns are now more likely to matter more because fewer voters base their choices on standing partisan predispositions—voters are beginning to choose.

Causes of Dealignment

There are several explanations for why fewer people develop party attachments. One explanation focuses on the *poor performance of political parties.* In the United States, the dramatic events of the 1960–70s turned many young people away from political parties. The antipartisan sentiments stirred by the Vietnam War, Watergate, and other scandals kept new voters from developing the early life partisan attachments that could build over time. The student protests in Europe and an apparently growing number of party scandals may have had a similar effect in these nations.

More generally, poor performance can perpetuate dealignment (Zelle 1995; Thomassen 2005). On the one hand, contemporary parties are struggling with problems of maintaining social services in the face of mounting government deficits. Some of the economic and welfare issues traditionally associated with the class cleavage have not been fully resolved. On the other hand, many of the New Politics issues—such as nuclear energy, minority rights, or local environmental problems—are difficult for established parties to accommodate along with their traditional political issues. The rise of single-issue interests doesn't translate well into partisan attachments, because the voting base and electoral impact of these issues are less predictable.

Although these performance factors are important, their ability to explain the dealignment trend is limited. Some failures in party performance may have initially stimulated a dealignment trend, but this trend didn't reverse when a new party won control of the government or when policy failure was replaced by policy success. Research in each nation typically points to a unique set of policy failures, but the dealignment trend is a common feature across these diverse experiences. Therefore, this suggests that more general forces are at work, even if a specific crisis or problem stimulated dealignment initially.

Another aspect of the performance thesis is that people's expectations about parties and electoral politics has changed, which is possibly linked to the value changes discussed in chapter 5. As younger, better-educated citizens have raised their expectations about politics, and become more skeptical of bureaucratic organizations, this has contributed to disenchantment with political parties. It is not so much that parties are performing a worse job than in the past, but that people have higher expectations—and by these higher expectations parties fall short. These changes in citizenship norms contribute to dealignment.

A *functionalist explanation* claims that the declining role of parties as political institutions contributes to the dealignment process. Other institutions have taken over many of the parties' traditional political functions. A myriad of special-interest groups and single-issue lobbies represent the public's issue interests, and political parties have little hope of incorporating all of them. Political parties thus see their critical programmatic function of aggregating and articulating political interests slipping away. In a creative study, Frode Berglund and colleagues (2005) showed that the extent of distinct policy choices between the parties is related to the strength of partisanship across six European democracies; as the distinction has blurred, partisanship has weakened.

Parties are no longer the patronage-giving organizations of the past. Party leaders are even losing some control over the selection of elected party representatives. The most advanced example is the United States, where the expansion of open primaries and nonpartisan elections has weakened the parties' hold on recruitment. The British Labour Party has experienced a similar shift in nominating power away from the party in Parliament to party conventions and local constituency groups. These and other developments lessen the role of parties in politics and therefore weaken the significance of parties as political reference points.

Changes in the mass media also may contribute to dealignment trends. The mass media now perform many of the information activities that political parties once controlled. Instead of learning about an election at a campaign rally or from party canvassers, prospective voters now turn to television and newspapers as the primary sources of campaign information (see chapter 2). Furthermore, the parties now share the political stage with other actors, and media reporting on campaigns places more attention on candidate over parties. For example, the American media have shifted their campaign focus away from the political parties toward the candidates, and a weaker parallel trend is evident in several parliamentary democracies (Dalton and Wattenberg 2000, ch. 3).

There is some truth to these claims. But again the breadth of the dealignment pattern—even in nations with different journalistic norms and different structures of party politics—suggests that the media are not the primary explanation. I believe that more fundamental changes in contemporary publics have contributed to partisan dealignment.

Cognitive Mobilization and Apartisans

The *cognitive mobilization* thesis accepts the importance of partisanship as a heuristic to help people orient themselves to politics (Shively 1979). However, because the public's cognitive sophistication is growing, more people can deal with the complexities of politics without passive reliance on external cues or heuristics (see chapter 2). The availability of political information through the media reduces the costs of making informed decisions. Cognitive mobilization therefore reduces some people's need to rely on PID or other cues to help them handle difficult and political choices. Indeed, the self-defined political interests and postmaterial/self-expressive values of the cognitively mobilized may drive them away from habitual party cues that provide less room for individual choice.

The cognitive mobilization theory implies that the growth in independents should be concentrated among a distinct group of citizens: the young, the better educated, and adherents of postmaterial values. In contrast, the early literature on partisanship held that nonpartisans were at the margins of the electoral process; they were unsophisticated about politics and uninvolved in elections (Campbell et al. 1960).

Party mobilization and cognitive mobilization are two alternative ways that citizens can connect themselves to the political process (Dalton 2012a; compare Arzheimer 2006). Some people orient themselves to politics based on their partisan attachments, which are a potent source of political cues.

Cognitive mobilization enables another group of people to orient themselves to politics on their own. The combination of these traits defines a typology of four types of citizens (figure 9.5). *Apolitical independents* are neither attached to a political party nor cognitively mobilized; this group conforms to the independents originally described by Campbell and his colleagues (1960, 143–45). *Ritual partisans* are mobilized into politics primarily by their strong party attachments and are not cognitively mobilized. *Cognitive partisans* are highly ranked on both mobilization dimensions: they have strong party attachments, and they are cognitively sophisticated even when party cues are lacking.

Apartisans are the "new independents." It is essential to distinguish them from apolitical independents. Apartisans possess high levels of political involvement and sophistication, though they remain unattached to any political party. Apartisans are also concentrated among the young, the better educated, and postmaterialists (Dalton 2012a). Social modernization is increasing the proportion of apartisans within contemporary publics, as well as shifting the ratio of ritual and cognitive partisans. Data from the American National Election Studies find that the number of apartisans has more than doubled since 1964—to a fifth of the electorate.[9] In addition, the number of cognitive partisans has grown, while the proportion of ritual

Figure 9.5	Mobilization Patterns

Party attachments and cognitive mobilization define categories of different types of citizens who vary in their electoral behavior.

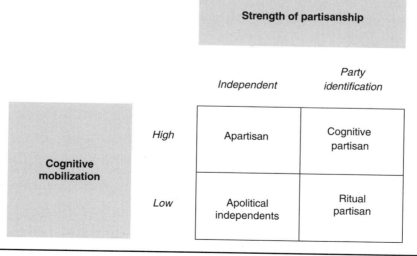

Source: Author.

partisans has decreased by almost half. Similar trends are observed in other established democracies, with the changes concentrated among younger generations (Dalton 2012a, ch. 9; Dalton 2012b). In most of these cases, the growth of independents is comprised almost entirely of an increasing number of apartisans.

Equally important, cognitive mobilization is also transforming the characteristics of partisans. The traditional ritual partisan who typically relied on party cues because of their limited political resources are becoming less and less common. Instead, most partisans today are more sophisticated and more able to understand the issues and principles of their parties rather than support them based on an inherited loyalty.

The growth of apartisans has several implications for citizen behavior. Because apartisans can follow the complexities of politics and are free of party ties, they voting patterns are more variable and reflect the changing context of elections—and they regularly turn out to vote in contrast to apolitical independents. The sources of apartisans' voting choice are also dramatically different from those of apolitical independents. Apartisans also place relatively greater weight on issues and candidate images in making their voting choices, and less attention to the characteristics of the parties. Apartisans may also press for an expansion of political involvement beyond the narrow channel of elections and other party-related activities. The political skills of apartisans encourage participation in public interest groups, community groups, protest demonstrations, and other contentious activities. The nonpartisan, issue-oriented characteristics of these activities make them ideal for apartisans.

Politics in a Dealigned Era

I regularly have lunch with a faculty member from engineering and another from economics. One is a strong Republican and the other is a strong Democrat. One believes George W. Bush was a very successful president and Barack Obama is continually making mistakes because of his inexperience. The other is supportive of Obama's policies on the economy, health care, and other issues—and he can't understand why anyone would have voted for Mitt Romney. There is little middle ground. This makes for sometimes testy lunch discussions. Such is the power of party identifications.

This chapter maintains that most people develop a psychological identification with a preferred political party, and these attachments are a potent guide for their attitudes and political actions. If one could ask just one question to understand the political behavior of a person, the question should ask about partisanship, because these attachments influence so many aspects of behavior.

And yet, party ties are eroding in virtually all the advanced industrial democracies, resulting in a new pattern of partisan dealignment. These new apartisans are concentrated among the better educated and the politically engaged.

It is as if many sophisticated fans of the sport of politics are becoming disengaged with the partisan players they see on the field.

Furthermore, as with the weakening of social group–based voting, the similarity of dealignment trends across various nations is striking. Long-term sources of partisan preferences—social characteristics and partisanship—are weakening in most of these democracies. In a single nation, we might explain such developments by the specific trials and tribulations of the parties in that nation. When a pattern appears across a wide variety of nations, however, it suggests that the causes are common to advanced industrial societies. Indeed, linking the process of cognitive mobilization to partisan dealignment seems to represent yet another aspect of the new style of citizen politics. Cognitively mobilized citizens are better able to make their own political decisions—and more interested in doing so—without relying on heuristics or external cues. These apartisans are the source the dealignment trend.

Weakening party bonds have real consequences for the political process. For example, partisan dealignment is part of a process that is transforming the relationship between voters and parties. The personal connection between parties and voters is being replaced by professional organizations that rely on the media and direct mailing to connect to voters. Instead of depending on party members for staffing, election campaigns have become professionalized activities run by hired specialists. Instead of drawing on membership dues to fund party activities, many party systems are turning to public funding sources. Such changes in organizational style may exacerbate dealignment trends by further distancing parties from the voters.

Weakened party-line voting also may contribute to split-party control of the federal and state governments in the United States. Between 1981 and 1986 different parties controlled the House and Senate for the first time since 1916; this pattern recurred from 1994 to 2000, and again in 2001–02. Most visible has been the division in partisan control of the presidency and Congress. From 1952 to 2012 the same party controlled the presidency and the House for only twenty-four out of sixty years.

The Federal Republic of Germany (FRG) also has a federal system, and the same pattern is found there. For the first twenty years of the FRG's history, the same party coalition controlled the Bundestag (the directly elected lower house of Parliament) and the Bundesrat (which represents the majority of state governments). However, between 1976 and 2005, and starting again in 2013, federal and state control was divided for more than a third of this period. There is a growing regionalization of voting patterns in Britain, as local electoral results are less closely tied to national patterns.

One of the strongest signs of dealigned politics is the rise of new political parties that can draw on independents for their initial support. The U.S. electoral system discourages new parties. Nevertheless, Ross Perot's candidacy in the 1992 and 1996 U.S. presidential elections and Ralph Nader's 2000 and 2004 campaigns illustrate the potential to appeal to nonpartisans.

And both of these candidates got disproportionate support from nonpartisans, despite the large ideological differences between the candidates. The number of political parties grew over the past several decades across the established parliamentary democracies. The success of "flash parties"— such as List Pym Fortuyn in the Netherlands, Beppe Grillo's *Five Star Movement* in Italy, and the Pirate Party in Sweden and Germany—and the general rise of New Left and New Right parties in Europe are additional indicators of the volatility we see in contemporary party systems. Local elections in Germany have seen the rise of *Freie Wähler* (free voters) who eschew party ties (Morlok, Poguntke, and Walther 2012).

Finally, the eroding influence of long-term sources of partisanship would suggest that factors further along the funnel of causality will play a larger role in voter choice. People are still voting, even if many don't rely on social group or party cues to the degree they once did. This new independence may encourage the public to judge candidates and parties on their policies and government performance—producing a deliberative public that more closely approximates the classic democratic ideal. But, the lack of long-standing partisan loyalties may also make electorates more vulnerable to manipulation and demagogic appeals (Holmberg 1994, 113–14). Dealignment has the potential to yield both positive and negative consequences for electoral politics, depending on how party systems and voters react in this new context. In the following chapters, we consider how the changing role of issues and candidate images is affecting the calculus of voting.

Suggested Readings

Bartle, John, and Paolo Bellucci, eds. 2009. *Political Parties and Partisanship: Social Identity and Individual Attitudes*. London: Routledge.

Dalton, Russell. 2012. *The Apartisan American: Dealignment and Electoral Change*. Washington, DC: Congressional Quarterly Press.

Dalton, Russell, and Martin Wattenberg, eds. 2000. *Parties without Partisans: Political Change in Advanced Industrial Democracies*. New York: Oxford University Press.

Green, Donald, Bradley Palmquist, and Eric Schickler. 2002. *Partisan Hearts and Minds: Political Parties and the Social Identities of Voters*. New Haven: Yale University Press.

Hajnal, Zoltan, and Taeku Lee. 2011. *Why Americans Don't Join the Party: Race, Immigration, and the Failure of Parties to Engage the Electorate*. Princeton: Princeton University Press.

Lewis-Beck, Michael, William Jacoby, Helmut Norpoth, and Herbert Weisberg. 2008. *The American Voter Revisited*. Ann Arbor: University of Michigan Press.

Rose, Richard, and Ian McAllister. 1990. *The Loyalties of Voters: A Lifetime Learning Model.* Newbury Park, CA: Sage.

Thomassen, Jacques, ed. 2005. *The European Voter.* Oxford, UK: Oxford University Press.

Wattenberg, Martin. 1998. *The Decline of American Political Parties, 1952–1996.* Cambridge, MA: Harvard University Press.

Notes

1. The standard U.S. party identification question asks, "Generally speaking, do you think of yourself as a Republican, a Democrat, an Independent, or what?" For those expressing a party preference: "Would you call yourself a strong Republican/Democrat or a not very strong Republican/Democrat?" For Independents: "Do you think of yourself as closer to the Republican or Democratic Party?"

   The question produces a seven-point scale measuring both the direction of partisanship and the strength of attachments, ranging from strong Democratic identifiers to strong Republican identifiers.
2. There is a debate on how closely aggregate levels of partisanship track current voting preferences. See MacKuen, Erikson, and Stimson (1989); Abramson and Ostrom (1991, 1994).
3. For example, the German version of the PID question specifically asks the respondent about long-term partisan leanings: "Many people in the Federal Republic lean toward a particular party for a long time, although they may occasionally vote for a different party. How about you?"
4. These data come from parent–child interviews of families with sixteen- to twenty-year-olds living in the parent's home. For additional analyses, see Jennings et al. (1979).
5. Researchers have debated whether age differences in American partisanship represent generational or life cycle effects (Converse 1976; Abramson 1979). We emphasize the life cycle (partisan learning) model because the cross-national pattern of age differences seems more consistent with this explanation (Dalton and Weldon 2007).
6. Part of these relationships is due to accumulated partisanship over the life cycle. In addition, the lower levels of partisanship among the young can be traced to decreasing initial attachments among younger generations.
7. Although we stress the stability of partisanship, we find evidence that this stability has eroded over the past several decades (Dalton and Wattenberg 2000, ch. 3).
8. Methodologically, measuring vote switching through a single interview is complicated because people tend to adjust their memories of the previous election to match their voting preferences. Ideally one wants to

interview the same people across two elections, but such surveys are rare. In addition, including nonvoters can substantially influence the results (Dalton 2012a; Norris 1997, ch. 5).

9. I define cognitively mobilized citizens as having a combination of interests and skills—that is, being "very interested" in politics and/or having at least some college education. The following table presents the distribution of types using data from the ANES (also see Dalton 20012a):

	1964–66	1968–78	1980–90	1992–2000	2002–08
Apolitical independent	16	20	21	20	18
Ritual partisan	47	37	36	29	24
Cognitive partisan	27	26	29	34	39
Apartisan	10	17	14	17	19

10 Attitudes and Voting Choice

Election Day is approaching, and you have to decide how you will vote. How do you make this decision as a good democratic citizen? The interview of one voter in the 2008 American National Election Study (ANES) illustrates the factors that this person considered:

(What do you like about Barack Obama?): He has the gumption to challenge the status quo and he is sensitive to human service issues, people in poverty, reentry of the incarcerated, job training, and health care for all.

(What do you dislike about Obama?): His lack of experience; I'm concerned that we are in a state of crises with war and the economy.

(What do you like about John McCain?): I believe he is a man of courage, ethics, and sincerity. He will research the issues and surround himself with the wisdom he needs to make crucial decisions on behalf of the nation. He has proven himself trustworthy by his years of experience.

(What do you dislike about McCain?): His age, his strong inclination to war as being the solution, and his health care reform is still unclear in terms of accessibility to all.

This person seems like a good citizen who has reasoned bases for voting. Most people are not as articulate in expressing their likes and dislikes about the candidates, but we think that most people have views on the issues that are important to them and how the parties and candidates differ on these issues. In addition, factors such as personality, experience, and party ties enter into these calculations.

Electoral politics may begin as the competition between rival social groups or party camps, as discussed in the previous chapters, but elections should revolve around the issues and candidates of the campaign. Deciding how to vote is complicated. People should judge the parties on their policy positions, whether they agree with one more than the others, and how they view each party's capacity to govern. Issues and candidate images give political meaning to the partisan attachments and social divisions that were discussed in earlier chapters.

207

---| **Internet Resource** |---

Visit the European Union (EU) Profiler that was designed for the 2009 European Parliament elections. The profiler allows you to become a temporary citizen of any EU member country, answer a set of policy questions, and then gives your policy agreement with the major political parties in the nation:

http://www.euprofiler.eu

Issue opinions and candidate images also matter because they represent the dynamic aspect of electoral politics. The distribution of partisanship may define the broad parameters of electoral competition—creating the stabilizing force in electoral politics. However, debates over the policies of the contenders, the images of the candidates, or the government's policy performance create the dynamic forces of electoral politics. Because the mix of these factors varies across elections, issue beliefs and candidate images explain the ebb and flow of election outcomes. The importance of issue beliefs and candidate images is why the funnel of causality locates them so close to voting choice (see figure 9.1).

Finally, because the electoral impact of long-term partisan attachments and social cues is waning, many political scientists expect a corresponding increase in the influence of issue opinions on voting choice. In addition, scholars in America and Europe argue that candidate images are becoming more salient in election campaigns and consequently are more important for voting choices (Wattenberg 1991; Dalton and Wattenberg 2000, ch. 3; Aarts, Blais, and Schmitt 2011; Bittner 2011).

This chapter examines how issues and candidate images influenced voting choices in recent elections. This evidence helps us to complete our model of voter choice and discuss the implications for democracies today.

Principles of Issue Voting

The extent of issue voting is closely intertwined with the debate on the political sophistication of the public. Issue voting can be linked to a sophisticated, rational electorate: the voters evaluate the government and the opposition and then thoughtfully cast a ballot for their preferred parties. For the skeptics of mass democracy, this theoretical ideal seldom exists in reality. They see voters as lacking knowledge of the parties' positions, sometimes unsure of their own positions, and often voting based on ill-formed or even incorrect beliefs (see chapter 2). The early voting studies thus criticized the electorate's ability to make informed choices.

The authors of *The American Voter* said that the potential for issue voting has to fulfill three requirements (Campbell et al. 1960, ch. 8):

- People should be interested in the issue.
- They should hold an opinion on the issue.
- They should know the party or candidate positions on the issue.

The American Voter maintained that on most policy issues, most voters fail to meet these criteria. It classified a third of the public, or less, as possible issue voters on each of a long list of policy topics. Some recent studies of issue voting came to similar conclusions (Lewis-Beck et al. 2008, ch. 8; Abramson, Aldrich, and Rohde 2010). Moreover, some experts claim that these small percentages reflect the conceptual and motivational limits of the electorate—the lack of issue voting is presumably an intrinsic aspect of mass politics (Converse 1990; compare Converse 2007). These views thus cast doubt that issue positions can exert a substantial influence on voting choices.

Since the beginning of voting research, however, critics have challenged this negative image of issue voting. V. O. Key showed that people were "moved by concern about the central and relevant questions of public policy, of government performance, and of executive personality." In short, Key's unorthodox argument was that "voters are not fools" (1966, 7–8). Key's position has become less unorthodox as our understanding of citizen voting choice has grown and the nature of mass publics has changed.

That only a minority of the public fulfills the issue voting criteria for each issue on a list doesn't mean that only a third of the total public is capable for any and all issues. Contemporary publics are comprised of overlapping *issue publics,* groups of people interested in a specific issue (see chapter 2). These issue publics vary in size and composition. A large and heterogeneous group of people may be interested in basic issues such as taxes, inflation rates, budget deficits, and education. On more specific issues—agricultural policy, nuclear energy, transportation policy, or foreign aid—the issue publics usually are smaller and socially distinct.

Most voters are attentive on at least one issue, and many belong to several issue publics. Using open-ended questions about the likes and dislikes of the parties and candidates, Amy Gershkoff (2005) classified Americans in terms of their issue interests. She found that about a quarter of the public does not belong to any issue public, and another quarter mentions an interest in only one specific issue. But half of the electorate belongs to two or more issue publics and a seventh belongs to four or more. Gershkoff concluded that voters are information specialists: they focus their attention on a few major issues, follow the news on these issues, and use them as a basis for electoral choice.

When citizens define their own issue interests, they are more likely to fulfill the issue-voting criteria for their issues. One classic study showed that only 5 percent of Americans were interested in medical programs for the elderly, but more than 80 percent of this small group could be classified as potential issue voters (RePass 1971). One may assume that this issue public would mostly consist of older Americans, since few college students follow the Medicare debate. If one asked about environmental sustainability and global warming, the generational patterns might be reversed.[1] Other studies have underscored the importance of issue salience in U.S. elections (Krosnick 1990; Anand and Krosnick 2003) and in Europe (Clarke et al. 2004; Mayer and Tiberj 2004). Adopting a diversified view of a diverse electorate—not all citizens must be interested in all issues—presents a more reasonable assessment of issue voting.

The conflicting claims about issue voting also may arise because researchers think of issue voting in different terms or use contrasting evidence to support their positions. Indeed, the literature describes various types of issues, their characteristics, the demands they place on voters, and their likely impact on voting choices.[2] Issue voting may be more likely for some sorts of issues than for others, and the implications of issue voting also may vary depending on the type of issue.

Figure 10.1 depicts a framework for thinking about issue voting. One important characteristic is the type of issue. *Position issues* involve conflicts over different policy goals (Stokes 1963). A typical position issue might concern whether the U.S. government should support stem cell research (or not), or whether France should support Turkey's entry in the European Union (or not). Discussions of issue voting often focus on position issues.

Performance issues involve judgments about how effectively a government pursues widely accepted political goals.[3] Most people favor a strong economy, but they may differ in how they evaluate a government's success in accomplishing this goal. Or they may differ in how they judge the challenger's prospect for success on this goal. In studies of the 2001 and 2005 British elections, Harold Clarke and his colleagues (2004, 2009) maintain that performance issues are the central basis of competition in elections. Conflicting claims about performance judgments often lie at the heart of electoral campaigns.

Voters may also judge the *attributes* of the parties or candidates: Do they possess desired traits or characteristics? For example, a voter might consider a party as trustworthy and believe its campaign promises (or not).

Figure 10.1	Types of Issues

There are different types of issues that may affect voting choices.

Type of issue

Time frame	Position	Performance	Attribute
Retrospective	Policy appraisal	Performance evaluation	Attribute voting
Prospective	Policy mandate	Anticipatory judgment	

Source: Author.

The nature of issue voting also varies by the time frame of the voters' judgments (Fiorina 1981). *Retrospective* judgments evaluate political actors on their past performance. Evaluating Chancellor Gerhard Schröder in the 2005 election based on the performance of the economy—something he encouraged German voters to do when he was first elected in 1998—is an example of retrospective voting. *Prospective* judgments are based on expectations of future performance. An evaluation of Schröder based on what his administration might do differently in the future would be an example of prospective voting.

Retrospective and prospective judgments have different implications for the nature of voting choice. Retrospective judgments should have a firmer base in the facts because they are based on experience. This can produce a relatively simple decision-making strategy: vote for the incumbents if times have been good; vote against them if times have been bad. But a pure reliance on retrospective judgments limits the scope of citizen evaluations. Elections allow voters to select a government for the future, and their decisions should include evaluations of a party's promises and its prospects for future policy success. Therefore, voting decisions should include prospective judgments as well as retrospective evaluations. Prospective judgments are somewhat speculative and complex. People have to make forecasts about the expected performance of political actors—which is a difficult task. How citizens balance retrospective and prospective judgments is an important aspect of issue voting.

These characteristics define a typology of the different types of issue calculations that voters may use in elections. Some issue voting involves a *policy appraisal* that assesses a party's (or candidate's) past position on a policy controversy. The voters who supported George W. Bush in 2004 because they approved of his strong measures against terrorists were making a judgment about the past policies of his administration. Other voters may base their voting decisions on what a party or candidate promises for policies in the future. When President Barack Obama called on voters to endorse his economic and policy plans in 2008, he was asking for a *policy mandate* from the electorate.

Policy appraisals and policy mandates represent a sophisticated form of issue voting in which citizens are making choices between alternative policy goals for their government. This process places high requirements on the voters: they must inform themselves about the policy issue, settle on a preferred policy, and see meaningful choices between the contenders. Voters might acquire this information directly or through surrogate information sources (see chapter 2).

Performance evaluations are judgments about how a political actor (party, candidate, or government) has been doing its job. If the actor has been successful, voters often support its return to office; if it has struggled, voters look for acceptable alternatives to the incumbents. In 1980 Ronald Reagan asked Americans to make a performance evaluation of Jimmy Carter's presidency when he asked, "Are you better off than you were four years ago?" In other instances, voters may make *anticipatory judgments* about the future performance of government. Most analysts say that François Hollande won the French presidency in 2012 because a majority of French voters agreed with his proposed policies for dealing with the recession in a new Socialist administration.

Finally, some aspects of issue voting are based on judgments about candidate or party attributes as a basis of choice. This type of voting often lacks a specific time frame. Voters judge candidates on their personal characteristics, which might not be immediately political in their content but are legitimate factors in selecting a candidate (Kinder et al. 1980). Just as Bill Clinton's "slick Willie" image hurt him at the polls in 1992, Barack Obama's likeability benefited him in 2008 and 2012—and both images were politically relevant, although they didn't involve explicit policy or performance calculations. Similar stylistic considerations can influence voter choices of a political party. Tony Blair's 1997 victory in Britain and Schröder's 1998 victory in Germany are attributed in part to each candidate's ability to project a more dynamic, forward-looking image than his opponents.

Electoral researchers consider attribute voting as an example of limited political sophistication because it doesn't involve explicit policy criteria. As discussed later in this chapter, however, many attributes involve traits that are directly relevant to the task of governing or to providing national leadership. I therefore consider attribute voting as a potentially meaningful basis of electoral choice.

The typology of figure 10.1 is a way to think about the different types of issue voting. For example, Martin Wattenberg's (1991, ch. 6) analysis of support for Reagan provided an especially insightful example of how policy positions and performance evaluations reflect distinct aspects of issue voting. Some candidates win because of their policy promises; others win because of their performance in office. This mix of factors is seen in the quotation from a 2008 voter at the start of this chapter.

Position Issues and the Vote

Changes in the nature of electorates (and politics itself) over the past several decades should facilitate issue voting. Cognitive mobilization has increased the number of voters who have the conceptual ability and the political skills necessary to fulfill the issue-voting criteria. The growth of public interest groups and new issue-oriented parties in Europe (on both the Left and Right) also stimulate (and reflect) greater issue awareness. The extensive use of public opinion polls probably contributes to the discussion of issues as pundits discuss these results in the media. In response, political elites have become more conscious of the public's preferences and more sensitive to the results of public positions as reflected in opinion polls.

Contemporary issue voting still involves many long-standing Old Politics debates. Economic cycles inevitably stimulate concerns about the government's role in the economy and how it affects the public's economic security. Indeed, economic controversies seem to arise frequently, such as the "free market" initiatives of the 1980s and now the policy consequences of the 2008 recession. Issues tapping religion or morals are often part of the political debate and electoral politics.

Issue controversies also arise from the changing political context, such as with foreign policy. The United States and other Western democracies are grappling with a new post–Cold War international system. The terrorist attacks of September 11, 2001, signaled the global threat of jihadist terrorism and other conflicts that challenge peace and stability throughout the world. For European nations, the development of the European Union has grown in importance in recent years, punctuated by the current Euro and debt crisis. The United States and most European nations are confronting issues arising from immigration and increasing racial diversity. Today, political controversies include New Politics concerns such as nuclear energy, gender equality, multiculturalism, and social justice. It was not so long ago that politicians and voters didn't even know that problems of global warming and ozone depletion existed. These new issues can provide a political base for fledgling parties and reorient the voting patterns of attentive citizens.

The diversity of issues across elections makes it difficult to compare the influence of issues across time or nations. Indeed, the impact of specific issues *should shift* across time because they are a dynamic part of elections. A much richer compendium of information on issue voting exists for each nation separately. Research finds that position issues often influence voters' choices, although debate continues about the role of specific issues and how this has changed over time (Aardal and van Wijnen 2005).

One can assess the general impact of policy preferences on voting choice by examining the relationship between Left/Right attitudes and the vote. Chapter 6 described Left/Right attitudes as a sort of "super issue," a summary of positions on the issues that are most important to each voter. To a French union member, for example, Left/Right attitudes may reflect positions on traditional economic conflicts; to a German university student, Left/Right attitudes may reflect positions on New Politics controversies. Left/Right attitudes can also signify a mix of different types of issues. Specific issue interests will vary across individuals or across nations, but Left/Right attitudes can summarize each citizen's overall policy views.[4]

Most people can position themselves along a Left/Right scale, and their attitudes are linked to specific policy views, fulfilling the first two criteria of policy voting (see chapter 6). Figure 10.2 shows that people can also fulfill the third requirement: positioning the major political parties on the Left/Right scale. For each of our four nations, the figure presents the voters' average self-placements and the average scores they assign to the major political parties in their respective nations.

Figure 10.2 | Parties and the Left/Right Dimension

People perceive parties as located along the Left/Right dimension, with the average citizen near the middle.

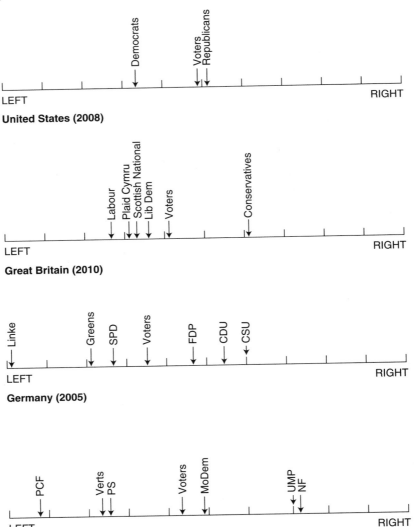

Sources: Comparative Study of Electoral Systems (CSES), United States (2008), France (2007), and Germany (2009): Britain, 2010 British Election Study, CSES supplement.

Note: Figure entries are public placement of parties on the Left/Right scale (mean scores on a 0–10 scale).

American voters are the most conservative, placing themselves to the right of the British, German, and French publics. Americans perceived modest political differences between the Democratic and Republican Parties in 2008, and this gap lessened slightly since the 2004 election.[5] This discrepancy suggests that the growing divisions of American political parties at the elite level exceed the differences within the electorate (Dalton 2012a; Abramowitz 2010; Fiorina 2005). Although specific presidential candidates may be seen as relatively more or less ideological, the positions of the U.S. parties change relatively little from election to election.

Perceived party differences are normally greater in European party systems. In France the political spectrum runs from the Communist Party on the far Left to the National Front on the far Right. By crude estimate, the French voter sees a range of party choices that extends more than four times as far across the political landscape than the span between the two major American political parties! The German partisan landscape ranges from the Linke on the far Left to the Christian Socialist Union (CSU) on the Right (with minor parties further right).[6] The British Labour and Conservative parties had distinctly different Left/Right positions in 2010, although under Blair's administration (1997–2007) the Labour Party had moved sharply toward the center (Clarke et al. 2008). Most political observers would agree that these party placements are fairly accurate portrayals of actual party positions.[7] Therefore, in overall terms, most people fulfill the third issue-voting criterion: knowing the party positions.

These findings lead to the question of how much Left/Right positions actually influence voting choice. Figure 10.3 shows the percentage voting for a Right party in each country according to the Left/Right attitudes of survey respondents. The impact of Left/Right attitudes is greatest where parties offer clear policy options. In France only 3 percent of self-identified leftists favored a rightist party (Democratic Movement [MoDem], Union for a Popular Movement [UMP], or National Front [NF]) in the 2007 legislative elections, compared to 92 percent among self-identified rightists. Because the parties offer more ideological choice in Europe, the influence of Left/Right attitudes is stronger in these three nations. Even in the United States, however, with only two major parties, there is a 56 percentage-point gap in the Republicans' share of the vote as a function of Left/Right attitudes. These voting differences are much larger than the effects of social characteristics noted in chapter 8. This is because policy evaluations are closer to the end of the funnel of causality and thus have more influence on voting choice.

A closer look at voting patterns confirms the relative positions of the parties along the Left/Right scale. As the most leftist party in France, the PC (Communist Party) attracts the greatest share of its vote among the most extreme leftists, while the Socialists do best among more moderate leftists; this pattern is mirrored in support for the UMP and the National Front on the right. Another significant contrast is between the Greens in Germany

| Figure 10.3 | The Power of Left/Right |

A person's Left/Right position is a powerful predictor of his or her voting choices in all four nations.

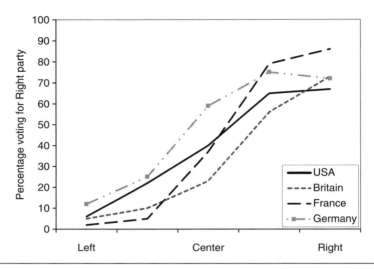

Sources: Comparative Study of Electoral Systems (CSES), United States (2008); France (2007); Germany (2009); Britain, 2010 British Election Study, CSES supplement.

Note: Figure entries are percentage voting for Right party based on the voter's self-placement on the Left/Right scale.

and France. The German Greens' strong support from leftists reflects their position on the continuum, while the French Greens typically draw more support from the center. When you ask people why they like a party or candidate, only a few say because they are liberal or conservative—but these terms are shorthand references for the specific issues that motivate voting choice.

As mentioned earlier, it is hard to compare the impact of issues across nations because the salient issues are changing to reflect current politics. Still, several surveys from the International Social Survey Program (ISSP) can illustrate the relative weight of broad policy domains (see chapter 6 for additional discussion of these items).

Table 10.1 describes the relationship between issue positions and party choices in our four nations (see appendix A on the interpretation of correlations).[8] We should be cautious about overinterpreting these data because the strength of each relationship reflects both the relative size of the relevant issue public and the clarity of party positions. Either of these factors, and therefore the impact of an issue, can change between elections. These data thus offer a snapshot of the relationship between issues and party preferences. Still, snapshots can provide a useful picture of reality.

Table 10.1	Issues and Vote			

Party preferences are linked to a wide range of issue interests.

OPINION	UNITED STATES	GREAT BRITAIN	FRANCE	GERMANY
Left/Right attitudes	0.43	0.27	0.38	0.37
Role of Government				
Government provides jobs	0.18	0.12	0.22	0.13
Government provides health care	0.20	0.09	0.17	0.10
Government provides for old age	0.18	0.11	0.17	0.11
Government provides for unemployed	0.19	0.15	0.27	0.14
Immigration				
Immigrants maintain traditions/ assimilate	0.14	0.17	0.28	0.29
Immigrants increase crime	0.11	0.13	0.26	0.17
Move to exclude illegal immigrants	0.14	0.12	0.26	0.16
Gender Issues				
Men have priority when jobs are scarce	0.08	0.17	0.14	0.14
University is better for boys	0.10	—	—	0.11
Men are better political leaders	0.14	—	—	0.08
Environmental Issues				
Pay more for environment	0.16	0.15	—	0.19
Pay more taxes for environment	0.14	0.12	—	0.14
Cut living standard for environment	0.10	0.12	—	0.04
Nuclear power is dangerous	0.16	0.15	—	0.14
Moral Issues				
Divorce is sometimes justified	0.14	0.11	0.11	0.12
Homosexuality is sometimes justified	0.17	0.11	0.12	0.12
Prostitution is sometimes justified	0.15	0.11	0.12	0.11
Abortion is sometimes justified	0.17	0.12	0.12	0.12
Foreign Policy				
Spend more on defense	0.16	0.16	0.19	0.12

Sources: Left/Right attitudes, Comparative Study of Electoral Systems (CSES), module II, and 2010 British Election Study, CSES module; Role of government, 2006 International Social Survey Program (ISSP); Immigration, 2003 ISSP; Gender, World Values Survey (WVS) waves 4 and 5; Environment, ISSP 2010; Moral issues, 2005–08 WVS and 2008 European Values Survey; Foreign policy, ISSP 2006.

Note: Table entries are Cramer's V coefficients between issue positions and party vote preference. See note 8 and appendix A for descriptions of how to interpret Cramer's V coefficients.

The strongest relationship in each nation is between Left/Right attitudes and party preferences. This is understandable because Left/Right summarizes a person's positions on the issues that are salient to her or him. Even in Britain, where the relationship is weakest, the correlation still indicates strong voting differences. For example, the far leftists cast 64 percent of their votes for Labour, compared to only 5 percent on the Right.

Economic issues of the Old Politics—such as a belief that government is responsible for health care, old age security, and the conditions of the unemployed—display modest to strong relationships with party preferences. This pattern occurs because economic topics have large issue publics, and most political parties have clear policies on the government's role in the economy and related economic policies (see figure 7.2). In the United States, for example, the Republican Party has challenged social spending policies as part of the party's core program, and Democrats defend these policies. There are similar party divisions in Great Britain, France, and Germany.

The public's issue interests now include a wide range of issues. In Britain, for example, the average correlation for role of government issues is comparable to the issues of immigration and environmental protection. Gender issues also have a modest relationship to party choice. Even support for defense spending influences party preference. The correlation in Germany, for example, represents a 15 percent difference in CDU/CSU support between those who want much more defense spending and those who want much less. We shouldn't make a precise comparison across issues, because the results depend on which questions were asked and the events immediately surrounding the survey. But these results show that many issues now affect the voting preferences of contemporary electorates.

The modest impact of each of these issues should not be interpreted as a limited role for issues, because not all issues are salient to all voters. In fact, issue interests have probably increased in diversity over time, and the linkage between issues and political parties has become more complex. A more refined analysis of specific issue publics would find that individual voting decisions are strongly influenced by each voter's specific issue interests—but these interests vary from person to person (Krosnick 1990; Gershkoff 2005). Correlations based on the total public combine those inside and outside of each issue public, which decreases the overall evidence of issue voting. If I limited our analysis to only members of the relevant issue public that is concerned with each issue, the correlations would be even stronger.

In addition, cognitively sophisticated voters are more likely to rely on issues in making their electoral choices, further magnifying the importance of issue voting. A simple example can illustrate this. If one uses liberal/conservative attitudes in the 2008 U.S. election as summarizing issue positions, this relationship increases from .37 among those lowest in cognitive mobilization to .57 among the highly mobilized.[9] As a reference standard, the correlation with party identification and vote is only weakly affected by the level of cognitive mobilization. Thus, those lowest in cognitive mobilization place greater reliance on party identification when making their vote choice (if they vote), and the cognitively mobilized balance issues and partisanship.

In summary, V. O. Key's positive assessments of the public's issue voting no longer appear so unorthodox.

Performance Issues and the Vote

Another form of issue voting involves performance evaluations. Many voters follow Ronald Reagan's advice to ask themselves if they are better off than they were four years ago—and vote for or against the incumbents on that basis (Anderson et al. 2005). Morris Fiorina (1981, 5) put it best: citizens "typically have one comparatively hard bit of data: they know what life has been like during the incumbent's administration. They do not need to know the precise economic or foreign policies of the incumbent administration in order to judge the results of those policies." In other words, performance-based voting offers people a reasonable shortcut for ensuring that unsuccessful policies are dropped and successful policies continued.

This argument holds that many voters dispense electoral rewards and punishments based on past performance of the government or the governing parties. Performance voting typically focuses on *valance issues* where people agree on the general outcome—such as favoring a strong economy or protecting the environment—so that differences in the achievement of these goals is important. Benjamin Page (1978, 222), for example, wrote, "Even if the Great Depression and lack of recovery were not at all [Herbert] Hoover's fault . . . it could make sense to punish him in order to sharpen the incentives to maintain prosperity in the future." Page acknowledged that blame may be placed unfairly, yet "to err on the side of forgiveness would leave voters vulnerable to tricky explanations and rationalizations; but to err on the draconian side would only spur politicians on to greater energy and imagination in problem solving." Therefore, performance voting requires that voters have a target for their blame when the government falters in some respect, whether it is economic slowdown or a foreign policy mistake.

Studies of performance-based voting often focus on the economic conditions (Lewis-Beck and Paldam 2000; MacKuen, Erikson, and Stimson 1992). An example of performance evaluation is when judgments about one's personal financial situation or the performance of the national economy are significantly related to voting choices. People want the economy to improve because they see their own well-being suffering or worry about the social effects of unemployment and growing debt—and they look for a party that they believe will improve the economy.

Figure 10.4 gives an example of performance voting in the relationship between reports on person's individual conditions over the past year and support for the incumbent party. In each case, worsening economic conditions hurt the incumbents, and improving conditions benefit them. In the 2009 German election, for example, the incumbent SPD-CDU/CSU government got only 35 percent of the vote from those who said they were much worse off versus 58 percent from those who were somewhat better off (because of the recession, there were only ten voters in the survey who felt "much better"). Similar patterns appear for American and British voters.

Research has asked whether these relationships are sufficient evidence of causality (Wlezien, Franklin, and Twiggs 1997). As noted in chapter 8, some people adjust their economic expectations to reflect their general images of the government. People who like the incumbent government for whatever reason are more likely to put a favorable spin on economic conditions; those who are critical of government for one aspect of policy may generalize this dissatisfaction to include their economic judgments. Such projections, which are a normal part of incumbent images, likely magnify the relationship between economic perceptions and party preferences. Nevertheless, the

| **Figure 10.4** | **Well-Being and Vote Choice** |

If people believe their economic conditions are worsening, they vote against the incumbents.

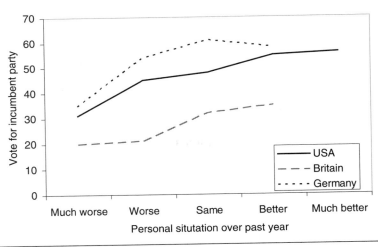

Sources: United States, 2008 American National Election Study; Britain, 2010 British Election Study; Germany, 2009 German Longitudinal Election Study.

Note: Figure entries are percentages of the vote for the incumbent party by the respondent's perception of his or her personal economic condition over past year.

underlying relationship is still important. A rising economic tide benefits the incumbents, while a failing economy often spells defeat at the next elections.

Another factor involves the scope of economic evaluations. Researchers have examined whether voters base their political evaluations on their personal economic situation (*pocketbook voting*) or on the broader national economy (*sociotropic voting*). Most studies find that voters generally follow the sociotropic model, which implies that policy outcomes rather than narrow self-interest are the driving force behind performance voting (Nadeau, Niemi, and Yoshinaka 2002; Listhaug 2005).

Another insight is that the strength of performance voting depends on the public's ability to assign credit or blame—which reflects the institutional structures (Hellwig 2011; Duch and Stevenson 2008; Brug, van der Eijk, and Franklin 2007). For instance, with the complex system of divided government and checks and balances in the United States, it is difficult to assign responsibility for governance. In contrast, in Britain's normally one-party-dominant system a citizen knows which party to hold responsible for the actions of government. And there is another irony for politicians: voters seem more likely to punish governments for bad economic times than reward them when the times are good. Thus, no single government was responsible for the 2008 recession, but incumbents in both Europe and North America have struggled at the polls as a result of the economic downturn.

The focus on economic voting is partially because economic conditions are important to many voters—but performance voting can be generalized to other policy areas (Clarke et al. 2009; Clarke, Kornberg, and Scotto 2009). If there is an obvious foreign policy blunder, it makes sense for the public to hold the government to account (such as the Carter administration's failure to rescue hostages at the U.S. embassy in Iran in 1979; or the eventual backlash to the George W. Bush administration's war policies). The governing party in Japan lost public support in the wake of the Fukushima nuclear disaster because of its mishandling of the crisis. On many issues the public can ask, Are things better off than they were four years ago?

A general illustration of performance effects comes from two questions in the Comparative Study of Electoral Systems survey. The survey first asked people what was the most important problem facing their nation. Then it asked which party or candidate would best deal with the problem. Typically a large majority of those who mention a party as most capable on the most important issue say that they voted for this party—but a significant percentage don't vote for the party they cited as most capable.[10] In some cases, contrasting preferences on other issues may push voters in a different direction. Or they might not favor the general policy positions of the first cited party.

The crucial aspect of performance voting is that it emphasizes the competency of the government (or a political party) to deliver a generally preferred policy goal.[11] This contrasts with position issues, where the policy goal is debated. At one time, democratic theorists discounted the meaningfulness of performance voting because it was a debate over political means rather than ends. But two recent studies of British voting choice make a persuasive case that performance voting is an important element of democratic choice (Clarke et al. 2004, 2008). Does it make sense, they ask, to pay attention to the policy positions of an ineffective administration that seemingly cannot make good on its promises and program? Such considerations can be applied to both candidates and political parties. They further argue that judging parties on valence issue is a meaningful heuristic for people who are "smart enough" to know they "are not smart enough" to figure out the complexity of policy choices on their own. Policy voting and performance voting have to coexist to ensure democratic accountability and representation. The most effective weapon of popular control in a democratic regime is the electorate's capacity to hold the government accountable for past actions as well as look toward the future.

Candidate Images and the Vote

The interview cited at the opening of this chapter highlighted the issue positions of this American voter. The responses also included comments about Barack Obama's personality and communication skills as factors affecting voting choice, as well as points about John McCain. Candidate images are inevitably part of the calculus of voting.

Democratic theorists describe issue voting in positive terms, but they often view candidate-based voting decisions less positively (Converse 1964; Page 1978). Candidates' images can be seen as commodities packaged by image makers who sway the public by emphasizing personal traits to appeal to the voters. People's judgments about alternative candidates can, in this view, rely on superficial criteria such as a candidate's style or looks. Indeed, many experimental studies demonstrate that it is possible to manipulate a candidate's personal appearance to affect voters' choices.

However, there is another view of the meaningfulness of candidate images. This position holds that candidate evaluations are not necessarily superficial, emotional, or purely short term. Voters may focus on the personal qualities of a candidate to gain important information about characteristics relevant to assessing likely performance in office. This approach suggests that people organize their thoughts about candidates into broad categories or "prototypes" that they use in making judgments when other information is limited. Donald Kinder and his colleagues (1980), for example, explored the features that citizens use to define an ideal president. They showed that people apply the attributes they believe would make for an ideal president in rating the incumbent president.

Arthur Miller, Martin Wattenberg, and Oksana Malanchuk (1986, 536) similarly argued for a rational interpretation of candidate-based voting: "Candidate assessments actually concentrate on instrumental concerns about how a candidate would conduct governmental affairs." They found that the three most important dimensions of candidate image for Americans are integrity, reliability, and competence. Bittner's (2011) recent cross-national study of candidate-based voting held that competence and character are the most important aspects of candidate evaluations. Such criteria are hardly irrational, for if a candidate is too incompetent to carry out policy promises or too dishonest for those promises to be trusted, it makes perfect sense for a voter to pay attention to these personal traits.

Another concern is whether candidate images are independent of party preferences or a projection of these preferences on the candidates. In the 2009 German election, among those who voted for the CDU/CSU, 91 percent said they liked Angela Merkel, but only 30 percent liked Frank-Walter Steinmeyer, who was the Social Democratic Party (SPD) chancellor-candidate; among SPD voters the patterns were reversed—83 percent liked Steinmeyer and 36 percent liked Merkel. Clearly party preferences and candidate preferences covary together.

The structure of the electoral system can also affect the level of candidate-based voting (Aarts, Blais, and Schmitt 2011; Tverdova 2011; Bittner 2011). In single-member district parliamentary systems, partisan and candidate preferences are often closely intertwined because the parties typically select loyal candidates. When people vote directly for parties in proportional electoral systems, candidate factors are lessened. Only in a system of direct election of candidates who are not selected by the party organization—such as through the primary system in the United States—is there likely to be much separation between party preferences and candidate preferences.

The United States is certainly in the lead in developing a pattern of candidate-centered electoral politics (Wattenberg 1991, 2011). Presidents are the focal point of the quadrennial elections, and the large shifts in vote shares between presidential elections often reflect the effects of candidate images. Presidents (and chief executives in state and local governments) are directly elected, and they often run on personal platforms as well as representatives of a party position. Candidate image is one of their major electoral resources. A similar personalization of politics occurs in France, where the president is directly elected and legislative elections are held at a separate time (Lewis-Beck, Nadeau, and Bèlanger 2012). The French president also functions separately from the legislative majority and even from his or her own party within the legislature.

Electoral research on parliamentary systems finds that candidate images have less impact on voting choice because people do not directly vote for the chief executive or district representative in most parliamentary systems. However, the importance of candidate images seems to be increasing even in parliamentary systems, although this point is still debated (Aarts, Blais, and Schmitt 2011; Curtice and Holmberg 2005; Poguntke and Webb 2005; compare Aardal and Binder 2011). Hayes and McAllister's findings for Britain, Australia, and the United States sum up this general pattern: "Election outcomes are now, more than at any time in the past, determined by voters' assessments of party leaders" (1997, 3).

Anyone who has watched modern parliamentary campaigns, with candidates staging walkabouts for television and hosting discussion sessions with voters (in front of the cameras), must recognize that candidate images are an important part of contemporary electoral campaigns in virtually all advanced industrial democracies (Ohr 2011; Mughan 2000). The focus on candidates has also led to the introduction of televised candidate debates, with the British finally adopting this model in the 2010 election. Elections are primarily about parties and their programs, but candidates put a public face on the campaign, and chief executives have a major impact on the style and content of governments.

The End of the Causal Funnel

Okay, the time has finally come—it is Election Day. When people are ready to vote, they inevitably weigh a mix of partisanship, issues, and candidate images to make their voting choices. Candidate images are at the very end of the funnel of causality, indicating that they are strongly related to voting preferences, at least in systems where voters cast ballots for specific candidates. At the same time, candidate images are themselves the culmination of prior influences. Long-term partisanship can have a potent effect in cuing voters on which politicians to like or dislike, just as voters' issue preferences can lead them toward specific candidates.

So, with overlapping candidate, party, and issue preferences, it is difficult to assess the independent effect of each. A simple comparison of the weight of issues and candidate orientations can illustrate the mix of factors at play. Figure 10.5 combines Left/Right attitudes, satisfaction with the government's performance, and images of the major party candidates to explain voting choices. (A full model should consider other factors, such as party identification and social group cues; the figure summarizes the variables at the very end of the causal funnel.) The left side of the figure presents the impact of these factors in predicting vote choices for the legislature. The right side of the figure presents the relationships for voting in the 2008 U.S. presidential election and 2007 French presidential election.

Each of the three factors significantly affects legislative voting in each nation. Candidate images strongly influence legislative voting in all four nations; in three nations it is the strongest predictor.[12] This is partly because candidate image is toward the end of the funnel of causality, close to the actual vote decision. Still, in parliamentary systems the voters do not select the prime minister (PM), but evaluations of the PM candidates is seemingly of growing importance as their personal images come to dominate the campaigns.

In addition, the impact of candidate image understandably varies with the type of election. In the United States, for example, feelings toward Barack Obama and John McCain were strongly related to congressional voting preferences in 2008—comparable to the effects in France and Britain. However, candidate images exerted an even stronger influence on presidential vote choice in the United States. The voting evidence on the French 2007 elections shows that candidate images are more important than Left/Right positions in determining voters' ballots in the legislative and presidential election, perhaps because of the visibility of the Sarkozy or Royale contest

Figure 10.5 Predicting the Vote

Candidate preferences and issue opinions are important predictors of voting choice, and candidate images are especially important in presidential elections.

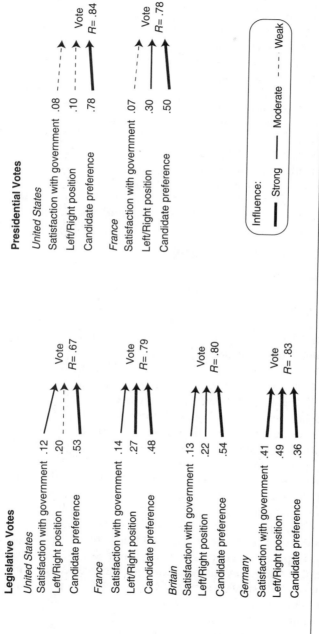

Legislative Votes

United States
Satisfaction with government .12
Left/Right position .20
Candidate preference .53
Vote
R= .67

France
Satisfaction with government .14
Left/Right position .27
Candidate preference .48
Vote
R= .79

Britain
Satisfaction with government .13
Left/Right position .22
Candidate preference .54
Vote
R= .80

Germany
Satisfaction with government .41
Left/Right position .49
Candidate preference .36
Vote
R= .83

Presidential Votes

United States
Satisfaction with government .08
Left/Right position .10
Candidate preference .78
Vote
R= .84

France
Satisfaction with government .07
Left/Right position .30
Candidate preference .50
Vote
R= .78

Influence:
——— Strong —— Moderate - - - Weak

Sources: Comparative Study of Electoral Systems (CSES), United States (2008), France (2007), Germany (2009); Britain, 2010 British Election Study, CSES supplement.

Note: Figure entries are standardized regression coefficients. Parties are coded by public's perceptions of their Left/Right position (figure 10.1). See appendix A for an explanation of these coefficients.

in 2007.[13] Although it is difficult to determine the exact impact of candidate images on voter choice, these results suggest that these images are a strong influence on voting choice.

Issues—represented in figure 10.5 by Left/Right attitudes and perceptions of the government's performance—also have significant influence on voting choice. Left/Right attitudes are more strongly related to vote choice in all three European democracies than in the United States. Because European parties offer clearer policy choices than American parties do, and Europeans vote (directly or indirectly) for a party more than for a candidate, it isn't surprising that policy positions are a stronger basis of voting in European elections. Despite the emphasis on performance voting, satisfaction with government policy has a limited impact on voting choice in these comparisons.

The specific mix of issue and candidate influences will be highly variable across elections because they are short-term elements of the vote, but these transatlantic differences reflect institutional structures that are likely to endure over time.[14] In contrast, it is striking that in neither U.S. congressional nor presidential elections do Left/Right positions have a strong independent relationship to vote, which repeats earlier findings for the 2004 election.

One Electorate or Many?

The increasing diversity of factors that people use in their voting decisions is fragmenting the public into separate electorates that have different views of the election and their voting decisions. For some people, the mere presence of a party label may be sufficient to decide their vote. As the old saying goes, some Americans would vote for a yellow dog if it were a Democrat. Other people focus on the candidates, their qualities to govern, or just their likeability. Even greater fragmentation occurs if one considers how the weight of different issues might vary across the electorate.

Combining all of the electorate in a single correlation—such as the relationship between social class and vote or Left/Right attitudes and vote—combines different voting calculations for different individuals. The impact of candidate image and issues in predicting vote in figure 10.5 doesn't mean that every voter gives the same weights to the predictors. Some more heavily base their vote on candidate image, while others disproportionately judge the election in Left/Right terms. The statistics in figure 10.5 and other similar analyses average together the calculations of distinct subpublics.

In theory, the number of distinct subpublics that may exist in any one election is unlimited. Part of the challenge is to determine which subgroups are most important to compare. The idea of issue publics suggests that issue interests are not evenly distributed. Some people see the campaign as a referendum on taxes, while others focus on foreign policy or social welfare policies. This is quite apparent if you ask people to discuss their issue interests or what they like or dislike about the parties. Single-issue voting occurs when some individuals focus on a limited set of issues (or a single issue) to decide their votes.

To illustrate the concept of subpublics, I use the political mobilization typology presented in chapter 9. Some people rely on their partisan identities as political cues, while others have the cognitive skills and resources to reach their own political judgments. And some have both—or neither. These different bases of political mobilization should affect the sources of voting choice. Better-educated and politically sophisticated voters place more weight on issues as a basis for their electoral decision making; less sophisticated voters rely more on partisanship and social cues (Dalton 2012a; Sniderman, Brody, and Tetlock 1991). And one would expect partisans to weight party cues more heavily than nonpartisans.

Figure 10.6 summarizes the influence of party cues and Left/Right policy preferences for voter choice in the 2008 U.S. presidential elections.[15] The weight of both factors is separately calculated for the four mobilization types of figure 9.5. The figure shows that relative affect toward the two major parties is most strongly related to vote choice, which is natural because the candidates are representatives of their respective parties. At the same time, apartisans place the greatest weight on Left/Right attitudes in making their voting choice. The voting choice of cognitive partisans and ritual partisans is very strongly related to their relative preference for the two parties, with Left/Right attitudes playing a distinctly secondary role. Finally, apolitical independents (who lack party cues or the political sophistication) show the weakest relationship for both factors as a basis for their voting choices—if they do vote.

A parallel analysis of the 2009 German elections found a similar pattern (Dalton 2012b). Apartisans were most likely to mention policy reasons for their votes, and least likely to cite party traits. Conversely, ritual partisans and cognitive partisans were most likely to cite party traits as an explanation for their votes. In summary, each of these groups uses a different decision-making calculus when making its choices.

Research would show a similar fragmentation of the electorate if it compared the impact of specific issues across issue publics. We would expect that members of an issue public would vote for the candidate who agrees with their views on that issue. For citizens not in that issue public, a candidate's stand on the issue is much less relevant to their voting choices. Campaigns are therefore fragmented in this way as well. Bartle (2005) showed similar patterns as a function of the salience of candidate images. Combining the variations by cognitive mobilization, issue publics, and candidate salience, one might conclude that there isn't one election campaign, but many; there isn't one electorate, but many.

Citizen Politics and Voting Behavior

The previous several chapters have described changes in the patterns of voting choice in advanced industrial democracies. Three major changes are intertwined. The first is a *general decline in the long-term determinants of voting*. Social class has a decreasing impact on voting in virtually all

| Figure 10.6 | Political Mobilization and Voting |

The bases of presidential choice vary systematically depending on the partisanship and sophistication of the voter.

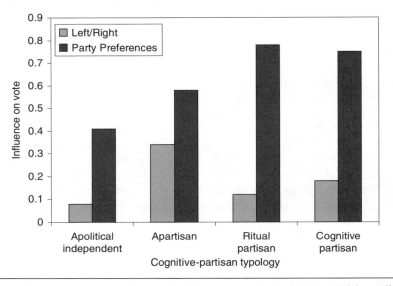

Source: 2008 American National Election Study; see note 14 for the calculation of these effects.

established democracies, along with similar declines in the impact of religion and other social characteristics (chapter 8). Similarly, dealignment has decreased the effect of party attachments on voting (chapter 9). Thus, fewer voters now approach elections with standing party predispositions based on either social characteristics or early learned partisan ties.

The second change is the *growth in the importance of short-term factors on voting,* such as issue opinions and candidate images. The most persuasive cross-national evidence comes from a study of voting behavior in seventeen Western democracies. In reviewing their findings, Mark Franklin, Tom Mackie, and Henry Valen (1992, 400) conclude, "If all the issues of importance to voters had been measured and given their due weight, then the rise of issue voting would have compensated more or less precisely for the decline in cleavage politics."

The trend toward greater issue voting and candidate voting is a self-reinforcing process. As party ties weaken, the potential for issues to influence voting choice increases. In addition, as issues become more important, this encourages some party defection and erodes the voter's party attachments still further.[16] Parties also respond to the developments and change their electoral messages to voters away from long-term loyalties. Thus, the rise of issue voting and the decline of partisanship are interrelated trends.

The shifting balance of long-term and short-term voting influences is another aspect of the new style of citizen politics. As modern electorates have become more sophisticated and politically interested, and as political information has become more available, many citizens can now reach their own voting decisions without relying on broad external cues such as social class or family partisanship. In short, more citizens now have the political resources to follow the complexities of politics; they have the potential to act as the independent issue voters described in classic democratic theory but seldom seen in practice.

These developments mean that basic electoral patterns are changing. For example, more people are deciding their vote later in campaigns to take issues and candidate images into account. This also means that more people are changing their voting preferences between elections as events change. Between the 1960s and today, electoral volatility has roughly doubled in the established democracies (Dalton 2012a, ch. 9). Split-ticket voting is also generally increasing in many democracies. The erosion of party loyalties and issue-based voting also contributes to the fragmentation of existing parties and the emergence of new parties to capture these new floating voters. Paraphrasing another study of voting behavior: voters are beginning to exercise real choice.

The third change is the *fragmentation of voter choice* into separate subpublics (also see Bartle 2005). Despite the changes noted here, some people remain politically disengaged: if they vote at all, they may base their choice on idiosyncratic criteria. Some people, although fewer and fewer in number, vote on the basis of social group identities such as class or religion. Other voters, whom I have labeled "ritual partisans," view the campaigns and candidates in terms of their party loyalties. More sophisticated voters may have strong issue beliefs and make their voting choice on which party or candidate best represents their views. This pattern of issue voting can further fragment the electorate and divide people into separate issue publics. Yet another group of voters might focus on candidate traits or other factors in making their voting choices. The most sophisticated voters consider a range of factors spanning issues and candidate characteristics. This diversity of decision making means that there isn't one election campaign, but many, as the voters focus on different factors. It also means there isn't one voting calculus, but many, as voters use different factors to make their choices.

The impact of economics on the vote illustrates these changes. Traditionally, social divisions defined economic conflicts: the working class versus the middle class, industrial versus agrarian interests. In this situation, one's social position was often a meaningful guide to voting choices. As social divisions have narrowed, the group bases of political interests have blurred, other issues attract voter attention, and social class is less relevant as a voting cue. Some people still vote on class or union cues, but they are fewer in number. This decline doesn't mean that economic issues are unimportant—quite the opposite: contemporary evidence of economic voting is widespread. But today, issue positions are more individually based rather than group derived. The political cues of a union leader or business association must compete with a voter's own opinions on economic policy and party programs. That a continuing concern for economic growth and security hasn't revived traditional class divisions even in the wake of the 2008 recession provides compelling evidence that a new style of citizen politics now guides many voters.

This new style of individually based voting decisions may signify a boon or a curse for contemporary democracies. On the positive side, sophisticated voters should inject more issue voting into elections, increasing the policy implications of electoral results. And politicians must become more responsive to public preferences if they want to win their votes; they cannot depend on hereditary loyalties as in the past. In the long term, greater issue voting may make candidates and parties more responsive to public opinion and move the democratic process closer to the democratic ideal. This may be why recent representation studies typically conclude that governments and parties are more representative of their voters in comparison to a generation or two ago (see chapter 11; Powell 2011).

On the negative side, many political scientists are concerned that the growth of issue voting and single-issue groups may place too many demands on democratic governments (see chapter 12). The demands of single-issue publics also may be irreconcilable if treated independently of other interests, and a focus on special issues can ignore the collective needs of society. Should the AARP (and seniors) have a decisive say on Social Security legislation, and should the Sierra Club (and environmentalists) dominate environmental policymaking and potentially exclude other societal interests? Without the issue-aggregating functions performed by political parties, democratic governments may face conflicting issue demands that they find difficult to satisfy.

Another concern involves the citizens who lack the political skills to meet the requirements of sophisticated issue voting. These people may become isolated from politics if traditional political cues (party and social groups) decline in usefulness. Lacking firm political predispositions or a clear understanding of politics, they may decide not to vote or they may be mobilized by demagogic elites or fraudulent party programs. Many political analysts see the rise of New Right and flash parties in Europe, especially those headed by charismatic party leaders, as a negative consequence of a dealigned electorate. Indeed, television facilitates direct, unmediated contacts between political elites and the public. Despite its potential for encouraging more sophisticated citizen involvement, television also offers the possibility of trivialized electoral politics in which video style outweighs substance in campaigning.

The trends discussed here do not lend themselves to a single prediction of the future of democratic party systems. The future is, however, within our control, depending on how political systems respond to these challenges. If elites improve the quality of discourse, democracy will benefit. If they attempt to exploit the erosion of long-term loyalties for their short-term advantage by populist appeals and limited accountability, democracy may suffer.

Suggested Readings

Aarts, Kees, André Blais, and Hermann Schmitt, eds. 2011. *Political Leaders and Democratic Elections*. Oxford, UK: Oxford University Press.

Bittner, Amanda. 2011. *Platform or Personality? The Role of Party Leaders in Elections*. Oxford, UK: Oxford University Press.

Clarke, Harold, et al. 2009. *Performance Politics and the British Voter*. Cambridge, UK: Cambridge University Press.

Clarke, Harold, et al. 2013. *Campaigning for Change: The Dynamics of Political Choice in Britain*. Cambridge, UK: Cambridge University Press.

Lau, Richard, and David Redlawsk. 2006. *How Voters Decide: Information Processing during Election Campaigns*. New York: Cambridge University Press.

LeDuc, Lawrence, Richard Niemi, and Pippa Norris, eds. 2010. *Comparing Democracies 3: Elections and Voting in the 21st Century*. 3rd ed. Thousand Oaks, CA: Sage.

Niemi, Richard, Herbert Weisberg, and David Kimball, eds. 2010. *Controversies in Voting*. 5th ed. Washington, DC: Congressional Quarterly Press.

Poguntke, Thomas, and Paul Webb, eds. 2005. *The Presidentialization of Politics: A Comparative Study of Modern Democracies*. New York: Oxford University Press.

Wattenberg, Martin. 1991. *The Rise of Candidate-Centered Voting*. Cambridge, MA: Harvard University Press.

Notes

1. The Pew Center (2012b) asked about party positions on seven current issues. Older Americans were more accurate in identifying the conservative party on raising taxes and reducing the deficit; younger Americans were more accurate on the issues of gay rights, citizenship for illegal immigrants, and reducing the budget.
2. Ted Carmines and James Stimson (1980) distinguished between "hard" issues, which are complex and difficult to evaluate, and "easy" issues, which present clear and simple choices. Donald Kinder and Rod Kiewiet (1981) contrasted personal issues, such as voting on the basis of economic self-interest, and issues that reflect national policy choices, such as voting on the basis of what will benefit most Americans.

3. Bernard Berelson, Paul Lazarsfeld, and William McPhee (1954) described these as style issues; Donald Stokes (1963) used the term "valence issue." Later research made the further distinction between performance and attributes (Miller and Wattenberg 1985; Shanks and Miller 1990).

4. Anthony Downs conceived of Left/Right labels as a way to reduce information costs rather than as fully informed ideological orientations. As he explained (1957, 98), "With this short cut a voter can save himself the cost of being informed upon a wide range of issues."

5. Those who voted for the Democratic congressional candidate locate themselves at 5.1 on the Left/Right scale, more toward the center than the average placement of the Democratic Party (4.4). Conversely, voters for the Republican candidate were more conservative (6.8) than the overall public's placement of the Republican Party (6.4). In 2008 the public saw both Obama (4.6) and McCain (5.9) as more moderate than their respective parties.

6. Surveys in 2011 found that Germans place the new Pirate Party to the left, perhaps because its voters typically supported leftist parties. However, the party hasn't developed a broad ideological program and instead focuses on a small subset of core issues.

7. Powerful evidence of the collective wisdom of the electorate comes from comparing the public's Left/Right placement of the parties with the judgments of political science experts in each nation (Dalton, Farrell, and McAllister 2011, ch. 5). These two Left/Right scores yields an extremely high correlation ($r = .92$ for 107 parties), which indicates almost complete agreement. PhDs are almost as good as average citizens in identifying party positions!

8. See appendix A. The relationship is described by a Cramer's V correlation: a value of .00 means that issue opinions are unrelated to party preference. (See appendix A for explanation.)

9. The following table gives the tau-b correlations for congressional vote choice in the United States with liberal/conservative self-placement and party identification.

Cognitive Mobilization	Liberal/ Conservative	Party Identification
Low	.37	.50
Medium	.48	.59
High	.57	.57

10. Using the 2010 British Election Study as an example, among those who said the Labour Party was best able to deal with the most important national problem, 22 percent voted for a party besides Labour. For those who felt the Conservatives were most competent, 21 percent voted for another party, and among those who felt the Liberal Democrats were most competent, 18 percent voted for another party.

11. Performance voting is similar to the thermostatic model of representation described in chapter 11 (Soroka and Wlezien 2010).

12. I measured affect toward Barack Obama and John McCain in the United States, Gordon Brown and James Cameron in Britain, Ségolène Royal and Nicolas Sarkozy in France, Frank-Walter Steinmeyer and Angela Merkel in Germany. The government performance question asked about how good a job the government had done since the last election.

13. The party and candidate choices in the French survey were rescored to equal the value of the public's Left/Right placement of each actor, and this was used as the dependent variable in Figure 10.5.

14. One productive new area of research examines how institutional context systematically affects the correlates of voting (Dalton and Anderson 2011). For example, candidate effects are predictably stronger in candidate-based systems than in party-based proportional representation (Tverdova 2011). Similarly, the impact of issues on voting choice is partly a function of the polarization of the party choices.

15. The partisan variable is the difference between feelings toward Obama and feelings toward John McCain (thermometer scores). The Left/Right variable is the respondent's self placement on this scale. For more information, see Dalton (2012a, ch. 7).

16. The conventional wisdom holds that partisanship strongly influences issue opinions, while the reverse causal flow is minimal (figure 9.1). As issue voting has increased, however, research has found that issues can be quite important in changing partisanship (Niemi and Jennings 1991; Fiorina 1981).

11 Political Representation

If you have ever watched the classic movie *Mr. Smith Goes to Washington*, you have seen representative democracy at its best and worst. An idealistic Jimmy Stewart is appointed to fill a vacancy in the U.S. Senate. He naïvely proposes the creation of a national boy's camp to aid youth in the midst of the Depression, but his idea creates conflict with entrenched interests and corruption in Washington. In the end, the film is about how democracy, freedom, and idealism can triumph over corruption and oppression.[1]

Contemporary democracies owe their existence to the invention of representative democracy, in which elected officials act in behalf of their constituents. From the ancient Greeks through the eighteenth century, *democracy* meant the direct participation of all the citizens in the affairs of government. The Greek city-state, the self-governing Swiss canton, and the New England town meeting exemplify this democratic ideal.

The invention of representative government freed democracies from these limits. Instead of directly participating in political decision making, the public selects legislators to represent them in government deliberations. The case for representative government is largely one of necessity. Democracy requires citizen control over the political process. But in large nations, the town meeting model is not feasible.[2] Proponents of representative government also stress the limited political sophistication of the average citizen and the need for professional politicians. Popular control over government occurs through periodic, competitive elections to select these elites. Elections should ensure that officials are responsive and accountable to the public. By accepting this electoral process, the public gives its consent to be governed by the elites selected. The democratic process therefore depends on the relationship between the representative and the represented.

Many early political philosophers criticized the concept of representative government because they believed it undermined the tenets of democracy by transferring political power from the people to a small group of selected officials. Voters had political power only on the day their ballots were cast, and then they had to wait in political servitude until the next election—four or five years hence—for the opportunity to exercise that power again. Under representative government, citizens may control, but elites rule. Rousseau warned, "The instant a people allows itself to be represented it loses its freedom."

235

---| **Internet Resource** |---

Visit the Eurobarometer website of the European Union for information on the latest citizen and elite surveys:

http://ec.europa.eu/public_opinion/index_en.htm

Contemporary proponents of direct democracy are equally critical of representative government. European Green parties criticize the process of representative government while calling for increased citizen influence through referendums, citizen action groups, and other forms of "basic" democracy. The German Pirate Party uses an online forum (liquid democracy) that allows members to instruct party delegates on current issues. Populist groups in the United States display a similar skepticism of electoral politics in favor of direct citizen participation. Benjamin Barber (1984, 145) expressed these concerns: "The representative government principle steals from individuals the ultimate responsibility for their values, beliefs, and actions. . . . Representation is incompatible with freedom because it delegates and thus alienates political will at the cost of genuine self-government and autonomy."

Such critics worry that the democratic principle of popular control has been replaced by a commitment to routinized electoral procedures—democracy is defined by its means, not its ends. Moreover, they claim governments resist efforts to increase public influence and control because elections provide the accepted standard of influence. These critics are not opposed to representative government, but they are critical of a political system that stops at representation and limits other (and perhaps more effective) methods of citizen input.

The linkage between the public and the political decision makers is one of the essential questions for the study of democratic political systems (Dalton, Farrell, and McAllister 2011). The commitment to popular rule is what sets democracies apart from other political systems. Although we cannot resolve the debate on the merits of representative government, we can address how well the representation process functions today.

Collective Correspondence

In the broadest sense of the term, the *representativeness* of elite attitudes is measured by their similarity to the attitudes of the overall public. Robert Weissberg (1978) referred to this comparison as "collective correspondence": when the public's policy preferences are matched by the preferences of elites, the public as a collective is well represented by elites as a collective.

The complexity of political representation obviously goes beyond a comparison of all citizens' opinions to all elites. Some elected officials may stress their role in educating the public instead of merely reflecting current public preferences. When voters hold contradictory opinions, the policymaking role of elites may lead them to adopt more consistent, but less representative, positions. Sometimes different issue publics hold opinions that are logically contradictory, and both cannot be represented—such as cutting taxes and expanding government spending. Policy preferences also are not necessarily equivalent to policy outcomes. We could add other qualifiers to this list. Still, citizen–elite agreement is a basic standard for judging the representativeness of a democratic system. Agreement is a meaningful test because it determines whether decision makers approach policymaking with the same overall policy preferences as the public, and as such it is a critical goal of representative democracy.

Cross-national data comparing the opinions of top-level political elites and the public are fairly rare. More common are studies that focus on public–elite comparisons in a single nation.[3] This chapter assembles a diverse mix of evidence comparing elite and public opinion within and across nations.

We begin with evidence from the United States. In 1998 the Pew Center (1998b) surveyed members of Congress, but it only asked a few items that were comparable to questions in public opinion surveys (table 11.1). Pew found that only 45 percent of members of Congress said that federal government programs should be maintained to deal with important problems, but 57 percent of the American public supported this position. On the standard liberal/conservative scale, Congress had more self-identified conservatives than the public at large, and fewer liberals, but the percentage differences were modest on each response. In the years since this survey there has been a growing polarization between Democratic and Republican members of Congress. It is not clear how this has affected collective correspondence, but it means that the choices facing voters have become more sharply distinct.

Table 11.1	Citizens and Members of Congress	

With a Republican majority in 1998, Congress was slightly more conservative than the American public.

	MEMBERS OF CONGRESS	CITIZENS
Maintain Government Programs	57	45
Liberal/Conservative Position		
Conservative	37	47
Moderate	40	31
Liberal	19	7

Sources: 1998 Pew Center survey of members of Congress and Pew public survey (Pew Center 1998b).

Note: Entries are percentages agreeing with policy statement and self-identifying on a liberal/conservative scale.

Previous comparisons of public opinion and opinions of members of Congress in 1978, 1982, and 1987 also found that the two groups differed by only a few percentage points (Bishop and Frankovic 1981; Erikson and Tedin 2010; Herrera, Herrera, and Smith 1992). In broad terms, the fit between the American public and congressional elites generally shows substantial collective correspondence.

Cross-national studies of mass and elite opinions in Europe are even rarer. Projects survey European public opinion and European elite opinion—but few projects regularly ask the same questions to both groups. The most recent available surveys asked about opinions for candidates in the 2009 European Parliament (EP) elections. Figure 11.1 compares the Left/Right attitudes of candidates for the European Parliament (CEPs) to those of their respective publics.

The two bars for each nation describe the Left/Right opinions of the overall public to the elites (CEPs) from the nation.[4] In general, the public is more likely to locate itself at the center of the Left/Right scale in each nation. In Britain, for example, 36 percent of the public positions themselves at the center of the scale compared to 21 percent of elites. Probably because we

| Figure 11.1 | Citizens, Elites, and Left/Right |

In broad terms, citizens and candidates for the European Parliament share similar Left/Right attitudes, except that citizens are more likely to call themselves centrists.

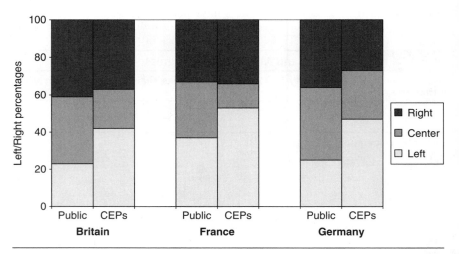

Sources: 2009 European Election Study and 2009 Candidates to the European Parliament Study.

Note: The figure displays the distribution of Left/Centrist/Right attitudes among the public in each nation and CEPs weighted by each party's seat share in the Parliament.

are comparing candidates to the European Parliament who are more liberal than national members of Parliament (MPs), elites in all three nations tend to have a higher proportion of leftists; the percentage of rightists is very similar between publics and elites. And in general terms, the results mirror patterns we saw in chapter 6. The French public is more to the left than either the British or Germans, and French elites are also more leftist.

National studies have compared citizens and elites on specific issue opinions. The 1997 British Election Study found that the average British citizen and member of the British Parliament position themselves at virtually the same position on the Left/Right scale (Norris 1999c). On traditional economic issues—taxes versus services, privatization, and jobs versus prices—the MPs are slightly to the right of the British public. On two noneconomic issues—European integration and the role of women—the British MPs are to the left of the public. When Bernhard Wessels (1993) compared the issue opinions of Bundestag deputies and the German public, he found close agreement on Old Politics issues such as economic growth and public order, and somewhat lower levels of agreement on New Politics goals.

In summary, collective correspondence on broad political orientations is fairly common in established democracies. This result should be expected, because the logic of the electoral process is to select legislators who are broadly consistent with public preferences. These patterns may, however, vary across issues and be affected by the nature of the electoral system. Thus, we turn to the processes of representation in the next section.

Dyadic Correspondence

Overall opinion agreement between the public and the political elites does not occur by chance. Some degree of popular control is necessary to ensure the responsiveness of elites. Citizen–elite agreement without popular control is representation by luck, not democracy. One method of popular control makes political elites electorally dependent on a specific geographic district. Weissberg (1978) defined the pairing of district opinion and elites as *dyadic correspondence*—in simple terms, liberal districts presumably select liberal representatives, and conservative districts select conservative representatives.

In studying the connection between citizens and elites, researchers initially treated the individual legislator as the basis of dyadic linkage. Traditionally, a *delegate* model defined the legislator's role in a deterministic fashion. Representative government implied that voters would formally instruct the delegates on district preferences before they went to Parliament, and the legislator was obliged to follow the district's mandate. Edmund Burke's classic "Speech to the Electors of Bristol" in 1774 offered a new model of representation that is still discussed today. Burke proposed a more independent *trustee* role for legislators. He argued that once elected, legislators should be allowed to follow their own beliefs about what they thought was best for their constituency and the nation.

American research on political representation reinforced this emphasis on the individual legislator. In part, this focus reflected the weakness of American parties and the open structure of the political process, in which many legislators seem to act as individual entrepreneurs. And, in part, it reflected the use of a single-member-district electoral system in the United States and Britain, where one legislator was elected to represent the district.

Warren Miller and Donald Stokes (1963) conducted the seminal study of political representation in America based on the trustee and delegate models of representation. They interviewed a small sample of the public in a set of congressional districts after the 1958 elections as well as the members of the House of Representatives from these same districts. They also collected the voting records of the members of Congress during the following legislative session, which allowed them to compare citizen opinions to the opinions and votes of these representatives.

Miller and Stokes built a creative model of the representation process (figure 11.2). Broadly speaking, they described two pathways by which a district could influence the legislative voting of its representative. One pathway defined the trustee model of representation: the district selects a legislator who shares its views (path *a*), so that in following his or her own convictions (path *b*) the legislator represents the district's will. In this case, the district's opinion and the legislator's actions are connected through the legislator's own policy attitudes. A second pathway reflects the delegate model. A legislator turns to citizens in his or her district for cues on their policy preferences (path *c*), and then follows these cues in making voting choices (path *d*). In this case, the legislator's perception of district attitudes is the link between district opinion and the legislator's voting behavior.

Figure 11.2	Constituency Influence in Congress

Citizens can influence legislator's actions either by the trustee linkages on the top or the delegate linkages on the bottom.

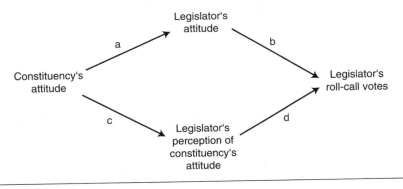

Source: Author.

Miller and Stokes applied the model to three policy areas: civil rights, social welfare, and foreign policy. They found a strong relationship between constituency opinion and the legislator's voting record for civil rights and social welfare issues and a weaker connection for foreign policy. In addition, the path of constituency influence varied between policy areas. Civil rights issues primarily functioned by a delegate model. Members of Congress accurately perceived the opinions of their constituents and voted in accord with these opinions. For social welfare issues, the trustee path through the legislator's own attitude was the most important means of district influence.

This study described the representation process at work. Moreover, the process seemed to work fairly well: most liberal districts were represented by liberal legislators, and most conservative districts chose conservative representatives. Many have criticized the methodology of this study, but most political scientists still support its essential conclusions (for further discussion, see Erikson and Tedin 2010, ch. 10; Warren Miller et al. 1999).

Cheryl Lyn Herrera, Richard Herrera, and Eric Smith (1992) partially repeated the Miller and Stokes analyses for the 1986–88 Congress. They compared the opinions of members of Congress from thirty-three districts to their constituents' opinions. They found that the fit between districts and their representatives was fairly high on most issues, especially those with sizable issue publics and polarized public opinion, such as abortion, minority aid, and government services. They concluded that "dyadic representation is better today than was true 30 years ago" (p. 201), meaning that the democratic process in the United States was working better than during the Miller and Stokes study in the late 1950s.

In another project, Stephen Ansolabehere and his colleagues (2001a, 2001b) measured the positions of congressional candidates from surveys by the Vote Smart project. They compared candidate positions to measures of district opinions and the roll-call votes of the elected representatives. Figure 11.3 shows the relationship between the liberal/conservative opinions of each district on the horizontal axis and the liberal/conservative opinions of the district's representative on the vertical axis.[5] The congruence between district and representative opinions is very strong, as one would expect if the democratic process is working. Moreover, when these researchers examined the next step in the representation process—path *b* in figure 11.2—they found an equally strong link between the representatives' attitudes and their overall voting pattern (r = .88 for Republicans and .85 for Democrats).[6] Elections thus are a means for voters to select candidates who broadly share their political values, and who then take these orientations to Washington.

The Miller and Stokes model was extended to representation studies in nearly a dozen other Western democracies (Miller et al. 1999), but these studies typically found limited policy agreement between districts and their legislators. For example, Samuel Barnes (1977) found virtually no correspondence between the issue opinions of Italian deputies and public opinion in their respective districts; there was a similar weak linkage for French

Figure 11.3   Democrats, Republicans, and Their Districts

District conservatism is strongly related to the representative's overall political position.

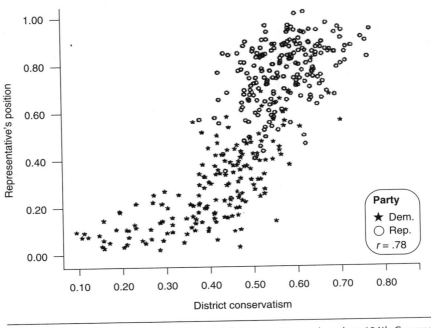

Source: Personal communication, Stephen Ansolabehere; data are based on 104th Congress, also see Ansolabehere et al. (2001a, 2001b).

legislators on specific policy issues (Converse and Pierce 1986, ch. 22).[7] It appeared that either political representation did not occur in these European democracies or that it worked through other means.

The Party Government Model

Research on political representation in non-American political systems gradually deemphasized a model based on individual legislators and focused instead on the actions of political parties as collectives (Dalton, Farrell, and McAllister 2011; Budge et al. 2012). This model of representation through parties—*responsible party government*—is built upon several principles:

- People possess informed political preferences and policy choices.
- Parties offer distinct policy options so voters can make meaningful choices about which party best represents their preferences.
- These perceptions of parties' positions guide voting choices.

In other words, national elections make judgments about the political parties and their activities, and representation occurs through parties rather than individual candidates. These principles are similar to the principles of issue voting discussed in chapter 10, now applied to parties as a collective.

The party government model seems more relevant for parliamentary systems with strong political parties. In most European systems, candidates are selected by party elites rather than through open primaries, so they are first and foremost representatives of their parties. The party government model presumes that a party's parliamentary delegation acts in unison. Parties vote as a bloc in parliament, although the members may have an internal debate before the party position is decided. Parties exercise control over the government and the policymaking process through party control of the national legislature. In sum, the choice of parties—rather than constituency-based representation—provides the electorate with a means of control over the actions of legislators and the affairs of government.

Political representation in Europe largely follows the party government model. In comparison to the United States, the multiparty systems of most European democracies offer the voters greater diversity in party programs, which gives more meaning to party labels (see chapter 7). Most democracies are parliamentary systems with unified legislative parties (Bowler 2000). When a party votes as a united bloc, it makes little sense to discuss the voting patterns of individual legislators. Giovanni Sartori (1968, 471) maintains that "citizens in Western democracies are represented *through* and *by* parties. This is inevitable" (emphasis in original).

The party government model therefore focuses the voters' attention on parties, rather than individual legislators, as representatives. Indeed, many Europeans (including Germans) vote directly for party lists instead of individual candidates. Dyadic correspondence is based more on a voters–party link than a district–legislator link. The voter half of the dyad is composed of all party voters in a nation, even if the country is organized by geographic electoral districts; the elite half is composed of party officials as a collective. If the party government model holds, we should expect a close match between the policy views of a party's voters and the party's elites.

I should stress one other point about dyadic correspondence. This chapter speaks in causal terms—voter opinions presumably influence party positions—but political influence runs in both directions. Voters influence parties, as parties try to persuade voters, which is why researchers have adopted the causally neutral term *correspondence*. The essence of the democratic marketplace is that like-minded voters and parties search out each other and join forces. Socialist voters and politicians find a common home in the German Social Democratic Party (SPD), and environmentalists find each other in the Greens. Even if one cannot determine the direction of causal flow, the similarity of opinions between party voters and party elites is a meaningful measure of the democratic representation.

As we have argued previously (chapters 6 and 10), the Left/Right scale is a reasonable way to summarize overall political positions. Using the 2009

European Election Study, I compared the average Left/Right position of party voters to the where candidates to the European Parliament CEPs from the same party would position the party (figure 11.4). The horizontal axis in the figure plots the average position of a party's supporters; the vertical axis plots the average position of the party elites.[8] These two coordinates define a party's location in the figure. The 45-degree line represents perfect agreement—where the positions of party elites exactly match that of their supporters.

This figure shows two important patterns. The first is the strong relationship between voters and party positions in Left/Right terms. Voters with leftist preferences and elites who share these views come together in the

Figure 11.4	Parties and Their Voters

Party voters have an average Left/Right position that is very close to the candidates' placement of the party's position.

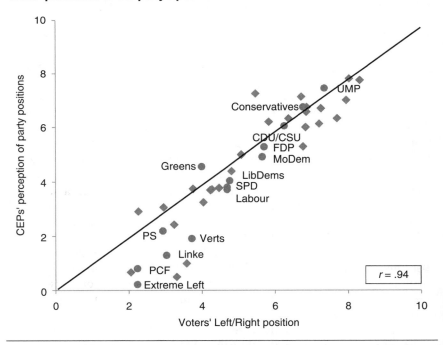

Sources: 2009 European Election Study and 2009 Candidates to the European Parliament Study. Parties are from the fifteen early European Union member states in Western Europe where there are sufficient respondents to plot party positions.

Note: The figure plots the mean Left/Right position of party voters and where candidates for the European Parliament perceive their party's position on the Left/Right scale.

leftist parties such as the French Socialists, the Communists (PCF) and the Linke. These traditional leftists are now joined by the French Verts and other New Left parties. Closer to the middle are the center-left German Social Democrats and the British Labour Party. At the other extreme are conservative parties and their supporters: the French UMP (Union for a Popular Movement), the British Conservatives, and the German CDU/CSU. Voters and parties broadly share their Left/Right attitudes, noted by the very strong correlation between them ($r = .94$). This pattern is the evidence of the distinct party positions that underlie the party government model of representation.

The 45-degree line in the figure also shows that candidates for the European Parliament tend to be more liberal than their own voters. This might be a general function of EP elections, since those who want to serve in the Parliament tend to be more internationalist than the rest of their parties. Other evidence suggests that there is a systematic tendency for political parties to be more extreme than their supporters. For example, those who vote for an extreme left (or right) party tend to locate themselves closer to the center than does the party itself (Dalton, Farrell, and McAllister 2011, ch. 5). This is important because it implies that in national elections political parties tend to accentuate the political position of their supporters.

Another advantage of the 2009 European Election Study is that both the public and CEPs surveys included a common battery of a dozen issue questions (Costello, Thomassen, and Rosema 2012). The issues cover a set of long-standing Old Politics concerns, such as state ownership of public services or government involvement in the economy, and redistribution to decrease income inequality. Because economic issues are so important in structuring political conflict, research generally suggests that congruence on these issues is substantial (Miller et al. 1999). In addition, other items tapped cultural, New Politics concerns, such as questions on immigration, same-sex marriage, or the role of women. We used a statistical technique to create two general issue indices: one emphasizing positions on the economic, Old Politics issues, and one measuring positions on the New Politics dimension.[9]

Figure 11.5 displays voter and party elite agreement on the economic issue scale. We plot voter and elite positions for thirty parties in eight nations. These comparisons demonstrate a strong correspondence on these issues, even though the exact interpretation of issues might vary a bit because the national policy context varies. The Socialist and Communist parties tend toward the lower-left quadrant, and their voters also hold liberal opinions on economic issues. For example, the voters for the German Linke and the party itself are positioned at the bottom left corner of the figure. Conversely, the economically conservative Free Democrats (FDP) are located at the opposite corner of this continuum. The correlation between voters and parties is high, but lower than for overall Left/Right orientations.

| Figure 11.5 | Economic Congruence |

Party voters and elites show substantial agreement on economic issues such as state ownership of public services and the redistribution of income to reduce inequality.

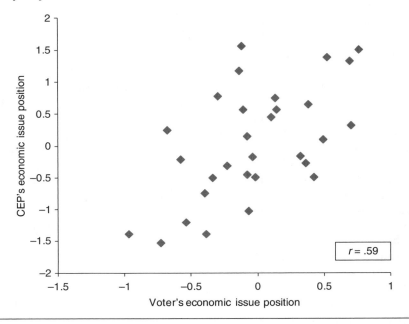

Sources: 2009 European Election Study and 2009 Candidates to the European Parliament Study. Parties are from the original nine EU member states where there are sufficient respondents to plot party positions.

Note: The figure entries represent party supporters' average score on economic issues on the horizontal axis and the average score of the party's candidates to the European Parliament on the vertical axis.

Figure 11.6 compares voter opinions on cultural issues to the opinions of party elites. This figure also shows a basic correspondence between party voters and party elites on these issues. A voter bloc that wants a more conservative response to immigration and other cultural issues is represented by party elites who generally share their concern, and vice versa. Again, the relationship is substantial but less than over overall Left/Right orientations. This makes sense; Left/Right is the average of the issues of most important to the individual, and as an average it likely combines opinions where voters-parties agree and opinions where they disagree. In addition, separate issue publics pull the parties in different directions, and Left/Right averages these patterns (Thomassen 2012).

Figure 11.6 Cultural Congruence

Party voters and elites show substantial agreement on cultural issues such as immigration, same-sex marriage, and social order.

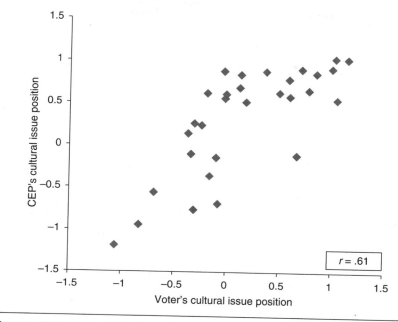

Sources: 2009 European Election Study and 2009 Candidates to the European Parliament Study. Parties are from the original nine EU member states where there are sufficient respondents to plot party positions.

Note: The figure entries represent party voters' average score on cultural issues on the horizontal axis and the average score of the party's candidates to the European Parliament on the vertical axis.

It is also significant that the cultural issues show the same level of congruence as traditional economic issues. The latter were the historic basis of many political parties and their ideologies; now these issues are sharing the political stage with new issues of multiculturalism and gender equality. In fact, among the public in these nine EU nations, positions on the cultural issues are more strongly related to their Left/Right positions ($r =. 30$) than are positions on economic issues ($.10$). Both relationships are much stronger for EP elites because it is their job to think about issues, and the two issue dimensions have about equal weight ($.59$ and $.56$).

Just as important as the overall level of correspondence are the factors affecting voter–party agreement. Some parties consistently achieve a close match between the opinions of voters and party elites, while other parties display less correspondence. These variations in party representation determine the efficiency of the party linkage process. Several studies have examined the overall fit between parties and their electorates. It appears that the clarity of party images helps voters find parties that match their positions. This clarity partially reflects the ideological position of a party, its visibility (size), a centralized organization, and the nature of the electoral system (Rohrschneider and Whitefield 2012; Wessels 1999; Dalton 1985).

The Impact of Representation

This chapter describes two distinct patterns of democratic representative government. Political representation in the United States has largely depended on the relationship between individual legislators and their constituencies. People in a congressional district or a state legislative district think of the individual legislator as their representative. In contrast, people in most other democracies are primarily represented through their choice of political parties at election time. In some ways, however, this contrast may be narrowing as polarized parties are becoming more obvious in American politics, and candidate-centered politics is increasingly salient in Europe.

Both models can provide effective means of citizen–elite linkage, but they emphasize different aspects of representation. The American system of representation, based on individual legislators, allows for greater responsiveness to the interests of each district. The political process is also more open to new political interests and the representation of minority groups because electoral control at the district level is more easily accomplished than control of an entire party.

The flexibility of the American style of representation also involves some costs. An entrepreneurial style of representation makes it more difficult for the public to monitor and control the actions of its representatives between elections. It also encourages campaigns to focus on personalities and district service rather than on policy and ideological orientations. Indeed, studies of congressional elections suggest that personality and constituency service are important influences on voting.

Nevertheless, empirical research shows that policy outcomes in the United States generally reflect the preferences of the public—although obviously this result is, and probably should be, an imperfect linkage. Benjamin Page and Robert Shapiro (1983, 1992) described a substantial correspondence between Americans' preferences for policy change and actual changes in public policy.[10] Sophisticated new empirical analyses are providing fresh insights into the public's overall impact on the policy process and how this influence interacts with the institutional structure of American politics (Stimson, McKuen, and Erikson 1995; Burstein 2003; Wlezien 2004). Brooks and Manza (2007) show that public sentiments on welfare state issues are strongly related to social spending levels cross-nationally.

Research on the party-government framework also finds that party choices have clear policy consequences. Hans-Dieter Klingemann, Richard

Hofferbert, and Ian Budge (1994) found that parties are meaningful vehicles for policy control in most democracies. More recent research finds a strong congruence between the Left/Right position of the public and the Left/Right position of the elected government—and a further impact on the policy outputs of government (Dalton, Farrell, and McAllister 2011; Soroka and Wlezien 2010). And, after demonstrating that changes in citizen spending preferences are generally translated into shifts in government spending policies in the United States, Britain, and Canada, Stuart Soroka and Christopher Wlezien (2010) come to a simple but powerful conclusion: "Democracy works."

In overall terms, I agree. Furthermore, there is evidence suggesting that government has improved its representativeness over time (Powell 2011; Golder and Stramski 2010). Presumably a more informed and active public prompts politicians to be more responsive to an alert citizenry. The advent of public opinion polling also provides timely information on what the public as a whole and voters of each party prefer. And an attentive media can further leverage the influence of public opinion.

Nevertheless, contemporary levels of representation do not ensure that people are satisfied by current politics. In fact, the complexity of politics and the vagaries of party actions mean that many people do not feel represented. Figure 11.7 displays the percentage who feel a party or a candidate represents their interests across several established democracies. Barely half the public in these nations feel they have some party or some candidate in their corner. Even among those who just voted for a party or candidate in the immediately previous election, the percentage who feel represented is only marginally higher.

This presents a mini-paradox. If democracy works, then why do so many people feel unrepresented by any party or candidate? There are many answers (Wessels 2011; Wagner and Wessels 2012). At least part of the answer is that parties do not always meet public expectations or even their own campaign promises. Another part of the answer is that citizen expectations for government have fragmented into multiple issue publics, and it has become harder for political parties to simultaneously represent conflicting issue demands. Indeed, as we argued in chapter 3, many people are turning to other forms of representation because they don't consider parties a sufficient or effective means of policy input.

Many roadblocks and pitfalls still stand in the way of representation, even within a democratic system. In these times of change and political turmoil, the evidence of government failures and party failures is often obvious. A large part of the observed correspondence must be attributed to a dynamic process of representation. Voters migrate to the party (candidate) that best represents their views, and the party convinces supporters to adopt these policies. When public interests change, or party positions change, people vote for the next best option. Overall Left/Right congruence also does not ensure that the public can control government. Beyond the general patterns described here, one can think of a host of specific policies on which

Figure 11.7 Do You Feel Represented?

Countries differ widely in the percentages of the public who feel represented by a party or candidate vote.

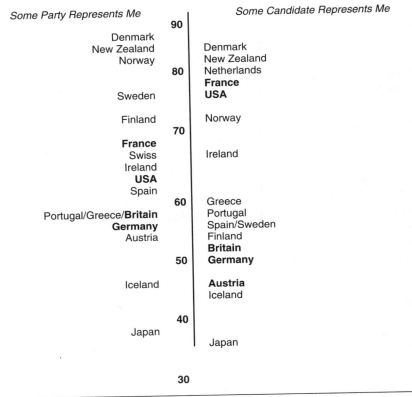

Sources: Comparative Study of Electoral Systems (module III); 2010 British Election Study.

Note: Figure entries are percentages of public who feel represented by a political party or a candidate.

the impact of public preferences is uncertain. Still, congruence indicates an agreement between public preferences and public policy that is expected under a democratic system. Moreover, congruence underscores our belief in the rationality of public action that elitist theories of democracy doubt exist.

Suggested Readings

Alonso, Sonia, John Keane, and Wolfgang Merkel, eds. 2011. *The Future of Representative Democracy.* Cambridge, UK: Cambridge University Press.

Budge, Ian, Michael McDonald, Paul Pennings, and Hans Keman. 2012. *Organizing Democratic Choice: Party Representation over Time.* Oxford, UK: Oxford University Press.

Converse, Philip, and Roy Pierce. 1986. *Representation in France.* Cambridge, MA: Harvard University Press.

Dalton, Russell, David Farrell, and Ian McAllister. 2011. *Political Parties and Democratic Linkage: How Parties Organize Democracy.* Oxford, UK: Oxford University Press.

Enns, Peter, and Christopher Wlezien, eds. 2011. *Who Gets Represented?* New York: Russell Sage Foundation.

Erikson, Robert, Michael MacKuen, and James Stimson. 2002. *The Macro Polity.* Cambridge, UK: Cambridge University Press.

Miller, Warren, et al. 1999. *Policy Representation in Western Democracies.* Oxford, UK: Oxford University Press.

Page, Benjamin, and Robert Shapiro. 1992. *The Rational Public: Fifty Years of Trends in Americans' Policy Preferences.* Chicago: University of Chicago Press.

Rohrschneider, Robert and Stephen Whitefield. 2012. *The Strain of Representation: How Parties Represent Diverse Voters in Western and Eastern Europe.* Oxford, UK: Oxford University Press.

Soroka, Stuart, and Christopher Wlezien. 2010. *Degrees of Democracy: Politics, Public Opinion and Policy.* New York: Cambridge University Press.

Notes

1. Ironically, there was pressure to delay the film's release, which coincided with the outbreak of World War II, because the film depicted political corruption and appeared to paint an unflattering picture of the U.S. government.
2. The development of Internet-based networking, teleconferencing, and other communication advances may lead democracies to reconsider the physical limits on direct citizen participation. Indeed, the technology exists for instantaneous national referendums and national town meetings (Bimber 2003).
3. Previous studies include the following: for the United States, Miller and Jennings (1986) and Miller (1987); for Germany, Wessels (1993); for France, Converse and Pierce (1986).
4. The citizen data are from the 2009 European Election Studies (www .piredeu.eu/public/EES2009.asp). The elite surveys are drawn from the

2009 Candidates from the European Parliament at the same website. The elite samples are weighted to reflect the percentage each party gained in the EP election. The figure plots the Left, Center, and Right percentages on a 10-point Left/Right scale.

5. The median district opinion was based on the difference between the percentages of the Democratic and Republican presidential vote in the district in 1996. The candidate position is an average of opinions on more than two hundred policy questions. See Ansolabehere, Snyder, and Stewart (2001a).

6. Steve Ansolabehere provided these data; I greatly appreciate his assistance.

7. Converse and Pierce (1986, ch. 23) also specified the conditions that strengthen or retard representation. They found that citizen–elite congruence varied by policy domain, competitiveness of the district, and the legislator's role conceptions.

8. This comparison is based on Western European parties in the 2009 European Parliament election. With only a few exceptions, it plots parties that had at least twenty-five voters in the election study and four or more elites in the candidate survey. The candidate study was relatively small, producing only a few candidates in many parties, so the estimates of party positions are less precise.

9. I used factor analysis to estimate two orthogonal dimensions that identify the issues most strongly related to each dimension. We did separate analyses for the public sample and the candidates sample. To maximize the comparability of results, we restricted our attention to only the eight early EU member states where the interpretation and comparability of issues was likely greatest even though this reduces the number of parties in figure 11.4 and 11.5. The two figures plot factor scores for voters and elites of each party.

10. State-level comparisons provide another opportunity to study the congruence between public opinion and public policy. Robert Erikson and his colleagues show a strong policy correspondence (Erikson, Wright, and McIver 1994).

Part Four
Democracy and the Future

12 Citizens and the Democratic Process

Politics today is like the opening line in a Dickens novel: We seem to live in the best of times . . . and the worst of times for the democratic process. In the last decade of the twentieth century, a wave of democratization swept across the globe. The citizens of Eastern Europe, South Africa, and several East Asian nations rose up against their autocratic governments. The Soviet Empire collapsed, and millions of people enjoyed new democratic freedoms. These events led a noted political analyst, Francis Fukuyama (1992), to claim that we were witnessing "the end of history." Humankind's evolution was supposedly converging on a single form of government—democracy—as the culmination of human development. Even some experts who had previously ruminated about the limits to democracy's expansion now trumpeted this third wave of democratization.[1]

The 1990s also brought unprecedented affluence and economic well-being to the United States, as Americans experienced their longest period of sustained economic growth in peacetime. Crime rates dropped, and progress was made on many policy fronts. To a lesser degree, Western Europe also enjoyed a peace dividend of economic stability and a new era of international security. This was, it seemed, a positive time for Western democracy. The Cold War was over, and we had won. In addition, the citizens in the former autocratic states of the Soviet Empire had won.

Despite these advances, public opinion surveys have found that people are now more critical of politicians, political parties, and political institutions than they were a generation ago (Dalton 2004; Norris 2011). This is not a recent development resulting from the 2008 recession. The malaise first appeared in the United States in the 1960s, and trust in government has remained low since the late 1970s. These trends have stimulated a chorus of voices claiming that American democracy is at risk (Macedo et al. 2005; Wolfe 2006). Political dissatisfaction is also common in other advanced industrial democracies. For example, if one is fortunate enough to browse through Paris bookshops, one sees titles such as *France in Freefall*, *Bankrupt*

France, and *France's Misfortune*. Even while enjoying the fruits of economic and political development, people have become more critical of their governments and other institutions of democracy.

Admittedly, anxiety about the health of democracy is a regular feature of political science and political punditry. An important discussion about America's postwar goals took place during the administration of President Dwight D. Eisenhower, and President John F. Kennedy asked Americans to renew their commitment to state and nation (see Mueller 1999, ch. 7). A prominent academic study of the 1970s nearly forecasted democracy's demise (Crozier, Huntington, and Watanuki 1975). "Declinism" is an enduring school of thought among French and German intellectuals. These earlier pessimistic accounts of democracy's future fortunately proved to be overstatements.

It does seem, however, that attitudes toward government are changing in basic ways, and citizens in most established democracies are no longer deferential and supportive of political elites. This development leads us to ask whether such changes in the political culture put democracy at risk and how they are affecting the democratic process.

This chapter looks at how people judge the democratic process today. How is it that as democracy celebrates its success at the beginning of a new millennium, its citizens are apparently expressing deep doubts about their political system? In addition, we consider how the new style of citizen politics may contribute to these misgivings and what the implications are for the democracy's future.

The Types of Political Support

Political support is a term with many possible meanings. Gabriel Almond and Sidney Verba (1963) referred to attitudes toward politics and the political system as the "political culture" of a nation. Political culture encompasses beliefs about the legitimacy of the system, the appropriateness of structures for political input, and the role of the individual in the political process. The most important of these attitudes is a generalized feeling toward the political system, or *system affect*. Such feelings are presumably socialized early in life, representing a positive attitude toward the political system that is relatively independent of the actions of the current government. Almond and Verba believed that affective feelings toward the political system assure the legitimacy of democratic governments and limit expressions of political discontent.

David Easton (1965, 1975) developed an influential theoretical frame-work describing the various objects of political support: political authorities, the regime, and the political community.

- *Political authorities support* includes opinions toward the incumbents of political office or, in a broader sense, the pool of political elites from which government leaders are drawn.

- *Regime support* refers to attitudes toward the institutions of government rather than the present officeholders—such as respect for the presidency rather than opinions about a specific president. This also involves attitudes toward the procedures of government, such as the principles of pluralist democracy and support for parliamentary government.

- *Political community support* implies a basic attachment to the nation and political system beyond the present institutions of government. A sense of being "English" or "Scottish" is an example of these attachments.

The differences among these levels of support are very significant. Discontent with the political authorities normally has limited systemic implications. People often become dissatisfied with political officeholders and act on these feelings by voting the rascals out and selecting new officials (rascals) at the next election. Dissatisfaction with authorities, within a democratic system, is not usually a signal for basic political change. Negative attitudes toward political officials can and do exist with little loss in support for the office itself or the institutional structure of government.

When the object of dissatisfaction becomes more general—shifting to the regime or the political community—the political implications increase. A decline in regime support might provoke a basic challenge to political institutions or calls for reform in government procedures. For example, when Americans became dissatisfied with government in the mid-1990s they enacted term limits on legislators and other reforms. Weakening ties to the political community might foretell eventual revolution, civil war, or the loss of legitimacy. Therefore, Easton said, "Not all expressions of unfavorable orientations have the same degree of gravity for a political system. Some may be consistent with its maintenance; others may lead to fundamental change" (1975, 437).

In addition to the objects of political support, Easton identified two kinds of support: diffuse and specific. According to Easton, *diffuse support* is a state of mind—a deep-seated set of political attitudes that are deeply engrained in belief systems. For example, the sentiment "America, right or wrong" reflects a commitment to the nation that is distinct from the actual behavior of the government. In contrast, *specific support* is more closely related to the actions and performance of the government or political elites. Specific support is object specific in two senses. First, it normally applies to evaluations of political authorities; it's less relevant to support for the political community. Second, specific support is typically based on the actual policies and governing style of political authorities or political institutions.

The distinction between diffuse and specific support is important in understanding the significance of different aspects of political support. A democratic political system must keep the support of its citizens if the system is to remain viable because it rules by the consent of the governed. However, because all governments occasionally fail to meet public expectations, short-term political failures must not directly erode diffuse support for the regime or political community. If one politician or government fails, this shouldn't be an indictment of the entire political system. In other words, a democratic political system requires a reservoir of diffuse support independent of immediate policy outputs (specific support) if it's to weather periods of public disaffection and dissatisfaction (Almond and Verba 1963).

German history in the twentieth century highlights the importance of diffuse support. The Weimar Republic (1918–33) was built on an unstable foundation. Many Germans felt that the creation of this government at the end of World War I had contributed to Germany's wartime defeat; from the outset, the regime was stigmatized as a traitor to the nation. Important sectors of the political elite—the military, the civil service, and the judiciary—and many citizens questioned the legitimacy of the new regime and favored a return to the former German Empire. The fledgling democratic state then faced a series of major crises: postwar economic hardships, attempted right-wing and left-wing coups, explosive inflation in the early 1920s, and the French occupation of the Ruhr. Because the political system was never able to build up a pool of diffuse support for the republic, the dissatisfaction created by the Great Depression in the 1930s easily eroded support for political authorities *and the democratic regime*. Communists and Nazis argued that the democratic political system was at fault, and the Weimar Republic succumbed to those attacks.[2]

The democratic transition in the German Democratic Republic in 1989–90 also illustrates the importance of cultural and institutional congruence. Surveys of East German youth found a marked decrease in support for the communist principles of the German Democratic Republic during the 1980s (Friedrich and Griese 1990). These youths led the populist revolt in the East that weakened the regime in the fall of 1989. Revelations in early 1990 about the Communist Party's abuses of power further eroded the regime's popular base and spurred the race toward unification with the West.

Early cross-national opinion studies argued that political support was a requisite of stable democracy. Almond and Verba (1963) found that system affect in the late 1950s was most widespread in the long-established democracies of the United States and Great Britain. For example, 85 percent of Americans and 46 percent of Britons spontaneously mentioned their political system as a source of national pride. In contrast, system support was more limited in West Germany and Italy: only 7 percent of West Germans and 3 percent of Italians mentioned their political system as a source of national pride. Low levels of support raised fears that democracy was still fragile in these two formerly fascist states.

A cross-national study by Hadley Cantril (1965) found a similar pattern in public opinion: positive national self-images were more common in the stable, well-run democracies than in fledgling democracies. A more recent set of comparative studies has similarly demonstrated that a democratic political culture is strongly correlated with the stability of a democratic system (Inglehart and Welzel 2005). Although one can never be certain whether stable government produces political support, or whether political support produces stable government, these two are interrelated. The support of its citizens is necessary if a democracy is to survive over the long term.

Declining Confidence in Authorities

A few years ago I was visiting Germany during its national elections. On the weekend before the vote I went to the town square with a friend to talk to the parties' representatives about the election. At one booth I was given a nice pen with a picture of the local candidate down the side. My friend leaned over and whispered: Hurry up and use the pen now, because after the election it will stop working—just like the politician. Such public skepticism of elected officials and other political authorities has become a common part of politics in most advanced industrial democracies.

Rather than focus on individual officeholders, we examine citizen images of political leaders in general. A variety of evidence points to Americans' growing skepticism about political officials and the government over time (figure 12.1). The early readings depicted a largely supportive public. In 1958 most Americans believed that officials care what people think (71 percent), that people in government are honest (68 percent), and that one can trust the government to do what is right (71 percent). These positive feelings remained relatively unchanged until the mid-1960s and then declined precipitously.

Beginning at about the time of the crises and political scandals of the 1960s and 1970s—Vietnam, urban unrest, and Watergate—Americans' trust in their politicians sank steadily lower. In 1979 President Jimmy Carter warned that declining public confidence "was a fundamental threat to American democracy." The upbeat presidency of Ronald Reagan temporarily improved Americans' image of politics. By the end of the Reagan-Bush era, however, trust in government was as low as it had been in 1980. These indicators had hit historic lows in 1994 during the Clinton administration, but they had partially improved by 2000. Yet even with the unprecedented economic growth of the 1990s and the consolidation of democracy around the globe, Americans' trust in government rebounded only to the levels of Reagan's first administration. Support for incumbents and the government briefly spiked upward after the September 2001 terrorist attacks on the United States but soon faded. By the 2008 elections, trust had decreased to the levels of the early 1990s. Media polls suggest that trust in government had declined to a new low point in 2010–11.

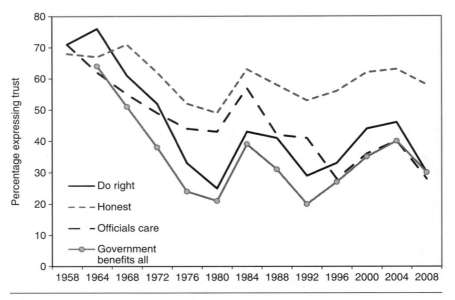

| Figure 12.1 | Trust in Government |

Americans' trust in government dropped in the 1960s–70s and has remained low since then.

Source: American National Election Studies, 1958–2008.

Virtually all long-term public opinion series show similar downward trends. For example, since 1966 the Harris poll asked, "The people running the country don't really care what happens to you." In 1966, only 29 percent shared this opinion; in 2011 a full 73 percent thought politicians didn't care. The Pew Center for People and the Press (2010) studied attitudes toward government in 2010 and concluded, "By almost every conceivable measure Americans are less positive and more critical of government these days."

Looking back at this span of U.S. history, it's easy to cite possible reasons for the public's growing doubts about their leaders (Nye, Zelikow, and King 1997). During any four-year electoral cycle, one can find multiple events that may have diminished the reputations of Congress and the executive branch: Watergate, the House banking scandal, Iran-contra, the Abramoff lobbying scandal, Bill and Monica, the invisible WMD in Iraq, and so on. In policy terms, candidates promise one thing at election time, but they regularly fail to deliver and may even violate their promises once in office (for example, George H. W. Bush's promise, "Read my lips, no new taxes"). In addition, some of the most distinguished members of Congress have resigned from office, offering stinging indictments of the institution. As one former representative said upon leaving the U.S. House: "May your mother never find out where you work."

Such explanations of decreasing trust focus on the peculiar history of the United States, or specific institutional features of American politics, but we are not alone. The same trends are occurring in Great Britain, France, Germany, and most other established democracies. Figure 12.2 tracks the decline in the belief that politicians care what people think in our set of four nations.[3] For example, 47 percent of the German public believed politicians cared what they thought in 1972; by 2002, only 13 percent shared this opinion. Similarly, in 1986 only 11 percent of the British public said they never trusted the government—by 2010 this group had tripled in size (Curtice 2013).Other trends from these four nations generally display the same pattern of decreasing trust in elected officials (Norris 2011; Mayer 2000).

Even more significant, public skepticism about politicians and government officials is spreading to virtually all the advanced industrial democracies. A cross-national inventory of questions measured support for politicians and

Figure 12.2	Do Politicians Care?

Belief that politicians care what people think has generally declined over time.

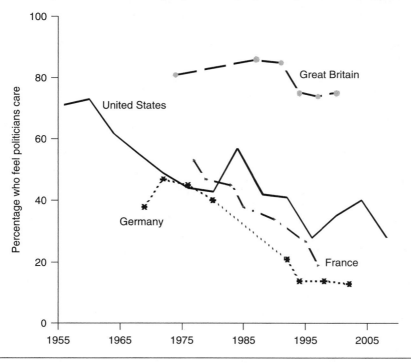

Sources: United States, American National Election Studies, 1956–2008; Great Britain, 1974 Political Action Survey and British Social Attitudes Surveys, 1987–2000; Germany, German Election Studies, 1969–2002; France, SOFRES Polls, 1977–97.

government from national surveys in sixteen Western democracies (Dalton 2004; also see Norris 1999a, 2011a). Typically beginning in the late 1960s or early 1970s, these trends show a downward slide in political support *in nearly all the countries for which systematic long-term data are available.* Decreasing trust in government and elected officials is now commonplace in contemporary democracies.

It would be understandable if people had become frustrated with government only after the 2008 recession and its consequences. However, the puzzle is that this trend toward negativity occurred at a time when the political systems of most advanced industrial societies were making real advances in addressing the needs of their nations (for example, Bok 1996). In addition, these trends have paralleled an apparent decrease in political corruption and an increase in citizen access to politics. It was the best of times and the worst of times. And now, when economic times are bad, dissatisfaction has deepened.

Views of Political Institutions

Why do employees in the White House use the term "Mr. President" when they talk to Barack Obama (I think Michelle can say "Barack")? In part, it's a matter of respect and etiquette. But this usage has a long tradition. The logic is that people should think of the president as making decisions for the nation rather than a person making individual decisions. Thus, people should respect the office of the president even if they don't like the person or disagree with the policies.[4]

So our next question asks whether skepticism about political elites has been generalized to more basic attitudes toward the institutions and structure of government. This question was first taken up by Arthur Miller (1974a, 1974b) and Jack Citrin (1974). Miller argued that Americans were generalizing their dissatisfaction with the repeated policy failures and political scandals of government officials into broader criticism of the political process. He spelled out the potentially grave consequences the loss of regime support could have for the American political process.

Citrin felt that Miller was overstating the problem. He interpreted the declines in political support as a sign of disenchantment with politicians in general, not distrust in the system of American government. Citrin (1974, 987) claimed that "political systems, like baseball teams, have slumps and winning seasons. Having recently endured a succession of losing seasons, Americans boo the home team when it takes the field." He maintained that these catcalls do not show deeper opposition to the game of government, but only to the players in the lineup and their recent performance on the field. Given a few new stars or a winning streak, the decline in public confidence would reverse.

Citrin's cautiousness seemed warranted in 1974, but now, about four decades later, public disenchantment continues. In addition, distrust has

spread to the institutions of democratic government. One set of survey questions taps public confidence in the people running major social, economic,
and political organizations: confidence in the leadership of virtually every
U.S. institution has tumbled downward. In the 1960s many Americans
expressed a fair amount of confidence in the executive branch (41 percent)
and Congress (42 percent), but these positive evaluations dropped substantially over time (table 12.1). In 2012 only 15 percent of Americans had
confidence in the executive branch, and Congress fared even worse (7 percent). Confidence in business, labor, higher education, organized religion,
the press, and the medical profession have suffered similar declines over the
past four decades. Separate trends from the Harris Poll show confidence in
Congress dropping to 6 percent in 2012 and confidence in the executive at
22 percent.

Table 12.1	**Institutional Confidence**							

Confidence in the leadership of most American institutions has decreased since the 1960s.

	1960s	1970s	1980s	1990s	2000s	2010	2012	DIFFERENCE
Medicine	72	54	50	45	41	42	39	−33
Higher education	61	38	32	16	24	20	26	−35
Banks and finance	—	37	26	20	27	10	11	−26
Military	62	37	33	41	49	54	55	−7
Organized religion	41	35	30	26	24	20	22	−19
Supreme Court	50	35	32	33	34	31	29	−21
Major corporations	55	26	27	25	20	13	17	−38
Press	29	25	18	11	10	11	9	−20
Executive branch	41	19	18	14	15	17	15	−26
Congress	42	17	14	10	13	10	7	−35
Organized labor	22	14	12	11	10	13	12	−10
Average	48	31	27	22	24	22	23	−25

Sources: 1966 from Harris Poll; 1973–2012, General Social Surveys.

Note: Table entries are the percentages expressing a "great deal" of confidence in the people running each institution.

Furthermore, the drop in confidence in democratic institutions is not unique to the United States. Opinion trends in other advanced industrial democracies show that trust in the national legislature has fallen in most democracies—including all four of our core nations (Dalton 2004, 37–39). In Germany, for example, the ALLBUS surveys find that those trusting the Bundestag decreased from 50 percent in 1984 to only 26 percent in 2008. Similar evidence is available for Britain and France.

The 2005–08 World Values Survey (WVS) compared confidence in institutions across our four nations (see table 12.2).[5] The question wording and set of institutions differ from those in table 12.1, so the results are not directly comparable. Still, the results present a familiar pattern: people have little confidence in the institutions of representative democracy. Roughly a third in each nation expresses "a great deal" or "quite a lot" of confidence in the national government or the national legislature. Perceptions of political parties are even more critical. Based on the original six European Union (EU) member states, the 2008 European Values Survey (EVS) found that only 16 percent had confidence in political parties—far below the average for the other social and political institutions it examined. In addition, despite the downward trend in political support in all four nations, Americans remain more trustful of political institutions.

People express more confidence in nonpolitical institutions of government, such as the judicial system or the civil service, than in the institutions of representative democracy. This finding is ironic. The members of the U.S. Supreme Court are not subject to election, and the justices serve for life; but people are more positive about the Court than about elected government

Table 12.2	Confidence in Institutions across Nations

Confidence in political institutions is low in all four nations, with Americans more positive than Europeans.

	UNITED STATES	GREAT BRITAIN	FRANCE	GERMANY
National government	41	34	29	27
National legislature	36	36	35	26
Courts	66	60	40	60
Civil service	61	46	54	34
Political parties	22	18	16	15
Press	26	14	39	34
Major companies	32	37	40	26
Labor unions	36	30	39	34
Environmental groups	59	70	65	60

Source: 2005–08 World Values Survey.

Note: Table entries are the percentages expressing "a great deal" or "quite a lot" of confidence in each institution. Missing data were excluded from the calculation of percentages.

officials. These numbers suggest a growing public dissatisfaction with the style of representative government and the actions of elected politicians.

Support for a Democratic Regime

If we return to Citrin's baseball analogy, the loss of trust in government and political institutions can have even more fundamental implications. It's not just that the home team has had a losing season (or two, or three). Rather, it's that people see most politicians and governments in most nations as suffering a long-term losing streak. Presidents, prime ministers, and chancellors alike have been replaced during this losing streak, but the skepticism continues.

At some point, we must worry that dissatisfaction about the team (the government or the political institutions) generalizes to dissatisfaction with the game itself (democracy and its values). Indeed, these doubts are growing. In 1973, the MORI poll showed that about half of the British public thought the political system could be improved quite a lot; in 2010 this had increased by two-thirds. Similarly, in 1988 the ALLBUS survey found that only 16 percent of Germans described the political system as needing much reform or as already broken; by 1994 almost three times as many people (44 percent) shared these sentiments. If politics were a baseball game, this implies that people want to see changes in the nature of the game and not just the players or managers in the dugout.

In earlier historical periods, dissatisfaction with politicians or political institutions often led to (or arose from) disenchantment with the democratic process itself. This was the case with the antidemocratic challenges that faced the United States and many European democracies in the 1920s and 1930s. Even during the years immediately following World War II, dissatisfaction with democracy in Europe was often concentrated among antidemocratic extremists on the Left or Right. If people lose faith in the norms and principles of the democratic process, they may reject government authority or question whether democracy is sustainable or desirable. Such sentiments would place democracy at risk.

But the news is not all bad. The available evidence suggests that the current situation is different from these historical examples. Support for democratic norms and procedures have grown over the past generation—even while trust in government has decreased. For example, long-term trends indicate that people have become more politically tolerant during the postwar period. Americans' tolerance of five potentially contentious social and political groups has trended upward during the past four decades, and expressed support for civil liberties is more common (Dalton 2009a, ch. 5; Nie, Junn, and Stehlik-Barry 1996).[6] The extension of democratic rights to women, racial and ethnic minorities, and homosexuals has profoundly altered the politics of advanced industrial democracies within the span of a generation (also see chapter 6). Other evidence points to the breadth of democratic values among contemporary publics, especially among the young (Thomassen 2007; Dalton 2009a). Ronald Inglehart's (1990, 1997) research on postmaterial value change also highlights the growing emphasis on political and social participation as core value priorities. At least in principle, there is widespread public endorsement of the political values and norms that underlie the democratic process.

To tap support for the principle of democracy and a democratic form of government, opinion surveys typically ask whether democracy is the best form of government compared to all the rest. Although we lack long-term time series for this question, the current high degree of support suggests no major erosion in these sentiments (table 12.3).[7] On average, about 90 percent of the public in advanced industrial democracies agree that democracy is better than other forms of government (also see Inglehart 2003; Dalton 2004, ch. 2). Another question in the WVS/EVS asked about support for the

Table 12.3	Support for Democracy	
The democratic ideal is almost universally supported in these nations.		
NATION	DEMOCRACY IS BETTER THAN OTHER GOVERNMENTS	DEMOCRATIC SYSTEM IS GOOD
Australia	87	89
Austria	96	92
Belgium	90	92
Canada	87	91
Denmark	99	99
Finland	96	92
France	93	91
Germany	94	90
Great Britain	89	87
Greece	97	97
Iceland	96	96
Ireland	85	83
Italy	96	97
Japan	92	88
Netherlands	93	92
New Zealand	87	94
Norway	95	95
Portugal	93	93
Spain	96	96
Sweden	95	94
Switzerland	96	97
United States	88	86

Sources: 2008 European Values Survey; 1999–2002 and 2005–08 World Values Survey for the United States, Australia, Canada, Japan, and New Zealand.

Note: Table entries are the percentages agreeing with each statement. Missing data were excluded from the calculation of percentages.

idea of democracy. Assent to the statement "The democratic system is good" shows that support is nearly universal in Western democracies. Moreover, in comparison to a Eurobarometer survey of the late 1980s, support for demo- cratic government has strengthened in most Western European nations.

In summary, this evidence suggests that current expressions of political dis- trust or disaffection are not a critique of democracy per se, as it was in the past, but exist among citizens who remain committed to the democratic ideal.

Community Support

A final aspect of political support concerns orientations toward the politi- cal community and society. Community support involves the system affect described by Almond and Verba (1963). A strong emotional attachment to the nation presumably provides a reservoir of diffuse support that can main- tain a political system through temporary periods of political stress. Most Western democracies endured at the start of the Great Depression because people had faith that democracy would address the problems, and such a reservoir of popular identification helps a political system endure during periods of crisis. One would expect national attachments to also help societ- ies manage the dislocations caused by the 2008 recession.

One measure of such feelings is pride in one's nation. Figure 12.3 dis- plays the percentages of citizens who feel very proud of their nation within the advanced industrial democracies in the early 1980s and again in the 2005–08.[8] Overall, feelings of national pride are relatively high, but with significant national differences (Smith 2009).

National pride is exceptionally high in the United States: 76 percent of the public in 1981 and 65 percent in 2005 felt "very proud" to be an American (nearly all the rest felt "proud"). Those chants of *USA! USA! USA!* are not lim- ited to Olympic competition; they signify a persistent feeling among Americans.

Most Europeans voice their national pride in more moderate tones; the relative raking of nations also has changed only marginally over time. Ger- mans, for example, were hesitant in their expressions of national pride in the 1980s and are still today; the trauma of the Third Reich burned a deep scar in the German psyche in both West and East. Young Germans espe- cially feel that the nationalist excesses of the past must never be repeated. The Federal Republic therefore has avoided many of the emotional national symbols that are common in other industrial nations. Germany celebrates few political holidays or memorials; the national anthem is seldom played; and even the anniversary of the founding of the Federal Republic attracts little public attention. Although most people are proud to be German, they refrain from any unquestioning emotional attachment to state and nation.

Beyond these cross-national variations, it's clear that national pride hasn't eroded over the past few decades. These surveys suggest that national pride is generally growing, which is surprising given the high baseline of opinions in the first survey in the early 1980s. When longer time series are available for specific nations, they too show a pattern or relative stability or growth in national pride over time (for example, Smith 2009). As one should expect from affective feelings of toward the nation, these sentiments have been relatively impervious to the erosion in other aspects of political support.

Figure 12.3	National Pride

Feelings of national pride vary widely across democracies.

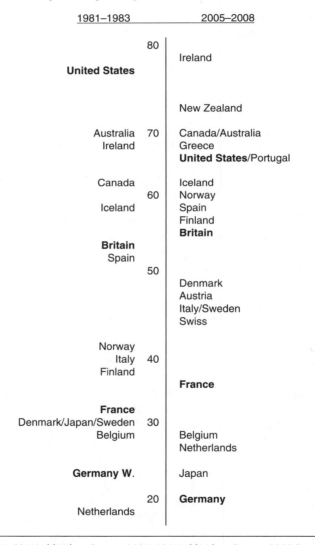

1981–1983		2005–2008
	80	Ireland
United States		
		New Zealand
Australia	70	Canada/Australia
Ireland		Greece
		United States/Portugal
Canada		Iceland
	60	Norway
Iceland		Spain
		Finland
		Britain
Britain		
Spain		
	50	
		Denmark
		Austria
		Italy/Sweden
		Swiss
Norway		
Italy	40	
Finland		
		France
France		
Denmark/Japan/Sweden	30	
Belgium		Belgium
		Netherlands
Germany W.		Japan
	20	**Germany**
Netherlands		

Sources: 1981–83 World Values Survey; 2005–08 World Values Survey; 2008 European Values Survey.

Note: Figure entries are the percentages feeling "very proud" of their nation. Missing data were excluded from the calculation of percentages.

Dissatisfied Democrats

As previously noted, by some measures this time may be considered the golden age of democracy. At the beginning of the twenty-first century, more nations in the world have become or strive to be democracies than at any other point in human history. Most of the other political ideologies that once stood as major rivals to democracy, such as fascism and communism, have lost their legitimacy. Democracy has brought peace, freedom, and prosperity to billions of people in the world.

At the same time, people have grown more critical of political elites, more negative toward political parties, and less confident of political institutions—and their attitudes represent a basic change in the political norms of democratic publics. The deference to authority and political allegiance that once was common in many of these nations has been partially replaced by skepticism about elites. In most democracies, people are more cynical about the key institutions of democratic governance. At the same time, however, people are simultaneously expressing strong support for the democratic creed.

These mixed sentiments produce a new pattern of "dissatisfied democrats"—people who are dissatisfied with political institutions but supportive of democratic principles (Klingemann 1999). Dissatisfied democrats appear to be another characteristic of the new style of citizen politics, although researchers debate this point.

The significance of the trends rests in part on what is shaping these new citizen orientations. Political scientists interpret these trends in dramatically different ways. The remainder of this section discusses the two contrasting views of the changes.

The Democratic Elitist Perspective

One group of scholars cites widespread political dissatisfaction as evidence of a crisis of democracy (Zakaria 2003; Macedo et al. 2005; Wolfe 2006). Some researchers claim that excessive public demands are overtaxing governments' ability to satisfy them. Thus, these analysts use the elitist theory of democracy (see chapter 2) to offer a solution to this crisis. In a crude exaggeration of democratic theory, they maintain that if a supportive and quiescent public ensures a smoothly functioning political system, then we must redevelop these traits in contemporary publics. The centrifugal tendencies of democratic politics (and the demands of the public) must be controlled, and political authority must be reestablished. Samuel Huntington assumed the ermine robes as spokesperson for this position when political trust first started to decline:

> The problem of governance in the United States today stems from an "excess of democracy." . . . [T]he effective operation of a democratic political system usually requires some measure of apathy and non-involvement on the part of some individuals and groups. The vulnerability of democratic government in the United States comes . . . from the internal dynamics of democracy itself in a highly educated, mobilized, and participatory society. (1975, 37–38)

More recently, Fareed Zakaria (2003, 248) is even blunter in his critique of American democracy: "What we need in politics today is not more democracy, but less." There is limited research on the Tea Party movement or the Occupy Wall Street movement, but I suspect these elitists would be critical of both as excesses of populism.[9]

In short, these analysts maintain that a crisis of democracy has developed because too many people want to apply its creed of liberty and equality to themselves but democratic systems cannot meet these expectations. The critics contend that democracy has become overloaded because minorities are no longer apathetic, women are demanding equality, students are no longer docile, and the average citizen is no longer deferential. If these groups would only leave politics to the politicians—and their expert advisers—"democracy" would again be secure.[10]

Another element of the elitist perspective calls for a reduction in the scale of government. These analysts argue that governments have assumed too large a role in society, which contributes to the overload. This tenet was one of the underpinnings of Thatcher's, Reagan's, and other neoconservatives' attempts to limit the size of government starting in the 1980s and has been revived in reaction to the economic strains we now face. However, such calls for retrenchment are often biased in determining which programs the government should no longer support; usually targeted for cuts are social services or environmental programs rather than programs that benefit conservative constituencies.

John Hibbing and Elizabeth Theiss-Morse (2002) claim that people want to be less involved in government; they suggest that democracy be reformed to spare them the burdens of democratic citizenship. This is a provocative argument, but it runs counter to the study's own evidence as well as the evidence presented here and in other research. Hibbing and Theiss-Morse's survey of American public opinion found that 86 percent favored more ballot initiatives and an expansion of democracy (2002, 75). Similarly, the British public strongly favors a variety of institutional reforms that will expand citizen access and input into the political process, such as greater use of referendums and direct election of local candidates (Curtice 2013).

Taken together, the cures offered by elitist theorists are worse than the problem they address; democracy's very goals are ignored in its defense. The critics of citizen politics forget that democracy means popular control of elites, not elite control over the populace.

The New Politics Perspective

The New Politics perspective offers a contrasting image of contemporary democracy. Political dissatisfaction has generally increased the most among the young and the better educated—those who disproportionately hold New Politics values and who benefit most from the social modernization of advanced industrial societies (Klingemann 1999; Dalton 2004, ch. 5; Dalton and Welzel 2013). These individuals have higher expectations of government: they are more demanding of politicians and more critical of how the process functions. Because they follow politics and are more concerned about what government does, they hold government to a higher standard than people did in the past.

Consequently, dissatisfied democrats may represent another step in democracy's progress toward its ideals. Just as earlier periods of dissatisfaction led to the expansion of the mass franchise, the granting of voting rights to women, and populist reforms that strengthened the democratic process, we may be in a new period of democratic reform.

The link between postmaterial value change and the growth of dissatisfied democrats is illustrated in figure 12.4. The figure shows that postmaterialists are distinctly *less likely* than materialists to express confidence in government. At the same time, postmaterialists are much *more likely* to believe that democracy is a good thing. Only 48 percent of materialists in our four core nations strongly agree that democracy is a good form of government, compared to 65 percent of postmaterialists.[11] Postmaterialists therefore illustrate the creedal passion in support for democracy that some analysts lament—but that offers the potential for democracy to move toward its theoretical ideal, on the horizon.

Figure 12.4	Changing Expectations

Postmaterialists are more supportive of democratic principles but express less confidence in their governments.

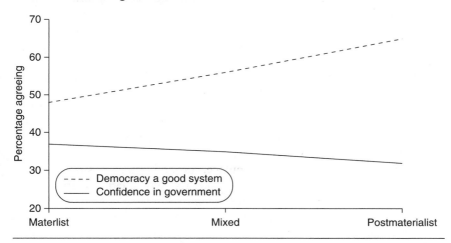

Source: Combined data from United States, Britain, France, and Germany from the 2005–08 World Values Survey.

Note: Figure plots the percentages of those strongly agreeing that democracy is a good system of government and those who are confident in the national government.

In short, the New Politics approach offers a different diagnosis of current patterns of political support. People today are better informed and more highly skilled than previous electorates, and they carry different expectations about how the democratic process should function. People are also more conscious of their political rights and more demanding in their individualism. The new style of citizen politics encourages a diversity of political interests (issue publics), instrumental choice in contrast to the affective partisan loyalty of the past, and more direct styles of political action.

Dissatisfied democrats are also likely to change their patterns of political participation to use protest, direct action, and other forms of contentious action (chapter 4). These new forms of activism often strain the democratic process, as demonstrators challenge established political elites and current government structures. The rise of new social movements and citizen interest groups further institutionalizes the changing nature of citizen politics. These groups change the style of interest representation, because people can focus their efforts on specific policy concerns—and work through methods of direct action. (One might add the creation of an omnipresent mass media to this change in the pattern of politics.) Public interest groups also present a challenge to political parties and the established processes of representative government. The structures of representative democracy that were created in the late 1800s often seem ill suited to deal with the plethora of new interests, articulated in new ways and functioning by new rules.

Democratic governments need to accommodate the changing patterns of citizen politics. For example, the structured system of representative democracy limits the potential for citizen participation, especially in Western Europe. Opportunities for electoral input are scandalously low for most Europeans; the option to cast only a few votes during a multiyear electoral cycle is not an admirable democratic record. Moreover, beyond elections, many democracies offer their citizens few ways to participate in the decisions of government that affect their lives. Indeed, governments often shielded themselves from public scrutiny and intentionally limited the direct impact of the citizenry—as in the constitutional structure initially devised by the founders of the United States (or the constitutional structure of many European parliamentary systems). The fundamental structure of contemporary democratic institutions was developed in the nineteenth century—and society has changed a good deal since then.

The emphasis on new forms of citizen access and influence is not simply a call for participation for participation's sake. Expanding citizen participation can open up political systems that have become sclerotized by corporatist policymaking, political cartels, and bureaucratized administration. The triumvirate of business-labor-government in many advanced industrial democracies often restricts the political interests of other groups. A system that distorts access to the political process is necessarily inefficient in meeting all of society's needs.

Opening up the political process may also prompt governments to become more responsive to a broader spectrum of political demands. This method doesn't increase the quantity of political demands—the needs of the environment, women, consumers, and other groups exist—but it ensures that the demands receive fair attention from the government and thereby improves the government's ability to address all societal needs.

Greater political involvement also educates citizens in the democratic process. James Wright (1976, 260) noted a basic irony in the elitists' criticisms of citizen participation. The democratic elitists believe that governments can generate more support by convincing citizens of a lie (a sense of political efficacy that is fictitious) than by encouraging citizens to participate and learn of the necessary limits to their influence. The "big lie" may work for a while, but as soon as someone points out the gap between myth and reality, the political credibility of the system falters. It happened to the Eastern European governments in 1989–91. Call it co-optation, pragmatism, or Jeffersonian idealism, but involving citizens in the democratic process is one method to increase their identification with the process.

Finally, greater citizen input ultimately ensures the quality of government decision making. There is some evidence that an active, critical citizenry leads to better governance (Geissel 2008; Putnam 1993). As we noted in chapter 1, Thomas Jefferson viewed the public as the major constraint on the potential excesses of government officials. Citizen participation is not, however, a panacea for all of modern society's ills; even educated, informed, and politically involved citizens will still make errors in judgment. As Benjamin Barber (1984, 151) also noted,

> Democracy doesn't place endless faith in the capacity of individuals to govern themselves, but it affirms with Machiavelli that the multitude will on the whole be as wise or wiser than princes, and with Theodore Roosevelt that "the majority of plain people will day in and day out make fewer mistakes in governing themselves than another smaller body of men will make in trying to govern them."

Since I presented this evaluation of contemporary democratic politics in the first edition of *Citizen Politics*, the calls for political reform have become more commonplace. And there are encouraging signs that politicians and governments are responding.

Significant institutional reforms are restructuring the democratic process (Cain, Dalton, and Scarrow 2003; G. Smith 2009). Many nations are reforming administrative procedures to give citizen groups access to the formerly closed processes of policy administration. In Germany local citizen action groups have won changes in administrative law to allow for citizen participation in local administrative processes. Similar reforms in the United States offer individual citizens and citizen groups greater access to the political process. New Freedom of Information laws and ombudsman offices are making government more transparent and accessible to its citizens (Cain, Fabrinni, and Egan 2003).

Other forms of direct democracy are also more apparent. Citizen groups in the United States and Europe are making greater use of referendums to involve the public directly in policymaking (Pállinger et al 2007; Bowler and Glazer 2008). More individual citizens and public interest groups are turning to the courts to guarantee their rights of democratic access and influence (G. Smith 2009; Cichowski and Stone Sweet 2003). Environmentalists in many nations have gained legal standing in the courts so they can sue to curb the harmful actions of municipalities or government agencies.

Reforms can be seen within the structured system of party government. The formation of new parties is one sign of adaptation, but even the established parties are changing internally to give their members more influence. The term limits movement is one expression of these reformist sentiments. A majority of U.S. states have now enacted some type of term limits legislation, normally through citizen initiatives.

These institutional changes are difficult to accomplish. They proceed at a slow pace and often have unintended consequences. But once implemented, they restructure the whole process of making policy that extends beyond a single issue or a single policy agenda. The degree of institutional change during the past three decades rivals the reformist surge of the Populist movement of the early 1990s (Cain, Dalton, and Scarrow 2003). The processes of contemporary democracies are being transformed to reflect the new style of citizen politics.

Indeed, these adaptations reflect the ability of democracy to grow and evolve; the lack of such adaptivity is what brought about the downfall of communism. As German sociologist Ralf Dahrendorf noted,

> What we have to do above all is to maintain that flexibility of democratic institutions which is in some ways their greatest virtue: the ability of democratic institutions to implement and effect change without revolution—the ability to react to new problems in new ways—the ability to develop institutions rather than change them all the time—the ability to keep the lines of communication open between leaders and led—and the ability to make individuals count above all. (1975, 194)

Such change in the style of representative democracy is not without risk. The political process may experience some growing pains as it adjusts to greater citizen participation, especially in the more tightly structured European political systems.

A skeptical public is likely to act differently (Hetherington 2005). Public opinion surveys suggest that people who think their government wastes tax money and is unresponsive to their interests may feel they are justified in fudging a bit on their taxes or bending the law in other ways. The skeptical citizen may also be hesitant to serve on a jury or perform other public service activities. In short, political support is part of the social contract that enables democracies to act without coercion and with the voluntary compliance of the citizenry. Decreasing support erodes this part of the social contract.

Another potential problem is the possibility of a growing participation gap between sophisticated and unsophisticated citizens (see chapter 3).

Because the resources required to lobby government directly or to organize a public interest group are greater than those required to vote, a change in the style of political activity may leave behind those in society who lack the education and other skills and resources needed for direct action politics.

Democracies must also face the challenge of balancing greater responsiveness to specific interests against the broader interests of the nation. In the vernacular of political science, we have seen a dramatic increase in the expression of interests over the past generation but an erosion in the ability to integrate these interests in coherent government programs. In other words, citizen interest groups, social movements, individual citizens, and various political groups are now more vocal about their political interests and have greater access to the democratic process. At the same time, political institutions struggle to balance contending interests—and to make interest groups sensitive to the collective needs of society. The collective interest is more than just the sum of individual interests, and one of the pressing needs for contemporary democracies is to find new ways to bring diverse interests together.

Participatory democracy can produce political overkill, but it also contains an equilibrium mechanism to encourage political balance. In the long political history of the United States, the process has generally succeeded in retaining the benefits of new ideas while avoiding the ominously predicted excesses of democracy. We should remember that democratic politics is not supposed to maximize government efficiency or to increase the autonomy of political elites. Just the opposite. In fact, efficiency is partially sacrificed to ensure a more important goal: popular control of elites. Expanding participation is not a problem but an opportunity for the advanced industrial democracies to come closer to matching their democratic ideals.

In summary, the current crisis of democracy is really just another stage in the ongoing history of democracy's development. Democracies need to adapt to present-day politics and to the new style of citizen politics. As Dahrendorf (2000, 311) has observed, "Representative government is no longer as compelling a proposition as it once was. Instead, a search for new institutional forms to express conflicts of interest has begun." This process of democratic experimentation and reform may be threatening to some, and it does present a risk—but change is necessary. The challenge to democracies is to discover whether they can continue to evolve, to guarantee political rights, and to increase the ability of citizens to control their lives. Can we move democracy closer to its theoretical ideals?

Suggested Readings

Dalton, Russell. 2004. *Democratic Challenges, Democratic Choices: The Erosion of Political Support in Advanced Industrial Democracies.* Oxford, UK: Oxford University Press.

Dalton, Russell, and Christian Welzel, eds. 2013. *The Civic Culture Transformed: From Allegiant to Assertive Citizens*. Cambridge, UK: Cambridge University Press.

Hetherington, Marc. 2005. *Why Trust Matters: Declining Political Trust and the Demise of American Liberalism*. Princeton: Princeton University Press.

Hibbing, John, and Elizabeth Theiss-Morse. 2002. *Stealth Democracy: Americans' Beliefs about How Government Should Work*. New York: Cambridge University Press.

Norris, Pippa. 2011. *Democratic Deficit: Critical Citizens Revisited*. Cambridge, UK: Cambridge University Press.

Norris, Pippa, ed. 1999. *Critical Citizens: Global Support for Democratic Governance*. Oxford, UK: Oxford University Press.

Nye, Joseph, Philip Zelikow, and David King. 1997. *Why People Don't Trust Government*. Cambridge, MA: Harvard University Press.

Pharr, Susan, and Robert Putnam, eds. 2000. *Disaffected Democracies: What's Troubling the Trilateral Countries?* Princeton: Princeton University Press.

Notes

1. In the mid-1980s, Samuel Huntington (1984) was explaining why there would be no more democracies in the world, a theme consistent with his elitist view of democracy. By the end of the decade, he was describing democratization as a wave that was transforming the international order (Huntington 1991).
2. The argument is also made that diffuse regime support existed in other Western democracies in the 1930s and that dissatisfaction focused only on the performance of political elites. These beliefs were channeled within the political process, and the basic structure of democratic government persisted in the United States, Britain, and France.
3. The question wording and coding categories differ slightly across nations, so one shouldn't directly compare the cross-national levels of support in the figure. For such comparisons, see Norris (2011) and tables 12.2 and 12.3 in this chapter.
4. Watch old episodes of the television program *West Wing*. In seven seasons, there are only a handful of times when anyone except his immediate family doesn't address Jed Bartlett as "Mr. President."
5. For a more extensive comparison of confidence in institutions, see Dalton (2004) and Norris (2011).
6. Some counter evidence is apparent for Britain, where the British Social Attitudes survey shows a drop in tolerance and civil liberties in 2005

(Johnson and Gearty 2007). But a good deal of time has passed since the previous survey, and the 2005 result may have been affected by the terrorist attacks in London that occurred in the midst of the interviewing for the survey.

7. The two questions were as follows: "Democracy may have problems but it's better than any other form of government. Do you agree or disagree?" and "Would you say it's a very good, fairly good, fairly bad, or very bad way of governing this country: Having a democratic political system?"

8. The 2005–08 World Values Survey shows little change for the four core nations: United States (93 percent), Britain (86 percent), France (86 percent), and Germany (68 percent). The question was asked, "How proud are you to be (nationality)?" The responses were (1) very proud, (2) quite proud, (3) not very proud, and (4) not at all proud. The figure presents the "very proud" and "proud" responses.

9. In fact, throughout 2011 Zakaria used his appearances on CNN to call the Tea Party antidemocratic and a threat to democracy; then various Fox News reporters were equally critical about Occupy Wall Street.

10. Huntington's advice on limiting political demands overlooks the possibility of constraining the input of Harvard professors, corporate executives, and the upper class. His focus solely on the participation of average citizens suggests that he has confused the definitions of plutocracy and democracy.

11. These results are from the 2005–08 World Values Survey combining results from the United States, Britain, France, and Germany. The democracy item asks about approval of a democratic form of government; the confidence in government question is the same as presented in table 12.2.

Appendix A

Statistical Primer

Most newspapers report on public opinion polls and publish tables and graphs to illustrate the results. The informed citizen needs to know how to read and interpret these tables and graphs.

This book provides this kind of information to describe the attitudes and behavior of contemporary publics. The tables and figures I present generally follow one of two patterns. The first pattern describes the differences in citizen opinions or behaviors across the four core nations in this study. As examples, table 2.1 describes the sources of information for citizens in each nation, and table 3.4 summarizes patterns of political participation. Surveys estimate public opinion, and typically the results in such a table are within a few percentage points of what the entire public actually thinks or does (Asher 2007).

In the second pattern, tables or figures describe the relationships between two or more questions from a public opinion survey. For example, what factors are related to different types of political participation, what are the correlates of voting choice, or what attitudes are related to trust in government? I often present these relationships in graphic terms; showing, perhaps, that as education goes up, so does voting turnout (figure 4.1), or, as church attendance increases, so does the share of the vote going to conservative parties (table 8.3). Implicitly, at least, there is a presumption of causality: when education is related to higher turnout, we can infer that education provides the skills and resources that allow people to be more politically active.

These presentations of relationships in a table or figure typically have the presumed predictor aligned along the horizontal axis, with categories of the predictor marked in the table or figure. The effect is arrayed along the vertical axis. In figure 4.1, the least educated group (less than a high school diploma) is on the left of the horizontal axis, and the most educated age group (some college or more) is on the right side of this axis. The figure then presents the voting turnout rates on the horizontal axis. Separate lines plot the increase in turnout with education in each nation.

Often tables and figures include multiple comparisons, such as many levels of education or church attendance—and it can become difficult to see the overall pattern amid a blur of numbers. Therefore, I often use correlation statistics to summarize relationships. Statistics are tools to help you understand relationships, even if you are not numerically inclined. These correlations summarize the extent to which responses on one survey question (such has higher levels of education) are related to responses on another question (such as higher voter turnout).

Statistics is a complex field, and data analysis is a complicated research methodology; statisticians might disapprove of the quick summaries that follow and the limited attention devoted to the assumptions underlying the use of these statistics. Nevertheless, this primer provides a guide on how to use the statistics presented in this book, with the hope that it helps you understand the presentation of findings.

I most commonly use three correlation statistics:

- **Cramer's V correlation.** This correlation measures the relationship between two variables when at least one of them is a "categoric" variable, that is, a set of categories with no distinct order. Examples of a categoric variable are region, race, religious denomination, or other measures that do not follow a natural order from low to high, agree to disagree, or some other underlying order.

- **Pearson's *r* correlation.** This correlation measures the relationship between two variables when both have an ordered pattern of categories, such as from low to high or agree to disagree. This statistic is more powerful and demanding because it does not just see whether categories differ on the predicted variable: it presumes an ordered pattern to these differences. See figure 4.1 for an example: as education level increases, the vote turnout also should increase. The larger differences by education in the United States imply that education has a stronger impact (correlation) than for the three European countries.

  The Pearson's *r* also measures the *direction* of a relationship because there is a distinction between positive and negative values. For example, age is positively related to voting turnout, but protest decreases with age. The first example would produce a positive correlation, and a negative correlation in the second.

  Several tables and figures present correlations to summarize relationships across different nations or groups rather than display each relationship in a separate graph. Figure 8.2 presents the relationship between social class and voting choice in seventeen nations. Figure 8.5 presents the relationship between postmaterial values and vote choice for a set of nations.

- **Regression coefficient (ß).** This statistic is the most complex. Often we want to examine the relationship between two variables, but we think the relationship might partially depend on one or more other variables. Multiple regression is a statistical method to simultaneously examine the relationships of several variables with a dependent variable, so that we can assess the separate effects of each. The regression coefficient describes the relationship between two variables while "statistically controlling for" the other variables in the model. For example, we can determine the effect of education on turnout while simultaneously controlling for (or statistically removing) age differences or ideological differences in turnout if all three variables are interrelated.

This book presents standardized regression coefficients from several such models (for example, figure 4.3 and table 4.1). These statistics are comparable to the Pearson r and are calculated in similar ways. They signify the direction and strength of a relationship, and the differences between a Pearson r and a regression coefficient indicate how much a relationship changes by controlling for the other variables in the model.

A simple example from this book illustrates the logic of regression analysis. We begin with the example of figure A.1, which is the same as figure 11.3. The ideological position of a district (the horizontal axis) is used to predict the ideological position of the member of Congress from that district (the vertical axis). The figure shows that there is a strong relationship between these two variables. The line in this figure summarizes the overall pattern and shows that as district ideology changes there is a marked change in the predicted ideology of the elected member of Congress. In addition, the

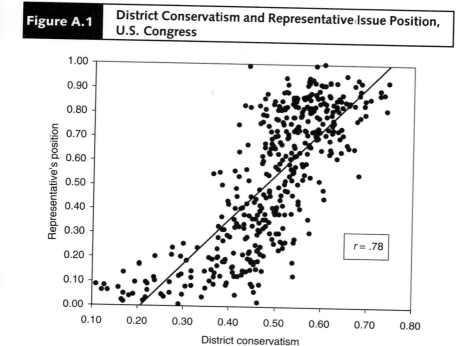

Figure A.1 | **District Conservatism and Representative Issue Position, U.S. Congress**

$r = .78$

Representative's position (vertical axis)

District conservatism (horizontal axis)

Sources: Personal communication, Stephen Ansolabehere; data are based on 104th Congress; also see Ansolabehere et al. (2001a, 2001b).

| Figure A.2 | District Conservatism and Representative Issue Position, Controlling for Representative's Partisanship |

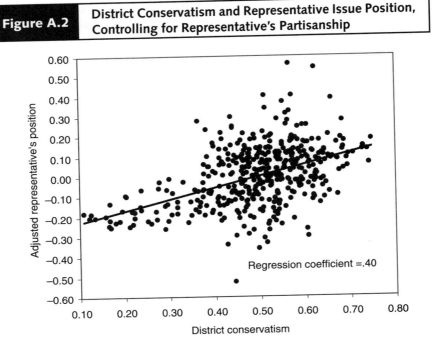

Source: Personal communication, Stephen Ansolabehere; data are based on 104th Congress; also see Ansolabehere et al. (2001a, 2001b).

points in the figure are relatively close to this summary line. The Pearson *r* is .78, which signifies a very strong relationship. (In part, the correlation is so high because we are dealing with aggregated units, electoral districts, and most relationships among individual attitudes are not so strong.)

If we stopped here, we would conclude that voters can perceive the ideological position of the candidates, and therefore most districts pick representatives who share their views. Liberal districts generally pick liberal candidates, and conservative districts generally pick conservative candidates. There is some variation, so points are spread out a bit in the figure. But the variation is limited, and hence the strong correlation.

One might ask, however, whether voters are really aware of the ideology of candidates or whether they are using political party as a cue. That is, if you look closely at figure 11.3, you see that Democratic legislators tend toward the liberal end of the dimension and Republican legislators toward the conservative end. In other words, both party and district ideology may predict the ideology of the elected representative. This potential joint effect of party and liberal/conservative ideology produces a two-variable regression model, using these two predictors.

Figure A.2 graphically illustrates the outcome from these analyses. The figure presents the ideology of the district and the ideology of the representative—while statistically holding constant party effects. One can see that the fit between the two variables is still substantial, but the line summarizing this relationship is now flatter, and the spread of points around the line is more dispersed. The statistic summarizing this relationship drops from the .78 correlation in the previous figure to the ß = .40 regression coefficient. The effect of district ideology has weakened by controlling for party, but it is still a significant predictor of the ideology of representatives. This, in brief, is the logic of multiple regression—to examine the independent impact of one variable while controlling for the effect of other variables.

What Is Big?

Correlations are designed to summarize the strength of the relationship between two variables. This raises the question of what is a strong relationship versus a weak relationship. I primarily rely on the three correlation statistics in this text because they give comparable values for similar relationships, even if they are calculated differently:

- **Cramer's V correlation.** This statistic ranges from a value of 0.0 when there are no differences across categories (that is, each comparison in a table has the same percentage distribution) to a values of 1.00 when categories in a table differ by a maximum possible 100 percent. Typically, we interpret coefficients of .10 or less as a weak relationship, .10–.20 as a modest relationship, and .20 or larger as a strong relationship.

- **Pearson's r correlation.** This statistic measures three properties that are apparent in figure A.1. First, how strongly does one variable predict differences in the dependent variable? In figure A.1 this means how steep is the angle of the line describing this relationship. Second, how closely are points clustered around this line; in other words, how well does the line represent the overall pattern? The points are more tightly clustered around the line in figure A.1 than in figure A.2. Third, relationships can be positive or negative. For example, voting turnout can increase with age (a positive relationship), while protest participation decreases with age (a negative relationship).

  Thus, the Pearson r ranges from a value of −1.0 when there is a perfect negative relationship (a sharp negatively sloped line with all the points clustered on the line), to 0.0 when there are no differences across categories (that is, scores of the predictor variable are unrelated to the dependent variable), to a value of 1.00 when there is a perfect positive correlation. As with Cramer's V, we interpret coefficients of .10 or less as a weak relationship, .10–.20 as a modest relationship, and .20 or larger as a strong relationship.

- **Regression coefficient (ß).** This statistic is comparable to the Pearson r, except that it measures the relationship between two variables while controlling for the relationships shared by other variables in the model. Like the Pearson r, it ranges from -1.0 for a perfect negative relationship to 1.0 for a perfect positive relationship. As with the other two statistics, we interpret coefficients of .10 or less as a weak relationship, .10–.20 as a modest relationship, and .20 or larger as a strong relationship.

Statistics, graphs, and tables can sometimes seem complex, but they are simply a shortcut for summarizing how much one variable is related to another. With this guide, these relationships should be easier to interpret than trying to understand all the percentages in a statistical table or points in a graph.

Appendix B

Major Data Sources

In 1948 researchers at the University of Michigan conducted one of the first national election surveys based on scientific sampling methods. The four scholars who eventually directed the early surveys—Angus Campbell, Philip Converse, Warren Miller, and Donald Stokes—wrote the landmark study of American electoral behavior, *The American Voter*. Since then, this election study series has been repeated at each biennial national election. The American National Election Studies (ANES) is a national resource in the social sciences and is used by researchers in hundreds of universities worldwide (www.electionstudies.org).

David Butler and Donald Stokes began a comparable series of British election studies with the 1964 election. They continued the series through the 1966 and 1970 elections, and then a team of researchers led by Ivor Crewe, at the University of Essex, continued the series in 1974 and 1979. Between 1983 and 1997, Anthony Heath, Roger Jowell, and John Curtice of Social and Community Planning Research (SCPR) in London conducted the British Election Studies. A new research team at the University of Essex conducted the 2001, 2005, and 2010 British Election Studies (www.essex.ac.uk/bes).

Academic studies of German elections trace their roots back to the 1961 study conducted by Gerhard Baumert, Erwin Scheuch, and Rudolf Wildenmann from the University of Cologne. The Cologne researchers and their students have established this series through the work of Max Kaase, Hans-Dieter Klingemann, Franz Pappi, and the Forschungsgruppe Wahlen (Manfred Berger, Wolfgang Gibowski, Dieter Roth, Mattias Jung, et al.). A new academic group centered at the Wissenschaftszentrum Berlin für Sozialforschung (WZB) has continued this election series (www.gles.eu/index.en.htm).

France has a less institutionalized series of election surveys. A number of individual scholars have conducted surveys of specific French elections, beginning with the 1958 election study by Georges Dupeaux and Philip Converse. The current French election studies are now conducted by CEVIPOF in Paris (http://www.cevipof.com).

Most of the data analyzed in this volume were drawn from the data sources mentioned previously and cross-national studies listed in the following section. We acquired most of these data from the Inter-university Consortium for Political and Social Research (ICPSR) at the University of Michigan in Ann Arbor (www.icpsr.umich.edu). Additional data were made available by the UK Data Archive at the University of Essex, England (www .data-archive.ac.uk); the British Election Study homepage (www.essex .ac.uk/bes); GESIS, which is part of the Leibnitz Institut für Sozialwissenschaften in Cologne, Germany (www.gesis.org); and the French National Center for Scientific Research (cdsp.sciences-po.fr/index.php?lang=ANG). Neither the archives nor the original collectors of the data bear responsibility for the analyses presented here.

Major Cross-National Studies

In addition to single nation surveys, there are an increasing number of cross-national surveys. This research method began with Gabriel Almond's and Sidney Verba's classic *Civic Culture* study in 1959.

This book also makes extensive use of the following cross-national surveys:

The Eurobarometer is an ongoing series of opinion surveys conducted by the Commission of the European Union starting in the mid-1970s (ec.europa.eu/public_opinion/index_en.htm).

The Political Action Study examined eight Western democracies in 1974–75 (Barnes, Kaase, et al. 1979).

The World Values Survey (WVS) began in 1981 and is now in its fifth wave; it includes surveys spanning most of the world's population (www.worldvaluessurvey.org).

The International Social Survey Program (ISSP) is a coordinated series of public opinion surveys conducted by various sociological institutes in the United States and Europe (www.issp.org).

The Comparative Study of Electoral Systems (CSES) is a coordinated set of postelection surveys conducted in twenty to forty democracies. There are now three waves of CSES surveys (www.cses.org).

The European Social Survey (ESS) began in 2002 to survey European publics about a range of political and sociological topics (www.europeanso cialsurvey.org).

Appendix C

World Values Survey
Codebook

One of the key sources of public opinion data in this book are the World Values Survey and European Values Survey (WVS/EVS). To assist students and instructors in understanding the causes and correlates of public opinion, I prepared a subset of WVS data to use in connection with *Citizen Politics*. For ease of student usage, these data were extensively recoded and reformatted, such as merging categories to ensure reasonable group sizes in cross-tabular analyses. Students can use these data for small research exercises designed by the instructor, or for larger research projects that explore the themes in this book or other public opinion topics.

This appendix includes a brief description of the World Values Survey and then an abbreviated codebook that describes the 130 variables in this subset. Data files for the Statistical Package in the Social Sciences (SPSS) are downloadable from the Congressional Quarterly Press website for this book (www.CQpress.com). There are separate files for the four core nations discussed in this book (the United States, Britain, Germany, and France). The files are described in this codebook.

The World Values Survey

The World Values Survey is a unique resource in the social sciences. The first wave of the project was a coordinated survey of twenty-one nations conducted in the early 1980s by the European Values Survey group (Inglehart 1990). The second wave, done in the early 1990s, expanded to forty-two nations, including many of the post-communist states in Eastern Europe (Inglehart 1997; Abramson and Inglehart 1995). The third wave in the mid-1990s included fifty-four nations, and the fourth wave surveyed seventy-one societies around 2000 (Inglehart and Welzel 2005). The fifth wave of the WVS (2006–08) includes representative national surveys examining the basic values and beliefs of publics in fifty-six societies on all six inhabited continents, containing almost 80 percent of the world's population (Welzel 2012).

An international network of social scientists carries out this project, coordinated by an international directorate. Most surveys are funded from national sources and conducted by leading survey research firms. An international board develops the questions to include in the survey, and these are translated in the national language by each research institute. The surveys are then assembled in a single dataset and made available to the international research community. Additional information about the WVS can be found on the website (www.worldvaluessurvey.org).

Variable List

V1 COUNTRY
V2 WEIGHT (must weight data)

Life Domains

V3 HOW IMPORTANT IS FAMILY
V4 HOW IMPORTANT ARE FRIENDS
V5 HOW IMPORTANT IS LEISURE TIME
V6 HOW IMPORTANT IS POLITICS
V7 HOW IMPORTANT IS WORK
V8 HOW IMPORTANT IS RELIGION

Quality of Life

V9 FEELING OF HAPPINESS
V10 ARE YOU SATISFIED WITH YOUR LIFE
V11 DO YOU FEEL HEALTHY
V12 HOW MUCH FREEDOM DO YOU FEEL

Group Membership

V13 MEMBER CHURCH ORGANIZATION
V14 MEMBER SPORTS GROUP
V15 MEMBER ARTS, MUSIC EDUCATION
V16 MEMBER LABOR UNION
V17 MEMBER POLITICAL PARTY
V18 MEMBER ENVIRONMENTAL GROUP
V19 MEMBER PROFESSIONAL ASSOCIATION
V20 MEMBER CHARITABLE GROUP
V21 MEMBER CONSUMER GROUP
V22 TOTAL MEMBERSHIPS

Information Sources

V23 USE A COMPUTER
V24 INFORMATION: DAILY NEWSPAPER
V25 INFORMATION: NEWS BROADCASTS
V26 INFORMATION: MAGAZINES
V27 INFORMATION: IN DEPTH REPORTS
V28 INFORMATION: BOOKS
V29 INFORMATION: INTERNET, EMAIL
V30 INFORMATION: TALK WITH FRIENDS

Political Involvement

V31 INTERESTED IN POLITICS
V32 DID YOU VOTE

V33 SIGN A PETITION
V34 JOIN IN BOYCOTTS
V35 ATTEND LAWFUL DEMONSTRATION
V36 PROTEST INDEX

Tolerance

V37 TOLERANCE: RACE/ETHNICITY
V38 TOLERANCE: DRUGS & DRINKING
V39 TOLERANCE: HOMOSEXUALS & AIDS

Social Trust

V40 MOST PEOPLE CAN BE TRUSTED
V41 PEOPLE TRY TO TAKE ADVANTAGE
V42 TRUST: YOUR FAMILY
V43 TRUST: YOUR NEIGHBORS
V44 TRUST: PEOPLE YOU KNOW
V45 TRUST: PEOPLE YOU FIRST MEET
V46 TRUST: PEOPLE OF ANOTHER RELIGION
V47 TRUST: PEOPLE OF ANOTHER NATIONALIT
V48 TRUST: BONDING TRUST
V49 TRUST: BRIDGING TRUST

Environment, Science and Technology

V50 ENVIRONMENT VS ECONOMIC GROWTH
V51 OPINION ABOUT SCIENCE ADVANCE
V52 MORE EMPHASIS ON TECHNOLOGY

Job Priorities

V53 MEN SHOULD HAVE PRIORITY FOR JOB
V54 NATIONALS SHOULD HAVE PRIORITY FOR JOB

Marriage, Gender and Children

V55 WOMAN AS A SINGLE PARENT
V56 BEING A HOUSEWIFE FULFILLING
V57 MEN MAKE BETTER POLITICAL LEADERS
V58 UNIVERSITY IS MORE IMPORTANT FOR A BOY
V59 MEN MAKE BETTER BUSINESS EXECUTIVES
V60 GENDER EQUALITY INDEX

Political Values

V61 POSTMATERIAL VALUES INDEX
V62 LEFT/RIGHT SCALE
V63 GREATER RESPECT FOR AUTHORITY

Economic Values

V64 INCOMES MORE EQUAL
V65 GOVERNMENT MORE RESPONSIBILITY
V66 COMPETITION IS GOOD
V67 HARD WORK GENERATES SUCCESS
V68 WEALTH ACCUMLATION
V69 ECONOMIC LIBERALISM INDEX

Personal Autonomy

V70 I SEEK TO BE MYSELF
V71 LIVE UP TO FRIENDS EXPECTATIONS
V72 DECIDE MY GOALS

Confidence in Institutions

V73 CONFIDENCE: CHURCHES
V74 CONFIDENCE: ARMED FORCES
V75 CONFIDENCE: PRESS
V76 CONFIDENCE: TELEVISION
V77 CONFIDENCE: LABOR UNIONS
V78 CONFIDENCE: THE POLICE
V79 CONFIDENCE: JUSTICE SYSTEM
V80 CONFIDENCE: GOVERNMENT
V81 CONFIDENCE: POLITICAL PARTIES
V82 CONFIDENCE: PARLIAMENT
V83 CONFIDENCE: THE CIVIL SERVICES
V84 CONFIDENCE: MAJOR COMPANIES
V85 CONFIDENCE: ENVIRONMENTAL MOVEMENT
V86 CONFIDENCE: WOMENS MOVEMENT
V87 CONFIDENCE: CHARITABLE ORGANIZATIONS
V88 CONFIDENCE: THE EUROPEAN UNION
V89 CONFIDENCE: THE UNITED NATIONS

Support for Democracy

V90 HAVING A STRONG LEADER
V91 HAVING EXPERTS MAKE DECISIONS
V92 HAVING THE ARMY RULE
V93 HAVING A DEMOCRATIC POLITICAL SYSTEM
V94 DEMOCRACY VS AUTOCRACY INDEX
V95 IMPORTANCE OF DEMOCRACY
V96 DEMOCRATICNESS OF COUNTRY

Political Community

V97 HOW PROUD OF NATIONALITY
V98 BE WILLING TO FIGHT FOR YOUR COUNTRY

Justifiable Actions

V99 JUSTIFIABLE: CLAIMING GOVERNMENT BENEFIT
V100 JUSTIFIABLE: AVOIDING A TRANSIT FARE
V101 JUSTIFIABLE: CHEATING ON TAXES
V102 JUSTIFIABLE: ACCEPTING A BRIBE
V103 JUSTIFIABLE: HOMOSEXUALITY
V104 JUSTIFIABLE: PROSTITUTION
V105 JUSTIFIABLE: ABORTION
V106 JUSTIFIABLE: DIVORCE
V107 JUSTIFIABLE: EUTHANASIA
V108 JUSTIFIABLE: SUICIDE

Ethnic Diversity

V109 IMPACT OF ETHNIC DIVERSITY

Party Preference

V110 LEFT/RIGHT PARTY PREFERENCE
V111A PARTY: UNITED STATES
V111B PARTY: GERMANY

Religious Values

V112 RELIGIOUS PERSON
V113 RELIGIOUS DENOMINATION
V114 HOW OFTEN ATTEND RELIGIOUS SERVICE
V115 HOW IMPORTANT IS GOD IN LIFE

Demographic Variables

V116 GENDER
V117 AGE RECODED
V118 ETHNIC IDENTITY
V119 MARITAL STATUS
V120 EDUCATIONAL LEVEL
V121 INCOME RECODED
V122 FINANCIAL SATISFACTION
V123 EMPLOYMENT STATUS
V124 R'S PROFESSION/JOB
V125 INSTITUTION OF OCCUPATION
V126 MANUAL TASKS ON JOB
V127 ROUTINE TASKS ON JOB
V128 INDEPENDENCE ON JOB
V129 SIZE OF TOWN
V130A REGION: USA
V130B REGION: BRITAIN
V130C REGION: FRANCE
V130D REGION: GERMANY

Codebook

V1 COUNTRY

1. United States

2. Britain

3. France

4. Germany

V2 WEIGHT

The World Values Survey provides a weight variable to correct the samples to reflect national distributions of key variables or to adjust for different sampling rates for population groups.

For instance, the German survey oversampled residents of the eastern states, and their responses should be appropriately weighted to yield a representation national sample. SPSS can use this weight variable to produce a representative sample; the weight is needed for the U.S., British, French, and German studies.

V3 HOW IMPORTANT IS FAMILY

For each of the following, indicate how important it is in your life. Would you say it is: Family:

1. Very important
2. Rather important
3. Not very important
4. Not at all important
0. Don't know; MD

V4 HOW IMPORTANT ARE FRIENDS

(How important are) Friends?
See V003 for response categories

V5 HOW IMPORTANT IS LEISURE TIME

(How important is) Leisure time?
See V003 for response categories

V6 HOW IMPORTANT IS POLITICS

(How important is) Politics?
See V003 for response categories

V7 HOW IMPORTANT IS WORK

(How important is) Work?
See V003 for response categories

V8 HOW IMPORTANT IS RELIGION

(How important is) Religion?
See V003 for response categories

V9 FEELING OF HAPPINESS

Taking all things together, would you say you are:

1. Very happy
2. Quite happy
3. Not very happy
4. Not at all happy
0. Don't know

V10 SATISFACTION WITH LIFE

All things considered, how satisfied are you with your life as a whole these days? Please use this card to help with your answer.

1. Dissatisfied (1–3)

2. Somewhat dissatisfied (4–5)

3. Somewhat satisfied (6–7)

4. Very satisfied (8–10)

0. Don't know; MD

V11 DO YOU FEEL HEALTHY

All in all, how would you describe your state of health these days? Would you say it is:

1. Very good

2. Good

3. Fair

4. Poor

0. Don't know; MD

V12 FEELING OF FREEDOM

How much freedom do you feel?

1. Not at all (1–3)

2. (4–5)

3. (6–7)

4. A great deal (8–10)

0. Don't know; MD

V13 MEMBER CHURCH ORGANIZATION

(Belong to) Religious or church organizations

0.   Not member

1. Inactive member

2. Active member

9. Missing data

V14 MEMBER SPORTS GROUPS

(Belong to) Sports or recreation group
See V13 for response categories

V15 MEMBER ARTS, MUSIC, EDUCATION GROUP

(Belong to) Arts, music, or education group
See V13 for response categories

V16 MEMBER LABOR UNION

(Belong to) Labor union
See V13 for response categories

V17 MEMBER POLITICAL PARTY

(Belong to) Political party or groups
See V13 for response categories (US includes informal party supporters)

V18 MEMBER ENVIRONMENTAL GROUP

(Belong to) Environmental group

See V13 for response categories

V19 MEMBER PROFESSIONAL ASSOCIATION

(Belong to) Professional association

See V13 for response categories

V20 MEMBER CHARITABLE GROUP

(Belong to) Charitable group

See V13 for response categories

V21 MEMBER CONSUMER GROUP

(Belong to) Consumer group

See V13 for response categories

V22 TOTAL MEMBERSHIPS

Number of organizations to which the respondent belongs:

0. No group
1. One group
2. Two groups
3. Three groups
4. Four or more groups
9. Missing data

V23 USE A COMPUTER

How often, if ever, do you use a personal computer?

1. Never
2. Occasionally
3. Frequently
0. Don't know

V24 INFORMATION: DAILY NEWSPAPERS

People use different sources to learn what is going on in their country and the world. For each of the following sources, please indicate whether you used it last week or did not use it last week to obtain information: Daily newspaper

1. Used in last week
2. Did not use
0. Missing data

V25 INFORMATION: NEWS BROADCASTS

(Did you get information from) News broadcasts on radio or TV

See V24 for response categories

V26 INFORMATION: MAGAZINES

(Did you get information from) Printed magazines
See V24 for response categories

V27 INFORMATION: IN DEPTH REPORTS

(Did you get information from) In depth reports on radio or TV
See V24 for response categories

V28 INFORMATION: BOOKS

(Did you get information from) Books
See V24 for response categories

V29 INFORMATION: INTERNET, EMAIL

(Did you get information from) Internet, Email
See V24 for response categories

V30 INFORMATION: TALK WITH FRIENDS

(Did you get information from) Talk with friends or colleagues
See V24 for response categories

V31 INTERESTED IN POLITICS

How interested would you say you are in politics?

1. Very interested
2. Somewhat interested
3. Not very interested
4. Not at all interested
0. Don't know

V32 DID YOU VOTE

Did you vote in your country's recent elections to the national parliament?

1. Yes
2. No
0. Missing data; don't know

V33 SIGN A PETITION

Now I'd like you to look at this card. I'm going to read out some different forms of political action that people can take, and I'd like you to tell me, for each one, whether you have actually done any of these things, whether you might do it or would never, under any circumstances, do it. Signing a petition:

1. Have done
2. Might do
3. Would never do
0. Don't know

V34 JOIN IN BOYCOTTS

(Have you) Joined in boycotts

See V33 for responses

V35 ATTEND LAWFUL DEMONSTRATION

(Have you) Attended lawful demonstrations

See V33 for responses

V36 PROTEST INDEX

This variable counts whether the respondent has participated in a boycott or demonstration (V34–35).

0. No protest activities

1. One

2. Both activities

V37 TOLERANCE: RACE/ETHNICITY

On this list are various groups of people. Could you please mention any that you would not like to have as neighbors? (This variable combines whether respondent would mind having a neighbor of a different race or who was an immigrant.)

1. Mentioned both of these groups

2. Mentioned one group

3. Mentioned neither group

0. Don't know

V38 TOLERANCE: CRIME & DRUGS

This variable combines those who mentioned people with drugs or drinking problems as people they would not like as a neighbor.

See V37 for response categories

V39 TOLERANCE: HOMOSEXUALS & AIDS

This variable combines those who mentioned homosexuals or people with AIDS as people they would not like as a neighbor.

See V37 for response categories

V40 MOST PEOPLE CAN BE TRUSTED

Generally speaking, would you say that most people can be trusted or that you need to be very careful in dealing with people?

1. Most people can be trusted

2. Need to be very careful

0. Don't know

V41 PEOPLE TAKE ADVANTAGE

Do you think most people would try to take advantage of you if they got a chance, or would they try to be fair? Please show your response on this card, where 1 means that "people would try to take advantage of you," and 10 means that "people would try to be fair":

1. People would try to take advantage of you (1–3)

2. 2 (4–5)

3. 3 (6–7)

4. People would try to be fair (8–10)

0. Missing data

V42 TRUST: YOUR FAMILY

I'd like to ask you how much you trust people from various groups. Could you tell me for each whether you trust people from this group completely, somewhat, not very much or not at all? Your family:

1. Trust completely

2. Trust somewhat

3. Do not trust very much

4. Do not trust at all

0. Missing data

V43 TRUST: YOUR NEIGHBORS

(Do you trust) Your neighborhood
See V42 for response categories

V44 TRUST: PEOPLE YOU KNOW

(Do you trust) People you know personally
See V42 for response categories

V45 TRUST: PEOPLE YOU FIRST MEET

(Do you trust) People you meet for the first time
See V42 for response categories

V46 TRUST: PEOPLE OF ANOTHER RELIGION

(Do you trust) People of another religion
See V42 for response categories

V47 TRUST: PEOPLE OF ANOTHER NATIONALITY

(Do you trust) People of another nationality
See V42 for response categories

V48 BONDING TRUST

Index combines three trust items (V42–V44) that deal with people who are close associates

1. High trust

2. 2

3. 3

4. Low trust

0. Missing; unknown

V49 BRIDGING TRUST

Index combines three trust items (V45–V47) that deal with people who are not close

1. High trust
2. 2
3. 3
4. Low trust
0. Missing; unknown

V50 ENVIRONMENT VS ECONOMY

Here are two statements people sometimes make when discussing the environment and economic growth. Which of them comes closer to your own point of view? (Read out and code one answer):

1. Protecting the environment should be given priority, even if it causes slower economic growth and some loss of jobs.
2. Economic growth and creating jobs should be the top priority, even if the environment suffers to some extent.
0. Missing; unknown

V51 OPINION ABOUT SCIENTIFIC ADVANCE

In the long run, do you think the scientific advances we are making will help or harm mankind?

1. Will help
2. Some of each
3. Will harm
0. Missing; unknown

V52 MORE EMPHASIS ON TECHNOLOGY

I'm going to read out a list of various changes in our way of life that might take place in the near future. Please tell me for each one, if it were to happen, whether you think it would be a good thing, a bad thing, or don't you mind? More emphasis on the development of technology.

1. Good
2. Don't mind
3. Bad
4. Missing; unknown

V53 MEN SHOULD HAVE PRIORITY FOR JOB

Do you agree or disagree with the following statements? When jobs are scarce, men should have more right to a job than women.

1. Agree
2. Neither
3. Disagree
0. Don't know

V54 NATIONALS SHOULD HAVE PRIORITY FOR JOB

When jobs are scarce, employers should give priority to [BRITISH] people over immigrants. See V53 for response categories

V55 WOMAN AS A SINGLE PARENT

If a woman wants to have a child as a single parent but she doesn't want to have a stable relationship with man, do you approve or disapprove?

1. Approve
2. Depends [IF VOLUNTEERED]
3. Disapprove
0. Don't know

V56 BEING A HOUSEWIFE FULFILLING

Being a housewife is just as fulfilling as working for pay.

1. Strongly agree
2. Agree
3. Disagree
4. Strongly disagree
0. Don't know

V57 MEN MAKE BETTER POLITICAL LEADERS

On the whole, men make better political leaders than women do.
See V56 for response categories

V58 UNIVERSITY IS MORE IMPORTANT FOR A BOY

A university education is more important for a boy than for a girl.
See V56 for response categories

V59 MEN MAKE BETTER BUSINESS EXECUTIVES

On the whole, men make better business executives than women do.
See V56 for response categories

V60 GENDER EQUALITY INDEX

This variable is a count of the questions on gender attitudes (from V56 to V59).

1. Low gender equality
2.
3.
4. High gender equality
0. Don't know; missing

V61 POSTMATERIAL VALUES INDEX

People sometimes talk about what the aims of this country should be for the next ten years. On this card are listed some of the goals which different people would give top priority. Would you please say which one of these you, yourself, consider the most important? And which would be the next most important?

1) Maintaining order in the nation, 2) Giving people more say in important government decisions, 3) Fighting rising prices, and 4) Protecting freedom of speech.

The postmaterial index counts items 1 and 3 as materialists, items 2 and 4 as postmaterialists, and those who select one from both listed are scored as mixed values.

1. Materialist

2. Mixed

3. Postmaterialist

0. Missing data

V62 LEFT RIGHT SCALE

In political matters, people talk of "the left" and "the right." How would you place your views on this scale, generally speaking?

1. Left (1–3)

2. Left-Center (4–5)

3. Right-Center (6–7)

4. Right (8–10)

0. Don't know; missing data

V63 GREATER RESPECT FOR AUTHORITY

Here is a list of various changes in our way of life that might take place in the near future. Please tell me for each one, if it were to happen whether you think it would be a good thing, a bad thing, or don't you mind? Greater respect for authority:

1. Good

2. Don't mind

3. Bad

0. Don't know

V64 INCOMES MORE EQUAL

Now I'd like you to tell me your views on various issues. How would you place your views on this scale? 1 means you agree completely with the statement on the left; 10 means you agree completely with the statement on the right; and if your views fall somewhere in between, you can choose any number in between.

1. Incomes should be made more equal (1–3)

2. (Values 4–5)

3. (Values 6–7)

4. We need larger income differences as incentives for individual effort (8–10)

0. Don't know

V65 GOVERNMENT MORE RESPONSIBILITY

The government should take more responsibility to ensure that everyone is provided for versus People should take more responsibility to provide for themselves

1. Government more responsible (1–3)

2. (Values 4–5)

3. (Values 6–7)

4. People more responsible for themselves (8–10)

0. Don't know

V66 COMPETITION IS GOOD

Competition is good. It stimulates people to work hard and develop new ideas versus
Competition is harmful. It brings out the worst in people

1. Competition is good (1–3)
2. (Values 4–5)
3. (Values 6–7)
4. Competition is harmful (8–10)
0. Don't know

V67 HARDWORK GENERATES SUCCESS

In the long run, hardwork usually brings a better life versus
Hardwork doesn't generally bring success—it's more a matter of luck and connections.

1. Hardwork brings a better life (1–3)
2. (Values 4–5)
3. (Values 6–7)
4. Hardwork doesn't matter (8–10)
9. Don't know

V68 WEALTH ACCUMULATION

People can only get rich at the expense of others versus
Wealth can grow so there's enough for everyone

1. Wealthy at others' expense (1–3)
2. (Values 4–5)
3. (Values 6–7)
4. Enough wealth for everyone (8–10)
0. Don't know

V69 ECONOMIC LIBERALISM INDEX

This variable is a measure of liberal/conservative responses on five economic policy questions
(V64–V68).

1. Economic conservative
2.
3.
4. Economic liberal
0. Missing data

V70 I SEEK TO BE MYSELF

I seek to be myself rather than to follow others

1. Strongly agree
2. Agree
3. Disagree
4. Strongly disagree
0. Don't know

V71 LIVE UP TO FRIENDS EXPECTATIONS

I make a lot of effort to live up to what my friends expect.
See V70 for response categories

V72 DECIDE MY GOALS

I decide my goals in life by myself.
See V70 for response categories

V73 CONFIDENCE: CHURCHES

I am going to name a number of organizations. For each one, could you tell me how much confidence you have in them: is it a great deal of confidence, quite a lot of confidence, not very much confidence or none at all? The churches

1. Great deal of confidence

2. Quite a lot of confidence

3. Not very much confidence

4. None at all

0. Don't know; missing

V74 CONFIDENCE: ARMED FORCES

(Confidence in) The armed forces
See V73 for response categories

V75 CONFIDENCE: THE PRESS

(Confidence in) the press
See V073 for response categories

V76 CONFIDENCE: TELEVISION

(Confidence in) television
See V73 for response categories

V77 CONFIDENCE: LABOR UNIONS

(Confidence in) labor unions
See V73 for response categories

V78 CONFIDENCE: THE POLICE

(Confidence in) the police
See V73 for response categories

V79 CONFIDENCE: JUSTICE SYSTEM

(Confidence in) justice system
See V73 for response categories

V80 CONFIDENCE: GOVERNMENT

(Confidence in) government
See V73 for response categories

V81 CONFIDENCE: POLITICAL PARTIES

(Confidence in) parties
See V73 for response categories

V82 CONFIDENCE: PARLIAMENT

(Confidence in) parliament
See V73 for response categories

V83 CONFIDENCE: THE CIVIL SERVICE

(Confidence in) the civil service
See V73 for response categories

V84 CONFIDENCE: MAJOR COMPANIES

(Confidence in) major companies
See V73 for response categories

V85 CONFIDENCE: ENVIRONMENTAL MOVEMENT

(Confidence in) environmental movement
See V73 for response categories

V86 CONFIDENCE: WOMEN'S MOVEMENT

(Confidence in) women's movement
See V73 for response categories

V87 CONFIDENCE: CHARITABLE ORGANIZATIONS

(Confidence in) charitable organizations
See V73 for response categories

V88 CONFIDENCE: THE EUROPEAN UNION

(Confidence in) the European Union
See V73 for response categories
0 Don't know; not asked in the United States

V089 CONFIDENCE: UNITED NATIONS

(Confidence in) United Nations
See V73 for response categories

V90 HAVING A STRONG LEADER

I'm going to describe various types of political systems and ask what you think about each as a way of governing this country. For each one, would you say it is a very good, fairly good, fairly bad or very bad way of governing this country? Having a strong leader who does not have to bother with parliament and elections

1. Very good
2. Fairly good
3. Fairly bad

4. Very bad

0. Don't know

V91 HAVING EXPERTS MAKE DECISIONS

(Do you feel good about) Having experts, not government, make decisions according to what they think is best for the country

See V90 for response categories

V92 HAVING THE ARMY RULE

(Do you feel good about) Having the army rule

See V90 for response categories

V93 HAVING A DEMOCRATIC POLITICAL SYSTEM

(Do you feel good about) Having a democratic political system

See V90 for response categories

V94 DEMOCRACY VS AUTOCRACY INDEX

This variable compares support for democracy (V93) with support for the most appealing autocracy option (V90–V92) to yield a measure of relative support for democracy versus autocracy

1. Autocracy good, democracy bad

2. Mixed; even

3. Democracy good, autocracy bad

0. Missing data

V95 IMPORTANCE OF DEMOCRACY

How important is it for you to live in a country that is governed democratically? On this scale where 1 means it is "not at all important" and 10 means "absolutely important" what position would you choose?

1. Not important (1–3)

2. (4–5)

3. (6–7)

4. Important (8–10)

0. Missing data

V96 DEMOCRATICNESS OF COUNTRY

And how democratically is this country being governed today? Again using a scale from 1 to 10, where 1 means that it is "not at all democratic" and 10 means that it is "completely democratic," what position would you choose?

1. Not democratic (1–3)

2. (4–5)

3. (6–7)

4. Completely democratic (8–10)

0. Missing data

V97 HOW PROUD OF NATIONALITY

How proud are you to be [FRENCH]? (substitute your own nationality)

1. Very proud
2. Quite proud
3. Not very proud
4. Not at all proud
0. Don't know

V98 BE WILLING TO FIGHT IN A WAR

Of course, we all hope that there will not be another war, but if it were to come to that, would you be willing to fight for your country?

1. Yes
2. No
0. Don't know; missing

V99 JUSTIFIABLE: CLAIMING GOVERNMENT BENEFIT

Please tell me for each of the following statements whether you think it can always be justified, never be justified, or something in between, using this card. Claiming government benefits to which you are not entitled:

1. Never justifiable (1)
2. 2–4
3. 5–7
4. Always justifiable (8–10)
0. Don't know; missing data

V100 JUSTIFIABLE: AVOIDING TRANSIT FARE

(Is it justifiable) Avoiding a fare on public transport
See V99 for response categories

V101 JUSTIFIABLE: CHEATING ON TAXES

(Is it justifiable) Cheating on taxes if you have a chance
See V99 for response categories

V102 JUSTIFIABLE: SOMEONE ACCEPTING A BRIBE

(Is it justifiable) Someone accepting a bribe in the course of their duties
See V99 for response categories

V103 JUSTIFIABLE: HOMOSEXUALITY

(Is it justifiable) Homosexuality
See V99 for response categories

V104 JUSTIFIABLE: PROSTITUTION

(Is it justifiable) Prostitution
See V199 for response categories

V105 JUSTIFIABLE: ABORTION

(Is it justifiable) Abortion
See V99 for response categories

V106 JUSTIFIABLE: DIVORCE

(Is it justifiable) Divorce

See V99 for response categories

V107 JUSTIFIABLE: EUTHANASIA

(Is it justifiable) Euthanasia—ending the life of the incurably sick

See V99 for response categories

V108 JUSTIFIABLE: SUICIDE

(Is it justifiable) Suicide

See V99 for response categories

V109 IMPACT OF ETHNIC DIVERSITY

Turning to the question of ethnic diversity, with which of the following views do you agree? Please use this scale to indicate your position (code one number):

1. Ethnic diversity erodes a county's unity (1–3)

2. 4–5

3. 6–7

4. Ethnic diversity enriches life (8–10)

0. Don't know; not asked in France or Britain

V110 LEFT/RIGHT PARTY PREFERENCE

If there were a national election tomorrow, for which party on this list would you vote? Just call out the number on this card. If you are uncertain, which party appeals to you most?

1. Left Party

2. Right Party

9. Other party; no answer; not asked in Britain or France

V111A PARTY PREFERENCE–US

1. Democrats

2. Independent

3. Republicans

0. Other party; no answer; other nations

V111B PARTY PREFERENCE–GERMANY

1. PDS

2. Greens

3. SPD

4. FDP

5. CDU/CSU

0. Other party; no answer; other nations

V112 RELIGIOUS PERSON

Independently of whether you go to church or not, would you say you are . . . (read out)

1. A religious person
2. Not a religious person
3. A convinced atheist
0. Don't know; missing data

V113 RELIGIOUS DENOMINATION (IF YES:) Which one?

1. Protestant
2. Catholic
3. Other
4. No religious denomination
0. No answer

V114 HOW OFTEN ATTEND RELIGIOUS SERVICES

Apart from weddings, funerals and christenings, about how often do you attend religious services these days?
1. Weekly or more often
2. Once a month
3. Only on special holy days
4. Never, practically never
0. Don't know; missing data

V115 HOW IMPORTANT IS GOD IN YOUR LIFE

How important is God in your life? Please use this scale to indicate—10 means very important and 1 means not at all important.
1. Not at all (1–3)
2. 4–5
3. 6–7
4. Very important (8–10)
0. Don't know

V116 GENDER

Sex of respondent:
1. Male
2. Female
0. Missing data

V117 AGE RECODED

Can you tell me your year of birth, please? 19__ This means you are __ years old.
1. 18–29
2. 30–44
3. 45–59
4. 60 and older
0. Missing data

V118 ETHNIC IDENTITY

Interviewer coded race/ethnicity:

1. White
2. Black
3. Hispanic
4. Asian; other
0. Don't know; missing data; not asked in Germany

V119 MARITAL STATUS

Are you currently. . . .

1. Married
2. Living together as married
3. Divorced Separated
4. Widowed
5. Single, never married
0. Missing data

V120 HIGHEST EDUCATIONAL LEVEL

What is the highest educational level that you have attained? (use functional equivalent of the following, in given society):

1. Primary education or less
2. High school diploma or less
3. Some college
4. University degree
0. Missing data

V121 INCOME RECODED

On this card is a scale of incomes on which 1 indicates the "lowest income decile" and 10 the "highest income decile" in your country. We would like to know in what group your household is. Please, specify the appropriate number, counting all wages, salaries, pensions and other incomes that come in.

1. Lower income
2. Lower middle income
3. Middle higher
4. Higher income
0. Don't know

V122 FINANCIAL SATISFACTION

How satisfied are you with the financial situation of your household? Please use this card again to help with your answer?

1. Dissatisfied (1–3)
2. (4–5)
3. (6–7)
4. Satisfied (8–10)
0. Missing data

V123 ARE YOU EMPLOYED NOW

Are you employed now or not? [IF YES:] About how many hours a week? If more than one job: only for the main job

1. Has paid employment full time (30 hours a week or more)

2. Part time (less than 30 hours a week)

3. Self employed

4. Retired/pensioned

5. Housewife not otherwise employed

6. Student

7. Unemployed

8. Other

0. Missing data

V124 R'S PROFESSION/JOB

In which profession/occupation do you or did you work? If more than one job, the main job? What is/was your job there?

1. Employer/manager

2. White-collar employee

3. Blue-collar employee

4. Other job

0. Missing data; not employed

V125 INSTITUTION OF OCCUPATION

Are you working for the government or for a private business or industry?

1. Government or public organization

2. Private business or industry

3. Private non-profit organization

0. Missing data; no answer

V126 MANUAL TASKS ON JOB

Are the tasks you perform at work mostly manual or non-manual? Use this scale where 1 means "mostly manual tasks" and 10 means "mostly non-manual tasks":

1. Mostly manual (1–3)

2. (4–5)

3. (6–7)

4. Mostly non-manual (8–10)

0. Missing data

V127 ROUTINE TASKS ON JOB

Are the tasks you perform at work mostly routine tasks or mostly not routine? Use this scale where 1 means "mostly routine tasks" and 10 means "mostly not routine tasks":

1. Mostly routine tasks (1–3)

2. (4–5)

3. (6–7)

4. Mostly not routine tasks (8–10)

0. Missing data

V128 INDEPENDENCE ON JOB

How much independence do you have in performing your tasks at work? Use this scale to indicate your degree of independence where 1 means "no independence at all" and 10 means "complete independence":

1. No independence (1–3)

2. (4–5)

3. (6–7)

4. Complete independence (8–10)

0. Missing data

V129 SIZE OF TOWN

Size of town:

1. Under 20,000

2. 20–500,000

3. 50–100,000

4. 100,000–500,000

4. 500,000 and more

0. Missing data

V130A REGION–US

USA: Region where the interview was conducted:

1. New England

2. Middle Atlantic states

3. South Atlantic

4. East South Central

5. West South Central

6. East North Central

7. West North Central

8. Rocky Mountain states

9. Northwest (& Alaska/Hawaii)

10. California

00. Missing data; other nation

V130B REGION–BRITAIN

Region where interview was conducted in Britain:

1. Northwest

2. Yorkshire and Humberside

3. East Midlands

4. West Midlands

5. Eastern

6. London

7. Southeast

8. Southwest

10. Wales

11. Scotland

12. North

00. Missing data; other nation

V130C REGION–FRANCE

Region where interview was conducted in France:

1. East

2. Mediterranean

3. North

4. West

5. South West

6. South East

7. Paris

8. Surrounding Paris West

9. Surrounding Paris East

00. Missing data; other nation

V130D REGION–GERMANY

Region (Land) in Germany where interview was conducted. Codes 1–10 are former Federal Republic; codes 12–16 are former German Democratic Republic. Berlin was divided:

1. Schleswig-Holstein

2. Hamburg

3. Lower Saxony

4. Bremen

5. Northrhine Westphalia

6. Hesse

7. Rhineland Pfalz

8. Baden-Wuerttemberg

9. Bavaria

10. Saarland

11. Berlin

12. Brandenburg

13. Mecklenburg-Vorpommern

14. Saxony

15. Saxony-Anhalt

16. Thueringen

00. Missing data; other nation

References

Aardal, Bernt, and Tanja Binder. 2011. Leader effects and party characteristics. In *Political Leaders and Democratic Elections*, eds. K. Aarts, A. Blais, and H. Schmitt. Oxford, UK: Oxford University Press.

Aardal, Bernt, and Pieter van Wijnen. 2005. Issue voting. In *The European Voter*, ed. J. Thomassen. Oxford, UK: Oxford University Press.

Aarts, Kees, André Blais, and Hermann Schmitt, eds. 2011. *Political Leaders and Democratic Elections*. Oxford, UK: Oxford University Press.

Abramowitz, Alan. 2010. *The Disappearing Center: Engaged Citizens, Polarization and American Democracy*. New Haven: Yale University Press.

Abramson, Paul. 1979. Developing party identification. *American Journal of Political Science*. 23:79–96.

Abramson, Paul, John Aldrich, and David Rohde. 2010. *Change and Continuity in the 2008 Elections*. Washington, DC: Congressional Quarterly Press.

Abramson, Paul, and Ronald Inglehart. 1995. *Value Change in Global Perspective*. Ann Arbor: University of Michigan Press.

Abramson, Paul, and Charles Ostrom. 1991. Macropartisanship: An empirical reassessment. *American Political Science Review*. 85:181–92.

———. 1994. Question wording and partisanship. *Public Opinion Quarterly* 58:21–48.

Alba, Richard, Peter Schmidt, and Martina Wasmer, eds. 2003. *Germans or Foreigners? Attitudes toward Ethnic Minorities in Post-reunification Germany*. New York: Palgrave Macmillan.

Almond, Gabriel, and Sidney Verba. 1963. *The Civic Culture*. Princeton: Princeton University Press.

Alonso, Sonia, John Keane, and Wolfgang Merkel, eds. 2011. *The Future of Representative Democracy*. Cambridge, UK: Cambridge University Press.

Alter, Jonathan. 2012. Republicans' voter suppression project grinds on. *Bloomberg News*. June 21. http://www.bloomberg.com

Alvarez, R. Michael, and Thad Hall. 2008. *Electronic Elections: The Perils and Promises of Digital Democracy*. Princeton: Princeton University Press.

Anand, Sowmya, and Jon A. Krosnick. 2003. The impact of attitudes toward foreign policy goals on public preferences among presidential candidates. *Presidential Studies Quarterly* 33:31–71.

Andersen, Robert, and Tina Fetner. 2008. Economic inequality and intolerance: Attitudes towards homosexuality in 35 democracies. *American Journal of Political Science* 52: 942–58.

Anderson, Christopher, et al. 2005. *Losers' Consent: Elections and Democratic Legitimacy*. Oxford, UK: Oxford University Press.

Anduiza, Eva, Michael Jensen, and Laia Jorba, eds. 2012. *Digital Media and Political Engagement Worldwide: A Comparative Study.* Cambridge, UK: Cambridge University Press.

Ansolabehere, Stephen, James Snyder, and Charles Stewart. 2001a. The effects of party and preferences on congressional roll-call voting. *Legislative Studies Quarterly* 26:533–72.

———. 2001b. Candidate positioning in the U.S. House elections. *American Journal of Political Science* 45:136–59.

Arnold, Douglas. 1990. *The Logic of Congressional Action.* New Haven: Yale University Press.

Arzheimer, Kai. 2006. Dead men walking? Party identification in Germany, 1977–2002. *Electoral Studies* 25:791–807.

Asher, Herbert. 2007. *Polling and the Public: What Every Citizen Should Know.* 7th ed. Washington, DC: Congressional Quarterly Press.

Bagehot, Walter. 1978. *The English Constitution.* Oxford, UK: Oxford University Press.

Baker, Kendall, Russell Dalton, and Kai Hildebrandt. 1981. *Germany Transformed: Political Culture and the New Politics.* Cambridge, MA: Harvard University Press.

Baker, Wayne. 2004. *America's Crisis of Values: Reality and Perception.* Princeton: Princeton University Press.

Banaszak, Lee Ann, Karen Beckwith, and Dieter Rucht, eds. 2003. *Women's Movements Facing the Reconfigured State.* New York: Cambridge University Press.

Barber, Benjamin. 1984. *Strong Democracy.* Berkeley: University of California Press.

Bardes, Barbara, and Robert Oldendick. 2012. *Public Opinion: Measuring the American Mind.* 4th ed. Lanham, MD: Rowman and Littlefield.

Barker, David, and Susan Hansen. 2005. All things considered: Systematic cognitive processing and electoral decision making. *Journal of Politics* 64:319–44.

Barnes, Samuel. 1977. *Representation in Italy.* Chicago: University of Chicago Press.

Barnes, Samuel, Max Kaase, et al. 1979. *Political Action.* Beverly Hills, CA: Sage.

Barnum, David, and John Sullivan. 1989. Attitudinal tolerance and political freedom in Britain. *British Journal of Political Science* 19:136–46.

Bartels, Larry. 2000. Partisanship and voting behavior. *American Journal of Political Science* 44:35–50.

———. 2003. Democracy with attitudes. In *Electoral Democracy*, ed. M. MacKuen and G. Rabinowitz. Ann Arbor: University of Michigan Press.

———. 2006. What's the matter with "What's the Matter with Kansas"? *Quarterly Journal of Political Science* 1: 201–26.

———. 2010. *Unequal Democracy: The Political Economy of the New Gilded Age.* Princeton: Princeton University Press.

Bartle, John. 2005. Homogeneous models and heterogeneous voters. *Political Studies* 53:653–75.

Bartle, John, Sebastian Avellaneda, and James Stimson. 2011. The moving centre: Preferences for government activity in Britain, 1950–2005. *British Journal of Political Science* 41:259–85.

Bartle, John, and Paolo Bellucci, eds. 2009. *Political Parties and Partisanship: Social Identity and Individual Attitudes.* London: Routledge.

Bauerlein, Mark. 2008. *The Dumbest Generation: How the Digital Age Stupefies Young Americans and Jeopardizes Our Future (Or, Don't Trust Anyone Under 30).* New York: Tarcher.

Baum, Matthew. 2003. *Soft News Goes to War: Public Opinion and American Foreign Policy in the New Media Age.* Princeton: Princeton University Press.

Baum, Matthew, and Angela Jamison. 2005. Oprah effect: How soft news helps inattentive citizens vote consistently. *Journal of Politics* 68:946–59.

Beck, Paul Allen, et al. 1992. Patterns and sources of ticket-splitting in subpresidential voting. *American Political Science Review* 86:916–28.

Beedham, Brian. 1993. What next for democracy? *The Economist*, September 11; special supplement: *The Future Surveyed.*

Bell, Daniel. 1973. *The Coming of Post-industrial Society.* New York: Basic Books.

Benoit, Kenneth, and Michael Laver. 2006. *Party Policy in Modern Democracies.* New York: Routledge.

Berelson, Bernard, Paul Lazarsfeld, and William McPhee. 1954. *Voting.* Chicago: University of Chicago Press.

Berglund, Frode, et al. 2005. Partisanship: Causes and consequences. In *The European Voter*, ed. J. Thomassen. Oxford, UK: Oxford University Press.

Berry, Jeffrey. 1999. *The New Liberalism: The Rising Power of Citizen Groups.* Washington, DC: Brookings Institution Press.

Bimber, Bruce. 2003. *Information and American Democracy: Technology in the Evolution of Political Power.* New York: Cambridge University Press.

Bishop, George, and Kathleen Frankovic. 1981. Ideological consensus and constraint among party leaders and followers in the 1978 election. *Micropolitics* 1:87–111.

Bittner, Amanda. 2011. *Platform or Personality? The Role of Party Leaders in Elections.* Oxford, UK: Oxford University Press.

Blais, André. 2000. *To Vote or Not to Vote: The Merits and Limits of Rational Choice Theory.* Pittsburgh: University of Pittsburgh Press.

Bobo, Lawrence, et al. 2012. The *real* record on racial attitudes. In *Social Trends in American Life*, ed. P. Marsden. Princeton: Princeton University Press.

Bok, Derek. 1996. *The State of the Nation: Government and the Quest for a Better Society.* Cambridge, MA: Harvard University Press.

Bowler, Shaun. 2000. Party cohesion. In *Parties without Partisans*, ed. R. Dalton and M. Wattenberg. Oxford, UK: Oxford University Press.

Bowler, Shaun, and Todd Donovan. 1998. *Demanding Choices: Opinion, Voting, and Direct Democracy.* Ann Arbor: University of Michigan Press.

Bowler, Shaun, and Amihai Glazer, eds. 2008. *Directing Democracy.* New York: Macmillan Palgrave.

Boy, Daniel, and Nonna Mayer, eds. 1993. *The French Voter Decides.* Ann Arbor: University of Michigan Press.

Braun, Michael, and Jacqueline Scott. 2009. Changing public views of gender roles in seven nations, 1988–2002. In *The International Social Survey Programme, 1984–2009*, ed. M. Haller, R. Jowell, and T. Smith. London: Routledge.

Brody, Richard. 1978. The puzzle of political participation in America. In *The New American Political System*, ed. A. King. Washington, DC: American Enterprise Institute.

Brooks, Clem, and Jeff Manza. 2007. *Why Welfare States Persist.* Chicago: University of Chicago Press.

Brooks, Clem, Paul Nieuwbeerta, and Jeff Manza. 2006. Cleavage-based voting behavior in cross-national perspective. *Social Science Research* 35:88–128.

Brug, Wouter van der, Cees van der Eijk, and Mark Franklin. 2007. *The Economy and the Vote: Economic Conditions and Elections in Fifteen Countries.* Cambridge, UK: Cambridge University Press.

Bryce, James. 1921. *Modern Democracies*. Vol. 1. New York: Macmillan.

Budge, Ian, Ivor Crewe, and David Farlie, eds. 1976. *Party Identification and Beyond*. New York: Wiley.

Budge, Ian, Michael McDonald, Paul Pennings, and Hans Keman. 2012. *Organizing Democratic Choice: Party Representation over Time*. Oxford, UK: Oxford University Press.

Burstein, Paul. 2003. The impact of public opinion on public policy: A review and an agenda. *Political Research Quarterly* 56(1):29–40.

Butler, David, and Donald Stokes. 1969. *Political Change in Britain*. New York: St. Martin's.

Cain, Bruce, Russell Dalton, and Susan Scarrow, eds. 2003. *Democracy Transformed? Expanding Political Access in Advanced Industrial Democracies*. Oxford, UK: Oxford University Press.

Cain, Bruce, Sergio Fabrinni, and Patrick Egan. 2003. Toward more open democracies: The expansion of freedom of information laws. In *Democracy Transformed?* ed. B. Cain, R. Dalton, and S. Scarrow. Oxford, UK: Oxford University Press.

Campbell, Angus, et al. 1960. *The American Voter*. New York: Wiley.

——. 1966. *Elections and the Political Order*. New York: Wiley.

Campbell, David. 2006. *Why We Vote: How Schools and Communities Shape Our Civic Life*. Princeton: Princeton University Press.

Campbell, Karen, and Peter Marsden. 2012. Gender attitudes since 1972. In *Social Trends in American Life*, ed. P. Marsden. Princeton: Princeton University Press.

Campbell, Rosie. 2006. *Gender and the Vote in Britain*. Colchester, UK: ECPR Press Monographs.

Cantril, Hadley. 1965. *The Patterns of Human Concern*. New Brunswick, NJ: Rutgers University Press.

Caplan, Bryan. 2007. *The Myth of the Rational Voter: Why Democracies Choose Bad Policies*. Princeton: Princeton University Press.

Carmines, Edward, and James Stimson. 1980. The two faces of issue voting. *American Political Science Review* 74:78–91.

Caul, Miki, and Mark Gray. 2000. From platform declarations to policy outcomes. In *Parties without Partisans*, ed. R. Dalton and M. Wattenberg. Oxford, UK: Oxford University Press.

Cautres, Bruno, and Anne Muxel, eds. 2011. *The New Voter in Western Europe: France and Beyond*. London: Palgrave Macmillan.

Central Intelligence Agency. 2012. *World Fact Book*. http://www.odci.gov/cia/publications/factbook/index.html

Chadwick, Andrew. 2006. *Internet Politics: States, Citizens, and New Communication Technologies*. Oxford, UK: Oxford University Press.

Charlot, Monica. 1980. Women in politics in France. In *The French National Assembly Elections of 1978*, ed. H. Penniman. Washington, DC: American Enterprise Institute.

Cichowski, Rachel, and Alec Stone Sweet. 2003. Participation, representative democracy, and the courts. In *Democracy Transformed?* ed. B. Cain, R. Dalton, and S. Scarrow. Oxford, UK: Oxford University Press.

Citrin, Jack. 1974. Comment. *American Political Science Review* 68:973–88.

Claggett, William, and Philip Pollack. 2006. Models of political participation revisited. *Political Research Quarterly* 59:593–600.

Clarke, Harold, and Nitish Dutt. 1991. Measuring value change in Western industrialized societies. *American Political Science Review* 85:905–20.

Clarke, Harold, Allan Kornberg, and Thomas Scotto. 2009. *Mapping Political Choices: Canada and the United States*. Toronto: University of Toronto Press.

Clarke, Harold, and Marianne Stewart. 1998. The decline of parties in the minds of citizens. *Annual Review of Political Science* 1:357–78.

Clarke, Harold, et al. 1999. The effect of economic priorities on the measurement of value change: New experimental evidence. *American Political Science Review* 93:637–47.

——. 2004. *Political Choice in Britain*. Oxford, UK: Oxford University Press.

——. 2008. *Journal of Elections, Public Opinion, and Parties*, 17, special issue, *Internet Surveys and National Election Studies*.

——. 2009. *Performance Politics and the British Voter*. Cambridge, UK: Cambridge University Press.

——. 2013. *Campaigning for Change: The Dynamics of Electoral Choice in Britain*. Cambridge, UK: Cambridge University Press.

Coleman, Stephen, and Jay Blumler. 2009. *The Internet and Democratic Citizenship*. Cambridge, UK: Cambridge University Press.

Coleman, Stephen, and Peter Shane. 2012. *Connecting Democracy: Online Consultation and the Flow of Political Communication*. Cambridge, MA: MIT Press.

Conover, Pamela, and Stanley Feldman. 1984. How people organize the political world. *American Journal of Political Science* 28:95–126.

Conradt, David. 2008. *The German Polity*. 9th ed. New York: Longman.

Converse, Philip. 1964. The nature of belief systems in mass publics. In *Ideology and Discontent*, ed. D. Apter. New York: Free Press.

——. 1966. The normal vote. In *Elections and the Political Order*, ed. Angus Campbell et al. New York: Wiley.

——. 1969. Of time and partisan stability. *Comparative Political Studies* 2:139–71.

——. 1970. Attitudes and nonattitudes. In *The Quantitative Analysis of Social Problems*, ed. E. Tufte. Reading, MA: Addison-Wesley.

——. 1972. Change in the American electorate. In *The Human Meaning of Social Change*, ed. A. Campbell and P. Converse. New York: Russell Sage Foundation.

——. 1976. *The Dynamics of Party Support*. Beverly Hills, CA: Sage.

——. 1990. Popular representation and the distribution of information. In *Information and Democratic Processes*, ed. J. Ferejohn and J. Kuklinski. Urbana: University of Illinois Press.

——. 2007. Democratic theory and electoral reality. *Critical Review* 18:297–329.

Converse, Philip, and Greg Markus. 1979. Plus ça change . . . The new CPS election study panel. *American Political Science Review* 73:32–49.

Converse, Philip, and Roy Pierce. 1986. *Representation in France*. Cambridge, MA: Harvard University Press.

Conway, Mary Margaret. 2000. *Political Participation in the United States*. 3rd ed. Washington, DC: Congressional Quarterly Press.

Costello, Rory, Jacques Thomassen, and Martin Rosema. 2012. European Parliament elections and political representation: Policy congruence between voters and parties. *West European Politics* 35:1226–48.

Crewe, Ivor. 1981. Electoral participation. In *Democracy at the Polls*, ed. D. Butler et al. Washington, DC: American Enterprise Institute.

Crouch, Colin. 1999. *Social Change in Western Europe*. Oxford, UK: Oxford University Press.

Crozier, Michel, Samuel Huntington, and Joji Watanuki. 1975. *The Crisis of Democracy*. New York: New York University Press.

Curtice, John. 2012. Political engagement: Bridging the gulf? Britain's democracy after the 2010 election. In Alison Park et al., *British Social Attitudes, 28th Report*. London: Sage.

——. 2013. Will the coalition's constitutional reforms re-engage a sceptical electorate? In Alison Park et al. *British Social Attitudes, 29th Report*. London: Sage.

Curtice, John, and Sören Holmberg. 2005. Leadership and voting decision. In *The European Voter*, ed. J. Thomassen. Oxford, UK: Oxford University Press.

Curtice, John, and Ben Seyd. 2002. Is there a crisis of political participation? In *British Social Attitudes: Public Policy, Social Ties*, ed. A. Park et al. Newbury Park, CA: Sage.

Cyert, Richard, and James March. 1963. *A Behavioral Theory of the Firm*. Englewood Cliffs, NJ: Prentice-Hall.

Dahl, Robert. 1971. *Polyarchy*. New Haven: Yale University Press.

——. 2003. *How Democratic is the American Constitution*. 2nd ed. New Haven: Yale University Press.

Dahrendorf, Ralf. 1975. Excerpts from remarks on the ungovernability study. In *The Crisis of Democracy*, M. Crozier et al. New York: New York University Press.

——. 2000. Afterword. In *Disaffected Democracies*, ed. S. Pharr and R. Putnam. Princeton: Princeton University Press.

Dalton, Russell. 1985. Political parties and political representation. *Comparative Political Studies* 17:267–99.

——. 2004. *Democratic Challenges, Democratic Choices: The Erosion of Political Support in Advanced Industrial Democracies*. Oxford, UK: Oxford University Press.

——. 2008. *Citizen Politics: Public Opinion and Political Parties in Advanced Industrial Democracies*. 5th ed. Washington, DC: Congressional Quarterly Press.

——. 2009a. *The Good Citizen: How the Young Are Reshaping American Politics*. Rev. ed. Washington, DC: Congressional Quarterly Press.

——. 2009b. Economics, environmentalism and party alignments. *European Journal of Political Research* 48:161–75.

——. 2012a. *The Apartisan American: Dealignment and Changing Electoral Politics*. Washington, DC: Congressional Quarterly Press.

——. 2012b. Partisan mobilization, cognitive mobilization and the changing German electorate. *Electoral Studies* 31:35–45.

Dalton, Russell, and Christopher Anderson, eds. 2011. *Citizens, Context and Choice: How Context Shapes Citizens' Electoral Choices*. Oxford, UK: Oxford University Press.

Dalton, Russell, David Farrell, and Ian McAllister. 2011. *Political Parties and Democratic Linkage: How Parties Organize Democracy*. Oxford, UK: Oxford University Press.

Dalton, Russell, Scott Flanagan, and Paul Beck, eds. 1984. *Electoral Change in Advanced Industrial Democracies*. Princeton: Princeton University Press.

Dalton, Russell, and Mark Gray. 2003. Expanding the electoral marketplace. In *Democracy Transformed*, ed. B. Cain, R. Dalton, and S. Scarrow. Oxford, UK: Oxford University Press.

Dalton, Russell, and Willy Jou. 2010. Is there a single German party system? *German Politics and Society* 28:34–52.

Dalton, Russell, and Hans-Dieter Klingemann, eds. 2007. *The Oxford Handbook of Political Behavior*. Oxford, UK: Oxford University Press.

Dalton, Russell, and Martin Wattenberg. 1993. The not so simple act of voting. In *The State of the Discipline,* ed. A. Finifter. Washington, DC: American Political Science Association.

———, eds. 2000. *Parties without Partisans: Political Change in Advanced Industrial Democracies.* Oxford, UK: Oxford University Press.

Dalton, Russell, and Steve Weldon. 2005. Public images of political parties: A necessary evil? *West European Politics* 28:931–51.

———. 2007. Partisanship and party system institutionalization. *Party Politics* 13:179–96.

Dalton, Russell, and Christian Welzel, eds. 2013. *The Civic Culture Transformed: From Allegiant to Assertive Citizens.* Cambridge, UK: Cambridge University Press.

Damon, William. 2001. To not fade away: Restoring civil identity among the young. In *Making Good Citizens: Education and Civil Society,* ed. D. Ravitch and J. Viteritti. New Haven: Yale University Press.

DeBardeleben, Joan, and Jon Pammett, eds. 2009. *Activating the Citizen: Dilemmas of Participation in Europe and Canada.* London: Palgrave Macmillan.

Delli Carpini, Michael, and Scott Keeter. 1996. *What Americans Know about Politics and Why It Matters.* New Haven: Yale University Press.

Downs, Anthony. 1957. *An Economic Theory of Democracy.* New York: Wiley.

Duch, Raymond, and Michael Taylor. 1993. Postmaterialism and the economic condition. *American Journal of Political Science* 37:747–79.

———. 1994. A reply to Abramson and Inglehart's "Education, security, and postmaterialism." *American Journal of Political Science* 38:815–24.

Duch, Raymond, and Randolph Stevenson. 2008. *The Economic Vote: How Political and Economic Institutions Condition Election Results.* Cambridge, UK: Cambridge University Press.

Dunlap, Riley. 2008. The globalization of environmental concern and the limits of the postmaterialist values explanation. *Sociological Quarterly* 49:529–63.

Dye, Thomas, and Harmon Ziegler. 1970. *The Irony of Democracy.* Belmont, CA: Duxbury.

Easterbrook G. 2003. *The Progress Paradox: How Life Gets Better While People Feel Worse.* New York: Random House.

Easton, David. 1965. *A Systems Analysis of Political Life.* New York: Wiley.

———. 1975. A reassessment of the concept of political support. *British Journal of Political Science* 5:435–57.

Edlund, Jonas. 2009. Attitudes toward state-organized welfare in twenty-two societies. In *The International Social Survey Programme, 1984–2009,* ed. M. Haller, R. Jowell, and T. Smith. London: Routledge.

Eichenberg, Richard. 2007. Citizen opinion on foreign policy and world politics. In *The Oxford Handbook of Political Behavior,* ed. R. Dalton and H.-D. Klingemann. Oxford, UK: Oxford University Press.

Eijk, Cees van der, and Mark Franklin. 2009. *Elections and Voters.* London: Palgrave Macmillan.

Elff, Martin, and Sigrid Rossteutscher. 2011. Stability or realignment? Class, religion and the vote in Germany. *German Politics* 20:111–31.

Ellis, Christopher, and James Stimson. 2012. *Ideology in America.* New York: Cambridge University Press.

Enns, Peter, and Christopher Wlezien, ed. 2011. *Who Gets Represented?* New York: Russell Sage Foundation.

Erikson, Robert, Michael MacKuen, and James Stimson. 2002. *The Macro Polity.* Cambridge, UK: Cambridge University Press.

Erikson, Robert, and Kent Tedin. 2010. *American Public Opinion.* 8th ed. New York: Allyn and Bacon.

Erikson, Robert, Gerald Wright, and John McIver. 1994. *State House Democracy: Public Opinion and Public Policy in the American States.* New York: Cambridge University Press.

Evans, Geoffrey, ed. 1999. *The End of Class Politics? Class Voting in Comparative Context.* New York: Oxford University Press.

——. 2000. The continued significance of class voting. *Annual Review of Political Science* 3:401–17.

Feldman, Stanley. 1989. Reliability and stability of policy positions. *Political Analysis* 1:25–60.

Fiorina, Morris. 1981. *Retrospective Voting in American National Elections.* New Haven: Yale University Press.

——. 2002. Parties and partisanship: A forty year retrospective. *Political Behavior* 24:93–115.

——. 2005. *Culture War? The Myth of a Polarized America.* New York: Pearson Longman.

Flanagan, Scott. 1982. Changing values in advanced industrial society. *Comparative Political Studies* 14:403–44.

——. 1987. Value change in industrial society. *American Political Science Review* 81:1303–19.

Flanagan, Scott, and Aie-Rie Lee. 2003. The new politics, culture wars, and the authoritarian-libertarian value change in advanced industrial democracies. *Comparative Political Studies* 36:235–70.

Florida, Richard, 2003. *The Rise of the Creative Class: And How It's Transforming Work, Leisure, Community, and Everyday Life.* New York: Basic Books.

Flynn, James. 2007. *What Is Intelligence?* Cambridge, UK: Cambridge University Press.

Frank, Thomas. 2004. *What's the Matter with Kansas? How Conservatives Won the Heart of America.* New York: Metropolitan Books.

Franklin, Mark. 2004. *Voter Turnout and the Dynamics of Electoral Competition in Established Democracies since 1945.* New York: Cambridge University Press.

Franklin, Mark, Tom Mackie, and Henry Valen, eds. 1992. *Electoral Change.* New York: Cambridge University Press.

Friedman, Jeffrey, and Shterna Friedman, eds. 2012. *The Nature of Belief Systems Reconsidered.* London: Routledge.

Friedrich, Walter, and Hartmut Griese. 1990. *Jugend und Jugendforschung in der DDR.* Opladen: Westdeutscher.

Fuchs, Dieter, and Hans-Dieter Klingemann. 1989. The Left-Right schema. In *Continuities in Political Action*, ed. M. K. Jennings and J. van Deth. Berlin: deGruyter.

——. 1995. Citizens and the state. In *Citizens and the State*, ed. H. Klingemann and D. Fuchs. Oxford, UK: Oxford University Press.

Fukuyama, Francis. 1992. *The End of History and the Last Man.* New York: Free Press.

Gabriel, Oscar, and Silke Keil, eds. 2012. *Society and Democracy in Europe.* London: Routledge.

Gabriel, Oscar, Silke Keil, and Eric Kerrouche, eds. 2012. *Political Participation in France and Germany.* Colchester, UK: ECPR Press.

Gallup, George. 1976a. *International Public Opinion Polls: Britain*. New York: Random House.

——. 1976b. *International Public Opinion Polls: France*. New York: Random House.

Geer, John. 2005. *Public Opinion and Polling around the World*. 2 vols. Santa Barbara, CA: ABC-CLIO.

Geissel, Brigitte. 2008. Do critical citizens foster better governance? *West European Politics* 31: 855–73.

German Marshall Fund. 2007. *Transatlantic Trends: Key Findings 2007*. http://www.transatlantictrends.org

Gershkoff, Amy. 2005. Not "Non-attitudes" but rather "non-measurement." Paper presented at the Southern Political Science Association Meeting, New Orleans.

Golder, Matt, and Jacek Stramski. 2010. Ideological congruence and electoral institutions. *American Journal of Political Science* 54:90–106.

Green, Donald, Bradley Palmquist, and Eric Schickler. 2002. *Partisan Hearts and Minds: Political Parties and the Social Identities of Voters*. New Haven: Yale University Press.

Gurr, T. Robert. 1970. *Why Men Rebel*. Princeton: Princeton University Press.

Hajnal, Zoltan, and Taeku Lee. 2011. *Why Americans Don't Join the Party: Race, Immigration, and the Failure of Parties to Engage the Electorate*. Princeton: Princeton University Press.

Haller, Max, Roger Jowell, and Tom Smith, eds. 2009. *The International Social Survey Programme, 1984–2009*. London: Routledge.

Hayes, Bernadette, and Ian McAllister. 1997. Gender, party leaders, and electoral outcomes in Australia, Britain and the United States. *Comparative Political Studies* 30:3–26.

Hellwig, Timothy. 2011. Context, information, and performance voting. In *Citizens, Context and Choice*, ed. R. Dalton and C. Anderson. Oxford, UK: Oxford University Press.

Henn, Matt, Mark Weinstein, and Dominic Wring. 2002. A generation apart? Youth and political participation in Britain. *British Journal of Politics and International Relations*. 4:167–92.

Herrera, Cheryl Lyn, Richard Herrera, and Eric R. A. N. Smith. 1992. Public opinion and congressional representation. *Public Opinion Quarterly* 56:185–205.

Hess, Robert, and Judith Torney. 1967. *The Development of Political Attitudes in Children*. Chicago: Aldine.

Hetherington, Marc. 2005. *Why Trust Matters: Declining Political Trust and the Demise of American Liberalism*. Princeton: Princeton University Press.

Hibbing, John, and Elizabeth Theiss-Morse. 2002. *Stealth Democracy: Americans' Beliefs about How Government Should Work*. New York: Cambridge University Press.

Höllinger, Franz, and Max Haller. 2009. Decline or persistence of religion? In *The International Social Survey Programme, 1984–2009*, ed. M. Haller, R. Jowell, and T. Smith. London: Routledge.

Holmberg, Sören. 1994. Party identification compared across the Atlantic. In *Elections at Home and Abroad*, ed. M. K. Jennings and T. Mann. Ann Arbor: University of Michigan Press.

——. 2007. Partisanship reconsidered. In *Oxford Handbook of Political Behavior*, ed. R. Dalton and H.-D. Klingemann. Oxford, UK: Oxford University Press.

Huntington, Samuel. 1975. The democratic distemper. *Public Interest* 41:9–38.

——. 1984. Will more countries become democratic? *Political Science Quarterly* 99:193–218.

——. 1991. *The Third Wave*. Norman: University of Oklahoma Press.

Hurwitz, Jon, and Mark Peffley. 1987. How are foreign policy attitudes structured? *American Political Science Review* 81:1099–1120.

Hutchings, Vincent. 2003. *Public Opinion and Democratic Accountability*. Princeton: Princeton University Press.

Inglehart, Ronald. 1977. *The Silent Revolution*. Princeton: Princeton University Press.

——. 1981. Post-materialism in an environment of insecurity. *American Political Science Review* 75:880–900.

——. 1984. Changing cleavage alignments in Western democracies. In *Electoral Change in Advanced Industrial Democracies*, ed. R. Dalton, S. Flanagan, and P. Beck. Princeton: Princeton University Press.

——. 1990. *Culture Shift in Advanced Industrial Society*. Princeton: Princeton University Press.

——. 1995. Political support for environmental protection. *PS—Political Science and Politics* 28:57–72.

——. 1997. *Modernization and Postmodernization: Cultural, Economic and Political Change in 43 Nations*. Princeton: Princeton University Press.

——. 2003. How solid is mass support for democracy—And how can we measure it? *PS: Political Science and Politics* 36:51–57.

——. 2008. Changing values among Western publics from 1970 to 2006. *West European Politics* 31:130–46.

Inglehart, Ronald, and Pippa Norris. 2003. *A Rising Tide: Gender Equality and Cultural Change around the World*. New York: Cambridge University Press.

Inglehart, Ronald, and Christian Welzel. 2005. *Modernization, Cultural Change, and Democracy: The Human Development Sequence*. New York: Cambridge University Press.

Jackman, Robert. 1972. Political elites, mass publics, and support for democratic principles. *Journal of Politics* 34:753–73.

Jacoby, William. 1991. Ideological identification and issue attitudes. *American Journal of Political Science* 35:178–205.

Jennings, M. Kent, and Thomas Mann, eds. 1994. *Elections at Home and Abroad*. Ann Arbor: University of Michigan Press.

Jennings, M. Kent, and Greg Markus. 1984. Partisan orientations over the long haul. *American Political Science Review* 78:1000–18.

Jennings, M. Kent, and Richard Niemi. 1973. *The Character of Political Adolescence*. Princeton: Princeton University Press.

Jennings, M. Kent, Laura Stoker, and Jake Bowers. 2009. Politics across generations: Family transmission reexamined. *Journal of Politics* 71:782–99.

Jennings, M. Kent, and Jan van Deth, eds. 1989. *Continuities in Political Action*. Berlin: deGruyter.

Jennings, M. Kent, et al. 1979. Generations and families. In *Political Action*, ed. S. Barnes, M. Kaase, et al. Beverly Hills, CA: Sage.

Johnson, Mark, and Conor Gearty. 2007. Civil liberties and the challenges of terrorism. In *British Social Attitudes: Perspectives on a Changing Society*, ed. A. Park et al. London: Sage.

Jowell, Roger, et al., eds. 1998. *British—and European—Social Attitudes: The 15th Report.* Brookfield, VT: Ashgate.

Judis, John, and Ruy Teixeira. 2002. *The Emerging Democratic Majority.* New York: Scribner.

Kagan, Robert. 2003. *Of Paradise and Power: America and Europe in the New World Order.* New York: Knopf.

Keil, Silke. 2012. Social participation. In Oscar Gabriel, Silke Keil, and Eric Kerrouche, eds. *Political Participation in France and Germany.* Colchester, UK: ECPR Press

Keith, Bruce, et al. 1992. *The Myth of the Independent Voter.* Berkeley: University of California Press.

Kenny, Charles. 2011. *Getting Better: Why Global Development Is Succeeding—and How We Can Improve the World Even More.* New York: Basic Books.

Key, V. O. 1966. *The Responsible Electorate.* Cambridge, MA: Belknap Press.

Kinder, Donald. 2007. Belief systems today. *Critical Review* 18:197–216.

Kinder, Donald, and D. R. Kiewiet. 1981. Sociotropic politics. *British Journal of Political Science* 11:129–61.

Kinder, Donald, et al. 1980. Presidential prototypes. *Political Behavior* 2:315–37.

Kitschelt, Herbert. 1994. *The Transformation of European Social Democracy.* Cambridge, UK: Cambridge University Press.

Kittilson, Miki, and Christopher Anderson. 2011. Electoral supply and voter turnout. In *Citizens, Context and Choice,* ed. R. Dalton and C. Anderson. Oxford, UK: Oxford University Press.

Klein, Markus, et al., eds. 2000. *50 Jahre empirische Wahlforschung in Deutschland: Entwicklung, Befunde, Perspektiven, Daten.* Opladen: Westdeutscher.

Klingemann, Hans-Dieter. 1998. Parteien im Urteil der Bürger: Eine Längsschnittanalyse 1969–94. In *Wahlen und Wähler,* ed. M. Kaase and H. Klingemann. Opladen: Westeutsche.

———. 1999. Mapping political support in the 1990s. In *Critical Citizens,* ed. P. Norris. Oxford, UK: Oxford University Press.

———, ed. 2008. *The Comparative Study of Electoral Systems.* Oxford, UK: Oxford University Press.

Klingemann, Hans-Dieter, Richard Hofferbert, and Ian Budge, eds. 1994. *Parties, Policy and Democracy.* Oxford, UK: Oxford University Press.

Klingemann, Hans-Dieter, et al. 2006. *Mapping Policy Preferences II: Estimates for Parties, Electors, and Governments in Eastern Europe, European Union, and OECD 1990–2003.* Oxford, UK: Oxford University Press

Knutsen, Oddbjørn. 2004. Religious denomination and party choice in Western Europe: A comparative longitudinal study from eight countries, 1970–97. *International Political Science Review* 25:97–128.

———. 2006. *Class Voting in Western Europe: A Comparative Longitudinal Study.* Lanham, MD: Lexington Books.

Knutsen, Oddbjorn, and Staffan Kumlin. 2005. Value orientations and party choice. In *The European Voter,* ed. J. Thomassen. Oxford, UK: Oxford University Press.

Koch, Achim, Martina Wasmer, and Peter Schmidt, eds. 2001. *Politische Partizipation in der Bundesrepublik Deutschland: Empirische Befunde und theoretische Erklärungen.* Opladen: Leske + Budrich.

Kohut, Andrew, et al. 2000. *The Diminishing Divide: Religion's Changing Role in American Politics.* Washington, DC: Brookings Institution Press.

Kriesi, Hanspeter, et al. 2008. *West European Politics in the Age of Globalization.* Cambridge, UK: Cambridge University Press.

Krosnick, Jon. 1990. Government policy and citizen passion: A study of issue publics in contemporary America. *Political Behavior* 12:59–92.

Kuklinski, James, and Buddy Peyton. 2007. Belief systems and political decision-making. In *Oxford Handbook of Political Behavior*, ed. R. Dalton and H. Klingemann. Oxford, UK: Oxford University Press.

Lane, Robert. 1962. *Political Ideology.* New York: Free Press.

———. 1973. Patterns of political belief. In *Handbook of Political Psychology*, ed. J. Knutson. San Francisco: Jossey-Bass.

Langenbacher, Eric, ed. 2010. *Between Left and Right: The 2009 Bundestag Elections and the Transformation of the German Party System.* Brooklyn, NY: Berghahn.

Lau, Richard, and David Redlawsk. 2006. *How Voters Decide: Information Processing during Election Campaigns.* New York: Cambridge University Press.

Layman, Geoffrey. 2001. *The Great Divide.* New York: Columbia University Press.

Lazarsfeld, Paul, Bernard Berelson, and Hazel Gaudet. 1948. *The People's Choice.* New York: Columbia University Press.

LeDuc, Lawrence. 1981. The dynamic properties of party identification. *European Journal of Political Research* 9:257–68.

LeDuc, Lawrence, Richard Niemi, and Pippa Norris, eds. 2010. *Comparing Democracies 3: Elections and Voting in the 21st Century.* 3rd ed. Thousand Oaks, CA: Sage.

Lewis-Beck, Michael, William Jacoby, Helmut Norpoth, and Herbert Weisberg. 2008. *The American Voter Revisited.* Ann Arbor: University of Michigan Press.

Lewis-Beck, Michael, Richard Nadeau, and Éric Bèlanger. 2012. *French Presidential Elections.* London: Palgrave Macmillan.

Lewis-Beck, Michael, and Martin Paldam, eds. 2000. *Electoral Studies* 19, special issue, *Economics and Elections.*

Lijphart, Arend. 2012. *Patterns of Democracy*, 2nd edition. New Haven, CT: Yale University Press.

Lippmann, Walter. 1922. *Public Opinion.* New York: Harcourt, Brace.

Lipset, Seymour Martin. 1981. *Political Man: The Social Bases of Politics.* Baltimore: Johns Hopkins University Press.

Lipset, Seymour Martin, and Stein Rokkan, eds. 1967. *Party Systems and Voter Alignments.* New York: Free Press.

Listhaug, Ola. 2005. Retrospective voting. In *The European Voter*, ed. J. Thomassen. Oxford, UK: Oxford University Press.

Lodge, Milton, and Kathleen McGraw. 1995. *Political Judgment: Structure and Process.* Ann Arbor: University of Michigan Press.

Lupia, Arthur. 1994. Shortcuts versus encyclopedias. *American Political Science Review* 88:63–76.

———. 2007. How elitism undermines the study of voter competence. *Critical Review* 18:217–32.

Lupia, Arthur, and Mathew McCubbins. 1998. *The Democratic Dilemma: Can Citizens Learn What They Need to Know?* Cambridge, UK: Cambridge University Press.

Luther, Richard, and Ferdinand Mueller-Rommel, eds. 2002. *Party Change in Europe.* Oxford, UK: Oxford University Press.

Macedo, Stephen, et al. 2005. *Democracy at Risk: How Political Choices Undermine Citizen Participation, and What We Can Do about It.* Washington, DC: Brookings Institution Press.

MacKuen, Michael, Robert Erikson, and James Stimson. 1989. Macropartisanship. *American Political Science Review* 83:1125–42.

MacRae, Duncan. 1967. *Parliament, Parties, and Society in France, 1946–1958.* New York: St. Martin's.

Manza, Jeff, and Clem Brooks. 1999. *Social Cleavages and Political Change.* New York: Oxford, UK: Oxford University Press.

Marien, Sophie, Marc Hooghe, and Ellen Quintelier. 2010. Inequalities in non-institutionalised forms of political participation: A Multi-level Analysis of 25 Countries. *Political Studies* 58:187–213.

Marsden, Peter, ed. 2012. *Social Trends in American Life.* Princeton: Princeton University Press.

Maslow, Abraham. 1954. *Motivations and Personality.* New York: Harper and Row.

Mayer, Nonna. 2000. The decline of political trust in France. Paper presented at the meetings of the International Political Science Association, Quebec, Canada.

Mayer, Nonna, and Vincent Tiberj. 2004. Do issues matter? In *The French Voter*, ed. M. Lewis-Beck. Basingstoke, UK: Palgrave Macmillan.

McClosky, Herbert, and Alida Brill. 1983. *Dimensions of Tolerance: What Americans Think about Civil Liberties.* New York: Russell Sage Foundation.

McDonald, Michael, and Samuel Popkin. 2001. The myth of the vanishing voter. *American Political Science Review* 95:963–74.

Micheletti, Michele, and Andrew McFarland, eds. 2011. *Creative Participation: Responsibility-Taking in the Political World.* Boulder, CO: Paradigm.

Miegel, Fredrik, and Tobias Olsson. 2008. From pirates to politicians: The story of the Swedish file sharers who became a political party. In *Democracy, Journalism and Technology: New Developments in an Enlarged Europe,* ed. N. Carpentier et al. Tartu, Estonia: Tartu University Press.

Miller, Arthur. 1974a. Political issues and trust in government. *American Political Science Review* 68:951–72.

———. 1974b. Rejoinder. *American Political Science Review* 68:989–1001.

Miller, Arthur, and Martin Wattenberg. 1985. Throwing the rascals out. *American Political Science Review* 79:359–72.

Miller, Arthur, Martin Wattenberg, and Oksana Malanchuk. 1986. Schematic assessments of presidential candidates. *American Political Science Review* 80:521–40.

———. 1987. *Without Consent: Mass–Elite Linkages in Presidential Politics.* Lexington: University Press of Kentucky.

Miller, Warren, and M. Kent Jennings. 1986. *Parties in Transition: A Longitudinal Study of Party Elites and Party Supporters.* New York: Russell Sage Foundation.

Miller, Warren, and J. Merrill Shanks. 1996. *The New American Voter.* Cambridge, MA: Harvard University Press.

Miller, Warren, and Donald Stokes. 1963. Constituency influence in Congress. *American Political Science Review* 57:45–56.

Miller, Warren, et al. 1999. *Policy Representation in Western Democracies.* Oxford, UK: Oxford University Press.

Morlok, Martin, Thomas Poguntke, and Jens Walther, eds. 2012. *Politik an den Parteien vorbei.* Baden-Baden: Nomos.

Morris, Richard. 1995. What informed public? *Washington Post National Weekly Edition,* April 10–16, 36.

Mueller, John. 1999. *Capitalism, Democracy, and Ralph's Pretty Good Grocery.* Princeton: Princeton University Press.

Mueller-Rommel, Ferdinand, and Thomas Poguntke. 2002. *Green Parties in National Governments.* London: Routledge.

Mughan, Anthony. 2000. *Media and the Presidentialization of Parliamentary Elections*, ed. B. Cautres and A. Muxel. Basingstroke, UK: Palgrave.

Muxel, Anne. 2011. Loyalties, mobilities, abstentions. In *The New Voter in Western Europe: France and Beyond.* London: Palgrave Macmillan.

Nadeau, R., Richard Niemi, and A. Yoshinaka. 2002. A cross-national analysis of economic voting. *Electoral Studies* 21:403–23.

National Conference on Citizenship. 2006. *America's Civic Health Index: Broken Engagement.* Washington, DC: National Conference on Citizenship.

Nevitte, Neil. 1996. *The Decline of Deference.* Petersborough, CAN: Broadview.

———. 2013. The decline of deference revisited. In *The Civic Culture Transformed: From Allegiant to Assertive Citizens*, ed. R. Dalton and C. Welzel. Cambridge, UK: Cambridge University Press.

Nie, Norman, Jane Junn, and Kenneth Stehlik-Barry. 1996. *Education and Democratic Citizenship in America.* Chicago: University of Chicago Press.

Nie, Norman, Sidney Verba, and John Petrocik. 1979. *The Changing American Voter.* Cambridge, MA: Harvard University Press.

Niedermayer, Oskar, and Richard Sinnott, eds. 1995. *Public Opinion and International Governance.* New York: Oxford University Press.

Niemi, Richard, and M. Kent Jennings. 1991. Issues and inheritance in the formation of party identification. *American Journal of Political Science* 35:970–88.

Niemi, Richard, Herbert Weisberg, and David Kimball, eds. 2010. *Controversies in Voting.* 5th ed. Washington, DC: Congressional Quarterly Press.

Nieuwbeerta, Paul. 1995. *The Democratic Class Struggle in Twenty Countries 1945–90.* Amsterdam: Thesis.

Nieuwbeerta, Paul, and Nan Dirk de Graaf. 1999. Traditional class voting in 20 postwar societies. In *The End of Class Politics?* ed. G. Evans. New York: Oxford University Press.

Nordhaus, Ted, and Michael Shellenberger. 2007. *Break Through: From the Death of Environmentalism to the Politics of Possibility.* New York: Houghton Mifflin.

Norris, Pippa. 1997. *Electoral Change since 1945.* London: Wiley Blackwell.

———, ed. 1999a. *Critical Citizens: Global Support for Democratic Governance.* Oxford, UK: Oxford University Press.

———. 1999b. New politicians? Changes in party competition at Westminster. In *Critical Elections*, ed. G. Evans and P. Norris. London: Sage.

———. 2000. *Virtuous Circle: Political Communications in Postindustrial Societies.* Cambridge, UK: Cambridge University Press.

———. 2002. *Democratic Phoenix: Reinventing Political Activism.* Cambridge, UK: Cambridge University Press.

———. 2011. *Democratic Deficit: Critical Citizen Revisited.* Cambridge, UK: Cambridge University Press.

Norris, Pippa, and Ronald Inglehart. 2011. *Sacred and Secular: Religion and Politics Worldwide.* 2nd ed. New York: Cambridge University Press.

Norris, Pippa, et al. 1999. *On Message: Communicating the Campaign.* London: Sage.

Norton, Philip. 2010. *The British Polity.* 6th ed. New York: Longman.

Nye, Joseph, Philip Zelikow, and David King, eds. 1997. *Why People Don't Trust Government*. Cambridge, MA: Harvard University Press.

Offe, Claus, and Susanne Fuchs. 2002. A decline of social capital? The German case. In *Democracies in Flux*, ed. R. Putnam. Oxford, UK: Oxford University Press.

Ohr, Dieter. 2011. Changing patterns of political communication. In *Political Leaders and Democratic Elections*, ed. K. Aarts, A. Blais, and H. Schmitt. Oxford, UK: Oxford University Press.

Oppenheimer, Daniel, and Michael Edwards. 2012. *Democracy Despite Itself: Why a System That Shouldn't Work at All Works So Well*. Cambridge, MA: MIT Press.

Oskarson, Maria. 2005. Social structure and party choice. In *The European Voter*, ed. J. Thomassen. Oxford, UK: Oxford University Press.

Page, Benjamin. 1978. *Choices and Echoes in Presidential Elections*. Chicago: University of Chicago Press.

Page, Benjamin, and Robert Shapiro. 1983. Effects of public opinion on public policy. *American Political Science Review* 77:175–90.

———. 1992. *The Rational Public: Fifty Years of Trends in Americans' Policy Preferences*. Chicago: University of Chicago Press.

Pállinger, Zoltán Tibor, et al., eds. 2007 *Direct Democracy in Europe: Developments and Prospects*. Wiesbaden: fuer Sozialwissenschaften.

Park, Alison, et al. 2004. *British Social Attitudes: Continuity and Change over Two Decades*. London: Sage.

Park, Alison, et al. 2011. *British Social Attitudes: The 28th Report*. NatCen Social Research. http://www.natcen.ac.uk/study/british-social-attitudes-28th-report

Parry, Geraint, George Moyser, and Neil Day. 1992. *Political Participation and Democracy in Britain*. Cambridge, UK: Cambridge University Press.

Patterson, Thomas. 2003. *The Vanishing Voter: Public Involvement in an Age of Uncertainty*. New York: Vintage.

Pattie, Charles, Patrick Seyd, and Paul Whiteley. 2004. *Citizenship in Britain: Values, Participation, and Democracy*. New York: Cambridge University Press.

Peffley, Mark, and Jon Hurwitz. 1985. A hierarchical model of attitude constraint. *American Journal of Political Science* 29:871–90.

Pew Center for People and the Press. 1998. *Public Appetite for Government Misjudged: Washington Leaders Wary of Public Opinion*. http://people-press .org/reports.

———. 2010. *Distrust, Discontent, Anger and Partisan Rancor: The People and Their Government*. http://www.people-press.org/2010/04/18/distrust-discontent-anger-and-partisan-rancor/

———. 2012a. *Cable Leads the Pack as Campaign News Source*. http://www.people-press.org/files/legacy-pdf/2012_Communicating_Release.pdf

———. 2012b. *What the Public Knows about the Political Parties*. http://www.people-press.org/files/legacy-pdf/04–11_Knowledge_Release.pdf

Pharr, Susan, and Robert Putnam, eds. 2000. *Disaffected Democracies: What's Troubling the Trilateral Countries?* Princeton: Princeton University Press.

Pinker, Steven. 2011. *The Better Angels of Our Nature: Why Violence Has Declined*. New York: Viking.

Piven, Frances Fox, and Richard Cloward. 2000. *Why Americans Don't Vote: And Why Politicians Want It That Way*. Rev. ed. Boston: Beacon Press.

Poguntke, Thomas, and Paul Webb, eds. 2005. *The Presidentialization of Politics: A Comparative Study of Modern Democracies.* New York: Oxford University Press.

Popkin, Samuel. 1991. *The Reasoning Voter.* Chicago: University of Chicago Press.

Popkin, Samuel, and Michael Dimock. 1999. Political knowledge and citizen competence. In *Citizen Competence and Democratic Institutions,* ed. S. Elkin and K. Soltan. University Park: Pennsylvania State University.

Powell, G. Bingham. 1986. American voting turnout in comparative perspective. *American Political Science Review* 80:17–44.

———. 2000. *Elections as Instruments of Democracy: Majoritarian and Proportional Visions.* New Haven: Yale University Press.

———. 2011. Institutions and the ideological congruence of governments. In *Citizens, Context and Choice: How Context Shapes Citizens' Electoral Choices,* ed. R. Dalton and C. Anderson. Oxford, UK: Oxford University Press.

Powell, G. Bingham, Russell Dalton, and Kaare Strom, eds. 2011. *Comparative Politics Today.* 10th ed. New York: Longman.

Prior, Markus. 2007. *Post-Broadcast Democracy: How Media Choice Increases Inequality in Political Involvement and Polarizes Elections.* New York: Cambridge University Press.

Putnam, Robert. 1993. *Making Democracy Work.* Princeton: Princeton University Press.

———. 2000. *Bowling Alone: The Collapse and Renewal of American Community.* New York: Simon and Schuster.

———, ed. 2002. *Democracies in Flux: The Evolution of Social Capital in Contemporary Society.* Oxford, UK: Oxford University Press.

Putnam, Robert, and David Campbell. 2010. *American Grace: How Religion Unites and Divides Us.* New York: Simon and Schuster.

RePass, David. 1971. Issue saliency and party choice. *American Political Science Review* 65:389–400.

Rohrschneider, Robert, Matthew Miles, and Mark Peffley. 2013. The structure and sources of global environmental attitudes. In *The Civic Culture Transformed: From Allegiant to Assertive Citizens,* ed. R. Dalton and C. Welzel. Cambridge, UK: Cambridge University Press.

Rohrschneider, Robert, and Stephen Whitefield. 2012. *The Strain of Representation: How Parties Represent Diverse Voters in Western and Eastern Europe.* Oxford, UK: Oxford University Press.

Rokeach, Milton. 1973. *The Nature of Human Values.* New York: Free Press.

Rootes, Christopher, ed. 1999. *Environmental Politics* 8, special issue, *Environmental Movements: Local, National, and Global.*

———. 2007. Britain. In *Environmental Protest in Western Europe,* ed. C. Rootes. 2nd ed. Oxford, UK: Oxford University Press.

Rose, Richard, ed. 1969. *Electoral Behavior.* New York: Free Press.

Rose, Richard, and Ian McAllister. 1990. *The Loyalties of Voters: A Lifetime Learning Model.* Newbury Park, CA: Sage.

Rose, Richard, and Derek Urwin. 1969. Social cohesion, political parties, and strains in regimes. *Comparative Political Studies* 2:7–67.

Rosenstone, Steven, and John Hansen. 1993. *Mobilization, Participation and Democracy in America.* New York: Macmillan.

Safran, William. 2008. *The French Polity.* 7th ed. New York: Longman.

Saggar, Shamit. 2007. Race and political behavior. In *The Oxford Handbook of Political Behavior*, ed. R. Dalton and H.-D. Klingemann. Oxford, UK: Oxford University Press.

Sartori, Giovanni. 1968. Representational systems. *International Encyclopedia of the Social Sciences* 13:470–75.

Schain, Martin. 2008. *The Politics of Immigration in France, Britain and the United States*. London: Palgrave Macmillan.

Schattschneider, E. E. 1942. *Party Government*. New York: Rinehart.

Schickler, Eric, and Donald Green. 1997. The stability of party identification in Western democracies. *Comparative Political Studies* 30:450–83.

Schlozman, Kay, Sidney Verba, and Henry Brady. 2012. *The Unheavenly Chorus: Unequal Political Voice and the Broken Promise of American Democracy*. Princeton: Princeton University Press.

Schoen, Harald. 2000. Stimmensplitting be Bundestagswahlen. In *50 Jahre empirische Wahlforschung in Deutschland*, ed. M. Klein et al. Wiesbaden: Westdeutscher.

Schuman, Howard, et al. 1997. *Racial Attitudes in America: Trends and Interpretations*. Rev. ed. Cambridge, MA: Harvard University Press.

Schumpeter, Joseph. 1943. *Capitalism, Socialism and Democracy*. London: Allen and Unwin.

Schwartz, Shalom. 2012. Basic personal values and political orientations. In *Improving Public Opinion Surveys: Interdisciplinary Innovation and the American National Election Studies*, ed. J. Aldrich and K. McGraw. Princeton: Princeton University Press.

Schwartz, Shalom, and A. Bardi. 2001. Value hierarchies across cultures. *Journal of Cross-Cultural Psychology* 32:268–90.

Schwarz, Norbert, and Gerd Bohner. 2001. The construction of attitudes. In *Blackwell Handbook of Social Psychology*, ed. A. Tesser and N. Schwarz. Oxford, UK: Blackwell.

Scott, Jacqueline, Michael Braun, and Duane Alwin. 1998. Partner, parent, worker: Family and gender roles. In *British—and European—Social Attitudes: The 15th Report*, ed. R. Jowell et al. Brookfield, VT: Ashgate.

Shanks, J. Merrill, and Warren Miller. 1990. Policy direction and performance evaluations. *British Journal of Political Science* 20:143–235.

Shively, W. Phillips. 1979. The development of party identification among adults. *American Political Science Review* 73:1039–54.

Skocpol, Theda, and Morris Fiorina, eds. 1999. *Civic Engagement in American Democracy*. Washington, DC: Brookings Institution Press.

Smith, Aaron, et al. 2009. *The Internet and Civic Engagement*. Pew Center for Internet and American Life. http://www.pewinternet.org/

Smith, Graham. 2009. *Democratic Innovations: Designing Institutions for Citizen Participation*. New York: Cambridge University Press.

Smith, Tom. 2009. National pride in comparative perspective. In *The International Social Survey Programme 1984–2009*, ed. M. Haller, R. Jowell, and T. Smith. London: Routledge.

Smith, Tom, and Paul Sheatsley. 1984. American attitudes toward race relations. *Public Opinion* 7:14ff.

Sniderman, Paul, Richard Brody, and James Kuklinski. 1984. Policy reasoning and political values. *American Journal of Political Science* 28:74–94.

Sniderman, Paul, Richard Brody, and Philip Tetlock. 1991. *Reasoning and Choice*. New York: Cambridge University Press.

Sniderman, Paul, and Louk Hagendoorn. 2007. *When Ways of Life Collide: Multiculturalism and Its Discontents in the Netherlands.* Princeton: Princeton University Press.

Sniderman, Paul, and Thomas Piazza. 1993. *The Scar of Race.* Cambridge, MA: Harvard University Press.

Sniderman, Paul, et al. 1991. The fallacy of democratic elitism. *British Journal of Political Science* 21:349–70.

———. 2001. *The Outsider: Prejudice and Politics in Italy.* Princeton: Princeton University Press.

Soroka, Stuart, and Christopher Wlezien. 2010. *Degrees of Democracy: Politics, Public Opinion and Policy.* New York: Cambridge University Press.

Stimson, James, Michael McKuen, and Robert Erikson. 1995. Dynamic representation. *American Political Science Review* 89:543–65.

Stokes, Donald. 1963. Spatial models of party competition. *American Political Science Review* 57:368–77.

Stolle, Dietlind, Marc Hooghe, and Michele Micheletti. 2005. Politics in the supermarket: Political consumerism as a form of political participation. *International Political Science Review* 26:245–70.

Stouffer, Samuel. 1955. *Communism, Conformity, and Civil Liberties.* New York: Doubleday.

Surowiecki, James. 2004. *The Wisdom of Crowds.* New York: Doubleday.

Taagepera, Rein, and Matthew Shugart. 1989. *Seats and Votes: The Effects and Determinants of Electoral Systems.* New Haven: Yale University Press.

Taber, Charles, and Milton Lodge. 2006. Motivated skepticism in the evaluation of political beliefs. *American Journal of Political Science* 50:755–69.

Teixeira, Ruy. 1992. *The Disappearing American Voter.* Washington, DC: Brookings Institution Press.

Teorell, Jan, Mariano Torcal, and José Ramon Montero. 2007. Political participation: Mapping the terrain. In *Citizenship and Involvement in European Democracies*, ed. J. van Deth, J. Montero, and A. Westholm. London: Routledge.

Thomassen, Jacques, ed. 2005. *The European Voter: A Comparative Study of Modern Democracies.* Oxford, UK: Oxford University Press.

———. 2007. Democratic values. In *Handbook of Political Behavior*, ed. R. Dalton and H.-D. Klingemann. Oxford, UK: Oxford University Press.

———. 2012. The blind corner of political representation. *Representation* 48:13–27.

Tocqueville, Alexis de. 1966. Reprint of 1835, 1840 editions. *Democracy in America.* New York: Knopf.

Tverdova, Yuliya. 2011. Follow the leader or follow the party? In *Citizens, Context and Choice*, ed. R. Dalton and C. Anderson. Oxford, UK: Oxford University Press.

Twenge, Jean, and W. Keith Campbell. 2010. *The Narcissism Epidemic: Living in the Age of Entitlement.* New York: Free Press.

Uhlaner, Carole. 1989. Rational turnout. *American Journal of Political Science* 33:390–422.

van Deth, Jan. 2001. Soziale und politische Beteiligung: Alternativen, Ergänzungen oder Zwillinge? In *Politische Partizipation in der Bundesrepublik Deutschland*, ed. A. Koch, M. Wasmer, and P. Schmidt. Opladen: Leske + Budrich.

van Deth, Jan, and Elinor Scarbrough, eds. 1995. *The Impact of Values.* New York: Oxford University Press.

van Deth, Jan, et al., eds. 2007. *Citizenship and Involvement in European Democracies: A Comparative Analysis.* London: Routledge.

Vassallo, Francesca. 2010. *France, Social Capital and Political Activism.* New York: Palgrave Macmillan.

Vedel, Thierry. 2011. Following the campaign. In *The New Voter in Western Europe: France and Beyond*, ed. B. Cautrès and A. Muxel. New York: Palgrave Macmillan.

Verba, Sidney, and Norman Nie. 1972. *Participation in America.* New York: Harper and Row.

Verba, Sidney, Norman Nie, and J. O. Kim. 1978. *Participation and Political Equality.* New York: Cambridge University Press.

Verba, Sidney, Kay Schlozman, and Henry Brady. 1995. *Voice and Equality: Civic Voluntarism in American Politics.* Cambridge, MA: Harvard University Press.

Wagner, Aiko, and Bernhard Wessels. 2012. Party representation and leader representation: Does it matter how it fits? *Electoral Studies* 31:72–82.

Wakefield, Jane. 2008 Google your way to a wacky office. *BBC News.* http://news.bbc.co.uk/2/hi/7290322.stm

Wald, Kenneth. 2003. *Religion and Politics in the United States.* 4th ed. Lanham, MD: Rowman and Littlefield.

Wattenberg, Martin. 1991. *The Rise of Candidate-Centered Politics.* Cambridge, MA: Harvard University Press.

———. 1998. *The Decline of American Political Parties, 1952–1996.* Cambridge, MA: Harvard University Press.

———. 2002. *Where Have All the Voters Gone?* Cambridge, MA: Harvard University Press.

———. 2011a. *Is Voting for Young People?* 3rd ed. New York: Longman.

———. 2011b. U.S. party leaders. In *Political Leaders and Democratic Elections*, ed. K. Aarts, A. Blais, and H. Schmitt. Oxford, UK: Oxford University Press.

Webb, Paul, David Farrell, and Ian Holliday, eds. 2002. *Political Parties in Advanced Industrial Democracies.* Oxford, UK: Oxford University Press.

Weisberg, Herbert, and Steve Greene. 2003. The political psychology of party identification. In *Electoral Democracy*, ed. M. MacKuen and G. Rabinowitz. Ann Arbor: University of Michigan Press.

Weisberg, Herbert, and Jerold Rusk. 1970. Dimensions of candidate evaluation. *American Political Science Review* 64:1167–85.

Weissberg, Robert. 1978. Collective versus dyadic representation in Congress. *American Political Science Review* 72:535–47.

Welzel, Christian. 2013. *Freedom Rising: Human Empowerment and the Quest for Emancipation.* New York: Cambridge University Press.

Wessels, Bernhard. 1993. Politische Repräsentation als Prozeß gesellschaftlich-parlamentarischer Kommunikation. In *Parlament und Gesellschaft*, ed. D. Herzog et al. Opladen: Westdeutscher.

———. 1999. System characteristics matter: Empirical evidence from ten representation studies. In *Policy Representation in Western Democracies*, ed. W. Miller et al. Oxford, UK: Oxford University Press.

———. 2011. Performance and deficits of present-day representation. In *The Future of Representative Democracy*, eds. S. Alonso, J. Keane, and W. Merkel. Cambridge, UK: Cambridge University Press.

Whiteley, Paul. 2012. *Political Participation in Britain: The Decline and Revival of Civic Culture.* New York: Palgrave Macmillan.

Whiteley, Paul, and Patrick Seyd. 2002. *High-Intensity Participation: The Dynamics of Party Activism in Britain.* Ann Arbor: University of Michigan Press.

Wlezien, Christopher. 2004. Patterns of representation: Dynamics of public preferences and policy. *Journal of Politics* 66:1–24.

Wlezien, Christopher, Mark Franklin, and Daniel Twiggs. 1997. Economic perceptions and vote choice. *Political Behavior* 19:7–17.

Wolfe. Alan. 2006. *Does American Democracy Still Work?* New Haven: Yale University Press.

Wolfinger, Raymond, and Steven Rosenstone. 1980. *Who Votes?* New Haven: Yale University Press.

World Bank. 2001. *World Development Report 2001*. Washington, DC: World Bank.

Wortham, Jenna. 2012. With Twitter, blackouts and demonstrations, Web flexes its muscle. *New York Times*, January 18.

Wright, Erik. 1997. *Class Counts: Comparative Studies in Class Analysis*. Cambridge, UK: Cambridge University Press.

Wright, James. 1976. *The Dissent of the Governed*. New York: Academic Press.

Zakaria, Fareed. 2003. *The Future of Freedom: Illiberal Democracy at Home and Abroad*. New York: Norton.

Zaller, John. 1992. *The Nature and Origins of Mass Opinion*. New York: Cambridge University Press.

Zelle, Carsten. 1995. Social dealignment vs. political frustration. *European Journal for Political Research* 27:319–45.

Zimmerman, Michael. 1990. Newspaper editors and the creation-evolution controversy. *Skeptical Inquirer* 14:182–95.

——. 1991. A survey of pseudoscientific sentiments of elected officials: A comparison of federal and state legislators. *Creation/Evolution* 29:26–45.

Zuckerman, Alan, and Martin Kroh. 2006. The social logic of bounded partisanship in Germany. *Comparative European Politics* 4:65–93.

Zukin, Cliff, et al. 2006. *A New Engagement? Political Participation, Civic Life, and the Changing American Citizen*. New York: Oxford University Press.

Index

⑤SAGE research**methods**
The Essential Online Tool for Researchers

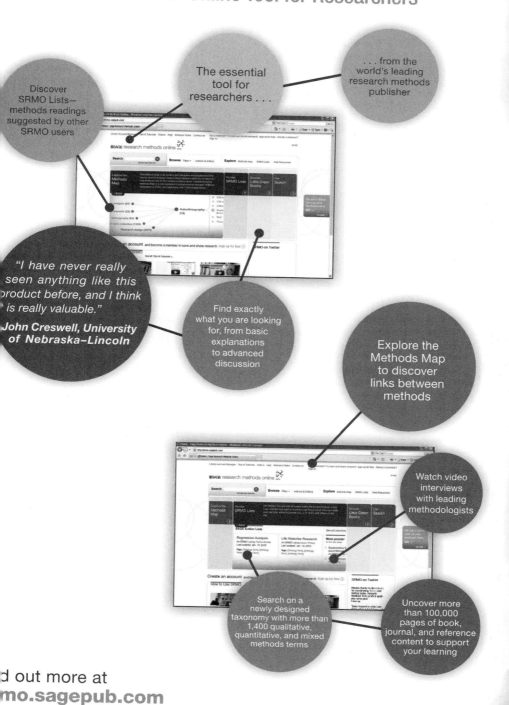

Discover SRMO Lists—methods readings suggested by other SRMO users

The essential tool for researchers . . .

. . . from the world's leading research methods publisher

"I have never really seen anything like this product before, and I think it is really valuable."

John Creswell, University of Nebraska–Lincoln

Find exactly what you are looking for, from basic explanations to advanced discussion

Explore the Methods Map to discover links between methods

Watch video interviews with leading methodologists

Search on a newly designed taxonomy with more than 1,400 qualitative, quantitative, and mixed methods terms

Uncover more than 100,000 pages of book, journal, and reference content to support your learning

d out more at
mo.sagepub.com